¡Ya verás! GOLD
~ Nivel 1 ~

John R. Gutiérrez

The Pennsylvania State University

Harry L. Rosser

Boston College

Marta Rosso-O'Laughlin

Tufts University

HH Heinle & Heinle Publishers

An International Thomson Publishing Company

I(T)P Boston, MA • 02116 • U.S.A.

Visit us on the Internet **http://yaveras.heinle.com**

The publication of *¡Ya verás! Gold, Nivel 1*, was directed by the members of the Heinle & Heinle School Publishing Team.

Team Leader: Vincent Duggan
Publisher: Denise St. Jean
Production Services Coordinator: Mary McKeon
Market Development Director: Pamela Warren

Also participating in the publication of this program were:
Assistant Editor: Sonja Regelman
Manufacturing Coordinator: Wendy Kilborn
Development, Design and Composition: Hispanex Inc.
Cover Art: Mark Schroder
Cover: Rotunda Design

Manufactured in the United States of America

ISBN 0-8384-8554-5 (student text)

10 9 8 7 6 5 4 3

To the Student

You are about to begin an exciting and valuable experience. Learning a new language will open up cultures other than your own: different ways of living, thinking, and seeing. In fact, there is an old Spanish proverb that underscores the importance of knowing another language. It states: *El que sabe dos lenguas vale por dos*—the person who speaks two languages is worth two people.

Today the Spanish language is spoken all over the world by more than 300 million people. Many of you will one day have the opportunity to visit a Spanish-speaking country. Your experience will be all the richer if you can enter into the cultures of those countries and interact with their people. However, even if you don't get to spend time in one of those countries, Spanish is very much alive right here in this country, for it is spoken every day by millions of Americans!

Do you already know some Spanish speakers in your community or have you ever been exposed to elements of Hispanic culture? Perhaps you have sampled some Mexican food or turned on the television to find a Spanish news broadcast. Perhaps you have listened to the music of Gloria Estefan or Rubén Blades or maybe seen a movie in Spanish with English subtitles. The possibilities are endless.

Once you begin to use the Spanish language in class, you will discover that you can interact with Spanish speakers or your classmates and teacher right away. Knowing that of over 80,000 words found in the Spanish language, the average Spanish speaker uses only about 800 on a daily basis might help to persuade you of this! Therefore, the most important task ahead of you is not to accumulate a large quantity of knowledge about Spanish grammar and vocabulary but rather to use what you learn as effectively and creatively as you can.

Communicating in a foreign language means understanding what others say and transmitting your messages in ways that avoid misunderstandings. As you learn to do this, you will find that making errors is part of language learning. Think of mistakes as positive steps toward effective communication. They don't hold you back; they advance you in your efforts.

Learning a language takes practice, but it's an enriching experience that can bring you a lot of pleasure and satisfaction. We hope your experience with *¡Ya verás! Gold, Nivel 1*, is both rewarding and enjoyable!

Acknowledgments

Creating a secondary program is a long and complicated process which involves the dedication and hard work of a number of people. First of all, we express our heartfelt thanks to the Secondary School Publishing Team at Heinle & Heinle for its diligent work on *¡Ya verás! Gold* and to Hispanex of Boston, MA for the many contributions its staff made to the program. We thank Kenneth Holman who created the textbooks' initial interior design and the designers at Hispanex who refined and created it.

Our thanks also go to Charles Heinle for his special interest and support and to Jeannette Bragger and Donald Rice, authors of *On y va!* We thank Jessie Carduner, Charles Grove, and Paul D. Toth for their contributions to the interdisciplinary sections in the student textbook. We also express our appreciation to the people who worked on the fine set of supporting materials available with the *¡Ya verás! Gold*, level 1, program: Greg Harris, Workbook; Chris McIntyre and Jill Welch, Teacher's Edition; Joe Wieczorek, Laboratory Program; Kristen Warner, Testing Program; Susan Malik, Middle School Activities and Teacher's Guide; Sharon Brown, Practice Software; and Frank Domínguez, Ana Martínez-Lage, and Jeff Morgenstein, the *Mundos hispanos 1* multimedia program.

Finally, a very special word of acknowledgment goes to our children:
— To Mía and Stevan who are always on their daddy's mind and whose cultural heritage is ever present throughout *¡Ya verás! Gold*.
— To Susan, Elizabeth, and Rebecca Rosser, whose enthusiasm and increasing interest in Spanish inspired their father to take part in this endeavor.

John R. Gutiérrez and Harry L. Rosser

The publisher and authors wish to thank the following teachers who pilot-tested the *¡Ya verás!, Second Edition,* program. Their use of the program in their classes provided us with invaluable suggestions and contributed important insights to the creation of *¡Ya verás! Gold.*

Nola Baysore
Muncy JHS
Muncy, PA

Barbara Connell
Cape Elizabeth Middle
  School
Cape Elizabeth, ME

Frank Droney
Susan Digiandomenico
Wellesley Middle School
Wellesley, MA

Michael Dock
Shikellamy HS
Sunbury, PA

Jane Flood Clare
Somers HS
Lincolndale, NY

Nancy McMahon
Somers Middle School
Lincolndale, NY

Rebecca Gurnish
Ellet HS
Akron, OH

Peter Haggerty
Wellesley HS
Wellesley, MA

José M. Díaz
Hunter College HS
New York, NY

Claude Hawkins
Flora Mazzucco
Jerie Milici
Elena Fienga
Bohdan Kodiak
Greenwich HS
Greenwich, CT

Wally Lishkoff
Tomás Travieso
Carver Middle School
Miami, FL

Manuel M. Manderine
Canton McKinley HS
Canton, OH

Grace Angel Marion
South JHS
Lawrence, KS

Jean Barrett
St. Ignatius HS
Cleveland, OH

Gary Osman
McFarland HS
McFarland, WI

Deborah Decker
Honeoye Falls-Lima HS
Honeoye Falls, NY

Carrie Piepho
Arden JHS
Sacramento, CA

Rhonda Barley
Marshall JHS
Marshall, VA

Germana Shirmer
W. Springfield HS
Springfield, VA

John Boehner
Gibson City HS
Gibson City, IL

Margaret J. Hutchison
John H. Linton JHS
Penn Hills, PA

Edward G. Stafford
St. Andrew's-Sewanee
  School
St. Andrew's, TN

Irene Prendergast
Wayzata East JHS
Plymouth, MN

Tony DeLuca
Cranston West HS
Cranston, RI

Joe Wild-Crea
Wayzata Senior High
  School
Plymouth, MN

Katy Armagost
Manhattan HS
Manhattan, KS

William Lanza
Osbourn Park HS
Manassas, VA

Linda Kelley
Hopkinton HS
Contoocook, NH

John LeCuyer
Belleville HS West
Belleville, IL

Sue Bell
South Boston HS
Boston, MA

Wayne Murri
Mountain Crest HS
Hyrum, UT

Barbara Flynn
Summerfield Waldorf
  School
Santa Rosa, CA

The publisher and authors wish to thank the following people who reviewed the manuscript for the *¡Ya verás!*, Second Edition, program. Their comments were invaluable to its development and of great assistance in the creation of *¡Ya verás! Gold*.

High School Reviewers

Georgio Arias, Juan De León, Luís Martínez (McAllen ISD, McAllen, TX); **Katy Armagost** (Mt. Vernon High School, Mt. Vernon, WA); **Yolanda Bejar, Graciela Delgado, Bárbara V. Méndez, Mary Alice Mora** (El Paso ISD, El Paso, TX); **Linda Bigler** (Thomas Jefferson High School, Alexandria, VA); **John Boehner** (Gibson City High School, Gibson City, IL); **Kathleen Carroll** (Edinburgh ISD, Edinburgh, TX); **Louanne Grimes** (Richardson ISD, Richardson, TX); **Greg Harris** (Clay High School, South Bend, IN); **Diane Henderson** (Houston ISD, Houston, TX); **Maydell Jenks** (Katy ISD, Katy, TX); **Bartley Kirst** (Ironwood High School, Glendale, AZ); **Mala Levine** (St. Margaret's Episcopal School, San Juan Capistrano, CA); **Manuel Manderine** (Canton McKinley Sr. High School, Canton, OH); **Laura Martin** (Cleveland State University, Cleveland, OH); **Luis Millán** (Edina High School, Minneapolis, MN); **David Moffett, Karen Petmeckey, Pat Rossett, Nereida Zimic** (Austin ISD, Austin, TX); **Jeff Morgenstein** (Hudson High School, Hudson, FL); **Rosana Pérez, Jody Spoor** (Northside ISD, San Antonio, TX); **Susan Polansky** (Carnegie Mellon University, Pittsburgh, PA); **Alva Salinas** (San Antonio ISD, San Antonio, TX); **Patsy Shafchuk** (Hudson High School, Hudson, FL); **Terry A. Shafer** (Worthington Kilbourne High School, West Worthington, OH); **Courtenay Suárez** (Montwood High School, Socorro ISD, El Paso, TX); **Alvino Téllez, Jr.** (Edgewood ISD, San Antonio, TX); **Kristen Warner** (Piper High School, Sunrise, FL); **Nancy Wrobel** (Champlin Park High School, Champlin, MN)

Middle School Reviewers

Larry Ling (Hunter College High School, New York, NY); **Susan Malik** (West Springfield High School, Springfield, VA); **Yvette Parks** (Norwood Junior High School, Norwood, MA)

Contenido

CAPÍTULO 1   *Vamos al café* •••••••••••• 2

CAPÍTULO 2   *¡Vamos a un bar de tapas!* •••••••••• 26

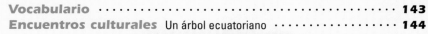

¡Bienvenidos al mundo hispánico!

Did you know that Spanish is spoken by more than 360 million people around the world and that is the third most widely spoken language after Chinese and English? In fact, Spanish, which originated in a tiny corner of Castile, Spain, is the principal language of 20 countries. After English, it is also the most commonly spoken language in the United States, boasting more than 22 million speakers! These simple facts, however, only hint at the vibrant diversity of the Spanish language and the rich tapestry of Hispanic cultures.

Like many languages, Spanish has been shaped by geography. The Spanish spoken by the Chileans living in the shadows of the snow-capped Andes has evolved differently from that of the Argentines herding cattle on the vast grass-filled plains known as the pampas. Even within a country as small as the Dominican Republic, the way Spanish sounds in the capital city of Santo Domingo differs from the way it is spoken in rural areas.

In many places, Spanish was also shaped by the cultures and languages of the indigenous peoples who lived there long before the arrival of Spanish-speakers—for example, the Maya of Mexico's Yucatan peninsula and Guatemala, and the Guaranis of Paraguay. Just as the United States is a "melting pot" of many cultures, the Spanish-speaking world represents a dynamic linguistic and cultural mosaic. ¡Bienvenidos al mundo hispánico! You are about to embark on a fascinating journey!

Te toca a ti

Examine the maps in your textbook to find the following information.

1. The twenty Spanish-speaking countries
2. The name of the river that separates Mexico from the United States
3. The only country in Central America that is not considered a Spanish-speaking country
4. The number and names of the countries in South America where Spanish is not the principal language
5. The Spanish-speaking island in the Caribbean that is part of the United States
6. A Spanish-speaking country in Africa

GUATEMALA — HONDURAS

MAR CARIBE

EL SALVADOR

NICARAGUA

Barranquilla
Cartagena

Lago de Maracaibo

Caracas

Río Orinoco

GUAYANA

SURINAM

GUAYANA FRANCESA

OCÉANO ATLÁNTICO

COSTA RICA

PANAMÁ

Manizales

VENEZUELA

★ **Bogotá**

Cali

COLOMBIA

ECUADOR

Quito

ECUADOR

Iquitos

Río Amazonas

PERÚ

ANDES

Lima

Machu Picchu
Cuzco

BRASIL

Ayacucho

Lago Titicaca

BOLIVIA

La Paz

Sucre

Potosí

Río Paraná

PARAGUAY

Salta

CHILE

Asunción

Iguazú

Río Uruguay

OCÉANO PACÍFICO

OCÉANO ATLÁNTICO

URUGUAY

A R G E N T I N A

Santiago ★

Buenos Aires

Montevideo

AMÉRICA DEL SUR

ISLAS MALVINAS (Br.)

Estrecho de Magallanes

TIERRA DEL FUEGO

0	1000 km.
0	600 millas

NIGERIA

ÁFRICA

CAMERÚN

Malabo ★

GUINEA ECUATORIAL

ECUADOR

GABÓN

ÁFRICA

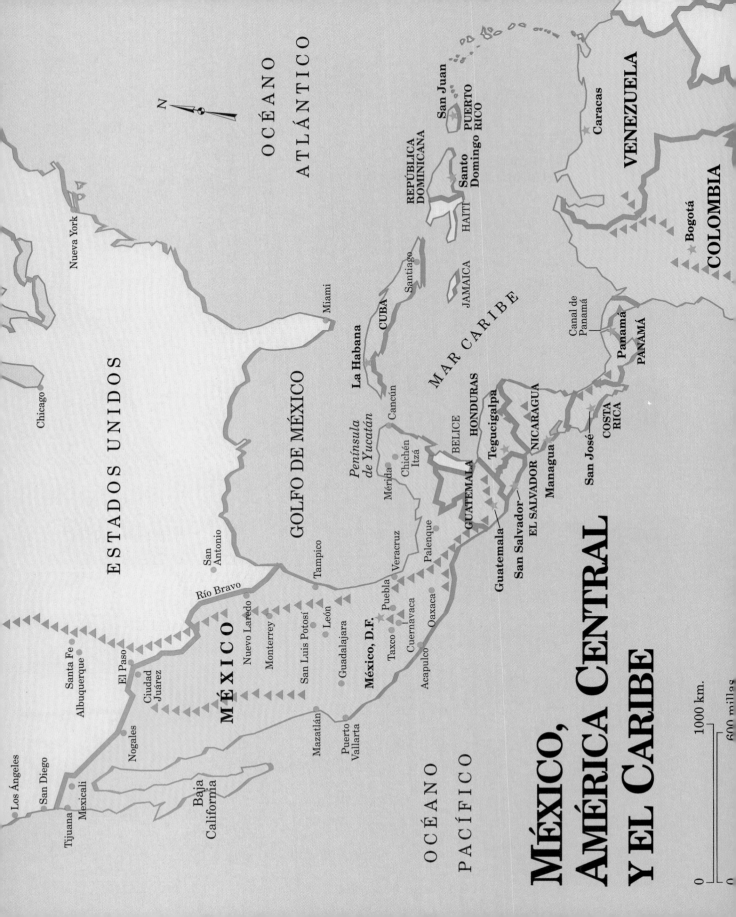

MÉXICO, AMÉRICA CENTRAL Y EL CARIBE

ESTADOS UNIDOS

MÉXICO

OCÉANO ATLÁNTICO

OCÉANO PACÍFICO

GOLFO DE MÉXICO

MAR CARIBE

CUBA

JAMAICA

REPÚBLICA DOMINICANA

HAITÍ

PUERTO RICO

GUATEMALA

BELICE

HONDURAS

EL SALVADOR

NICARAGUA

COSTA RICA

PANAMÁ

VENEZUELA

COLOMBIA

Los Ángeles
San Diego
Tijuana
Mexicali
Nogales
Baja California
Santa Fe
Albuquerque
El Paso
Ciudad Juárez
Chicago
Nueva York
San Antonio
Río Bravo
Nuevo Laredo
Monterrey
San Luis Potosí
León
Guadalajara
México, D.F.
Taxco
Puebla
Cuernavaca
Oaxaca
Acapulco
Mazatlán
Puerto Vallarta
Tampico
Veracruz
Palenque
Miami
La Habana
Cancún
Mérida
Chichén Itzá
Península de Yucatán
Santiago
Guatemala
San Salvador
Tegucigalpa
Managua
San José
Panamá
Canal de Panamá
San Juan
Santo Domingo
Caracas
Bogotá

N

0   1000 km.
0   600 millas

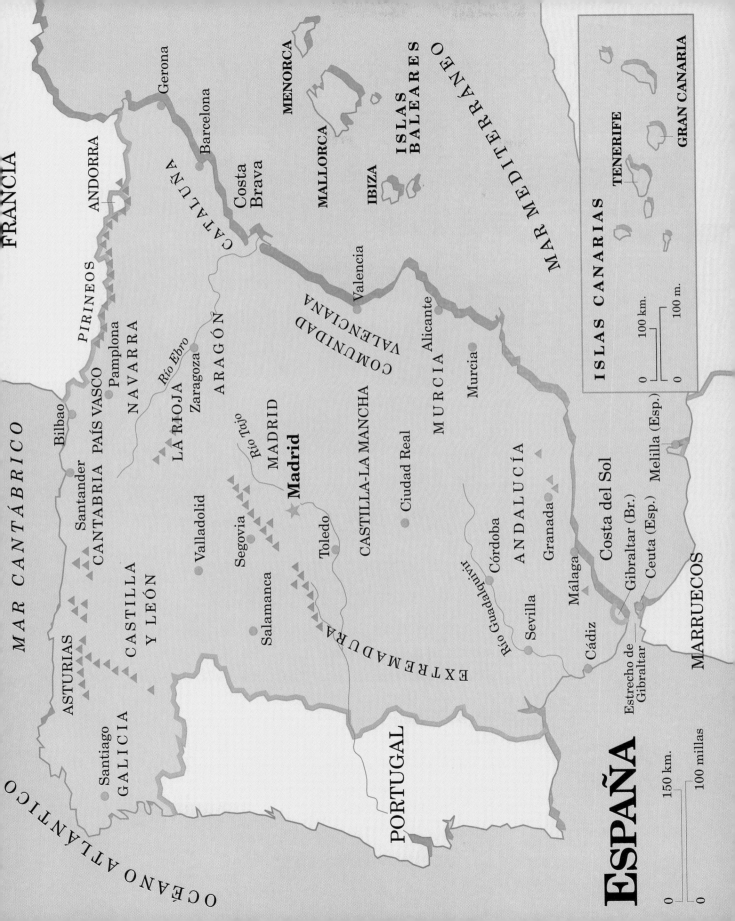

UNIDAD 1

Vamos a tomar algo

Objectives

In this unit you will learn:

- to meet and greet people
- to discuss and express your likes and dislikes about common activities
- to get something to eat and drink
- to read a café menu
- to express how well or how often you do something
- to understand meal-time customs in the Spanish-speaking world

¿Qué ves?

- Where are the people in these photographs?
- What are they doing?
- What kinds of beverages are they having?
- Where do you like to go for something to eat or drink?

Vamos al café

Primera etapa: ¡Hola! ¿Qué tal?
Segunda etapa: ¡Un refresco, por favor!
Tercera etapa: ¡Vamos a comer algo!

¡Vamos a un bar de tapas!

Primera etapa: Las tapas españolas
Segunda etapa: ¡Buenos días!... ¡Hasta luego!

¿Te gusta la comida mexicana?

Primera etapa: ¡Vamos a un restaurante
Segunda etapa: ¡Qué comida más rica!

CAPÍTULO 1

Vamos al café

—Yo quisiera un refresco.
—Entonces, vamos al café.

Objectives

- ordering food and drink
- greeting, introducing, and leavetaking with friends
- expressing likes and dislikes
- asking and answering yes/no questions

PRIMERA ETAPA

- What do you think these teenagers are saying to each other as they meet on the street or in a public place?

- What gestures are they making?

- When you introduce a friend to someone, what do you usually do?

- What are some expressions that you use in English when you meet people?

- What do you say when you are about to leave?

¡Hola! ¿Qué tal?

Alba:	**Buenos días**, Teresa.
Teresa:	Buenos días, Alba. **¿Cómo estás?**
Alba:	**Muy bien, gracias. ¿Y tú?**
Teresa:	**Más o menos.**

Laura:	**¡Hola**, Anita! **¿Qué tal?**
Anita:	Muy bien, Laura. ¿Y tú?
Laura:	**Bien**, gracias. Anita, **te presento a** Juan. Juan, Anita.
Anita:	¡Hola!
Juan:	**Mucho gusto.**

Buenos días *Good morning* **¿Cómo estás?** *How are you?* **Muy bien, gracias.** *Very well, thank you.* **¿Y tú?** *And you?* **Más o menos.** *So-so.* **Hola** *Hello* **¿Qué tal?** *How are you? How is it going?* **Bien** *Well, fine* **te presento a...** *let me introduce you to...* **Mucho gusto.** *Nice to meet you.*

¡Hola!

¿Cómo estás?

¿Qué tal?

Hasta luego.

Saludos (Greetings)

Buenos días.

Buenas tardes. *Good afternoon.*
Buenas noches. *Good evening.*
  Good night.
¡Hola!
¿Cómo estás?
¿Cómo te va? *How's it going?*
¿Qué hay? *What's new?*
¿Qué pasa? *What's going on?*
¿Qué tal?

Respuestas (Answers)

Buenos días.

Buenas tardes.
Buenas noches.
¡Hola!
Bien, gracias. ¿Y tú?
Muy bien, gracias. ¿Y tú?
Más o menos. ¿Y tú?
Regular. *OK.*
Bastante bien. *Pretty good.*

Despedidas (Farewells)

Adiós. *Good-bye.*

Hasta luego. *See you later.*
Nos vemos. *See you.*

Respuestas

Adiós.
¡Chao! *Bye!*

¡Te toca a ti!

A. Saludos Answer these greetings appropriately.

1. ¡Hola!
2. Buenos días.
3. ¿Cómo estás?

4. ¿Qué tal?
5. Buenas tardes.
6. ¿Cómo te va?

7. Buenas noches.
8. ¿Qué pasa?
9. ¿Qué hay?

B. ¡Hola! ¿Qué tal? You are talking to a new Spanish-speaking student in the hallway of your school. A friend of yours approaches and you greet each other. You introduce the new student. Then you all say good-bye to each other. Working in groups of three, act out the situation. Follow the model.

MODELO

Tú:	*¡Hola! ¿Qué tal?*
Amigo(a):	*Bien, gracias, ¿y tú?*
Tú:	*Bien, gracias. Te presento a Marilú.*
Amigo(a):	*¡Hola!*
Marilú:	*Mucho gusto.*
Tú:	*Hasta luego.*
Amigo(a):	*Nos vemos.*
Marilú:	*Adiós.*

Comentarios CULTURALES

Saludos y despedidas

The body language that accompanies greetings and good-byes in Hispanic cultures is somewhat different from North American customs. In both situations, it is customary for Spanish-speaking men to shake hands formally or even exchange an **abrazo;** a brief embrace with a pat or two on the back. Among women, the custom is to kiss each other: on both cheeks in Spain and on only one cheek in Latin America. When a young man and woman who know each other meet, they generally kiss on one or both cheeks. Older people will usually shake hands unless they know each other well. When Spanish speakers of any age greet each other or engage in conversation, they generally stand closer to each other than do speakers of English.

PRONUNCIACIÓN THE SPANISH ALPHABET

A good place to start your study of Spanish pronunciation is with the alphabet. Listed below are the letters of the Spanish alphabet along with their names.

a	a	**j**	jota	**r**	ere
b	be	**k**	ka	**rr**	erre
c	ce	**l**	ele	**s**	ese
ch	che[1]	**ll**	elle[1]	**t**	te
d	de	**m**	eme	**u**	u
e	e	**n**	ene	**v**	ve
f	efe	**ñ**	eñe	**w**	doble ve
g	ge	**o**	o	**x**	equis
h	hache	**p**	pe	**y**	i griega
i	i	**q**	cu	**z**	zeta

[1] When looking up words in Spanish dictionaries and publications with alphabetical listings such as telephone directories, entries beginning with **ñ** are listed separately, following those beginning with **n.** Entries for **ch** and **ll** also used to be listed separately. For simplicity and to make Spanish more computer compatible internationally, the Association of Spanish Language Academies voted in 1994 to eliminate separate alphabetical lists for **ch** and **ll.** Such entries are now listed under **c** and **l,** respectively.

Práctica

C. Spell the following words using the Spanish alphabet.

1. pan
2. refresco
3. mantequilla
4. leche

5. aceitunas
6. bocadillo
7. naranja
8. limón

9. mermelada
10. calamares
11. sándwich
12. desayuno

13. jamón
14. pastel
15. tortilla

ESTRUCTURA

The verb gustar + infinitive

—**Me gusta** bailar.
—**¿Te gusta** cantar?
—**No me gusta** cantar; **me gusta** escuchar música.

—**¿Te gusta** hablar español?
—Sí, pero **no me gusta** estudiar y practicar.

I like to dance.
Do you like to sing?
I don't like to sing; I like to listen to music.

Do you like to speak Spanish?
Yes, but I don't like to study and practice.

1. To express in Spanish certain activities that you like or do not like to do, you can use the construction **gustar** + infinitive.

2. An infinitive is the simple form of a verb. It is not conjugated, that is, it shows no subject or number (singular or plural). For example, in English *to introduce* is an infinitive, while *introduces* is a conjugated form of the verb. Note that the Spanish infinitives in the preceding sentences all end in **-ar**.

Aquí practicamos

D. ¿Qué (What) te gusta? Answer the following questions, according to the model.

> **MODELO** ¿Te gusta estudiar?
> *Sí, me gusta estudiar.* o: *No, no me gusta estudiar.*

1. ¿Te gusta bailar?
2. ¿Te gusta hablar español en clase?
3. ¿Te gusta cantar ópera?

4. ¿Te gusta practicar el español?
5. ¿Te gusta estudiar matemáticas? ¿historia?
6. ¿Te gusta escuchar música rock? ¿clásica?

PALABRAS ÚTILES

Expressing likes and dislikes

Here are some words that can be used to express whether you like something very much or just a little. These words are called *adverbs*. They are used after the verb **gustar.**

mucho	*a lot*	**poco**	*a little*
muchísimo	*very much*	**muy poco**	*very little*

Me gusta **mucho** bailar.
Me gusta **muy poco** escuchar
  música clásica.

I like dancing a lot.
I like listening to classical music
  very little.

Aquí practicamos

E. ¿Muchísimo o muy poco? Say how much or how little you like these activities. Follow the model.

> **MODELO** cantar
> *Me gusta mucho cantar.* o: *Me gusta muy poco cantar.*

1. bailar
2. hablar en clase
3. hablar español
4. escuchar música rock

5. escuchar música clásica
6. estudiar
7. cantar

Aquí escuchamos

¡Hola y adiós! *Some friends run into each other on the street.*

Antes de escuchar Think of some of the common expressions, questions, and responses typically used in Spanish when meeting friends or acquaintances.

 A escuchar Listen twice to the two exchanges between friends before answering the questions about them on your activity master.

Después de escuchar Answer the following questions based on what you heard.

Conversación 1
1. What are the names of the two people in the conversation?
2. What does the boy respond when asked how he is?
3. Do the two people already know each other? How do you know?
4. What expression do they both use when they say good-bye?

Conversación 2
1. In general, what time of day is it when the people meet?
2 What country is one of the speakers from?
3. Who makes a reference at the end to someone's family?

¡Mucho gusto! You and a friend are sitting in a café when another friend arrives. 1) Greet the arriving friend. 2) Introduce him (her) to your other friend. 3) Discuss which refreshments on the menu you each like. 4) One of the two friends who have just met should ask the other a question about his (her) likes or dis-

likes. (**¿Te gusta escuchar música rock?**) 5) The other one should respond. (**Sí, me gusta escuchar música rock. Me gusta cantar también.**) 6) Finally, after finishing your drink you get up and say good-bye to your two friends.

 Una postal Write a postcard to a friend. Make sure it includes a greeting, a list of three things you like to do, a question about your friend's likes or dislikes, and a farewell.

Perú

SEGUNDA ETAPA

Preparación

- What beverages can you order at a restaurant or a café?

- Think about what you drink at different times during the day. What do you normally drink at breakfast time? At lunch? In the evening?

- When you are really thirsty, what do you most like to drink?

¡Un refresco, por favor!

Two girls at a café want to have a drink (**un refresco**).

María:	Pst, camarero.
Camarero:	Sí, señorita, ¿qué desea tomar?
María:	Una limonada, por favor.
Camarero:	Y usted, señorita, ¿qué desea?
Yolanda:	**Yo quisiera un licuado** de banana, por favor.

A few seconds later...

Camarero:	**Aquí tienen ustedes.** Una limonada y un licuado de banana.
María:	**Muchas gracias, señor.**
Camarero:	**De nada.**

camarero *waiter*   **señorita** *miss*   **¿qué desea tomar?** *what do you want to drink?*   **Una limonada** *A lemonade*
Yo quisiera *I would like*   **un licuado** *a milkshake*   **Aquí tienen ustedes.** *Here you are.*   **Muchas gracias** *Thank you very much*   **señor** *sir*   **De nada.** *You're welcome.*

Unas bebidas calientes *(Hot drinks)*

un café

un café con leche

un chocolate

un té

un té con leche

un té con limón

Unas bebidas frías *(Cold drinks)*

una botella de agua mineral, un vaso de agua con limón

una granadina con agua mineral

un jugo de naranja

un licuado de banana

una limonada

un refresco

¡Te toca a ti!

A. En el café You are in a café. A classmate will play the role of the waiter (waitress). When he (she) asks what you want, order the following drinks. Follow the model.

> **MODELO** un café con leche
>
> **Camarero(a):** *¿Qué desea, señorita (señor)?*
>
> **Tú:** *Un café con leche, por favor.*

1. un refresco
2. un té con limón
3. una botella de agua
4. un chocolate
5. un licuado de banana
6. una granadina con agua mineral
7. una limonada
8. un café
9. un vaso de agua con limón
10. un jugo de naranja
11. un té con leche
12. un té

B. Camarero(a), por favor Get the waiter's (waitress's) attention and order the drink of your choice. A classmate will play the role of the waiter (waitress). Follow the model.

> **MODELO**
>
> Tú: *Pst, camarero(a).*
> Camarero(a): *Sí, señor (señorita), ¿qué desea tomar?*
> Tú: *Un licuado de banana, por favor.*

C. Aquí tienen Play the role of the waiter (waitress) or one of two students at a café. Each student orders a drink, but the waiter (waitress) forgets who ordered what. Work in groups of three. Follow the model.

> **MODELO**
>
> Camarero(a): *¿Qué desean tomar?*
> Estudiante 1: *Una granadina con soda, por favor.*
> Camarero(a): *¿Y Ud., señor (señorita)?*
> Estudiante 2: *Yo quisiera un refresco, por favor.*
>
> Camarero(a): *Aquí tienen. Un refresco para Ud....*
> Estudiante 1: *No, señor(ita), una granadina.*
> Camarero(a): *¡Ah, perdón (sorry)! Una granadina para Ud., y un refresco para Ud.*
> Estudiante 2: *Sí, gracias.*
> Camarero(a): *De nada.*

PRONUNCIACIÓN THE VOWEL a

The sound of the vowel **a** in Spanish is pronounced like the *a* of the English word *father* except that the sound is shorter in Spanish.

Práctica

D. Listen and repeat as your teacher models the following words.

1. hola	5. tapas	9. calamares
2. va	6. canta	10. cacahuetes
3. pan	7. habla	
4. patatas	8. hasta	

Repaso ♻

E. Hola, te presento a... The Spanish Club has organized a meeting so that new members can get to know each other. Select a partner and introduce yourself and your partner to three people.

ESTRUCTURA

Gender of nouns and the indefinite articles

	Singular		Plural	
Masculine	**un refresco**	*a soft drink*	**unos refrescos**	*some soft drinks*
Feminine	**una botella**	*a bottle*	**unas botellas**	*some bottles*

1. Almost every noun in Spanish has a grammatical gender; that is, it is either masculine or feminine. Most nouns that end in –o are masculine (**un jugo**), and most nouns that end in –a are feminine (**una granadina**). In general, nouns that refer to male people or animals are masculine (**un señor**), and nouns that refer to female people or animals are feminine (**una señorita**). However, other words, like **té** and **café**, do not fall into these categories, so you should learn the gender of nouns as you learn their meanings.

2. In Spanish, the indefinite article has four forms. The form used depends on the noun's gender and on whether it is singular or plural. Masculine singular nouns use **un** *(a, an)*; feminine nouns use **una** *(a, an)*; masculine plural nouns use **unos** *(some)*; and feminine plural nouns use **unas** *(some)*. Note that if a noun is plural in Spanish, it usually ends with an –s whether it is masculine or feminine.

Aquí practicamos

F. ¿Un o unos? ¿Una o unas? Add the correct indefinite article to these nouns. Follow the model.

> **MODELO** botella de agua mineral
> *una botella de agua mineral*

1. jugo de naranja
2. botellas de agua mineral
3. té
4. vaso de agua
5. refrescos
6. café con leche

G. Yo quisiera... ¿Y tú? You and a friend are deciding what to have to drink. Express what you want to order and then ask your friend what she (he) would like. Follow the model.

> **MODELO** té / café con leche
> **Tú:** *Yo quisiera un té, ¿y tú?*
> **Amigo(a):** *Un café con leche.*

1. chocolate / refresco
2. té / limonada
3. vaso de agua mineral / jugo
4. granadina con agua mineral / café
5. licuado de banana / chocolate
6. té con leche / té con limón

Comentarios CULTURALES

Los cafés

In the Spanish-speaking world, young and old people enjoy meeting at cafés for a drink and a snack at different times during the day. In many neighbor-hoods of a town or city one can find cafés, each with its own particular clientele and atmosphere. In a café near a school or university, for example, it is possible to see groups of students sitting at tables discussing their studies and politics or just laughing and chatting with friends. Older people may prefer sitting in a quieter café where they can listen to music while they read the newspaper, play cards or domi-noes, or simply relax watching the passersby. In the summertime, tables are often set outside for the enjoyment of the customers.

Aquí escuchamos

En un café *Clara and her friends are having something to drink at a café.*

Antes de escuchar Based on the information you have learned in this chapter, answer the following questions.

1. What are some beverages you expect Clara and her friends will order?

2. What do you say to order something in Spanish?

 A escuchar Listen to the conversation that Clara and her friends have with the waiter at the café, paying special attention to what each young person orders.

Después de escuchar On your activity master, circle the items Clara and her friends ordered.

agua mineral	licuado	té
café	limonada	
leche	refresco	

¿Qué desean tomar? You and two friends are in a café. Decide what each person will order, call the waiter (waitress), and place your order. Work in groups of four and follow the model.

MODELO		
	Tú:	*¿Qué desean tomar?*
	Amigo(a) 1:	*Yo quisiera una limonada.*
	Amigo(a) 2:	*Un café para mí (for me).*
	Tú:	*Pst, camarero(a).*
	Camarero(a):	*Sí, señorita (señor), ¿qué desean?*
	Tú:	*Una limonada, un café y un té con limón, por favor.*
	Camarero(a):	*Muy bien, señorita (señor).*

 A mí me gusta... Get together with a classmate to do the following.

1. Make your own separate lists of six different beverages ranked in the order of your personal preferences.

2. Exchange lists and compare your preferences.

3. Identify three beverages that both of you like, adding to your original lists if necessary.

Café El Parnaso

Calle Mayor 27

Bahía Blanca, Argentina

(831-6517)

un café con leche	*1.00*
un café con leche	*1.00*
una limonada	*1.50*
un chocolate caliente	*1.75*

TERCERA ETAPA

- What are some of the things you can order for breakfast in a restaurant?
- What is your favorite breakfast food?
- What do you generally like to eat for lunch?
- What do you have for a snack now and then?

¡Vamos a comer algo!

un bocadillo

un croissant *(Spain)*

un pan dulce

un pastel de fresas

una rebanada de pan

mermelada

mantequilla

un pan tostado

un desayuno

un sándwich de jamón y queso

*Two friends (**amigas**), Ana and Clara, are at a café.*

Ana: Quisiera tomar un café. ¿Y tú?
Clara: Yo quisiera **comer algo**.
Ana: En **este** café **tienen** bocadillos, sándwiches y pasteles.
Clara: **Pues**, **voy a comer** un pastel, mm… **con** un café con leche.
Ana: Y para mí un sándwich de jamón y queso.

un bocadillo: *a sandwich made with a French roll; may have different fillings, such as cheese, ham, sausage, an omelette, etc.; most common in Spain.*

un pan dulce: *any kind of sweet roll, cinnamon roll, danish, etc.; usually eaten with hot chocolate; this expression is commonly used in Mexico.*

comer algo *to eat something* **este** *this* **tienen** *they have* **Pues** *Then* **voy a comer** *I'm going to eat* **con** *with*

¡Te toca a ti!

A. ¿Vas (Are you going) a comer algo?
You and a friend are at a snack bar. Decide what snack you will each have from the suggested items. Follow the model.

> **MODELO**   un sándwich de queso / un sándwich de jamón
> **Tú:**   *¿Vas a comer algo?*
> **Amigo(a):**   *Yo quisiera un sándwich de queso.*
> **Tú:**   *Yo voy a comer un sándwich de jamón.*

1. un bocadillo de jamón / un bocadillo de queso
2. un pastel de fresas / un pastel de banana
3. un croissant / un pan dulce
4. un sándwich de queso / un sándwich de jamón y queso
5. un pan tostado / una rebanada de pan
6. un licuado de banana / un pan con mantequilla
7. un pan con mermelada / un pan dulce
8. un sándwich de jamón / un sándwich de queso

B. El desayuno
You are having breakfast in a café in Condado, Puerto Rico. What would you like to order from the waiter (waitress)? Work with a partner and follow the model.

> **MODELO**   **Camarero(a):**   *¿Qué desea, señor (señorita)?*
> **Tú:**   *Un café y un pan tostado, por favor.*

PRONUNCIACIÓN   THE VOWEL e

The sound of the vowel **e** in Spanish is pronounced like the *e* of the English word *bet* except that the sound is shorter in Spanish.

Práctica

C.
Listen and repeat as your teacher models the following words.

1. que	5. café	9. es
2. leche	6. tres	10. ese
3. Pepe	7. nene	
4. este	8. té	

D. Después de clase (After class) You are meeting a friend in a nearby café. She (he) arrives with a person that you have never met before. 1) Greet your friend. 2) She (he) introduces you to the new person, and the three of you sit down for a drink. 3) The waiter (waitress) comes and takes your orders. While you wait, 4) you ask the new person what things she (he) likes to do. Work in groups of four, assigning one role to each person.

ESTRUCTURA

Subject pronouns and the present tense of regular –ar verbs: First and second persons

Subject Pronouns

	Singular		Plural
yo	*I*	**nosotros**	*we* (masculine)
tú	*you* (informal)	**nosotras**	*we* (feminine)
usted	*you* (formal)	**vosotros(as)**	*you* (informal)
		ustedes	*you*

1. **Tú** is used to address a friend, a child, a family member, or anyone with whom you are on a first-name basis. **Usted** (abbreviated **Ud.**) is used with older people, teachers, or anyone that you do not know very well. In general, the use of **usted** indicates a respectful or formal relationship.

2. **Nosotras** is used to refer to a group of all women; **nosotros** refers to a group of males and females or a group of all males.

3. **Vosotros(as)** is used as the plural of **tú** only in Spain. **Ustedes** (abbreviated **Uds.**) is used as the plural of both **usted** and **tú** throughout Latin America.

Present tense of regular –ar verbs: First and second persons

Subject Pronoun	Verb Ending	Conjugated form of the verb **tomar**
yo	**–o**	tom**o**
tú	**–as**	tom**as**
usted	**–a**	tom**a**
nosotros (as)	**–amos**	tom**amos**
vosotros (as)	**–áis**	tom**áis**
ustedes	**–an**	tom**an**

ESTRUCTURA (continued)

4. The infinitives of Spanish verbs end in **–ar, –er,** or **–ir.** Verbs consist of two parts: a stem (**tom–** for the **–ar** verb **tomar**), which carries the meaning, and an ending, which indicates the subject or person the verb refers to (**–as** for **tú**), as well as the tense. In Spanish, verb endings are very important because each one must agree in person (first, second, or third) and number (singular or plural) with its subject.

5. To conjugate any regular **–ar** verb, drop the **–ar** and replace it with the ending that corresponds to the subject. In addition to **tomar,** you already know some other regular **–ar** verbs: **bailar, cantar, desear, escuchar, estudiar, hablar,** and **practicar.** Two new verbs are **trabajar** *(to work)* and **viajar** *(to travel).*

6. The Spanish present tense has three English equivalents. When a statement is made negative in the present tense by adding **no** in front of the conjugated form of the verb, there are two English equivalents.

Yo canto en el café.   *I sing at the café. I am singing at the café.*

Nosotros no bailamos aquí.   *We are not dancing here. We do not dance here.*

Aquí practicamos

E. Todos (Everyone) cantan   Replace the subjects in italics and make the necessary changes in the verbs. Follow the model.

> **MODELO**   Yo bailo mucho. (tú / usted / nosotros / ustedes)
> *Tú bailas mucho.*
> *Usted baila mucho.*
> *Nosotros bailamos mucho.*
> *Ustedes bailan mucho.*

1. *Tú* cantas en el café. (usted / yo / nosotros / ustedes)
2. *Nosotros* practicamos en la clase. (tú / usted / yo / ustedes)
3. *Usted* habla español. (ustedes / yo / nosotras / tú)
4. *Yo* viajo a Guatemala. (tú / usted / nosotros / ustedes)
5. *Ustedes* estudian mucho. (yo / tú / usted / nosotras)
6. *Nosotras* escuchamos música. (tú / yo / usted / ustedes)

F. ¡Muy bien! Say whether you do or do not do the following activities. Follow the model.

> **MODELO**   bailar bien
> *Yo no bailo bien.* o: *Yo bailo bien.*

1. cantar muy bien
2. hablar mucho
3. practicar el piano
4. trabajar mucho
5. escuchar música rock
6. hablar en clase
7. estudiar poco
8. viajar a Paraguay

PALABRAS ÚTILES

Expressing frequency

You can use the following words and phrases to express how well or how often you do something.

bien	well	todos los días	every day
muy bien	very well	siempre	always
mal	poorly	a veces	sometimes

Aquí practicamos

G. Hablo español todos los días Say how well or how often you engage in the following activities. Follow the model.

> **MODELO**   estudiar
> *Yo estudio todos los días.*

1. hablar español
2. bailar
3. cantar en clase
4. estudiar
5. escuchar música popular
6. trabajar

H. Preguntas personales (Personal questions)
Answer the following questions. Follow the model.

> **MODELO**   ¿Cantas bien?
> *No, canto mal.* o: *Sí, canto bien.*

1. ¿Bailas mucho?
2. ¿Trabajas después de *(after)* clase?
3. ¿Hablas español muy bien?
4. ¿Estudias mucho o poco?
5. ¿Practicas el tenis?
6. ¿Escuchas música popular? ¿rock? ¿clásica?
7. ¿Cantas todos los días?
8. ¿Viajas todos los días a Nueva York?

I. Mi amigo(a) y yo Talk with a classmate about what you each do in a typical week. Then compare these activities with what your parents do. Using **-ar** verbs that you know, think of at least three pairs of examples. Follow the models.

Tú:	*Mi amigo y yo estudiamos mucho.*
Amiga(o):	*Y nuestros padres trabajan mucho.*
Amiga(o):	*Yo escucho música rock.*
Tú:	*Y mi madre escucha música clásica.*

Comentarios CULTURALES

Las comidas

In Spanish-speaking countries, there are often cafés near schools and universities where students meet before or after class. It is common to have a snack at mid-morning and at mid-afternoon, because lunch and dinner are frequently served late. Lunch is the largest meal of the day in many countries, including Colombia, and it is often served later than in the U.S. Traditionally, people would return home from work for a long lunch, although this custom is now changing. People who take long lunches usually start their work day earlier in the morning and finish later in the evening than is common in the U.S. Dinner may be served as late as 10:00 P.M. in some countries, such as Spain.

Aquí escuchamos

¡A comer! *Luis and his friends are having a bite to eat at a café.*

Antes de escuchar Based on what you have learned about food in this chapter, answer the following questions.

1. What are some of the things you expect Luis and his friends to order?
2. What question does a waiter (waitress) usually ask when first taking an order?

A escuchar Listen to the conversation Luis and his friends have with the waitress, paying special attention to what each person orders.

Después de escuchar On your activity master, put a check mark next to each item that Luis and his friends ordered.

__ agua mineral	__ croissant	__ pan dulce	__ pastel
__ bocadillo	__ jugo	__ pan tostado	__ sándwich

La merienda (Snack time) You go to a café at mid-morning for a snack and run into a classmate whom you don't know very well.

1. Greet each other.
2. Order something to eat.
3. While waiting for your food, ask each other questions to get acquainted. You can find out if the other person likes to travel, dance, and sing. Ask how well and how frequently he (she) does these activities. Finally, ask if he (she) works, how often, and if he (she) likes to work or not.

 ¿Qué vamos a tomar? With a classmate, write a list of your favorite beverages.

1. Make your own separate lists of six different beverages ranked in the order of your personal preferences.
2. Exchange lists and compare your preferences.
3. Identify three beverages that both of you like, adding to your original lists if necessary.

EN LÍNEA

Connect with the Spanish-speaking world!
Access the **¡Ya verás!** *Gold* home page for
Internet activities related to this chapter.

http://yaveras.heinle.com

VOCABULARIO

The Vocabulario *section consists of the new words and expressions presented in the chapter. When reviewing or studying for a test, you can go through the list to see if you know the meaning of each item. In the glossary at the end of the book, you can check the words you do not remember.*

Para charlar

Para saludar

Buenos días.
Buenas tardes.
Buenas noches.
¡Hola!
¿Cómo estás?
¿Cómo te va?
¿Qué hay?
¿Qué pasa?
¿Qué tal?

Para contestar

Buenos días.
Buenas tardes.
Buenas noches.
¡Hola!
Bien, gracias. ¿Y tú?
Muy bien, gracias.
Bastante bien.
Más o menos.
Regular.

Para despedirse

Adiós.
Chao.
Hasta luego.
Nos vemos.

Para presentar

Te presento a…

Para contestar

Mucho gusto.
¡Hola!

Para expresar gustos

Me gusta…
Te gusta…
No me gusta…
No te gusta…

Para hablar en un restaurante

¿Qué desea tomar?
¿Qué desean tomar?
Yo quisiera…
¿Y Ud.?
Voy a comer…
Para mí…
Aquí tienen ustedes.
por favor
Vamos al café.
Vamos a tomar algo.

Temas y contextos

Bebidas

una botella de agua
  mineral
un café
un café con leche
un chocolate
una granadina (con
  agua mineral, con
  soda)
un jugo de naranja
un licuado de
  banana
una limonada
un refresco
un té
un té con leche
un té con limón
un vaso de agua
  (con limón)

Comidas

un bocadillo
un croissant
un desayuno
mantequilla
mermelada
un pan dulce
un pan tostado
un pastel de fresas
una rebanada de
  pan
un sándwich de
  jamón y queso

Vocabulario general

Sustantivos

un(a) amigo(a)
abrazo
un(a) camarero(a)
el español
una merienda
la música
un señor
una señorita

Pronombres

yo
tú
usted (Ud.)
nosotros(as)
ustedes (Uds.)

Verbos

bailar
cantar
comer
desear
escuchar
estudiar
gustar
hablar
practicar
tomar
trabajar
viajar

Adverbios

a veces
bien
después de
mal
muchísimo
mucho
muy
muy bien
muy poco
poco
siempre
todos los días

Otras palabras
(words) y
expresiones

algo
caliente
con
De nada.
este
frío(a)
Muchas gracias.
no
perdón
pues
sí
un(a)
unos(as)

Mesón del Pirata

Reading Strategies
- Examining format for content clues
- Skimming for the gist
- Scanning for specific information
- Recognizing cognates

Antes de leer

1. Study the format of the following document. Can you tell what type of document it is? For whom is it intended?

2. Skim the very top part of the document. Can you guess where the restaurant is located?

3. Scan the middle of the document and find at least five cognates (words spelled similarly in English and Spanish that have the same meaning). Then, guess what type of restaurant is being described.

Restaurante
Mesón del Pirata
¡Donde comer es una aventura!

 Situado en el viejo San Juan

Calle del Cristo 137
Tel 258-9553 • Fax 258-9221

Tenemos las más exquisitas comidas puertorriqueñas de toda la isla. Nuestro chef, Don Tico, ha sido aclamado como el mejor chef de comida criolla de San Juan. Nuestras especialidades criollas son incomparables.

•••••••••••••• PLATOS TÍPICOS ••••••••••••••

tostones con mariscos • tostones rellenos con mariscos • queso frito del país • arafritas de plátano • surullitos de maíz rellenos con

queso • quesitos fritos • fricasé de conejo • filete relleno con chorizos • arroz con pollo • asopao de pollo

Guía para la lectura

1. Here are some words and expressions to keep in mind as you read.

   Tenemos   *We have*

   ha sido aclamado como   *Has been acclaimed, praised as*

   el mejor   *the best*

2. **La comida criolla** is the term used in a number of
   Latin American countries to describe prepared
   food that is considered typical or national. In
   Puerto Rico **comida criolla** is similar to Spanish
   food but with Puerto Rican ingredients and spices.

Después de leer

1. Why do you think the restaurant chose the name
   Mesón del Pirata?

2. Where is the restaurant located?

3. Which of the following statements accurately
   describes the foods that are served at the restaurant? More than one statement may be correct.

   ❑ Mostly American dishes are served.
   ❑ The restaurant claims to have an entertaining and
     lively atmosphere.
   ❑ The restaurant specializes in Puerto Rican dishes.
   ❑ The chef is well-known and has been recognized
     as one of the best.
   ❑ Dancing and live music are offered.

4. Would you like to go to the restaurant?
   Why or why not?

¡Vamos a un bar de tapas!

El bar de tapas es muy popular en España.

Objectives

- ordering something to eat
- greeting, introducing, and saying good-bye

PRIMERA ETAPA

Preparación

- As you noticed in Chapter 1, people eat different kinds of food when it is time for a snack. Here are some typical snacks from Spain, called **tapas.**

- Try to identify the different **tapas** in the picture. Do you recognize any of them?

- Have you ever had a **tapa?** Would you like to try this kind of snack? Why or why not?

Las tapas españolas

Aquí hay (Here are) *algunas tapas españolas típicas.*

aceitunas

cacahuetes

calamares

pan con chorizo

patatas bravas

queso

tortilla (de patatas)

patatas bravas: *cooked potatoes diced and served with a spicy sauce*

tortilla (de patatas): *a thick Spanish omelette made with eggs, potatoes, and onions; served in small bite-sized pieces*

¡Te toca a ti!

A. ¡Camarero(a), más (more) aceitunas, por favor!

You are in a **bar de tapas** with your friends, and you want to order more **tapas.** Ask the waiter (waitress) to bring you some. Follow the model.

> **MODELO**   aceitunas
> *Camarero(a), más aceitunas, por favor.*

1. cacahuetes
2. tortilla
3. patatas bravas
4. aceitunas
5. pan con chorizo
6. queso
7. calamares

B. Pasa (Pass) las patatas, por favor.

Your friend offers you some **tapas,** but the ones that you want to eat are too far away from you. Ask your friend to pass them to you. Work in pairs and follow the model.

> **MODELO**   Amigo(a):   ¿Deseas la tortilla? (las patatas)
> Tú: *No, pasa las patatas, por favor.*

1. ¿Deseas los cacahuetes? (las aceitunas)
2. ¿Deseas el queso? (el chorizo)
3. ¿Deseas la tortilla de patatas? (el pan)
4. ¿Deseas los calamares? (la tortilla)
5. ¿Deseas las aceitunas? (el queso)
6. ¿Deseas el chorizo? (las patatas bravas)
7. ¿Deseas el pan? (los calamares)

C. ¡Qué hambre! (I'm starving!)

You are very hungry and want something more to eat than **tapas.** What do you order? Work in groups of four. One person is the waiter (waitress) and the others are customers. Take turns ordering something to eat. Use some of the vocabulary that you already know from Chapter 1. Follow the model.

> **MODELO**   Camarero(a):   *¿Qué desean comer?*
> Tú: *Yo quisiera un sándwich de jamón y queso.*

 PRONUNCIACIÓN THE VOWEL **i**

The sound of the vowel **i** in Spanish is pronounced like the *ee* of the English word *beet,* except it is shorter in Spanish.

Práctica

D. Listen and repeat as your teacher models the following words for you.

1. sí
2. mi
3. silla
4. allí
5. y
6. mira
7. hija
8. mochila
9. ti
10. tiza
11. Lili
12. libro

Comentarios CULTURALES

Las tapas

In Spain, one of the most popular meeting places for friends is the **bar de tapas.** Spaniards commonly stop in these places after work or before dinner for a snack and something to drink. These snacks are called **tapas** and include such things as peanuts, olives, cheese, and bite-sized pieces of **tortilla española.** Sometimes these **tapas** are provided at no charge with each beverage order. The menu also includes more substantial food, such as **bocadillos** and different kinds of fried fish. **La Chuleta** is one of the better-known **tapas** bars in Madrid.

Repaso

E. Mis actividades Say whether or not you do the following activities. If you do them, say how often or how well. Follow the model.

> **MODELO**   cantar
> *Yo no canto muy bien.*

1. trabajar
2. escuchar música
3. viajar
4. cantar
5. hablar inglés
6. bailar
7. hablar español
8. estudiar matemáticas

¿Qué crees?

In Spain, a typical breakfast would be:

a) bacon and eggs
b) coffee and toast
c) pancakes with hot syrup

respuesta ☞

F. Una conversación en un café You meet two friends at a café for a snack. 1) One of you should make introductions. 2) Then place your order. While waiting for the waiter (waitress) to bring your food and beverages, 3) ask each other questions about the things you like to do. On a signal from your teacher, 4) end your conversation and say good-bye.

ESTRUCTURA

Subject pronouns and the present tense of regular -ar verbs: Third person

¿Miguel? Él **viaja** mucho.

¿Anita? Ella **habla** español muy bien.

¿Jaime y Tomás? Ellos **cantan** bien.

¿Paquita y Laura?
Ellas no **estudian** mucho.

¿Juan y Clara? Ellos **bailan**.

Subject Pronouns

	Singular		Plural
él	*he*	**ellos**	*they* (masculine)
ella	*she*	**ellas**	*they* (feminine)

1. **Ellas** is used to refer to groups of females; **ellos** refers to groups of males or groups of males and females.

Present Tense of Regular *-ar* Verbs

Subject Pronoun	Verb Ending	Conjugated form of the verb **trabajar**
él	**–a**	trabaj**a**
ella	**–a**	trabaj**a**
ellos	**–an**	trabaj**an**
ellas	**–an**	trabaj**an**

2. To form the present tense of any regular -**ar** verb in the third person, add to the stem the verb ending that corresponds to the subject. Remember that the stem is found by dropping the -**ar** from the infinitive (**trabaj-** for the -**ar** verb **trabajar**).

3. The endings for **él** and **ella** are the same as these used for **usted**, and the ones for **ellos** and **ellas** are the same as those used for **ustedes**.

4. Some additional -**ar** verbs and expressions that you should learn are **ganar dinero** *(to earn money)*, **mirar** *(to look at, to watch)*, and **tocar** *(to touch, to play a musical instrument)*.

5. In Spanish, since verb endings indicate the subject, subject pronouns are frequently omitted.

Escuchas música clásica.　　　*You listen to classical music.*
Hablan español.　　　*They speak Spanish.*

6. Subject pronouns are, however, used with conjugated verb forms for emphasis or clarification.

Usted toma un café y **yo tomo** un té.　　　*You are having a coffee and I am having a tea.*

Aquí practicamos

G. Las actividades Describe the activities that the people in the left-hand column are doing by forming sentences with phrases from the other two columns.

A	B	C
ellos	cantar	en un café
yo	hablar	una limonada
Juan y Alicia	trabajar	en clase
nosotras	escuchar	inglés
Carlos	mirar	dinero
Patricia y yo	bailar	música clásica
ustedes	tomar	todos los días
tú	viajar	en casa
ellos	desear	patatas bravas
el señor Suárez	estudiar	a San Salvador
el (la) profesor(a)	practicar	la televisión
mis hermanos	necesitar	

H. Mis amigos colombianos (My Colombian friends) Your Colombian friends have some questions for you and your classmates. Answer their questions using subject pronouns and the expressions in parentheses. Follow the model.

MODELO
    Amigo(a): ¿John habla español mal? (muy bien)
    Tú: *No, él habla español muy bien.*

1. ¿Jack baila muy poco? (muchísimo)
2. ¿Nancy y Kay estudian poco? (mucho)
3. ¿Helen trabaja todos los días? (a veces)
4. ¿Julie y Tom cantan bien? (mal)
5. ¿Ed y Andy escuchan música clásica todos los días? (a veces)
6. ¿Lisa gana mucho? (muy poco)

PALABRAS ÚTILES

Asking and answering yes/no questions

—¿Tú estudias mucho?	*Do you study a lot?*
—Sí, yo estudio mucho.	*Yes, I study a lot.*
—¿Hablan ustedes francés?	*Do you speak French?*
—No, nosotros no hablamos francés.	*No, we don't speak French.*
—Ellos trabajan mucho, ¿no?	*They work a lot, don't they?*
—Sí, ellos trabajan mucho.	*Yes, they work a lot.*
—Ella no toca la guitarra, ¿verdad?	*She doesn't play the guitar, does she?*
—No, ella no toca la guitarra.	*No, she doesn't play the guitar.*

1. There are three basic ways to ask these kinds of questions in Spanish.

   • Make your voice rise at the end of a group of words: **¿Usted baila bien?**

   • Invert the order of the subject and verb: **¿Practican ellas** español en clase?

   • Add the words **¿no?** or **¿verdad?** after the statement. In such questions, **¿no?** and **¿verdad?** are equivalents of expressions like *don't you?, aren't you,? isn't he (she)?* at the end of English sentences. Note that **¿no?** or **¿verdad?** can be used at the end of an affirmative statement, but only **¿verdad?** is used at the end of a negative statement.

Nosotras cantamos bien, **¿no?**	*We sing well, don't we?*
Tú **no ganas** mucho dinero, **¿verdad?**	*You don't earn much money, do you?*

2. To answer these kinds of questions negatively, place **no** before the conjugated verb.

Yo **no viajo** mucho.	*I do not travel a lot.*

Aquí practicamos

I. **¿Usted desea un café?**   Change each statement to a question by making your voice rise at the end of the sentence.

1. Usted desea un café.

2. Tú miras mucho la TV.

3. Román trabaja poco.

4. La señorita Ruiz gana mucho dinero.

5. Ustedes estudian mucho.

6. Ester toca el piano.

7. Nosotros viajamos a Ecuador.

8. Ellos cantan bien.

J. ¿Verdad? Now use **¿no?** or **¿verdad?** to change the following statements into questions.

1. Paquita habla bien el alemán *(German)*.
2. Ana y Rosa cantan muy mal.
3. Tú hablas español en el laboratorio.
4. Ella no estudia mucho.
5. Ellos trabajan poco.
6. Ustedes toman té.
7. Usted no gana mucho dinero.
8. Reynaldo toca el violín todos los días.

K. Hagan preguntas (Ask questions) You want to find as many people as you can who participate in the following activities. Ask your classmates and your teacher questions based on the model. On your activity master, keep track of who answers **sí** by writing their names in the blanks beside each activity. Be prepared to report the results of your poll.

MODELO   hablar francés
Tú hablas francés, ¿verdad? o:
¿Señor (Señorita), habla usted francés?

1. cantar muy bien				
2. viajar mucho				
3. estudiar poco				
4. estudiar todos los días				
5. no tomar té				
6. hablar español en casa				
7. tocar un instrumento				
8. mirar la TV mucho				
9. trabajar a veces				
10. escuchar música clásica				
11. practicar el tenis				

Aquí escuchamos

En un bar de tapas *Beatriz, Linda, and Cristina are at a **tapas** bar. It's 1:30 in the afternoon.*

Antes de escuchar Think about vocabulary you might hear in the conversation.

 A escuchar As you listen to the conversation, put a check mark on your activity master next to each of the following words every time you hear it.

___aceitunas	___pan con chorizo
___agua mineral	___refresco
___calamares	___tortilla de patatas

Después de escuchar On your activity master, indicate which food items each girl ordered. Be aware that Beatriz speaks first, then Linda, then Cristina.

	1. Beatriz	2. Linda	3. Cristina
a. agua mineral			
b. tortilla			
c. calamares			
d. pan con chorizo			
e. refresco			

¡ADELANTE!

 Chismes (Gossip) Your friend knows the new student in the class better than you do. Invite your friend to have a snack so you can ask some questions. Find out if the new student is a good singer and dancer, if she travels a great deal, if she watches TV a lot, if she works, etc. Order something to eat and drink as well.

 Más actividades Working with a partner, ask each other questions in Spanish. Use them to write nine sentences describing nine different activities. Include three that you both do on a regular basis, three that only you do regularly, and three that your partner does regularly. Your first three sentences should begin with **Nosotros...**, the next three should begin with **Yo...**, and the last three will have your partner's name as the subject. Be prepared to report all the information to the class.

- In Spanish-speaking cultures, certain courtesies are generally observed between people who meet for the first time. A certain degree of respectful formality by a younger person toward an older person is usually expected.

- How would you address a person who is older than you, or someone you haven't met before or don't know very well?

- How would you expect an older person who doesn't know you very well to address you in a public place?

- When people meet on the street and introductions are in order, who should take the responsibility to make them, as a courtesy?

¡Buenos días! ... ¡Hasta luego!

At the café, Lucas Pereda and his friend Jaime Torres run into two friends of Lucas' parents, **el señor** and **la señora** García.

el señor *Mr.*   la señora *Mrs.*

Sr. y Sra. García:	Buenos días, Lucas.
Lucas:	¡Oh! Buenos días, señor García. Buenos días, señora. **¿Cómo están ustedes?**
Sra. García:	Muy bien, gracias. ¿Y tú?
Lucas:	Estoy muy bien, gracias. **Quisiera presentarles a mi amigo** Jaime Torres. El señor y la señora García.
Sr. y Sra. García:	Mucho gusto, Jaime.
Jaime:	**Encantado,** señora. Mucho gusto, señor.
Sr. García:	¿Van a tomar un café?
Lucas:	No, **acabamos de** tomar unos refrescos.
Sr. García:	¡Ah! Pues, hasta luego. **Saludos a tus padres.**
Lucas:	Gracias.
Lucas y Jaime:	Adiós, señor, señora.
Sr. y Sra. García:	Adiós.

Saludos	Presentaciones (Introductions)
Buenos días.	Quisiera presentarle(s) a...
¿Cómo están ustedes?	Encantado(a).
¿Cómo está usted?	Mucho gusto.
(Estoy) Bien, gracias. ¿Y Ud.?	Igualmente. *Likewise.*

¿Cómo están ustedes? *How are you?* **Estoy** *I am* **Quisiera presentarles a mi amigo** *I would like to introduce you to my friend* **Encantado** *Delighted* **Van a** *Are you going to* **acabamos de** *we've just finished* **Saludos a tus padres.** *Greetings to your parents.*

Comentarios CULTURALES

Saludos informales y formales

When greeting people and making introductions, different expressions denote different degrees of formality or informality: **¡Hola!, ¿Qué tal?, ¿Cómo estás?, ¿Cómo te va?, Te presento a...** are used informally with people you know well and with peers. **¿Cómo está usted?, ¿Cómo están ustedes?, Quisiera presentarles(le) a...** are more formal and are used with older people or people you do not know very well. It is not uncommon for older people or superiors to speak informally to a younger person who addresses them as **usted,** as you saw in the conversation between Lucas, Jaime, and **el señor** and **la señora** García.

¡Te toca a ti!

A. ¿Qué respondes? (How do you answer?)
Respond to each question or statement with an appropriate expression. Address the person in parentheses by name. Follow the model.

> **MODELO**   Buenos días, Alberto. (Sr. Pérez)
> *Buenos días, señor Pérez.*

1. ¿Cómo estás, Adela? (Sr. Carrillo)
2. ¡Hola, Lourdes! (Sra. Ramírez)
3. Quisiera presentarle a mi amigo Pepe. (Sra. Ruiz)
4. ¿Cómo están ustedes, señores? (Margarita)
5. Mucho gusto, Raquel. (Sra. Castillo)

B. Buenos días, señor (señora, señorita)
Greet and shake hands with your teacher, introduce a classmate to him (her), and then say good-bye.

PRONUNCIACIÓN   THE VOWEL o
The sound of the vowel **o** in Spanish is pronounced like the *o* in the English word *open*, except it is much shorter in Spanish.

Práctica

C. Listen and repeat as your teacher models the following words.

1. ojo	4. chorizo	7. jugo	10. vaso
2. con	5. año	8. política	11. nosotros
3. algo	6. como	9. por	12. disco

Repaso

D. Escuchen bien (Listen carefully)
Play the roles of the following students and enact their conversation according to the model. Anita asks Marcos a question. After Marcos answers, Claudia asks Ada what he said, and Ada tells her.

> **MODELO**   hablar inglés
> **Anita:** *Marcos, ¿tú hablas inglés?*
> **Marcos:** *No, yo no hablo inglés.*
> **Claudia:** *Ada, ¿habla inglés Marcos?*
> **Ada:** *No, él no habla inglés.*

1. tocar la guitarra
2. bailar muy bien
3. viajar a Bolivia
4. tomar café con leche todos los días
5. mirar mucho la TV
6. estudiar francés *(French)*
7. cantar muy mal
8. trabajar muchísimo

E. Mi amigo(a)   In pairs, 1) ask your partner questions to gather information about him (her). 2) Then, create a profile of the two of you on your activity master. Put an X under each activity that each of you does well or often. 3) Prepare to report on your similarities and differences. Follow the model.

	hablar	estudiar	cantar	bailar	viajar	trabajar	tocar
yo							
mi amigo(a)							

MODELO

Tú: *Carmencita, cantas bien, ¿verdad?*
Carmencita: *Sí, canto bien.*
Tú: *Mi amiga Carmencita canta bien.*
Yo no canto bien, pero bailo muy bien.

ESTRUCTURA

The conjugated verb followed by the infinitive

¿Deseas trabajar?   *Do you want to work?*

Ellas no **necesitan estudiar** mucho.   *They don't need to study a lot.*

1. When two verbs are used with each other, the first verb is conjugated to agree with the subject and the second verb remains in the infinitive form. This construction occurs frequently with some verbs and expressions you already know: **desear** and **yo quisiera**. It also occurs with **acabar de** *(to have just done something)*, **necesitar** *(to need)*, and **tú quisieras** *(you would like)*.

2. To make this construction negative, place **no** in front of the conjugated verb form.

3. To confirm an affirmative statement someone has just said, use the word **también** *(also, too)* after the infinitive. For a negative statement, use **tampoco** *(neither, either)*.

—Deseo bailar.   *I want to dance.*
—Deseo bailar **también**.   *I want to dance too.*

—No deseo estudiar.   *I don't want to study.*
—No deseo estudiar **tampoco**.   *I don't want to study either.*

Aquí practicamos

F. **¿Quisieras tú...?** At a party, you try to impress a boy (girl) whom you like by asking in Spanish if he (she) would like to do certain things. Use the following expressions to form your questions. He (she) can answer affirmatively or negatively. Follow the model.

> **MODELO**　　comer algo *(something)*
>
> 　　　　　　**Tú:**　*¿Quisieras comer algo?*
>
> 　　　　**Amigo(a):**　*Sí, quisiera comer unas patatas bravas. o: No, quisiera bailar.*

1. bailar
2. cantar
3. escuchar música española *(Spanish)*
4. tomar algo
5. hablar español
6. comer unas tapas

G. **¿Deseas o necesitas?** On your activity master, indicate whether you want or need to do the following activities. Mark your answers by writing **sí** or **no** in each space. Then see if your classmate wants or needs to do the same things as you. If your classmate gives the **same** sí response as you, he (she) should add **también** to the answer on the activity master. If your classmate gives the same **no** response as you, he (she) should add **tampoco**. Look at the models for examples. Be prepared to report 1) one activity you both want to do, 2) one you both need to do, 3) one that neither one of you wants to do, and 4) one that neither of you needs to do.

> **MODELOS**　　Gathering information:
>
> 　　　　　　　　estudiar
>
> 　　　　　　**Tú:**　*Necesito estudiar.*
>
> 　　**Compañero(a):**　*Yo necesito estudiar también. o: No deseo estudiar.*
>
> 　　　　　　**Tú:**　*No necesito estudiar.*
>
> 　　**Compañero(a):**　*Yo sí necesito estudiar. o: Yo no necesito estudiar tampoco.*

> **MODELO**　　Reporting:　*Mi amiga Ana y yo deseamos viajar a Sudamérica. Necesitamos ganar dinero. No deseamos trabajar mucho. No necesitamos gastar mucho.*

	Yo necesito	Yo deseo	Mi amigo(a) necesita	Mi amigo(a) desea
viajar a Sudamérica (South America)				
hablar español				
tomar un refresco				
trabajar mucho				
tocar el piano				
mirar la TV				
estudiar mucho				
ganar mucho dinero				

H. Consejos (Pieces of advice)

Your mother (**mamá**) tells you what you need to do. Tell her that you have already done everything she mentions. Follow the model.

> **MODELO** estudiar matemáticas
>
> **Mamá:** *Necesitas estudiar matemáticas.*
> **Tú:** *Pero (But) acabo de estudiar matemáticas.*

1. estudiar inglés
2. trabajar mucho
3. comer bien
4. hablar en español
5. ganar dinero
6. practicar el piano

Aquí escuchamos

El señor y la señora Jiménez *Alicia and her friend Reynaldo meet some friends of her parents in the park.*

 Antes de escuchar Think of some of the set formal and informal phrases you know in Spanish for greetings, introductions, and farewells (page 37).

A escuchar Listen twice to the conversation, and pay particular attention to the formal and informal phrases Alicia, Reynaldo, and **señor** and **señora** Jiménez use.

Después de escuchar Answer the following questions about the conversation you just heard.

1. Who uses the more formal **usted** forms in the conversation? Why is this so?
2. Who uses the more informal **tú** forms? Why?
3. What do the two couples decide to do?
4. What are some of the set courtesy phrases that you hear more than once in the conversation?

¡ADELANTE!

 Buenos días, señor (señora) While walking with a friend, you run into a Venezuelan colleague of your parents, Sr. (Sra.) Ruiz. Introduce your friend to him (her). Sr. (Sra.) Ruiz will ask the two of you about what you like to do.

 Preferencias Write six different things that you prefer doing as opposed to other activities. Follow the model.

> **MODELO**   *No deseo mirar la televisión, pero deseo escuchar música.*

EN LÍNEA

Connect with the Spanish-speaking world! Access the *¡Ya verás! Gold* home page for Internet activities related to this chapter.

http://yaveras.heinle.com

VOCABULARIO

Para charlar	Temas y contextos	Vocabulario general
Para saludar	**Tapas españolas**	**Pronombres**
¿Cómo está Ud.?	unas aceitunas	él
¿Cómo están Uds.?	unos cacahuetes	ella
Buenos días.	unos calamares	ellos
Saludos a tus	chorizo	ellas
padres.	pan	
	unas patatas bravas	**Verbos**
Para contestar	queso	acabar de
Bien, gracias. ¿Y	una tortilla (de patatas)	ganar
Ud.?		mirar
Estoy bien, gracias.		necesitar
Muy bien, gracias.		pasar
		tocar
Para presentar		
Quisiera presentar-		**Otras palabras y**
le(les) a…		**expresiones**
		mi amigo(a)
Para contestar		aquí hay
Encantado(a).		dinero
Igualmente.		español(a)
		mamá
		más
		¿no?
		pero
		preguntas
		presentación
		¡Qué hambre!
		¿Quisieras…?
		el señor
		la señora
		Sudamérica
		también
		tampoco
		Van a…?
		¿verdad?

Así lo decimos

Antes de leer

1. The Spanish paragraph below contains several cognates. Scan the paragraph for cognates and identify their meanings.

2. Glance at the boxed list below. Based on the way the information is organized, can you guess what kind of list it is?

3. In this reading you will see several synonyms in Spanish for the words *attractive, crazy,* and *money,* among others. Can you think of synonyms for these words in English? Name some of the synonyms and explain in which situation each one would be used.

El español se habla en muchos países diferentes. Las personas que hablan español pueden comprenderse unas a otras, pero frecuentemente usan palabras o expresiones diferentes para referirse a las mismas cosas. Aquí hay unas palabras que las personas usan en diferentes países.

Attractive Atractivo, guapo, mono, ser una monada, estar bueno

Avocado Aguacate, palta

Banana Plátano, banana, banano, guineo

Bean Ejote, frijol, habichuela, haba, judía

Bus Autobús, camión, guagua, omnibús

Car Automóvil, carro, coche, máquina

Crazy Loco, chiflado, chalado, ido, pirado, tocado

Drinking straw Paja de sorber, pajita, pajilla, popote, sorbeto

Gossip Chisme, cotorreo, cháchara, parloteo

Grapefruit Pomelo, toronja

Kite Cometa, papalote, chiringa, barrilete, birlocha, milocha, volantín

Money Dinero, plata, buenamoza, chavos, duros, pasta, pelas

Orange *(fruit)* Naranja, china

Peach Durazno, melocotón

Peas Guisantes, arvejas

Pineapple Ananás, piña

Shrimp Camarón, gamba, esquila, quisquilla

Suitcase Maleta, valija

Trunk *(car)* Baúl, cajuela, maletero, portaequipajes

Guía para la lectura

Here are some words and expressions to keep in mind as you read.

se habla	*is spoken*
pueden	*can*
comprenderse unas a otras	*understand each other*
las mismas cosas	*the same things*

Los nombres para las frutas varían mucho de país a país

Después de leer

1. Why do you think there are many ways of saying the same thing in Spanish?

2. Can people from different Spanish-speaking countries understand each other? Why do you think that is?

3. Find out the countries in which some of the synonyms listed are used. You can use dictionaries, ask Spanish-speaking classmates or friends, or interview your teacher.

Aquí se venden judías... ¿O son habichuelas?... ¿O son ejotes?...

¿Te gusta la comida mexicana?

—Quisiera comer algo.
—¿Te gusta la comida mexicana?

Objectives

- ordering something to eat
- finding out information about people

PRIMERA ETAPA

Preparación

- Before you start working on this **etapa,** think about what you already know about Mexican food. You may already be familiar with some of the dishes you are going to learn about in this **etapa.** Make a list of all the Mexican dishes you know.

- Now think of several features that describe or characterize this kind of food; for example, colors, spices, vegetables, meats, the kinds of dishes and utensils used for serving and eating them, etc.

¡Vamos a un restaurante!

Rafael y Pablo **están** (are) *en un restaurante en México.*

Camarero:	Buenos días, señores. **¿Qué van a pedir?**
Rafael:	Yo quisiera comer un **taco de pollo** con **frijoles.**
Pablo:	Para mí, una **enchilada de carne** con **arroz.**
Camarero:	¿Y para tomar?
Rafael:	Un vaso de agua con limón.
Camarero:	¿Y para Ud., señor?
Pablo:	Una limonada, **bien** fría, por favor.
Camarero:	Muy bien.

¿Qué van a pedir? *What will you have?*   **taco de pollo** *chicken taco*   **frijoles** *beans*   **enchilada de carne** *meat enchilada*
arroz *rice*   **bien** *very*

enchilada: *soft corn **tortilla** filled with cheese, meat, or chicken, and served with hot sauce*

frijoles: *pinto or black beans cooked until tender; may be served mashed, most often as a side dish*

taco: *a corn tortilla filled with meat, chicken, or other fillings, and topped with lettuce, tomato, grated cheese, and sauce*

tortilla: *made of corn meal and shaped like a pancake; in Mexico, the **tortilla** is served with most meals and takes the place of bread*

¡Te toca a ti!

A. ¿Qué va a pedir? You are in a Mexican restaurant. Look at the pictures and decide what you are going to order based on the cues. A classmate will play the role of waiter (waitress). Follow the model.

> **MODELO** enchilada de queso
>
> **Camarero(a):** *¿Qué va a pedir?*
> **Tú:** *Yo quisiera comer una enchilada de queso.*
> **Camarero(a):** *Muy bien.*

1. enchilada de carne

2. enchilada de queso

3. tacos de pollo

4. tacos de carne

5. arroz con frijoles

6. frijoles

B. ¿En España o en México? Do you think these people are in Spain or in Mexico? Decide based on the food they are eating.

1. A mí me gusta mucho comer tapas con un refresco.
2. Yo quisiera un bocadillo de jamón, por favor.
3. Para mí una enchilada de carne con salsa, por favor.
4. Yo voy a tomar un chocolate.
5. Voy a comer un sándwich de jamón y queso.
6. Yo deseo un taco de pollo con frijoles.

C. ¿Vamos (Are we going) a comer algo? When asked this question, the people pictured below all answered **sí,** but they all wanted different things. Match each statement with the appropriate drawing.

1.

2.

3.

4.

a. Yo quisiera comer unas tapas y tomar algo bien frío.

b. A mí me gusta la comida mexicana… Mm…, ¡tacos y frijoles con arroz!

c. Yo deseo un café con leche y un sándwich.

d. Nosotros deseamos unos licuados de fresas con unos bocadillos.

PRONUNCIACIÓN THE VOWEL u

The sound of the vowel **u** in Spanish is pronounced like the **u** of the English word *rule,* except it is shorter in Spanish.

Práctica

D. Listen and repeat as your teacher models the following words.

1. tú	5. gusta	9. jugo
2. lunes	6. saludos	10. música
3. Perú	7. Cuba	
4. un	8. mucho	

Repaso ♻

E. ¡Hola! ¿Qué tal? With classmates, play the roles of the people depicted in each of the following situations. Pay attention to the level of language—whether it should be formal or informal according to the situation. Follow the model.

Silvia   Cristina

MODELO

Silvia:	*¡Hola, Cristina!*
Cristina:	*¡Hola! ¿Qué tal, Silvia?*
Silvia:	*Muy bien. ¿Y tú?*
Cristina:	*Mm… más o menos.*

1. Sr. González   Srta. Díaz   2. Enrique   Antonio   3. Héctor   Teresa   Samuel

4. Amalia   Clara   Sra. Rivas   5. Aldo   Luis   6. Sra.   Gerardo
                                                                        Mendoza

F.   ¿Te gusta bailar?   For each activity listed, survey three class-mates. Ask them whether they like the activity. Keep track of their answers on your activity master, writing their names in the appropriate columns. Follow the model.

> **MODELO**   bailar
>   **Tú:**   *Luisa, ¿te gusta bailar?*
>   **Luisa:**   *Sí, me gusta mucho bailar.* o: *Sí, yo bailo mucho.*
>
>   **Tú:**   *Tomás, ¿te gusta bailar?*
>   **Tomás:**   *No, me gusta muy poco bailar.* o: *No, yo bailo muy poco.*
>
>   **Tú:**   *Rafael, ¿te gusta bailar?*
> **Rafael:**   *No, me gusta poco bailar.*

	muy poco	**poco**	**mucho**	**muchísimo**
bailar	Tomás	Rafael	Luisa	
cantar				
estudiar				
hablar español				
tomar café				
mirar la TV				
viajar				
trabajar en clase				
ganar dinero				

ESTRUCTURA

The present tense of the verb ser

Pablo: ¡Hola! **Yo soy** Pablo Hernández.
Y tú, ¿quién *(who)* **eres?**
Tomás: **Yo soy** Tomás García.

Pablo: ¿De dónde **eres,** Tomás?
Tomás: **Soy** de Bogotá, Colombia.
¿Y tú?
Pablo: **Yo soy** de Lima, Perú.

Pablo: ¡Mira! Allí están *(There are)*
Luisa y Raquel.
Tomás: ¿También **son** de Lima?

Luisa: No, **nosotras somos** de los
Estados Unidos.
Raquel: Sí, **somos** de Miami.

ser *(to be)*			
yo	**soy**	nosotros(as)	**somos**
tú	**eres**	vosotros(as)	**sois**
él ella Ud.	**es**	ellos ellas Uds.	**son**

1. Some important Spanish verbs like the verb **ser** are irregular. This means that they do not follow a regular conjugation pattern, so you need to memorize their forms.

2. To ask where someone or something is from, use the expression ¿**de dónde + ser?** To express place of origin, use **ser + de** followed by the name of a country or city.

—¿**De dónde son Uds?**   *Where are you from?*
—**Somos de Bolivia.**   *We are from Bolivia.*

PALABRAS ÚTILES

Names of countries

Here are the names of places and countries in the world where Spanish is spoken, as well as the names of some other countries.

Países de habla hispana (Spanish-speaking countries)

(la) Argentina	Honduras
Bolivia	México
Chile	Nicaragua
Colombia	Panamá
Costa Rica	(el) Paraguay
Cuba	(el) Perú
(el) Ecuador	Puerto Rico
El Salvador	(la) República Dominicana
España	(el) Uruguay
Guatemala	Venezuela

Otros países

Alemania *Germany*	Inglaterra *England*
(el) Canadá	Italia
(la) China	(el) Japón
(los) Estados Unidos	Rusia
Francia	Vietnam

The Spanish term for the United States (**los Estados Unidos**) is often abbreviated **los EE.UU.** *(the U.S.).*

Aquí practicamos

G. Ellos no son de los Estados Unidos   Even though a great number of Spanish-speaking people live in the United States, many were not born here. When you ask them if they are from the U.S., they tell you where they are from originally. Using the cues, ask and answer questions with a partner according to the model.

> **MODELO**   Julia / Cuba
> **Tú:** *Julia, ¿eres de los Estados Unidos?*
> **Julia:** *No, no soy de los Estados Unidos. Soy de Cuba.*

1. Jorge / Guatemala
2. Patricia / Ecuador
3. Ángela / Argentina
4. Mercedes / Colombia

5. Daniel / Paraguay
6. Luisa / Bolivia
7. Francisco / Venezuela

H. ¿De dónde eres?
Find out where five of your classmates were born. Then be prepared to report the results to the class. Follow the model.

> **MODELO**
>
> **Tú:** *Anita, ¿de dónde eres?*
> **Anita:** *Soy de Nueva York.*
> **Tú:** *Anita es de Nueva York.*

Aquí escuchamos

En un restaurante mexicano
Carolina and her friends are at a Mexican restaurant.

Antes de escuchar Think about vocabulary you might hear in the conversation at the restaurant. Then, answer the following questions.

1. What do people often eat for lunch or dinner in Mexico?
2. What Mexican dishes would you order if you were with Carolina and her friends?

 A escuchar Listen twice to the conversation, and pay attention to what is ordered and to what the friends reveal about themselves.

Después de escuchar Answer the following questions based on what you heard.

1. At approximately what time of day does the conversation take place?
2. Name one of the drinks you heard ordered.
3. Does Pepe order anything to eat or drink?
4. Does Pepe like hot and spicy food?
5. What nationalities are represented in the group of friends?

Intercambio (Exchange) Ask a classmate the following questions. After answering them, he (she) will ask you the same set of questions.

1. ¿De dónde eres tú?

2. ¿Quisieras viajar a México?

3. ¿Te gusta la comida mexicana?

4. ¿Deseas comer en un restaurante mexicano?

5. ¿Qué quisieras comer?

 Mis actividades Write a list of six different activities that you like to do. Be prepared to report them back to the class.

> ### Preparación
>
> - Can you describe the difference between an **enchilada** and a **taco?**
>
> - Do you like **salsa de chile?** Do you prefer **salsa** that is hot, medium, or mild?
>
> - Have you ever had **flan** for dessert? If so, do you like it? Why or why not?

¡Qué comida más rica!

Sara y Carlos van a pedir comida mexicana.

Sara:	Mm... **¡Qué comida más rica!** **¿Qué** es?
Señora:	Son enchiladas con **salsa de chile.**
Carlos:	¡Ay!... **¡Qué picante!** No me gusta. Es muy picante para mí.
Señor:	**Aquí hay otra** enchilada que no es picante.
Carlos:	Mm... ¡Sí! **¡Ésta** es **riquísima!**
Sara:	Carlos, el **flan** es delicioso también.
Carlos:	Sí. ¡Qué **bueno!**
Sara:	Me gusta mucho la comida mexicana. Es muy diferente de la comida **norteamericana.**

chile: *a pepper ranging from mild to very hot; used to make sauces*

flan: *common dessert in Hispanic countries; baked custard topped with caramel sauce*

¡Qué comida más rica! *What delicious food!* **Qué** *What* **salsa de chile** *hot pepper sauce* **¡Qué picante!** *How hot (spicy)!* **Aquí hay otra** *Here is another* **Ésta** *This one* **riquísima** *delicious* **flan** *custard* **bueno** *good* **norteamericana** *from the U.S.*

¡Te toca a ti!

A. ¿Qué tal es? (What is it like?)
Complete and rewrite the sentences according to your food preferences. If the noun is masculine, use the ending **-o** for the adjective; if it is feminine, use the ending **-a**. Follow the model.

> **MODELO**   *El flan es* delicioso.

1. _____ riquísimo(a).
2. _____ rico(a).
3. _____ malo(a) *(bad)*.
4. _____ horrible.
5. _____ bueno(a).
6. _____ picante.

B. ¿Cómo (How) son?
What is your opinion of the following foods? Tell what you think about each one. Follow the model.

> **MODELO**   un taco con salsa
> *Un taco con salsa es muy picante. No me gusta.*

1. una hamburguesa
2. un pastel de fresas
3. una enchilada de queso
4. un croissant
5. un flan
6. un bocadillo de jamón

Repaso ♺

C. ¿De dónde son estas comidas?
Ask a classmate where these foods come from. He (she) should answer accordingly. Follow the model.

> **MODELO**   la salsa de chile
>   **Tú:**   *¿De dónde es la salsa de chile?*
>   **Compañero(a):**   *Es de México.*

1. las enchiladas
2. la tortilla de patatas
3. el croissant
4. las hamburguesas
5. las patatas bravas

ESTRUCTURA

Adjectives of nationality and noun-adjective agreement

País	Adjetivo	País	Adjetivo
Alemania	**alemán (alemana)**	Chile	**chileno(a)**
Argentina	**argentino(a)**	China	**chino(a)**
Bolivia	**boliviano(a)**	Colombia	**colombiano(a)**
Canadá	**canadiense**	Costa Rica	**costarricense**

ESTRUCTURA (CONTINUED)

País	Adjetivo	País	Adjetivo
Cuba	**cubano(a)**	Nicaragua	**nicaragüense**
Ecuador	**ecuatoriano(a)**	Panamá	**panameño(a)**
El Salvador	**salvadoreño(a)**	Paraguay	**paraguayo(a)**
España	**español(a)**	Perú	**peruano(a)**
Estados Unidos	**estadounidense**	Puerto Rico	**puertorriqueño(a)**
Francia	**francés (francesa)**	la República	**dominicano(a)**
Guatemala	**guatemalteco(a)**	Dominicana	
Honduras	**hondureño(a)**	Rusia	**ruso(a)**
Inglaterra	**inglés (inglesa)**	Uruguay	**uruguayo(a)**
Italia	**italiano(a)**	Venezuela	**venezolano(a)**
Japón	**japonés (japonesa)**	Vietnam	**vietnamita**
México	**mexicano(a)**		

In Spanish, adjectives agree in gender (masculine or feminine) and number (singular and plural) with the person or thing to which they refer.

1. Adjectives that end in **-o** are masculine. Change the **-o** to **-a** to obtain the feminine form.

    Él es **argentino**.   Ella es **argentina**.

2. Singular adjectives that end in a consonant (**-l, -n, -s**) form the feminine by adding an **-a**. Note that, if there is a written accent on the final vowel of the masculine singular adjective, it is dropped in the feminine singular form.

    Él es **español**.   Ella es **española**.

    Él es **alemán**.   Ella es **alemana**.

    Él es **japonés**.   Ella es **japonesa**.

3. Some adjectives have identical masculine and feminine forms.

    Él es **estadounidense**.   Ella es **estadounidense**.

    Él es **vietnamita**.   Ella es **vietnamita**.

4. To form the plural of adjectives that end in a vowel, simply add **-s** to the masculine or feminine singular forms. If the singular form ends in a consonant, add **-es** for masculine adjectives and **-as** for feminine adjectives.

    Ellos son **mexicanos**.   Ellas son **mexicanas**.

    Ellos son **españoles**.   Ellas son **españolas**.

    Ellos son **canadienses**.   Ellas son **canadienses**.

5. All inhabitants of North, Central, and South America live in the Americas (**las Américas**) and are, thus, Americans (**americanos**). Therefore, to express that someone or something is from the United States, use either **estadounidense** or **norteamericano(a)**.

Aquí practicamos

D. ¿Y David? Answer the questions according to the model. In the first four items, the first person is female and the second is male.

> **MODELO** Alicia es venezolana. ¿Y Alberto?
> *Él es venezolano también.*

1. Gladis es colombiana. ¿Y Fernando?

2. Ester es cubana. ¿Y José?

3. Adelita es peruana. ¿Y Pepito?

4. Marilú es española. ¿Y Paco?

In the next four items, the first person is male and the second person is female.

> **MODELO** Pancho es boliviano. ¿Y Marta?
> *Ella es boliviana también.*

5. Luis es costarricense. ¿Y Clara?

6. Pedro es argentino. ¿Y Luisa?

7. Miguel es panameño. ¿Y Teresa?

8. Tomás es puertorriqueño. ¿Y Elena?

E. Las nacionalidades You are with a group of young people from all over the world. Find out their nationalities by making the assumptions indicated, asking a friend, and then correcting your mistakes. Follow the model.

> **MODELO** Margarita — argentina / Nueva York
> **Tú:** *¿Margarita es argentina?*
> **Amiga(o):** *No, ella es de Nueva York.*
> **Tú:** *Ah, ella es estadounidense entonces* (then).
> **Amiga(o):** *Claro, es estadounidense.*

1. Lin-Tao (m.) — japonés / Pekín

2. Sofía — mexicana / Roma

3. Jean-Pierre — francés / Quebec

4. Jill — canadiense / Londres

5. Hilda y Lorena — colombianas / Berlín

6. Olga y Nicolás — venezolanos / Moscú

NOTA GRAMATICAL

Nouns for professions

Most nouns that refer to work or occupation follow the same patterns as adjectives of nationality.

1. If the masculine ends in **-o**, the feminine form changes **-o** to **-a**.

Él es **abogado** *(lawyer)*.	Ella es **abogada**.
Él es **secretario** *(secretary)*.	Ella es **secretaria**.
Él es **ingeniero** *(engineer)*.	Ella es **ingeniera**.
Él es **enfermero** *(nurse)*.	Ella es **enfermera**.
Él es **médico** *(doctor)*.	Ella es **médica**.

2. Nouns that end in the consonant **-r** form the feminine by adding **-a** to the end of the word.

Él es **contador** *(accountant)*.	Ella es **contadora**.

3. Nouns that end in the vowel **-e,** as well as those that end in **-ista,** have the same masculine and feminine forms.

Él es **estudiante**.	Ella es **estudiante**.
Él es **periodista** *(journalist)*.	Ella es **periodista**.

4. Nouns for professions form their plural in the same way as the adjectives of nationality. Add **-s** to the masculine or feminine singular form if the noun ends in a vowel. If the singular form ends in a consonant, add **-es** or **-as**.

Ellos son **abogados**.	Ellas son **abogadas**.
Ellos son **estudiantes**.	Ellas son **estudiantes**.
Ellos son **profesores**.	Ellas son **profesoras**.

Aquí practicamos

F. ¿El señor Martínez? Él es... You and a friend are attending a function with your parents. You point out to your friend various acquaintances of your parents and state their professions. Follow the models.

> **MODELOS**   Sr. Martínez / abogado
> *¿El señor Martínez? Él es abogado.*
>
> Sr. y Sra. Martínez / ingeniero
> *¿El señor y la señora Martínez? Ellos son ingenieros.*

1. Sr. y Sra. Herrera / médico
2. Sr. Pérez / profesor
3. Sr. y Sra. López / abogado
4. Sra. Quintana / secretario
5. Sra. Dávila / ingeniero

6. Sr. y Sra. Valdés / profesor
7. Patricio / estudiante de universidad
8. Sra. González / contador
9. Roberta / estudiante de colegio
10. Sr. y Sra. Chávez / periodista

¿Qué crees?

Approximately how many people of Spanish-speaking origin are there in the United States?

a) fewer than 10 million
b) 15 million
c) more than 20 million

respuesta ☞

G. Yo quisiera ser abogado(a) From the following list, choose several careers or jobs that you would like and several that you would not like. Which of these careers or jobs would you most like to have? Which of these careers or jobs would you not want to have? Follow the model to answer these questions.

> **MODELO**   *Yo quisiera ser médico(a), pero no quisiera ser abogado(a).*

periodista	hombre (mujer) de negocios	médico(a)
dentista	(*businessman, businesswoman*)	ingeniero(a)
profesor(a)	abogado(a)	enfermero(a)
secretario(a)	camarero(a)	contador(a)

Aquí escuchamos

Descripción personal *María Victoria Rodríguez, a Mexican-American, introduces herself.*

Antes de escuchar Based on what you have learned in this **etapa,** think about the sort of information that you might hear in a personal description.

A escuchar Listen twice to the description before answering the true-or-false questions about it on your activity master.

Después de escuchar On your activity master, indicate whether the following statements are true or false. If a statement is false, provide the correct information in English.

1. María Victoria is from New Mexico.
2. María Victoria's parents are originally from Mexico.
3. Playing the guitar is one of María Victoria's favorite activities.
4. Studying is an important part of María Victoria's routine.

 c

5. Someday María Victoria would like to be an actress.
6. María Victoria is concerned about the needs of other people.

¡ADELANTE!

 En la feria de la comida You and a friend are at an international food fair.

1. You each name three foods that you wish to sample, describing each one. Choose foods from two different countries.
2. Each of you then describes someone from another country who is at the fair, telling the person's name, nationality, profession, and two interesting things that the person likes to do. Follow the model.

MODELO *Allí está Juan. Él es cubano. Él es fotógrafo. Juan canta y baila bien.*

Mini-descripción Interview an adult. Write four to six sentences in Spanish describing her (him). Include basic information about the person, such as her (his) interests, activities, and profession. Be prepared to report back to the class on what you learned about this person.

EN LÍNEA

Connect with the Spanish-speaking world! Access the *¡Ya verás! Gold* home page for Internet activities related to this chapter.

http://yaveras.heinle.com

VOCABULARIO

Para charlar   Temas y contextos

Para comentar sobre la comida

bueno
malo(a)
¡Qué comida más rica!
¡Qué picante!
riquísimo(a)

Las nacionalidades

alemán (alemana)
argentino(a)
boliviano(a)
canadiense
chileno(a)
chino(a)
colombiano(a)
costarricense
cubano(a)
dominicano(a)
ecuatoriano(a)
español(a)
estadounidense
francés (francesa)
guatemalteco(a)
hondureño(a)
inglés (inglesa)
italiano(a)
japonés (japonesa)
mexicano(a)
nicaragüense
norteamericano(a)
panameño(a)
paraguayo(a)
peruano(a)
puertorriqueño(a)
ruso(a)
salvadoreño(a)
uruguayo(a)
venezolano(a)
vietnamita

Los países

Alemania
Argentina
Bolivia
Canadá
Chile
China
Colombia
Costa Rica
Cuba
Ecuador
El Salvador
España
(los) Estados Unidos
Francia
Guatemala
Honduras
Inglaterra
Italia
Japón
México
Nicaragua
Panamá
Paraguay
Perú
Puerto Rico
la República Dominicana
Rusia
Uruguay
Venezuela
Vietnam

Vocabulario continued

Temas y contextos

La comida mexicana

arroz
carne
chile
una enchilada
flan
unos frijoles
una hamburguesa
pollo
salsa (de chile)
un taco
una tortilla

Las profesiones

un(a) abogado(a)
un(a) contador(a)
un(a) dentista
un(a) enfermero(a)
un(a) estudiante
un hombre (una mujer) de negocios
un(a) ingeniero(a)
un(a) médico(a)
un(a) periodista
un(a) profesor(a)
un(a) secretario(a)

Vocabulario general

Verbos

ser

Otras palabras y expresiones

Allí está(n)…
Aquí hay otro(a)…
bien
bienvenidos(as)
cómo
¿De dónde es (eres)?
ésta
está(n)
intercambio
¡Mira!
¿Qué tal es?
¿Qué es?
¿Qué va(n) a pedir?
¿quién?
ser de
vamos

¡Qué delicioso!

Antes de leer

1. Look at the title above. Then look at the photos and the document on page 66. Based on these things, what do you expect the reading to be about?

2. Briefly skim the first paragraph of the reading. What kind of food do you think the reading is about?

3. This reading mentions dishes eaten in Cuba, Puerto Rico, the Dominican Republic, and Colombia. Look at a map of Latin America and locate each place.

Para los españoles y los mexicanos, el plátano es lo mismo que la banana. Pero en la región del Caribe, el plátano es una fruta con una textura, tamaño y sabor muy diferente. También es un aspecto muy importante de la cultura. Muchas familias, especialmente las familias en áreas rurales, tienen un árbol de plátano en el patio de su casa.

Hay muchas maneras de preparar el plátano. Como parte de una fiesta internacional, un grupo de estudiantes en una escuela secundaria de Providence, Rhode Island celebra la comida criolla con unos platos que contienen plátano. En su mesa hay platos de Cuba, de Puerto Rico, de Colombia y de la República Dominicana. El menú para la fiesta está en la página 66.

LA COCINA CRIOLLA

- **Los platanutres**
  como papitas, pero de plátano verde

- **Los tostones**
  plátanos fritos, como *french fries*

- **El piñón**
  un plato como lasaña, pero se usa
  plátano maduro en vez de pasta

- **El mofongo**
  después de cocinar el plátano verde,
  se le muele con tocino y especias

- **Los pasteles, o pastelones**
  como tamales pero se rellena la hoja
  del plátano con papas, plátano, carne
  y/o queso

- **Plátano con frijoles**
  una combinación rica de plátano,
  frijoles y tomate

- **Plátanos con salsa de caramelo**
  un plato dulce; se cocina plátano
  maduro en mantequilla, jugo de
  naranja y azúcar. Se sirve con
  helado de vainilla.

Guía para la lectura

1. Here are some words and expressions to keep in mind as you read.

plátano	*plantain*	**papitas**	*potato chips*
mismo	*same*	**se muele**	*it is ground*
tamaño	*size*	**tocino**	*bacon*
sabor	*taste*	**se rellena**	*one fills*
maneras	*ways*	**se cocina**	*one cooks*
platos	*dishes*	**azúcar**	*sugar*
mesa	*table*	**helado**	*ice cream*

2. **Papas** is the word for potatoes in Latin America. In Spain, they are
   called **patatas.**

Después de leer

1. Do you know anyone who prepares foods that include **plátano**? If
   so, compare and contrast these foods with those on the menu.

2. Which of the dishes mentioned on the menu sounds the most appetizing to you? Explain why.

3. If you were planning an international party for your school, what
   kinds of foods would you include? Explain your choices.

¡SIGAMOS ADELANTE!

Conversemos un rato

A. **En el café** Role-play the following situations with three other classmates.

1. You are in Puerto Rico on an exchange program in order to improve your Spanish. You run into a friend you've met at your daily language classes.

    a. Greet your friend and invite him (her) to join you at a nearby café.

    b. As you stroll to the café, talk about how things are going.

    c. At the café, interact with the waiter (waitress) to order something to eat and drink.

    d. Introduce your friend to another friend who arrives at the café.

2. With the same classmates, reenact your café conversation, but this time extend it so that you and your two friends get to know each other better.

    a. Find out what your newly arrived friend wants to eat and/or drink and place the order with the waiter (waitress).

    b. As your friends ask each other about their nationalities and origins, listen and try to encourage the conversation.

    c. Find out what languages all three of you are studying or know how to speak.

B. **¡Vamos a comer algo!** You are with a group of friends chatting in a mall on a Saturday evening. With three or four classmates, role-play the following discussion about where you want to eat.

1. All members of the group suggest a place where they would like to go. Each suggestion should be supported by details that make the choice appealing.

2. As each person makes a suggestion, you and your friends react by indicating what you like and dislike about the place and its menu.

3. Reach an agreement with your friends about where the group will go.

Taller de escritores

Writing extended picture captions

Como un pastel o un croissant todos los días. Son deliciosos, especialmente con chocolate o café con leche.

A. Reflexión

You are going to increase your writing skills in Spanish by writing extended picture captions. Begin by drawing four illustrations or selecting four photos from magazines. Your art/selections should depict food you like and dislike. As you look at each food item, on a separate sheet of paper, write as many key words or phrases in Spanish as you can think of to express your feelings about the food.

Deseo un sándwich de jamón.
No me gusta comer comida
dulce. Quisiera agua mineral
con el sándwich.

B. Primer borrador Keeping in mind that the readers of your captions will be your classmates and teacher, write three to four related sentences for each picture you drew or selected. Refer back to Chapters 1-3 for vocabulary.

C. Revisión con un(a) compañero(a) Exchange papers with a classmate. Read each other's work and comment on it, based on the questions below.

1. What do you like best about your classmate's first draft?

2. What part do you find the clearest?

3. What part do you find the most interesting?

4. Does the first draft keep the audience in mind?

5. Does the writing reflect the task assigned?

6. Does the first draft raise questions that, if answered, you think would make the writing clearer, more interesting, or more complete?

D. Versión final At home, revise your first draft, incorporating changes based on the feedback from your classmate. Revise content and check your grammar, spelling, punctuation, and accent marks. Bring your final draft to class.

E. Carpeta After you turn in your art with captions, your teacher may choose to place it in your portfolio, display it on a bulletin board, or use it to evaluate your progress.

Conexión con las ciencias

Las meriendas y la buena nutrición

Para empezar Reading about science in Spanish is not as difficult as you might think. English and Spanish have many cognates. These are words that are spelled similarly in both languages and share the same meaning. For example, **nutrición, minerales,** and **proteínas** are cognates of *nutrition, minerals,* and *proteins,* respectively. Looking purposely for cognates will help you understand more easily what you read.

Thinking about the title of a reading will also improve your reading skills. Based on the title, what do you think this reading is about? Can you predict what the author will say about the topic? What words might be important to know when reading about this topic?

Es importante **tener en cuenta** la buena nutrición al seleccionar lo que comemos. Las meriendas más **saludables tienen** menos calorías y poca **grasa**. La leche **descremada**, por ejemplo, tiene los **mismos** minerales vitaminas y proteínas que la leche normal, pero con menos grasa, colesterol y calorías. Es una buena idea comer una dieta variada y balanceada. Los **alimentos** con fibra, como las **palomitas de maíz** (sin mantequilla), las frutas y los vegetales, deben también formar parte de nuestra dieta diaria.

Merienda/alimento	Calorías	Grasa total (gramos)	Colesterol (miligramos)
Galletitas de chocolate (4)	205	12,0	17
Galletas Graham (2)	55	1,3	0
Helado de vainilla (1/2 **taza**)	175	11,8	44
Mantequilla de cacahuete (2 **cucharadas**)	188	16,0	0
Barra de chocolate (1 onza)	145	9,0	5
Pizza (1 tajada)	109	2,5	7
Mayonesa (2 cucharadas)	198	22,0	8
Lechuga	0	0	0
Tomate (1)	25	0	0
Naranja (1)	50	0	0
Palomitas de maíz (1 taza)	25	0	0

tener en cuenta *to take into account* saludables *healthy, nutritious* tienen *have* grasa *fat* descremada *skimmed* mismos *same* alimentos *food* palomitas de maíz *popcorn* helado *ice cream* taza *cup* mantequilla de cacahuete *peanut butter* cucharadas *tablespoons* lechuga *lettuce*

A. ¿Verdadero o falso? Indicate whether the following statements are true (**verdadero**) or false (**falso**), based on what you read.

1. La lechuga y el tomate son alimentos que tienen fibra.
2. La mayonesa es un alimento muy saludable porque tiene poca grasa y pocas calorías.
3. Es una buena idea tomar helado todos los días.
4. Es importante tener una dieta variada y balanceada.
5. Las palomitas de maíz con mantequilla son más saludables que las palomitas sin mantequilla.
6. La leche descremada tiene las mismas proteínas que la leche normal.

B. Las meriendas Work with a partner and the chart to complete the activities below.

1. First, rank the snacks in the chart from most nutritious (a), to least nutritious (h), based on the information provided in the reading. Then, tell your partner about your rankings in Spanish. Use the following model as a guide.

    MODELO   *La mantequilla de cacahuete no tiene mucho colesterol, pero sí tiene mucha fibra. Para mí, es a.*

2. Now rank the snacks from the one you think has the best taste (sabor) (a) to the one you think has the worst taste (h). Then, explain your rankings to your partner. Use the following models as a guide.

    MODELOS   *¡Qué delicioso! Como galletitas Graham todos los días. Para mí, son a.*

    No me gusta comer uvas. Son horribles. Para mí, son h.

Meriendas

	Nutrición		Sabor	
	Yo	Mi compañero(a)	Yo	Mi compañero(a)
4 galletitas Graham	___	___	___	___
un sándwich de mantequilla de cacahuete	___	___	___	___
una taza de palomitas de maíz	___	___	___	___
una pizza de tomate y queso	___	___	___	___
helado de vainilla	___	___	___	___
15 uvas	___	___	___	___
4 galletitas de chocolate	___	___	___	___
un bocadillo de jamón y queso	___	___	___	___

Vistas
de los países hispanos

Puerto Rico

Capital: San Juan

Ciudades principales: Bayamón, Ponce, Carolina, Caguas, Mayagüez

Población: 3.500.000

Idiomas: español

Área territorial: 9.104 km²

Clima: moderado, temperatura promedio es de 24° C

Moneda: dólar

moderado *moderate*   promedio *average*

EXPLORA

Find out more about Puerto Rico! Access the **Nuestros vecinos** page on the *¡Ya verás! Gold* web site for a list of URLs.

http://yaveras.heinle.com/vecinos.htm

En la comunidad

Using Spanish in your Community

Spanish is more than just words you study. It connects you to millions of people in the U.S. and in other countries. Whether you hear it in the mall, in your favorite sitcom, need it for work, or for travel, it can prove more useful than you ever imagined. As you will learn throughout these sections, Spanish is a rich, colorful thread that links culture to culture and helps you get ahead in the world of work.

¡Bienvenidos a Randy's Diner!

"When I started this business, I never dreamed I'd learn Spanish. Back then, there were hardly any Spanish-speakers in St. Paul. Today, most of my customers speak Spanish. I've expanded my menu to suit their tastes. This year I'm even taking a Spanish class at the University of Minnesota so that I can communicate better with my new neighbors and customers. So if you'd like to try a delicious **licuado**, *a tasty* **churro**, *or some* **huevos revueltos**, *you've come to the right place. ¡Estamos aquí para servirles!"*

¡Ahora te toca a ti!

In your community, choose a restaurant that serves typical food from Latin America or Spain. With a classmate, visit the restaurant and order your meal in Spanish. Before going, review food vocabulary listed in the **Vocabulario** section at the end of Chapters 1-3. After your visit, in Spanish, write or make an audio recording of a description of your meal.

If there are no Hispanic restaurants in your community, imagine that you own one similar to Randy's. With a classmate, name your restaurant. Then, research Spanish and Latin American dishes. Decide which to include on your menu and be prepared to explain your choices. Present your restaurant and menu to the class. Your classmates will discuss your menu in Spanish, ask you questions about it, and vote on the dish they find most appealing.

huevos revueltos *scrambled eggs*
churros *sweet, fried-dough pastries*

UNIDAD 2

¡*Vamos a conocernos!*

Objectives

In this unit you will learn:

- to talk about your possessions
- to express your likes and dislikes
- to describe your family
- to read a short descriptive text about people
- to understand people who are talking about themselves and their families

¿Qué ves?

- Where are the people in these photographs?
- Who are they with?
- What are they doing?

CAPÍTULO 4

¿De quién es?

Primera etapa: ¿Qué llevas a la escuela?
Segunda etapa: ¿Qué hay en tu casa?
Tercera etapa: En nuestra casa

CAPÍTULO 5

Me gusta mucho...

Primera etapa: Mis gustos
Segunda etapa: ¿Qué te gusta más?

CAPÍTULO 6

Ésta es mi familia

Primera etapa: Yo vivo con...
Segunda etapa: Tengo una familia grande

75

CAPÍTULO 4

¿De quién es?

—¿Cuántos discos compactos tienes?
—Tengo veinte. Éste es mi favorito.

Objectives

- identifying personal belongings
- obtaining information about other people

Preparación

- As you get ready to begin this **etapa,** think about the items you take to school. Make a list of at least five items that you usually take to school.

- In this **etapa** you will also learn to say that something belongs to someone else. If you have borrowed a calculator from a friend, how would you say, in English, whose calculator it is?

¿Qué llevas a la escuela?

Me llamo Elena. **Llevo** muchas **cosas** a la escuela.

borrador
cuaderno
libro
lápiz
sacapuntas
mochila
bolígrafo
pluma
cartera
calculadora
llave
portafolio

¿Qué llevas a la escuela? *What do you take to school?*   Me llamo *My name is*   Llevo *I take*   cosas *things*   la escuela *school*

¡Te toca a ti!

A. ¿Qué es?
Identify the objects in the numbered drawings. Follow the model.

| MODELO | *Es un lápiz.* |

1.

2.

3.

4.

5.

6.

7.

8.

B. No es...
Based on the numbered drawings in the previous exercise, correct the initial assumptions. Follow the model.

| MODELO | ¿Es un libro?
No es un libro. Es un lápiz. |

1. ¿Es un bolígrafo? 5. ¿Es un sacapuntas?

2. ¿Es una cartera? 6. ¿Es un borrador?

3. ¿Es un cuaderno? 7. ¿Es un portafolio?

4. ¿Es un lápiz? 8. ¿Es una llave?

C. ¿Qué llevas tú a la escuela?
Indicate what each person takes to school according to the drawings. Follow the model.

| MODELO | Juan
Juan lleva un libro a la escuela. | |

1. Julia 2. Jaime 3. tú 4. nosotros

5. yo   6. él   7. ella   8. Ud.

PRONUNCIACIÓN   THE CONSONANT p

The sound of the consonant **p** is similar to the sound of *p* in English, but is pronounced without the puff of air that accompanies the English sound. Put your hand in front of your mouth and note the puff of air that is produced when you pronounce the English word *pan* and the absence of this puff of air when you say *speak*. The Spanish **p** is more like the *p* in the English word *speak*.

Práctica

D. Listen and repeat as your teacher models the following words.

1. papa
2. política
3. pájaro
4. pintura

5. problema
6. póster
7. pronto
8. pluma

9. lápiz
10. sacapuntas

ESTRUCTURA

The definite article

	Singular	Plural
Masculine	**el** libro	**los** libros
Feminine	**la** mochila	**las** mochilas

1. In Spanish, the definite article has four forms. The form used depends on whether the noun is masculine or feminine and singular or plural.

ESTRUCTURA (continued)

2. One of the two main uses of the definite article is to designate nouns in a specific sense. In this situation, the English equivalent of **el, la, los,** and **las** is *the.*

Necesito **los** libros.
I need the books. (that is, the specific books already mentioned)

Aquí está **la** llave.
Here is the key. (that is, the specific key that someone is referring to)

3. The other main use of the definite article is to designate nouns in a general or collective sense. In this situation, English usually does not use an article.

El café es una bebida popular aquí.
Coffee is a popular drink here. (that is, coffee in general)

Me gusta **la** música.
I like music. (that is, music in general)

4. When talking about someone who has a title, always use the definite article in front of the title. However, when you talk directly to such a person, the definite article is not used with his (her) title.

El señor Herrera es ecuatoriano.
Mr. Herrera is Ecuadorian.

La señora Martínez lleva un libro a la escuela.
Mrs. Martínez takes a book to school.

Buenas tardes, **señorita Díaz.**
Good afternoon, Miss Díaz.

Aquí practicamos

E. **¿Un o el?** Replace the indefinite article with the appropriate definite article (**el, la, los, las**). Follow the models.

MODELOS   un cuaderno   unos libros
                 el cuaderno   *los libros*

1. un café
2. una estudiante
3. un sándwich
4. una mochila
5. unas bebidas
6. unos médicos
7. un bolígrafo
8. una cartera

9. unos refrescos
10. un jugo
11. una profesora
12. unos estudiantes
13. una llave
14. una calculadora
15. un borrador
16. un sacapuntas

F. ¿Qué necesita cada (each) persona? Based on the activities and people mentioned in Column A of the chart on your activity master, decide which items from Column B the people need. Follow the models to write your responses on your activity master. You may want to use some items from Column B more than once.

MODELOS   Yo quisiera leer.   Tina va a casa.
Tú necesitas un libro. *Ella necesita la llave.*

A	B
1. Ana estudia matemáticas.	bolígrafo(s)
2, Nosotros vamos a escribir.	calculadora(s)
3. Juan lleva muchos cuadernos a la escuela.	cuaderno
4. Miguel y María quisieran leer.	llave(s)
5. Tú vas a escribir (*write*) mucho con un lápiz.	libro(s)
6. Ustedes estudian mucho las matemáticas.	mochila
	sacapuntas

NOTA GRAMATICAL

Expressing possession with de

el libro de Ana	*Ana's book*
la calculadora de Juan	*Juan's calculator*
los cuadernos de Marta	*Marta's notebooks*
las llaves de Jorge	*Jorge's keys*

1. The following construction is often used in Spanish to express possession in the third person:

> *the definite article* + *noun* + **de** + *the name of the possessor*

2. To ask to whom a singular noun belongs, use **¿De quién es...?** Use **¿De quién son...?** to ask to whom a plural noun belongs.

¿De quién es la pluma?   *Whose pen is it?*

¿De quién son las plumas?   *Whose pens are they?*

G. Es de... After class one day, you and a friend notice that your classmates have left behind several of their belongings. You show these objects to your friend, who identifies the owners. With a singular noun, use **es.** With a plural noun, use **son.** Follow the models.

> **MODELOS**   un libro (Beatriz)   unos libros (Juan)
> *Es el libro de Beatriz.*   *Son los libros de Juan.*

1. un cuaderno (Vicente)
2. una mochila (Marcos)
3. una calculadora (Bárbara)
4. una llave (Victoria)

5. unos bolígrafos (María)
6. unas llaves (Pedro)
7. unos cuadernos (José)
8. unos lápices (Juanita)

H. ¿De quién es...? You are trying to sort out who owns each of several items that have been left in the classroom. Ask a question and have a classmate answer according to the model.

> **MODELO**   **Tú:**   *¿De quién es el lápiz?*   Carlos
>   **Compañera(o):**   *Es de Carlos.*

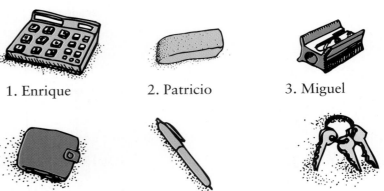

1. Enrique   2. Patricio   3. Miguel

4. Anita   5. Emilia   6. Mercedes

Aquí escuchamos

¿Qué llevas a la escuela? *Carmen describes her life as a high-school student.*

Antes de escuchar Think about items Carmen might take to school every day.

A escuchar As you listen to the monologue, put a check mark on your activity master next to each of the following words when you hear it.

__bolígrafo	__cuaderno
__calculadora	__libro
__cartera	__mochila

Después de escuchar On your activity master, check the appropriate column to show how often Carmen takes each thing she mentions to school.

	Todos los días	A veces
bolígrafo		
calculadora		
cartera		
cuaderno		
libro		
mochila		
lápices		

¡ADELANTE!

 Yo llevo... Make a list of five items that you usually take to school with you. Then interview three classmates to find out what they have on their lists. Keep track of their answers so that you can report whose list is most like yours and whose list is most different.

 ¿Qué llevas tú a la escuela? Write a short paragraph telling what you take to school with you. Mention...

1. something that you sometimes take.
2. something that you take every day.
3. something that you like to take (**me gusta llevar**).
4. something that you do not like to take.

For at least one of the items you mention, offer an explanation; for example: **Siempre llevo el libro de español porque estudio el español todos los días.**

- As you get ready to begin this **etapa,** think about what you have in your room at home.

- Make a list of at least eight items you have in your room.

¿Qué hay en tu cuarto?

Marta Gómez y Jorge de Vargas son **una muchacha** *y* **un muchacho** *que son estudiantes en una escuela en Quito, Ecuador.*

Me llamo Marta. **En mi cuarto hay...**

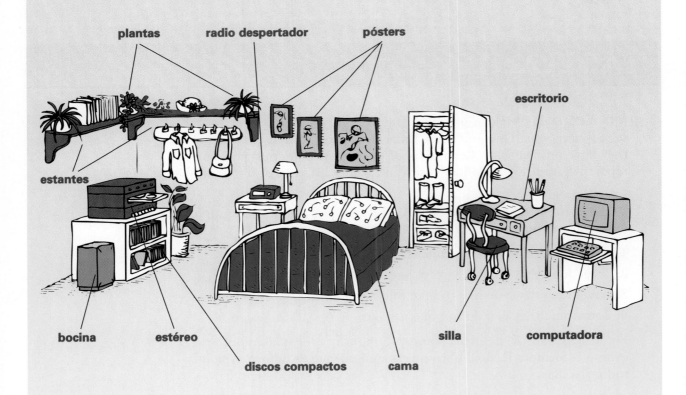

plantas radio despertador pósters escritorio

estantes

bocina estéreo discos compactos cama silla computadora

¿Qué hay en tu cuarto? *What is there in your room?* Una muchacha *a young woman* un muchacho *a young man*
En mi cuarto hay... *In my room there is/are . . .*

Me llamo Jorge. En mi cuarto hay...

cómoda   cámara   cintas   grabadora   televisor   estantes

cama   alfombra   silla   máquina de escribir   escritorio

¡Te toca a ti!

A. ¿Dónde hay...? (Where is/are there . . . ?)   Based on the pictures, answer the following questions about Marta's and Jorge's rooms. Follow the models.

> **MODELOS**   ¿un televisor?
> *En el cuarto de Jorge hay un televisor.*
>
> ¿una cama?
> *En el cuarto de Marta hay una cama y en el cuarto de Jorge hay una cama también.*

1. ¿una computadora?
2. ¿una grabadora?
3. ¿un radio despertador?
4. ¿una cama?
5. ¿un estéreo?
6. ¿unos pósters?
7. ¿una máquina de escribir?
8. ¿una cámara?
9. ¿unas cintas?
10. ¿unos discos compactos?
11. ¿unas plantas?
12. ¿unos estantes?
13. ¿una silla?
14. ¿una alfombra?

B. ¿Y tú?   Indicate what you have and do not have in your room at home. Follow the model.

> **MODELO**   *En mi cuarto, hay una cama y una cómoda, pero no hay un escritorio. También hay pósters en la pared* (on the wall).

PRONUNCIACIÓN THE CONSONANT t

The sound of **t** in Spanish is produced by placing the tip of the tongue behind the back of the upper front teeth, while *t* in English is pronounced by placing the tip of the tongue on the gum ridge behind the upper front teeth. Pronounce the English word *tea* and note where the tip of your tongue is. Now pronounce the Spanish word **ti** being careful to place the tip of the tongue on the back of the upper front teeth.

Práctica

C. Listen and repeat as your teacher models the following words.

1. tú
2. tomo
3. tapas
4. taza
5. tipo
6. tenis
7. tonto
8. política
9. fútbol
10. cinta

Repaso ☯

D. ¿Qué llevan a la escuela? Look at the drawings that follow and tell what each person takes to school.

Martín   Julio

PALABRAS ÚTILES

Numbers from 0 to 20

cero	0	seis	6	doce	12	dieciocho	18
uno	1	siete	7	trece	13	diecinueve	19
dos	2	ocho	8	catorce	14	veinte	20
tres	3	nueve	9	quince	15		
cuatro	4	diez	10	dieciséis	16		
cinco	5	once	11	diecisiete	17		

Aquí practicamos

E. Cuenta (Count) mucho Follow the directions in Spanish.

1. Cuenta del 0 al 10. Cuenta del 11 al 20.
2. Cuenta los números pares (even): 0, 2, 4, 6, 8, 10, 12, 14, 16, 18, 20.
3. Cuenta los números impares (odd): l, 3, 5, 7, 9, 11, 13, 15, 17, 19.

F. Sumar y restar (Adding and subtracting) Solve the following addition and subtraction problems, forming complete sentences with the solved problems. Follow the models.

MODELOS	$2 + 1 =$	$3 - 1 =$
	Dos más (plus)	Tres menos (minus)
	uno son tres.	uno son dos.

1. $2 + 5 =$ 5. $4 - 1 =$ 9. $7 + 13 =$ 13. $3 + 5 =$
2. $6 - 3 =$ 6. $0 + 4 =$ 10. $18 - 2 =$ 14. $1 + 2 =$
3. $6 + 10 =$ 7. $5 + 4 =$ 11. $8 - 3 =$ 15. $9 - 4 =$
4. $17 - 2 =$ 8. $19 - 6 =$ 12. $12 + 5 =$ 16. $19 - 8 =$

PALABRAS ÚTILES

Hay + noun

Hay lápices en el escritorio.	*There are pencils on the desk.*
Hay un libro en mi cuarto.	*There is a book in my room.*
Hay tres pósters en mi cuarto.	*There are three posters in my room.*

1. The Spanish word **hay** (there is, there are) may be followed by either a singular or a plural noun. **Hay** may also be followed by an indefinite article or a number.

2. When **hay** is used in the negative, the indefinite article is usually omitted.

No hay plantas en mi cuarto.	*There are no plants in my room.*

3. To ask how many people or things there are, use **¿Cuántos(as)... hay?**

¿Cuántos pósters hay en la pared?	*How many posters are there on the wall?*
¿Cuántas sillas hay aquí?	*How many chairs are there here?*

Aquí practicamos

G. El cuarto de Marta Indicate whether each item is or is not found in the room pictured on page 84. Follow the models.

> **MODELOS**
> una cama   unas grabadoras
> *Hay una cama.*   *No hay grabadoras.*

1. unos pósters
2. una silla
3. unas cintas
4. una computadora
5. un televisor
6. un estéreo
7. unos libros
8. unos lápices
9. unos bolígrafos
10. un escritorio
11. unas plantas
12. una cómoda
13. unos cuadernos
14. unas cámaras
15. una máquina de escribir

H. Hay... Working with another student, take turns pointing out items in the room pictured below. Each of you should also point out one item that is not in the room. Each of you should mention five items. Follow the model.

> **MODELO**
> *Hay una cama allí* (there).

Aquí escuchamos

¿Qué hay en tu cuarto? *Miguel mentions some items he has in his room.*

Antes de escuchar Think about what you have in your room at home. Then, think about the items Miguel might have in his room.

 A escuchar Listen twice to the monologue before checking off the mentioned items on your activity master.

Después de escuchar Check off on your activity master the items that Miguel has in his room.

cama	estéreo
cintas	grabadora
computadora	plantas
discos compactos	póster
escritorio	silla
estantes	

¡ADELANTE!

 ¿Qué hay? Find out from several of your classmates what they have and do not have in their rooms at home. Then tell them what you have and do not have in your own room. Follow the model.

MODELO

Tú: *¿Qué hay en tu cuarto?*
Compañero(a): *En mi cuarto hay dos plantas, una cama…*

Cosas importantes A foreign exchange student has just arrived at your school. A couple with no children has agreed to host the student. They have asked for help in furnishing their guest's room appropriately for a teen. With a partner, decide on the six most important items to include.

Preparación

- As you get ready to begin this **etapa,** think about where you and your friends and relatives live (house, apartment, condominium, etc.); what you have where you live; and how you get around town.

- Make a list with the headings *house, apartment, condominium* and/or *townhouse*; then list one to three acquaintances under each heading who live in that type of residence.

- Next to each name, list three interesting items that your friend or relative has at home.

- Name the different modes of transportation that each of you uses to get to school, go shopping, and to go to a friend's house.

En mi casa

Vivo en...

una casa

un apartamento

En mi casa *In my house*   **Vivo en...** *I live in...*

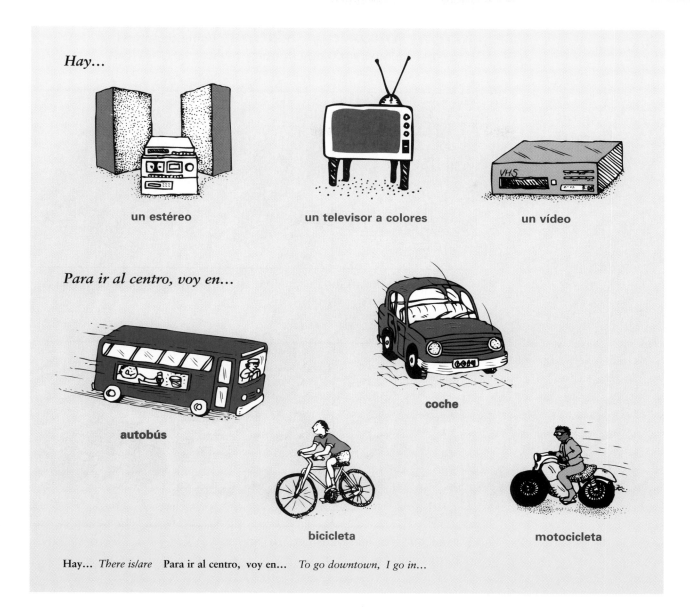

Hay...

un estéreo   un televisor a colores   un vídeo

Para ir al centro, voy en...

autobús   coche

bicicleta   motocicleta

Hay... *There is/are*   **Para ir al centro, voy en...** *To go downtown, I go in...*

¡Te toca a ti!

A. Mi casa   Answer the following questions about where you live.

1. ¿Vives tú *(Do you live)* en una casa o en un apartamento?
   Vivo...

2. ¿Hay un estéreo en tu casa? ¿Y un televisor? ¿Y una computadora?
   ¿Y un vídeo?
   Hay...

3. ¿Cómo vas *(How do you go)* al centro? ¿En coche? ¿En moto?
   ¿En bicicleta? ¿En autobús?
   Yo voy...

B. María, Antonio y Cristina Using the drawings, complete each person's description of where he (she) lives.

1. Me llamo María González. Vivo en… Allí hay…, pero no hay…
   Para ir al centro, voy en…

2. Me llamo Antonio Martínez. Yo vivo en… Allí hay… y… Pero no hay…
   Para ir al centro, voy en…

3. Me llamo Cristina Sánchez. Yo vivo en… Allí hay…, pero no hay…
   Para ir al centro, voy en…

PRONUNCIACIÓN THE SOUND OF /k/

In Spanish the sound of /k/ can be spelled with a **c** before the vowels **a, o,** and **u,** as in **caso, cosa, culpa,** or before the consonants **l** and **r** as in **clase** and **cruz.** It can also be spelled with **qu** as in **Quito** and **queso;** in this combination, the **u** is always silent. A few Spanish words that have been borrowed from other languages are spelled with the letter **k**—for example, **koala, kimono,** and **kilómetro.** In all of these cases the sound of /k/ in Spanish is identical to the sound of /k/ in English.

Práctica

C. Listen and repeat as your teacher models the following words.

1. casa
2. cómoda
3. cama
4. computadora
5. calculadora
6. que
7. quien
8. queso
9. pequeño
10. kilómetro

Repaso

D. ¿Qué hay? Ask a classmate the following questions, and have him (her) answer them.

1. En tu cuarto, ¿hay libros? ¿Hay plantas? ¿Hay pósters en la pared?
2. ¿Hay un estéreo en tu casa? ¿Hay discos compactos? ¿Hay discos compactos de jazz? ¿Y de rock? ¿Y de música clásica?
3. ¿Hay un radio despertador en tu cuarto? ¿Hay un estéreo? ¿Hay cintas?
4. En tu casa, ¿hay una máquina de escribir? ¿Hay una computadora? ¿Hay una cámara?

ESTRUCTURA

Possessive adjectives: First and second persons

—¿Necesitas **tu** lápiz?   *Do you need your pencil?*
—Sí, necesito **mi** lápiz.   *Yes, I need my pencil.*

—¿Es **su** coche?   *Is this your car?*
—Sí, es **nuestro** coche.   *Yes, it is our car.*

—¿Escuchan **mis** cintas?   *Are they listening to my tapes?*
—Sí, escuchan **sus** cintas.   *Yes, they are listening to your (formal) tapes.*

Possessive Adjectives

	Singular		Plural	
yo	**mi**	*my*	**mis**	*my*
tú	**tu**	*your*	**tus**	*your*
usted	**su**	*your*	**sus**	*your*
nosotros(as)	**nuestro(a)**	*our*	**nuestros(as)**	*our*
vosotros(as)	**vuestro(a)**	*your*	**vuestros(as)**	*your*
ustedes	**su**	*your*	**sus**	*your*

1. Like articles and other adjectives, possessive adjectives agree in gender and number with the noun they modify. This means that they agree with what is possessed or owned.
2. Note that possessive adjectives are placed before the noun they modify.

Aquí practicamos

E. ¿Es mi libro? Replace the nouns in italics and make changes if necessary.

1. Es mi *libro*. (lápiz / apartamento / bolígrafo)
2. Es mi *casa*. (calculadora / cámara / máquina de escribir)
3. Son mis *discos compactos*. (llaves / amigos / plantas)
4. Allí está tu *casa*. (apartamento / cuaderno / cámara)
5. Quisiera escuchar tus *discos compactos*. (cintas / estéreo / grabadora)
6. Nosotros necesitamos nuestros *libros*. (cuadernos / calculadoras / computadora)
7. Es nuestro *coche*. (cuarto / mochila / calculadora)
8. ¿Son sus *libros*? (cintas / amigos / llaves)
9. Es nuestra *escuela*. (disco compacto / llave / televisor)
10. Llevamos nuestros *libros* a clase. (calculadoras / cuadernos / mochilas)

F. ¡Qué confusión! Everyone seems confused about what belongs to whom. First, someone you don't know tries to take your things, but you politely set him (her) straight. Remember to use **es** with a singular noun and **son** with a plural noun. Follow the models.

> **MODELO**   Ah, mi lápiz.
> *Perdón. No es su lápiz. Es mi lápiz.*

1. Ah, mi cuaderno.
2. Ah, mi mochila.
3. Ah, mi calculadora.
4. Ah, mi borrador.

> **MODELO**   Ah, mis libros.
> *Perdón. No son sus libros. Son mis libros.*

5. Ah, mis cintas.
6. Ah, mis llaves.
7. Ah, mis cuadernos.
8. Ah, mis discos compactos.

Now your neighbors are confused about what belongs to them and what belongs to your family.

> **MODELO**   ¿Es nuestro coche?
> *No, no es su coche. Es nuestro coche.*

9. ¿Es nuestro televisor a colores?
10. ¿Es nuestra cámara?
11. ¿Es nuestro radio despertador?
12. ¿Es nuestra computadora?

> **MODELO**   ¿Son nuestras plantas?
> *No, no son sus plantas. Son nuestras plantas.*

13. ¿Son nuestros discos compactos?
14. ¿Son nuestras bicicletas?
15. ¿Son nuestras llaves?
16. ¿Son nuestras cintas?

Finally, your friend thinks your things belong to him (her).

> **MODELO**   Dame *(Give me)* mi llave.
> *Perdón. No es tu llave. Es mi llave.*

17. Dame mi cuaderno.
18. Dame mi cinta.
19. Dame mi borrador.
20. Dame mi mochila.

> **MODELO**   Dame mis libros.
> *Perdón. No son tus libros. Son mis libros.*

21. Dame mis pósters.
22. Dame mis discos compactos.
23. Dame mis llaves.
24. Dame mis cuadernos.

? ¿Qué crees?

Spanish television often features **telenovelas**, both here in the United States and in other parts of the Spanish-speaking world. Telenovelas are:

a) TV plays
b) novels read on TV
c) soap operas
d) game shows

respuesta ☞

G. No, no es mi libro

Now *you're* confused! When you point out the following items and ask a classmate if they belong to him (her), your classmate responds negatively. Follow the models.

MODELOS

Tú: *¿Es tu cámara?*
Compañera(o): *No, no es mi cámara.*

Tú: *Son tus plantas?*
Compañera(o): *No, no son mis plantas.*

☞ c

1.

2.

3.

4.

5.

6.

7.

8.

9.

10.

11.
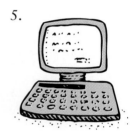

12.

13.

14.

15.

Aquí escuchamos

¿Dónde vives? *Carmen describes her home.*

Antes de escuchar Think about where Carmen might live, what she might have there, and how she might get around town.

 A escuchar Listen twice to the monologue and check off on your activity master the items that Carmen mentions.

__ apartamento	__ coche	__ motocicleta	__ televisor
__ bicicleta	__ estéreo	__ plantas	__ vídeo
__ casa	__ libros	__ pósters	

Después de escuchar On your activity master, write down some notes on what Carmen says about where she lives, what she has there, and how she gets around.

¡ADELANTE!

 Mi casa y tu casa Share information with a partner about your home and belongings.

1. Ask what he (she) has at home. (**¿Qué hay en tu casa?**)

2. Describe your own home. (**En mi casa hay…**)

3. While listening to your partner's description, point out something he (she) has that you also have at home. (**Hay un coche japonés en mi casa también.**)

4. Listen for something that there is at your partner's home but not at yours and comment on it. (**No hay moto en mi casa, pero hay tres bicicletas.**)

Finally, prepare a report together in which you identify…

1. a few items that are in both of your homes. (**En nuestras casas hay…**)

2. other items that are only in your home. (**En mi casa hay…, pero no hay… en su casa.**)

3. items that are only in his (her) home. (**En su casa hay…, pero no hay… en mi casa.**)

Mi cuarto y mis actividades   Prepare your own personal picture strip story describing your own home, what you have in it, and how you travel when you go out, based on the models in activity B on page 92. In your writing, include things you have in your home or room and mention what you like to do with those things. You may wish to start out with: **En mi casa** (or **cuarto**) **hay…**. Include in your description things you do not have at home (**En mi casa no hay…**). Follow the model.

MODELO   *En mi cuarto hay un estéreo y muchos discos compactos Mis discos compactos son de música rock. Me gusta escuchar música cuando estudio. Hay un teléfono también en mi cuarto. Me gusta mucho hablar con mis amigos. También me gusta visitar a mis amigos. A veces voy a casa de mis amigos en bicicleta.*

En mi cuarto hay muchas muñecas (dolls).

Connect with the Spanish-speaking world! Access the *¡Ya verás! Gold* home page for Internet activities related to this chapter.

http://yaveras.heinle.com

VOCABULARIO

Para charlar

Para expresar posesión

¿De quién es…?
¿De quién son…?
Es(Son) de…
mi(s)
tu(s)
su(s)
nuestro(s)
nuestra(s)

Para contar

cero
uno
dos
tres
cuatro
cinco
seis
siete
ocho
nueve
diez
once
doce
trece
catorce
quince
dieciséis
diecisiete
dieciocho
diecinueve
veinte

Temas y contextos

En la escuela

un(a) alumno(a)
un bolígrafo
un borrador
una calculadora
una cartera
un cuaderno
un lápiz
un libro
una llave
una mochila
una pluma
un portafolio
un sacapuntas

Los medios de transporte

un autobús
una bicicleta
un coche
una motocicleta

Las viviendas

un apartamento
una casa
un cuarto

En mi cuarto

una alfombra
una bocina
una cama
una cámara
una cinta
una cómoda
una computadora
un disco compacto
un escritorio
un estante
un estéreo
una grabadora
una máquina de escribir
una planta
un póster
un radio despertador
una silla
un televisor (a colores)
un vídeo

Vocabulario general

Verbos

llevar

Artículos

el
la
los
las

Otras palabras y expresiones

allí
cosa
¿Cuántos hay?
¿Dónde hay?
En mi cuarto hay…
éstos
más
Me llamo…
menos
muchacha
muchacho
Para ir al centro, voy en…
¿Qué hay en tu cuarto?
¿Qué llevas (tú) a la escuela?
telenovelas
Vivo en…

"Caballo de acero"

Antes de leer

1. What sports do you enjoy the most? The least?

2. What kind of format is the reading in?

3. Do you participate in cycling, either recreationally or competitively?

D e: reinaroja@arols.com

P a r a: Pedro "El Pollo" Villar, Club de ciclismo "Caballo de acero"<pollovila@arols.com>

F e c h a: 5 de febrero 19... 11:50AM

T e m a: Carreras de bicicleta

¡Hola pollo!

¿Cómo estás? Y los padres, ¿qué tal? Yo tengo una fuerte gripe. Mi bicicleta está en el garaje y estoy aquí, en la cama, sin apetito. Solo tomo té con limón y pan tostado. Me gustan tus cartas, pero especialmente ahora.

Te envío pronto una copia de una revista que compro aquí todos los meses. Tiene un artículo muy interesante sobre el ciclismo. Gracias por la información que enviaste por correo electrónico sobre la "Vuelta a Colombia" de este año. Yo también pienso que esta es una competencia muy importante para el ciclismo latinoamericano. La "Vuelta a México" es muy importante también. Me parece que es bueno saber que si no ganas un campeonato de bicicleta en Colombia o en México, a lo mejor ganas en Ecuador, en Uruguay o en Argentina. ¡Hay tantas competencias para escoger! Los campeonatos de primavera están cerca y todos tenemos que entrenar mucho. Yo estoy muy nerviosa, pues tengo demasiado trabajo de la escuela y no hay mucho tiempo más para entrenar bien este año.

Bueno pollo, chao, te escribo pronto.

Un abrazo,

Isabel, "La Reina Roja"

Guía para la lectura

Here are some words and expressions to keep in mind as you read.

Caballo de acero	*name of a cycling club (literally, "iron horse")*
pollo	*chicken, used here as a nickname*
gripe	*common cold—also known by other names in Spanish: catarro, resfriado*
revista	*magazine*
correo electrónico	*e-mail*
competencia	*competition*
campeonato	*championship*
a lo mejor ganas	*maybe you'll win*
primavera	*spring (season)*
todos tenemos que entrenar	*everyone has to to train*

Después de leer

1. According to the context of the reading, what do you think the "Vuelta a Colombia" and the "Vuelta a México" are?

2. What is the author's opinion about these two events? And about participating in cycling events in Latin America in general?

3. Is cycling popular in the United States? Would you say that it is more popular in the United States than in other countries? Why?

4. Would you rather own a bicycle or a car? Why? What are the advantages of each?

CAPÍTULO 5

Me gusta mucho...

—¿Te gusta la música?
—Claro. Me gusta mucho la música.

Objectives

- talking about preferences
- getting information about other people

Preparación

- As you get ready to begin this **etapa,** think about your likes and dislikes. On a sheet of paper, make headings for two lists: 1) *I like . . .* and 2) *I don't like . . . .*

- Write each of the following interests under the appropriate heading to express your personal tastes: music, animals, sports, nature, art, school subjects (science, history, foreign language, math).

Mis gustos

*Buenos días. Me llamo José. **Ésta** es Ana. Es mi **novia**, pero nuestros gustos son muy diferentes.*

José: No me gusta la música.
Ana: Me gusta la música.

José: Me gustan los animales.
Ana: No me gustan los animales.

Mis gustos *My tastes* **Ésta** *This* **novia** *girlfriend*

José: Me gustan los **deportes.**
Ana: No me gustan los deportes.

José: Me gusta la **naturaleza.**
Ana: No me gusta la naturaleza.

José: No me gusta el arte.
Ana: Me gusta el arte.

José: Me gustan las **lenguas.**
Ana: No me gustan las lenguas.

José: No me gustan las **ciencias…**
no me gusta la **química.**
Ana: Me gustan las ciencias…
me gusta la química.

José: No me gusta la biología.
Ana: Me gusta la biología.

deportes *sports* **naturaleza** *nature* **lenguas** *languages* **ciencias** *science* **química** *chemistry*

¡Te toca a ti!

A. ¡(No) Me gusta! Indicate how you feel about each activity pictured. Follow the model.

> **MODELO**   *Me gusta la música.* o:
> *No me gusta la música.*

1.

2.

3.

4.

5.

6.

B. ¿Y tú? Ask a classmate whether he (she) likes the activities pictured in the previous activity. Follow the model.

> **MODELO**   **Tú:**   *¿Te gusta la música?*
> **Compañera(o):**   *No, no me gusta la música.*

ESTRUCTURA

The verb *gustar*

Me gusta el disco compacto.	*I like the compact disc.*
Te gusta la cinta.	*You like the tape.*
Me gusta estudiar.	*I like to study.*
Te gusta trabajar.	*You like to work.*
Me gustan los discos compactos.	*I like the compact discs.*
Te gustan las cintas.	*You like the tapes.*

1. **Gustar** is different from other Spanish verbs you know in that it does not use subject pronouns. As you learned in Chapter 1, to express *I like* and *you like*, you use the pronouns **me** and **te** in front of a form of the verb **gustar**.

2. Only two forms of **gustar** are used—the singular form **gusta** and the plural form **gustan**. Use **gusta** if what is liked is a singular noun or an infinitive. If what is liked is a plural noun, use **gustan**.

Aquí practicamos

C. Los gustos Create a sentence by combining an element from Column A, one from Column B, and one from Column C. Follow the model.

> **MODELO**   *Me gustan los licuados.*

A	B	C
me	gusta	el sándwich
te	gustan	los licuados
		los refrescos
		el póster
		el disco compacto
		los deportes
		la música clásica
		las ciencias
		las lenguas
		los animales

D. ¡Me gustan muchísimo los deportes! An exchange student from Peru will be living with your family for the next six months. You are getting to know each other and she (he) is asking you about your likes and dislikes. Be as specific as possible in your answers. Follow the model.

> **MODELO**   ¿Te gustan los deportes?
> *¡Sí, me gustan muchísimo los deportes!* o:
> No, *no me gustan los deportes.*

1. ¿Te gusta estudiar?
2. ¿Te gusta bailar?
3. ¿Te gusta la química?
4. ¿Te gustan las lenguas?
5. ¿Te gustan los animales?
6. ¿Te gusta la música?

E. Me gustan los deportes, pero no me gusta la política
You and your friends are talking about what you like and dislike. In each case, say that the person indicated by the pronoun likes the first activity or item but dislikes the second one. Follow the model.

> **MODELO**   me / deportes / política
> *Me gustan los deportes, pero no me gusta la política.*

1. me / naturaleza / animales
2. te / música / arte
3. me / lenguas / literatura
4. me / lenguas / ciencias
5. te / política / matemáticas
6. te / música / deportes

PRONUNCIACIÓN   The Consonant d

In Spanish, when **d** is the first letter of a word or comes after **l** or **n**, it is produced by placing the tip of the tongue behind the back of the upper front teeth. In English, *d* is pronounced by placing the tip of the tongue on the gum ridge behind the upper front teeth. Pronounce the English word *dee* and note where the tip of your tongue is. Now pronounce the Spanish word **di** being careful to place the tip of the tongue on the back of the upper front teeth.

Práctica

F. Listen and repeat as your teacher models the following words.

1. disco
2. de
3. domingo
4. dos
5. diez
6. grande
7. aprender
8. Donaldo
9. Aldo
10. donde

Repaso ♻

G. ¿Cuántos hay?   Tell how many objects are in each of the drawings below. Follow the model.

> **MODELO**   *Hay dos lápices.*

1.

2.

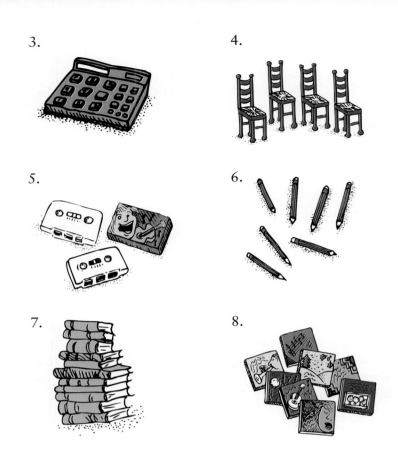

3.

4.

5.

6.

7.

8.

H. Nosotros llevamos... Make a list of five things you take to school every day. Compare your list with those of several other students in class. When you find that an item on your list is also on someone else's list, put a check mark beside it. Count the marks and report which items are most and least popular.

ESTRUCTURA

Ser + de for possession

El libro **es de Juan**.	*The book is Juan's.*
La calculadora **es de María**.	*The calculator is María's.*
Los lápices **son de él**.	*The pencils are his.*
Las mochilas **son de ellas**.	*The knapsacks are theirs* (female).

In Chapter 4, you learned two ways to express possession—the preposition **de** with nouns and possessors' names for the third person, and the possessive adjectives for first and second persons. You can also use the verb **ser + de** followed by the possessor's name or by a pronoun (**él, ella, ellos,** or **ellas**) to express possession in the third person.

Aquí practicamos

I. El libro es de...
Look at the drawings and indicate to whom the items belong. Follow the models.

MODELOS
El cuaderno es de José.
Los libros son de Bárbara.

José   Bárbara

1. Anita   2. Elena   3. Juan   4. ella   5. Tomás

6. Julián   7. él   8. Carmen   9. Alicia y Susana   10. ellos

J. ¿De quién es?
A classmate asks you to whom each of the following items belongs. Use **ser + de** to answer. Take turns asking and answering questions. Follow the models.

MODELOS

Compañera(o):	¿De quién es la mochila?
Tú:	La mochila es de María.
Tú:	¿De quién son los cuadernos?
Compañera (o):	Los cuadernos son de José.

María

José

1. Juan   2. ella   3. Catarina   4. Alicia

5. Miguel   6. él   7. Anita   8. Lorenzo

Capítulo 5 Me gusta mucho... **109**

Aquí escuchamos

Mis gustos *Carmen talks about her likes and dislikes.*

Antes de escuchar Think about how Carmen might say that she likes something, how she might say that she doesn't like some thing, and how the words **también, tampoco, y,** and **pero** are used.

 A escuchar As you listen, check the appropriate column on your activity master to show Carmen likes and what she doesn't like.

	She likes	She doesn't like
animales		
arte		
biología		
lenguas		
literatura		
matemáticas		
música		
química		

Después de escuchar On your activity master, answer the following question.

Which subject area do you think is Carmen's favorite: liberal arts, science, or technology?

Los gustos de la clase Form pairs and prepare a profile of your partner's likes and dislikes using the chart on your activity master. Interview your partner and rate how much he (she) likes each activity or item with the numbers on the following scale. Write the appropriate number next to each item on your activity master. Be ready to report on your partner's favorite and least favorite activities and items.

no = 0   poco = 1   bastante *(okay,*
mucho = 3   muchísimo = 4   *pretty well)* = 2

MODELO   **Tú:** *¿Te gusta mucho la biología?*
           Compañera(o): *No, me gusta la biología muy poco.*
                              (1 la biología) o:
                              No, pero me gusta la química
                              bastante. (2 la química)

___ la biología	___ la música clásica	___ los animales
___ la química	___ el jazz	___ los deportes
___ las ciencias	___ el arte moderno	___ la comida italiana
___ la historia	___ el arte clásico	___ la comida vietnamita
___ la literatura	___ los pósters	___ bailar
___ las lenguas	___ la política	___ viajar
___ la música rock	___ la naturaleza	___ cantar

Entrevista Using the list in the previous activity, along with other Spanish vocabulary you have learned, write a description of your likes and dislikes. Mention...

1. at least three things you like a lot

2. at least two that you don't like very much

Among them, mention...

3. something that you do well

4. something that you do every day

5. something else that you do occasionally

Use **también, tampoco, y,** and **pero** to connect your ideas. Compare your paragraph with that of a classmate. What are the similarities? What are the differences?

SEGUNDA ETAPA

Preparación

In this **etapa** you will continue to learn to talk about your likes and dislikes. Before you begin, think more specifically about the things you like and dislike. For example:

- Various sports
- Kinds of movies
- Types of art
- Types of animals
- Kinds of music
- Your school subjects

¿Qué te gusta más?

Un muchacho y una muchacha hablan de sus gustos.

Muchacho: Me gustan las **películas.**
Muchacha: ¿Qué te gusta más—las películas cómicas, las películas de horror, las películas de aventura o las películas de ciencia ficción?
Muchacho: Me gustan más las películas de horror.

¿Qué te gusta más? *What do you like more?* películas *movies*

Muchacho:	Me gusta el arte.
Muchacha:	¿Qué te gusta más—la **pintura** o la **escultura**?
Muchacho:	Me gusta más la escultura.

Muchacha:	Me gustan los animales.
Muchacho:	¿Qué te gusta más—los **perros**, los **gatos** o los **pájaros**?
Muchacha:	Me gustan más los pájaros.

Muchacha:	Me gustan los deportes.
Muchacho:	¿Qué te gusta más—el **fútbol**, el fútbol americano, el básquetbol, el béisbol o el vólibol?
Muchacha:	Me gusta más el béisbol.

Muchacho:	Me gusta mucho la música.
Muchacha:	¿Qué te gusta más—la música rock, el jazz o la música clásica?
Muchacho:	Me gusta más la música rock.

pintura *painting* **escultura** *sculpture* **perros** *dogs* **gatos** *cats* **pájaros** *birds* **fútbol** *soccer*

¡Te toca a ti!

A. ¿Qué te gusta más?
Of the following items, indicate which you like more. Follow the model.

> **MODELO**   el fútbol o el básquetbol
> *Me gusta más el básquetbol.*

1. el fútbol americano o el béisbol
2. los perros o los gatos
3. la pintura o la escultura
4. las películas de ciencia ficción o las películas cómicas
5. la música clásica o la música rock
6. la biología o la química
7. las lenguas o las matemáticas
8. la historia o el español

B. Me gusta más...
Ask two of your classmates to choose from the following sets of items. Follow the model.

> **MODELO**   la música clásica, el jazz, la música rock
>
> **Tú:** *¿Te gusta más la música clásica, el jazz o la música rock?*
> **Compañero(a) 1:** *Me gusta más la música clásica.*
> **Tú:** *¿Y a ti?* (And you?)
> **Compañero(a) 2:** *Me gusta más la música rock.*

1. el fútbol, el fútbol americano, el básquetbol
2. la pintura, la escultura, la arquitectura
3. la música, el baile *(dancing),* las películas
4. la música rock, el jazz, la música clásica
5. las hamburguesas, los sándwiches de jamón, las hamburguesas con queso
6. las películas de horror, las películas de aventura, las películas cómicas
7. el tenis, el golf, la natación *(swimming)*
8. la historia, las lenguas, las ciencias
9. el español, el francés, el inglés
10. la biología, la química, la física

PRONUNCIACIÓN THE CONSONANT **d**

The consonant **d** also has a sound that is similar to *th* in the English words *these, them, the, those,* etc. When you say these words note that the tip of the tongue touches the upper teeth. In Spanish, **d** is pronounced this way when it is between vowels or after any consonant except **l** or **n** or when it is the last letter in a word.

Práctica

C. Listen and repeat as your teacher models the following words.

1. todo
2. cada
3. madre
4. apellido
5. cuaderno

6. gordo
7. padre
8. universidad
9. verdad
10. usted

Repaso ♻

D. ¿De quién es? Identify each item. When a classmate asks you to whom each belongs, respond with the name of the person indicated under each picture. Follow the models.

MODELOS

Tú:	*Es un coche.*
Compañero(a):	*¿De quién es?*
Tú:	*El coche es de María.*

Tú:	*Son unos lápices.*
Compañero(a):	*¿De quién son?*
Tú:	*Los lápices son de Felipe.*

María   Felipe

1. Juan

2. Jaime

3. Rosa

4. Marta

5. Mario

6. Susana

7. Ana

8. José

ESTRUCTURA

The present tense of regular -er and -ir verbs

Yo **como** en la cafetería.   *I eat in the cafeteria.*

¿**Vives** tú aquí?   *Do you live here?*

Él **lee** siempre.   *He is always reading.*

Nosotros **comprendemos** inglés.   *We understand English.*

Uds. no **escriben** francés.   *You do not write French.*

Present Tense of Regular -er and -ir Verbs

Subject Pronoun	Verb Ending	Conjugated Verb Forms **correr** *(to run)*	**vivir** *(to live)*
yo	**-o**	corro	vivo
tú	**-es**	corres	vives
él ella Ud.	**-e**	corre	vive
nosotros(as)	**-emos/-imos**	corremos	vivimos
vosotros(as)	**-éis/-ís**	corréis	vivís
ellos ellas Uds.	**-en**	corren	viven

1. Note that, except for the **nosotros(as)** and **vosotros(as)** forms, the endings for **-er** and **-ir** verbs in the present tense are exactly the same. To conjugate any regular **-er** or **-ir** verb, drop the **-er** or **-ir** and replace it with the ending corresponding to its subject.

2. Here are some common **-er** and **-ir** verbs that you should learn.

aprender	*to learn*	**comer**	*to eat*
correr	*to run*	**vender**	*to sell*
compartir	*to share*	**recibir**	*to receive*
beber	*to drink*	**comprender**	*to understand*
leer	*to read*	**vivir**	*to live*
escribir	*to write*		

Aquí practicamos

E. ¿Comprenden español? Create original sentences using words from each column.

A	B	C
Raúl	comer	en la cafetería
Teresa y Sara	vivir	en un apartamento
yo	comprender	español
nosotros	compartir	un cuarto
Uds.		
tú		

F. Durante el verano... (During the summer...)

Tell what you and five friends do and don't do during the summer. Write one sentence about each of your classmates, using the words in Columns A, B, and C. Use a different verb from Column B in each sentence. Follow the model.

MODELO   *John corre todos los días. o:*
                John no corre todos los días.

A	B	C
(no)	comer	en la cafetería
	correr	todos los días
	leer	muchos libros
	beber	muchas cartas *(letters)*
	recibir	en Cuba
	vivir	leche cada mañana
	escribir	en un restaurante

G. ¿Qué hacen? (What are they doing?) Look at the drawings that follow and indicate what these people are doing.

1. Miguel

2. Rogelio y Lilia

3. Adela y Nívea

4. Leo

5. nosotros

6. Antonio

Aquí escuchamos

¿Qué te gusta más? *Carmen and José discuss their likes and dislikes.*

Antes de escuchar Think about how Carmen and José might say that they like or don't like something.

A escuchar Listen twice to the conversation and pay attention to each person's preferences.

Después de escuchar Write down on the chart on your activity master what Carmen and José say they like and don't like.

	José	Carmen
animales		
básquetbol		
béisbol		
deportes		
fútbol americano		
música		

	José	Carmen
películas		
de aventura		
de ciencia ficción		
de horror		
tenis		

¡ADELANTE!

 Yo me llamo...   Imagine this is your first day in an international school where the common language is Spanish.

1. Go up to another student and introduce yourself.
2. Say where you are from.
3. Ask his (her) name.
4. Ask the other student where he (she) is from.

Then share information about yourselves.

5. Indicate at least three things that you like.
6. Mention one thing that you do not like.

 Mi familia y yo   Write a short paragraph in which you describe where you and your family live and what you have in your home.

1. Mention where you are from if you do not live in your birthplace.
2. Say whether you live in a house or apartment.
3. Name at least three items in your home.
4. Mention the mode of transportation that each family member uses to go to work or to school. Follow the model.

MODELO   *Mi familia y yo somos de Nueva York, pero vivimos en Pennsylvania. Vivimos en una casa. En nuestra casa hay un estéreo, un televisor y una grabadora. No hay una computadora. Yo voy al centro en bicicleta, pero mis padres van al centro en coche.*

EN LÍNEA

Connect with the Spanish-speaking world! Access the *¡Ya verás! Gold* home page for Internet activities related to this chapter.

http://yaveras.heinle.com

VOCABULARIO

Temas y contextos

Los animales
un gato
un pájaro
un perro

El arte
la escultura
la pintura

Las ciencias
la biología
la química

Los deportes
el básquetbol
el béisbol
el fútbol
el fútbol americano
el tenis
el vólibol

La música
el jazz
la música clásica
la música rock

Las películas
cómicas
de aventura
de ciencia ficción
de horror

Vocabulario general

Verbos
aprender
beber
compartir
comprender
correr
escribir
leer
recibir
vender
vivir

Otras palabras y expresiones
¡Claro!
Me gusta(n) más…
gustos
las lenguas
la naturaleza
una novia
la política
¿Qué te gusta más?

La agenda de Mabel

Antes de leer

1. Look at the document below. Can you identify it? Do you use something similar?

2. Scan the document to find at least five cognates.

3. What extracurricular activities do you take part in during the week? Where do they take place?

4. What do you usually do on weekends? With whom do you spend time on weekends?

LUNES **20 de abril**	4:00	Clase de arte -Academia Sabrina. (Tengo una nueva profe.)
MARTES **21 de abril**	4:00	Clase de Badminton - Club El Frontón. A jugar con el "chistoso" de Max. Afortunadamente Loli y Jan aceptan su sentido de humor.
MIÉRCOLES **22 de abril**	4:30	Café Colón - Encontrarme con Sonia, Jochi y Gil antes de ir al cine para ver la nueva película de Disney. Me encantan nuestras sesiones de chismarreo.
JUEVES **23 de abril**	5:00	Café el Parisino - Encontrarme con la pandilla para 1) planear la fiesta, 2) decidir adónde ir para la excursión de clase. Si no presentamos opciones al profe Martínez mañana, no hay viaje; ¡Horror de horrores!
VIERNES **24 de abril**	9:00	¡Fiesta en casa de Jorge! ¡Toda la pandilla y otros amigos! También sus padres, claro. No son muy pesados pero se dejan ver.

SÁBADO **25 de abril**	9:00-2:00 p.m. Comprar el traje largo para la quinceañera de Sandra. 8:00-1:00 a.m. Quinceañera de Sandra en el Hotel El Conquistador. El guaperas de Nando es mi acompañante.	**DOMINGO** **26 de abril**	3:00-8:00 p.m. Discoteca Amazonas, Matiné Juvenil. ¡Bailar, bailar y bailar de todo y sin padres! Ánimos para el lunes...

Guía para la lectura

1. Here are some words to keep in mind as you read.

chistoso	*joker*
encontrarme con	*to meet up with*
me encantan	*I love (literally, they enchant me)*
chismarreo	*gossip*
pandilla	*the gang, group of friends (coll.)*
no pesados pero se dejan ver	*not heavy (i.e. smothering), but they let themselves be seen*
traje largo	*ballgown, formal dress for a dance*
guaperas	*handsome*
Ánimos	*courage*

2. **La quinceañera,** *or fifteenth birthday party, is a very important "coming of age" celebration for young women in Latin America. It is considered the official entry into society, and usually includes a formal dance party and a lavish dinner.*

Después de leer

1. Where does Mabel take her art and her badminton classes?

2. Why might this week's art class be particularly interesting?

3. What personality trait is Max known for?

4. What does Mabel think of Jorge's parents?

5. Where is Sandra celebrating her fifteenth birthday? Who do you think will be there?

6. Did you find any of Mabel's activities or their locations surprising or unusual? If so, which ones and why?

7. Are **quinceañeras** held in your community? What similar celebrations do you know of in the United States?

CAPÍTULO 6

Ésta es mi familia

Ésta es mi familia: mi madre, mi hermano y mi hermana con su esposo.

Objectives

- talking about one's family
- getting information about other people

Preparación

As you get ready to begin this **etapa,** think about the various members of your immediate family.

- Do you have a traditional family?
- Do you have stepparents?
- Do you have brothers and sisters?
- Do you have stepbrothers or stepsisters?

Yo vivo con...

Ésta es la familia de Ernesto.

madre   padre   hermano   hermana

abuelo   abuela

Buenos días. Me llamo Ernesto Torres. Ernesto es mi **nombre** y Torres es mi **apellido.** Hay siete personas en mi familia. **Tengo** un **padre,** una **madre,** un **hermano** y una **hermana.**

Mi **padre se llama** Alberto, y mi madre se llama Catalina. Mi hermano se llama Patricio, y mi hermana se llama Marta. Vivimos en una casa en la **Ciudad de México** con mi **abuelo** y mi **abuela.**

nombre *first name* **apellido** *last name* **Tengo** *I have* **padre** *father* **madre** *mother* **hermano** *brother* **hermana** *sister* **Mi padre se llama** *My father's name is* **Ciudad de México** *Mexico City* **abuelo** *grandfather* **abuela** *grandmother*

¡Te toca a ti!

A. Tu familia Complete these sentences with information about you and your family. Some additional words are listed for your use.

hermanastra *stepsister*   **madrastra** *stepmother*
hermanastro *stepbrother*   **padrastro** *stepfather*

1. Me llamo…
2. Mi nombre es…
3. Mi apellido es…
4. Hay… personas en mi familia.
5. Mi padre se llama…
6. Mi madre se llama…
7. Tengo… hermanos.
   (o: No tengo hermanos.)
8. Ellos se llaman…
9. Tengo… hermanas.
   (o: No tengo hermanas.)
10. Ellas se llaman…
11. Vivo con…

B. La familia de un(a) compañero(a) Ask a classmate these following questions about himself (herself) and his (her) family.

1. ¿Cómo te llamas?
2. ¿Cuál *(What)* es tu nombre?
3. ¿Cuál es tu apellido?
4. ¿Cuántas personas hay en tu familia?
5. ¿Cómo se llama tu padre?
6. ¿Cómo se llama tu madre?
7. ¿Cuántos hermanos tienes?
8. ¿Cómo se llaman?
9. ¿Cuántas hermanas tienes?
10. ¿Cómo se llaman?
11. ¿Cuántos abuelos tienes?
12. ¿Cuántas abuelas tienes?

Comentarios CULTURALES

Los apellidos

Perhaps you have noticed that Spanish speakers often use more than one last name. This is because many use their mother's maiden name after their father's last name. For example, Mario González Cruz would use the last name of his father first (González), followed by his mother's last name (Cruz). Mario might also use the initial instead of the complete maiden name (Mario González C.). When addressing someone, you use the first of the two last names (Mario González). What would be your complete name according to this tradition?

PRONUNCIACIÓN THE SOUND OF /b/

In Spanish the sound of /b/ can be spelled with the letter **b** or **v** and is pronounced like the *b* in *Bill* when it is the first letter of a word or after **n** or **m**.

Práctica

C. Listen and repeat as your teacher models the following words.

1. bueno
2. bien
3. bocadillo
4. vaso
5. vamos

6. hombre
7. un video
8. un beso
9. también
10. hambre

Repaso ♻

D. ¿Qué hacen? Describe what the people in the drawings are doing.

1. Alicia y Carlos

2. Ana

3. Alberto

4. Marirrosa y Juan

5. el Sr. García

6. Sofía

E. ¿Qué te gusta más? From the choices below, ask a classmate what he (she) likes more.

1. el fútbol, el fútbol americano, el básquetbol
2. la música, el baile, las películas
3. la música rock, el jazz, la música clásica
4. las hamburguesas, los sándwiches de jamón, las hamburguesas con queso
5. las películas de horror, las películas de aventura, las películas cómicas
6. la historia, las lenguas, las ciencias

?¿Qué crees?

When a woman marries she usually adds **de** plus her husband's last name to her own name. If María Pérez Clemente married José Román Caño, what would her name be?

a) María Clemente de Caño
b) María Pérez de Román
c) María Clemente de Román
d) María Pérez de Cañorespuesta

respuesta 🖙

ESTRUCTURA

The verb tener

Yo **tengo** dos hermanas.	*I have two sisters.*
¿**Tienes tú** un hermano?	*Do you have a brother?*
Él **tiene** un abuelo en Miami.	*He has a grandfather in Miami.*
Nosotros **tenemos** dos gatos.	*We have two cats.*
Ellos **no tienen** un perro.	*They don't have a dog.*

tener *(to have)*			
yo	**tengo**	nosotros(as)	**tenemos**
tú	**tienes**	vosotros(as)	**tenéis**
él ella Ud.	**tiene**	ellos ellas Uds.	**tienen**

In Spanish, the irregular verb **tener** can be used to talk about possessions.

Aquí practicamos

F. Tienen muchas cosas Tell what your friends have and do not have, using words from Columns A, B, C, and D.

A	B	C	D
José	(no)	tener	dos hermanos
yo			una hermana
nosotros			un gato
Juan y Catarina			dos perros
tú			un pájaro
Uds.			

☞ b

G. ¿Qué tienen Ana y Esteban? Look at the drawings below and tell what Ana and Esteban have and do not have. Follow the model.

MODELO
Ana tiene una cámara, pero Esteban no tiene una cámara. o: Ellos tienen unos lápices.

PALABRAS ÚTILES

Tener que + infinitive

Yo **tengo que** comer.   *I have to eat.*

Tú **tienes que** estudiar.   *You have to study.*

Él **tiene que** escribir la lección.   *He has to write the lesson.*

In Spanish, when you want to say that you have to do something, you do so by using the expression **tener que** followed by the infinitive form of the verb that expresses what must be done.

Aquí practicamos

H. ¿Qué tengo que hacer? Replace the words in italics and make the necessary changes.

1. Yo tengo que *comer*. (trabajar / estudiar / correr)
2. *Ellos* no tienen que estudiar. (Juan / Bárbara y Alicia / tú)
3. ¿Tienes *tú* que trabajar hoy *(today)?* (Julio y Santiago / Elena / Uds.)

I. Tenemos que... Tell what you and your friends have to do, using words from Columns A, B, and C.

A	B	C
yo	tener que	trabajar después de la escuela
nosotros(as)		estudiar para un examen
Jaime		hablar con un(a) amigo(a)
tú		comprar un disco compacto
Uds.		hacer un mandado *(errand)* para su padre (madre)

Aquí escuchamos

Mi familia *Carmen is going to provide some basic information about her family.*

Antes de escuchar What information about her family do you expect Carmen to include in her monologue?

 A escuchar Listen twice to the monologue before circling on your activity master the words that describe Carmen's family.

Después de escuchar On your activity master, circle the choices that match what Carmen says about her family.

familia	padre	madre	hermanos	animales
grande	contador	enfermera	gatos	uno
pequeña	ingeniero	periodista	perros	dos
	mecánico	profesora		

Tengo que estudiar para un examen, mirar una película y jugar al fútbol con mis amigos. Y tú, ¿qué tienes que hacer?

Esta semana (This week) tengo que... Make a list of at least three things that you have to do this week. Then ask several classmates what they have to do this week. When someone mentions an activity that is not on your list, add it to a second list labeled **Mis compañeros** *(classmates)* **tienen que...**

 ¿Qué tienes en tu casa? Tengo... Write a paragraph about your family and their activities, interests, and belongings.

1. Begin by telling how many people are in your family.

2. State their relationship to you.

3. Tell something that each person does or likes.

4. Tell something that each person has or would like to have that relates to his (her) activities or interests.

Use **le gusta(n)** for *he (she) likes* and **les gusta(n)** for *they like.*

MODELO   *Hay cuatro personas en mi familia: mi padre, mi madre, mi hermano y yo. Mi padre es contador y tiene una calculadora. Mi madre es abogada y escribe mucho. Ella tiene una computadora en su oficina, pero quisiera una computadora en casa también. Mi hermano tiene muchas cintas porque le gusta mucho la música. Me gusta la música también. Yo quisiera una grabadora.*

Family Picnic

Preparación

- As you begin this **etapa,** think about your extended family.
- Do you have grandparents? Uncles? Aunts? Cousins?

Tengo una familia grande

*La familia de Jaime es **grande** (large).*

Yo me llamo Jaime y ésta es mi familia. Mi abuelo se llama Sergio y mi abuela se llama Guadalupe. Mi abuela es la **esposa** de mi abuelo. Mis abuelos tienen un **hijo** y una **hija.** La hija se llama Rosa y el hijo se llama Juan. Rosa es mi madre y **está casada con** mi padre. Él se llama Fernando. Mi hermana se llama Diana.

Juan, el hermano de mi madre, es mi **tío.** Él está casado con mi **tía.** Ella se llama Elena. Mi tío Juan y mi tía Elena tienen dos hijas que se llaman Teresa y María Catarina. Ellas son mis **primas. Cada domingo** nosotros vamos a la casa de mis abuelos.

esposa *wife* **hijo** *son* **hija** *daughter* **está casada con** *is married to* **tío** *uncle* **tía** *aunt* **primas** *(female) cousins*
Cada domingo *Every Sunday*

¡Te toca a ti!

A. ¿Quién es? (Who is it?) Fill in the blanks to express the correct family relationships based on the information on page 132. Follow the model.

> **MODELO**   María Catarina es _la hija_ de Juan.

1. Rosa es _____ de Juan.
2. Fernando es _____ de Jaime.
3. Juan es _____ de Jaime.
4. Teresa es _____ de Juan.
5. Guadalupe es _____ de Rosa.
6. Sergio es _____ de Juan.
7. Sergio es _____ de Jaime.
8. Elena es _____ de Juan.
9. Guadalupe es _____ de María Catarina.
10. Fernando es _____ de Rosa.

B. Mi familia Draw a family tree of your own family. Using your family tree as a reference, tell your partner the name of each member on your family tree and their relationship to you.

PRONUNCIACIÓN   THE SOUND OF /b/

When the letter **b** or **v** is between vowels or after any consonant except **n** or **m,** it is pronounced with the lips coming together but not allowing the lips to stop the passage of air.

Práctica

C. Listen and repeat as your teacher models the following words.

1. favor
2. acabar
3. ¡Qué bueno!
4. cubano
5. jueves

6. a veces
7. una botella
8. abogado
9. noviembre
10. el vaso

Comentarios CULTURALES

La familia

When Hispanics talk about their families, they do not just mean their parents, brothers, and sisters as we often do in the United States. Many Hispanic families are very close and include many other relatives **(parientes),** such as grandparents, uncles and aunts, cousins, godparents, and in-laws. Sometimes one set of grandparents will live in the same house with one of their children and their grandchildren. This is becoming less common, especially in modern cities, but families generally remain very close.

Repaso ♻

C. Quisiera..., pero tengo que... Make a list of five things you would like to do but cannot because you have to do something else. Compare your list with a classmate's. Follow the model.

> **MODELO**   *Quisiera mirar la TV, pero tengo que estudiar.*

ESTRUCTURA

Information questions: dónde, cuántos, cuántas, quién, qué, por qué

You have already learned how to ask and answer *yes/no* questions. Frequently, however, you ask a question because you seek specific information. In Chapter 4 you learned to ask to whom something belongs, using **¿De quién es?** and **¿De quién son?** The following words are commonly used in Spanish when seeking information. Note that each of these words has an accent mark in its written form.

1. To find out *where* something is or someone is located, use **¿dónde?**

   —**¿Dónde** vive tu hermano?   *Where does your brother live?*
   —Él vive en Pittsburgh.   *He lives in Pittsburgh.*

   —**¿Dónde** está mi libro?   *Where is my book?*
   —Tu libro está en la mesa.   *Your book is on the table.*

2. To find out *how many* there are, use **¿cuántos?** if what you are asking about is masculine and **¿cuántas?** if what you are asking about is feminine.

   —**¿Cuántos** hermanos tienes?   *How many brothers do you have?*
   —Tengo dos.   *I have two.*

   —**¿Cuántos** perros tienes?   *How many dogs do you have?*
   —Tengo uno.   *I have one.*

   —**¿Cuántas** hermanas tiene él?   *How many sisters does he have?*
   —Él tiene seis.   *He has six.*

   —**¿Cuántas** cintas tienes?   *How many tapes do you have?*
   —Tengo una.   *I have one.*

3. To find out *who* does something, use **¿quién?**

   —**¿Quién** come en la cafetería?   *Who eats at the cafeteria?*
   —Bárbara come en la cafetería.   *Bárbara eats at the cafeteria.*

   —**¿Quién** estudia en la biblioteca? *Who studies at the library?*
   —Roberto estudia en la biblioteca.   *Roberto studies at the library.*

4. To find out *what*, use **¿qué?**

   —**¿Qué** buscan ellos?   *What are they looking for?*
   —Ellos buscan la casa de Marta.   *They are looking for Marta's house.*

   —**¿Qué** compran ellos?   *What are they buying?*
   —Ellos compran una mochila.   *They are buying a knapsack.*

ESTRUCTURA (continued)

5. To find out *why*, use **¿por qué?** The answers to such questions often includes **porque** *(because)*, which is one word and does not have an accent mark.

—**¿Por qué** estudias?　　　　　*Why are you studying?*
—**Porque** tengo un examen mañana.　*Because I have a test tomorrow.*

—**¿Por qué** comes pizza?　　　　*Why do you eat pizza?*
—**Porque** me gusta.　　　　　　*Because I like it.*

Me llamo Lourdes. Ahora estoy en los Estados Unidos pero vivo en Bogotá, Colombia. Tengo dos hermanos y una hermana. Mis hermanos trabajan en Cartagena y mi hermana es estudiante de escuela secundaria (high school).
¿Cuántos hermanos tienes tú?
¿Qué hacen?

Aquí practicamos

E. ¿Cuándo estudia Josefina? Create original questions using words from each column.

A	B	C
dónde	trabajar	Josefina
qué	tener	tu padre
por qué	buscar	tú
quién	estudiar	Juan y Pablo
cuándo	comer	ellas
	correr	Uds.

F. Más detalles (More details) You are talking with some of the Spanish-speaking exchange students in your school. After a student makes a statement, ask a follow-up question that makes sense. Follow the model.

> **MODELO**   Esteban: No vivo en Valencia.
> Tú: *¿Dónde vives?*

1. **Esteban:** Tengo hermanos, pero no tengo hermanas.
2. **Esteban:** Mis hermanos no viven con nosotros.
3. **Esteban:** Ellos no estudian ciencias.
4. **Bárbara:** Mi padre y mi madre trabajan.
5. **Bárbara:** Mi hermana estudia muchas horas todos los días.
6. **Bárbara:** Mi hermano tiene muchos discos compactos.
7. **Carlos:** No tengo el libro de química.
8. **Carlos:** Como en la cafetería.
9. **Carlos:** No vivo aquí.

G. ¿Dónde vives? Ask a classmate questions in order to get the information listed. Do not translate word for word. Instead, find a Spanish expression that will help you get the information. Your classmate will answer your questions. Follow the models.

<table>
<tr><td>**MODELOS**</td><td colspan="2">where he (she) lives</td></tr>
<tr><td></td><td>Tú:</td><td>¿Dónde vives?</td></tr>
<tr><td></td><td>Compañera(o):</td><td>Vivo en Los Ángeles.</td></tr>
<tr><td></td><td colspan="2">where his (her) father and mother work</td></tr>
<tr><td></td><td>Tú:</td><td>¿Dónde trabajan tu padre y tu madre?</td></tr>
<tr><td></td><td>Compañera(o):</td><td>Mi padre trabaja en First National Bank of Los Ángeles, y mi madre trabaja en City Hospital.</td></tr>
</table>

1. where his (her) grandparents live
2. how many brothers and sisters he (she) has
3. how many pets (dogs, cats, birds) he (she) has
4. what he (she) is studying

ESTRUCTURA

Descriptive adjectives

Él es **alto**.	He is tall.
Ella es **alta**.	She is tall.
Juan y José son **altos**.	Juan and José are tall.
María y Carmen son **altas**.	María and Carmen are tall.

1. Remember that, in Spanish, adjectives agree in gender and number with the noun they modify. Masculine singular adjectives that end in **-o** have three other forms—feminine singular that ends in -a, masculine plural that ends in **-os,** and feminine plural that ends in **-as.** Here are some adjectives of this type used to describe people and things:

aburrido	boring, bored	**guapo**	handsome
alto	tall	**malo**	bad
antipático	disagreeable	**moreno**	dark-haired, brunette
bajo	short	**pelirrojo**	red-haired
bonito	pretty	**pequeño**	small, little
bueno	good	**rubio**	blond
delgado	thin	**serio**	serious
divertido	fun, amusing	**simpático**	nice
feo	plain, ugly	**tonto**	stupid, foolish
gordo	fat		

ESTRUCTURA (continued)

pelirroja   moreno   rubia

2. Adjectives that end in -e have only two forms—one singular and one plural. Some common adjectives of this type are **inteligente** *(intelligent)*, **interesante** *(interesting)*, and **grande** *(big, large)*.

Alina y Bárbara son **inteligentes**.   *Alina and Bárbara are intelligent.*

Nuestra casa es **grande**.   *Our house is big.*

3. **¿Cómo es…?** and **¿Cómo son …?** are used to ask what someone or something is like.

—¿**Cómo es** el libro?   *What is the book like?*
—Es aburrido.   *It is boring.*

El libro es muy interesante.

4. In Spanish, when adjectives are used with the nouns they modify, they usually follow the noun.

Me gustan **los restaurantes italianos**.   *I like Italian restaurants.*

Mi primo es **un estudiante serio**.   *My cousin is a serious student.*

El español es una **lengua interesante**.   *Spanish is an interesting language.*

Aquí practicamos

H. ¿Cómo son? Describe the following people, using words from Columns A, B, and C. Follow the model.

MODELO *Él es alto.* o: *Él no es alto.*

A	B	C
él	(no)ser	alto
tú		inteligente
Elizabeth		bajo
Linda y Paula		rubio
Javier y Roberto		moreno
nosotros		pelirrojo
		aburrido
		tonto
		antipático
		bueno

I. No, no es..., es... A classmate asks you whether one of your friends has a certain quality. You respond by saying that your friend is the opposite. Follow the model.

MODELO alto / María
Compañera(o): *¿Es alta María?*
Tú: *No, no es alta, es baja.*

1. gordo / Juan
2. rubio / Anita
3. inteligente / David
4. divertido / Marina
5. simpático / Antonio
6. feo / Miguel y Luis
7. bajo / Éster y Marisa
8. simpático / ellos
9. aburrido / ellas
10. bueno / los hijos

J. ¿Cómo es?
Use the adjectives in parentheses to tell something about the words in italics. Make any necessary changes to the adjective. Follow the model.

> **MODELO**   (delicioso) Maribel come unas *patatas.*
> *Maribel come unas patatas deliciosas.*

1. (simpático) Leo y Jorge son dos *muchachos.*
2. (gordo) Mi amiga tiene un *perro.*
3. (divertido) Quisiera mirar una *película.*
4. (interesante) Clara lee un *libro.*
5. (pelirrojo) Tu primo tiene una *novia.*

Aquí escuchamos

La familia de Isabel   *Isabel, a friend of Carmen's, is going to give some information about her family.*

Antes de escuchar   Given what you have learned in this **etapa,** what information about Isabel's family do you think she will include in her description?

 A escuchar   Listen twice to the monologue before choosing on your activity master the items that match Isabel's description of her family.

Después de escuchar   On your activity master, circle the items that match what Isabel says about her family.

familia	padre	madre	animales	hermanos
grande	contador	enfermera	gatos	uno
pequeña	ingeniero	periodista	perros	dos
	mecánico	profesora		

Una fiesta Describe the people pictured in the following image.

 Tu familia Choose three members of your extended family. Write a description of each one, including at least three adjectives for each.

EN LÍNEA

Connect with the Spanish-speaking world! Access the *¡Ya verás! Gold* home page for Internet activities related to this chapter.

http://yaveras.heinle.com

VOCABULARIO

Para charlar	Temas y contextos	Vocabulario general	

Para preguntar

¿Cómo es(son)?
¿Cuántos(as)?
¿Dónde?
¿Qué?
¿Por qué?
¿Quién?

La familia

una abuela
un abuelo
una esposa
un esposo
una hermana
un hermano
una hija
un hijo
una madre
un padre
un pariente
una prima
un primo
una tía
un tío

Sustantivos

un apellido
una ciudad
un nombre
unas personas

Adjetivos

aburrido(a)
alto(a)
antipático(a)
bajo(a)
bonito(a)
bueno(a)
delgado(a)
divertido(a)
feo(a)
gordo(a)
grande
guapo(a)
inteligente
interesante
malo(a)
moreno(a)
pelirrojo(a)
pequeño(a)
rubio(a)
serio(a)
simpático(a)
tonto(a)

Verbos

tener

Otras expresiones

cada domingo
Está casado(a) con…
Se llama(n)…
tener que

Un árbol ecuatoriano

Antes de leer

1. Look at the illustration. What kind of diagram is this?

2. Do you know where your grandparents and great-grandparents came from?

3. How many last names do you use? Do you use a hyphenated family name? Do you know people who do? Explain the changes that a person's last name sometimes undergoes when he or she gets married.

Queridos papás:

¿Cómo están? Escribo esta nota porque quiero mostrarles el árbol genealógico que preparo para la clase de historia. Como se presentan los apellidos es bien diferente aquí, en los Estados Unidos. Mamá, ¿sabes que en los Estados Unidos mucha gente no usa el apellido materno? Es como un secreto. También, ¡cómo se sorprende a veces la gente de que mis parientes vengan de tantas partes del mundo! Quizás es que la gente no se acuerda de que en América Latina muchas personas también vinieron de otras partes del mundo, igual que por acá. Bueno, chau, me voy a hacer los deberes. Les escribo pronto.

Un beso,

Carlos

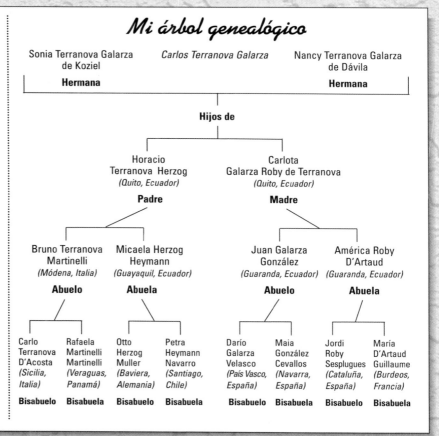

Mi árbol genealógico

Sonia Terranova Galarza de Koziel	Carlos Terranova Galarza	Nancy Terranova Galarza de Dávila
Hermana		**Hermana**

Hijos de

Horacio Terranova Herzog *(Quito, Ecuador)*	Carlota Galarza Roby de Terranova *(Quito, Ecuador)*
Padre	**Madre**

Bruno Terranova Martinelli *(Módena, Italia)*	Micaela Herzog Heymann *(Guayaquil, Ecuador)*	Juan Galarza González *(Guaranda, Ecuador)*	América Roby D'Artaud *(Guaranda, Ecuador)*
Abuelo	**Abuela**	**Abuelo**	**Abuela**

Carlo Terranova D'Acosta *(Sicilia, Italia)*	Rafaela Martinelli Martinelli *(Veraguas, Panamá)*	Otto Herzog Muller *(Baviera, Alemania)*	Petra Heymann Navarro *(Santiago, Chile)*	Darío Galarza Velasco *(País Vasco, España)*	Maia González Cevallos *(Navarra, España)*	Jordi Roby Sesplugues *(Cataluña, España)*	María D'Artaud Guillaume *(Burdeos, Francia)*
Bisabuelo	**Bisabuela**	**Bisabuelo**	**Bisabuela**	**Bisabuelo**	**Bisabuela**	**Bisabuelo**	**Bisabuela**

Guía para la lectura

1. Here are some words and expressions to keep in mind as you read.

quiero mostrarles	*I want to show you*
sabes	*do you know*
vengan	*might possibly come*
Quizás	*perhaps*
no se acuerda	*do not remember (reflex.)*
vinieron	*came*
los deberes	*homework (used in Ecuador)*

2. In Spanish-speaking countries, **de** is sometimes used after a woman's maiden name to separate it from her husband's last name.

Después de leer

1. Why do you think Carlos says that "el apellido materno en los Estados Unidos es como un secreto"? Are you known by both your mother's maiden name and your father's last name? What is the usefulness of using the last name of both one's parents?

2. Why does it bother Carlos that people in the United States are surprised that his ancestors came from all over the world?

3. A diagram depicting the growth of a family through several generations is often called "a family tree." Why do you think this term is used? Why do you think family trees might be useful? Have you or other family members ever prepared a family tree?

Conversemos un rato

A. Vamos a conocernos Role-play the following situation with a classmate.

1. Imagine that you are at a party feeling lonely and bored. You strike up a conversation with an interesting person sitting next to you. Work with a partner to prepare a dialogue based on the suggestions below.

   a. Greet each other using any of the **saludos y respuestas** you learned in the first chapter. Find out your classmate's first and last names.

   b. Find out where your classmate lives.

   c. Ask your partner to describe his or her family members (*parientes*). Ask how many brothers and sisters your partner has, and whether he or she has a small or large family.

   d. Find out the names of your friend's grandparents (*abuelos*).

   e. Ask if there are dogs or cats at home. Find out their names.

   f. Ask your partner to describe his or her parents and what do they do for a living.

B. Un diálogo de contrarios After reviewing pp. 103-104 and 112-113 in your textbook, prepare a dialogue with a classmate, based on the following scenario.

1. Imagine your family is hosting an exchange student from Bolivia. Discuss likes and dislikes with the exchange student.

   a. Greet each other using your full names and shake hands.

   b. Offer your new friend some snacks. Your friend should decline politely.

   c. For each of the categories below, express differing opinions.

      The type of movies you like

      The sports you watch

      Your favorite subjects in school

      What type of pet you like

   d. Dinner is ready and finally you find there's something you agree on; you both love to eat!

Taller de escritores

Writing a paragraph

For practice, write a paragraph in Spanish to a pen pal or email-pal, describing your room at home or another room you like.

> Mi cuarto es pequeño pero bonito. Tiene una ventana grande donde uno ve la próxima casa. Tiene mucha luz. Contiene muchas cosas para su tamaño: mi estéreo, mi ropa, mi computadora. Hay una cama, un escritorio, un estante con mis libros...

Writing Strategy
- List writing

A. Reflexión Choose a room to describe, then list as many details about it as you can think of. Narrow your list to a few main points.

B. Primer borrador Write a first draft of the paragraph.

C. Revisión con un(a) compañero(a) Exchange paragraphs with a classmate. Read each other's work and comment on it, based on these questions: What aspect of the description is the most interesting? What part of the room can you most easily visualize? Is the paragraph appropriate for its audience? Does the paragraph reflect the task assigned? What aspect of the paragraph would you like to have clarified or made more complete?

D. Versión final Revise your first draft at home, based on the feedback you received. Check grammar, spelling, punctuation, and accent marks. Bring your final draft to class.

E. Carpeta Your teacher may choose to place your work in your portfolio, display it on a bulletin board, or use it to evaluate your progress.

Conexión con la sociología

La familia en nuestra sociedad

Para empezar La familia es la base de nuestra **sociedad** humana. Algunas familias son grandes y otras son pequeñas. Nuestra sociedad es interesante y diversa porque todos tenemos familias diferentes.

A. ¿Con quién vives? Look over the following list of people.

1. Write down relatives you live with.
2. Write down how many of each you have in your family.

madre	tía	hijo
padre	primo	hija
hermano	prima	**sobrino**
hermana	padrastro	**sobrina**
abuelo	madrastra	**cuñado**
abuela	hermanastra	**cuñada**
tío	hermanastro	otros: _____

3. Tengo _____ personas en mi familia.

Tipos de familias

La familia nuclear: es ahora el tipo de familia más común en el mundo. En esta familia, hay dos esposos que viven con sus hijos o **hijastros**. Otros **parientes** llegan de visita pero no viven con ellos.

La familia extendida: Cuando otros parientes viven con dos esposos y sus hijos, es una familia extendida. En muchas familias extendidas, los abuelos, y a veces los primos, tíos y **parientes políticos** viven en la misma casa. En Latinoamérica todavía hay muchas familias extendidas.

La familia monoparental: En una familia monoparental, **sólo** hay una madre o un padre que vive con sus hijos o hijastros. No hay dos padres. A veces la madre o el padre está divorciado(a). A veces la madre o el padre es **viudo(a)**.

---

sociedad *society*   sobrino(a) *nephew (niece)*   cuñado(a) *brother-in-law (sister-in-law)*
hijastros *stepchildren*   parientes *relatives*   parientes políticos *relatives by marriage*   sólo *only*
viudo(a) *widower (widow)*

B. ¿Qué tipo de familia es?
Now complete the chart below using your knowledge from the reading to identify the kinds of families that the following people have. The first one is done for you.

persona	vive con	tipo de familia
Carmen	su madre y padre, sus hermanos y hermanas	*nuclear*
Luis	sus abuelos, padres y hermanos	
Elena	su esposo y su hijo	
Carlos	su hijo	
Mónica	su hijo y sus dos hijas	
Yo	¿?	¿?

C. ¿Verdadero o falso?
Answer **verdadero** or **falso** based on the information in the chart below.

1. En esta gráfica, hay información sobre personas solteras (*single*).
2. La gráfica tiene información sobre las familias extendidas.
3. El 12% de las personas viven con su madre, pero no con su padre.
4. El 15% de las personas viven en familias monoparentales.
5. La sección azul (*blue*) representa las familias nucleares.

FAMILIAS EN LOS ESTADOS UNIDOS

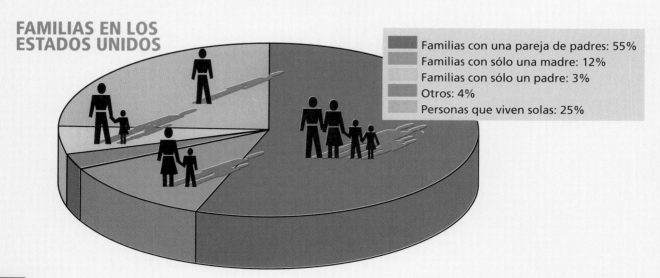

Familias con una pareja de padres: 55%
Familias con sólo una madre: 12%
Familias con sólo un padre: 3%
Otros: 4%
Personas que viven solas: 25%

Vistas

de los países hispanos

Ecuador

Capital: Quito

Ciudades principales: Guayaquil, Cuenca, Ambato

Población: 10.500.000

Idiomas: español, quechua

Área territorial: 270.670 km²

Clima: la costa mantiene una temperatura de 23° a 25° C; en la región de la sierra de 20° a 26° C

mantiene *maintains*   sierra *mountains*

Chile

Capital: Santiago

Ciudades principales: Concepción, Valparaíso,
Viña del Mar,

Población: 13.200.000

Idiomas: español

Área territorial: 756.626 km²

Clima: seco en el norte, templado en la region central,
frio y húmedo en el sur

seco *dry*   templado *temperate, moderate*   húmedo *humid*

EXPLORA

Find out more about Ecuador and Chile!
Access the **Nuestros vecinos** page on the
¡Ya verás! *Gold* web site for a list of URLs.

http://yaveras.heinle.com/vecinos.htm

Honduras

Capital: Tegucigalpa

Ciudades principales: San Pedro Sula, Choluteca

Población: 5.800.000

Idiomas: español, dialectos indígenas

Área territorial: 112,492 km²

Clima: tropical en la costa, templado en el interior

indígenas *indigenous, native*

EXPLORA

Find out more about Honduras! Access the **Nuestros vecinos** page on the *¡Ya verás! Gold* web site for a list of URLs.

http://yaveras.heinle.com/vecinos.htm

En la comunidad

¡Programa tu carrera!

"*My name is Adam Weiss. The summer of my junior year in high school, I took three years of high school Spanish and one big bag and went to Madrid on a cultural exchange. A month later, I brought home a passion for languages and a lifelong friendship with a Spanish family. It was exciting to actually use a foreign language!*

A background in Spanish and computer science turned out to be a requirement for my first job. Now I work as an international software engineer at a company that creates voice recognition software. If you want to talk to your computer in Spanish or in other European languages and have it do your typing for you, you'll use our software. Although my primary responsibility is programming, I've also traveled to Mexico and South America for trade shows to show off our products. I also collect voice and accent samples for our programs so they can recognize varying ways to pronounce the same words. My career has been a lot more interesting because I've learned Spanish!"

¡Ahora te toca a ti!

Adam's cultural exchange led to "a passion for languages and a lifelong friendship with a Spanish family." Why do you think he enjoyed the exchange program so much?

Do you think that spending time in Spain improved his Spanish? Why?

If you have visited a Spanish-speaking country or participated in an exchange program, you may want to prepare a short presentation in Spanish about your experiences. If you wish, bring photographs to class to help you describe the country as well as the people you met there.

If you haven't participated in an exchange program or traveled to a Spanish-speaking country, you might like to interview someone who has. Be prepared to share with your classmates what you find out.

You might also want to imagine that you're going on a cultural exchange program to a Spanish-speaking country. At the library, research places you would like to visit and choose a destination. Be prepared to discuss with your classmates why you want to visit that particular country.

UNIDAD 3

¿Dónde y a qué hora?

Objectives

In this unit you will learn:

- to identify and locate places in a city
- to express your desires and preferences
- to talk about age
- to ask for and give directions
- to give orders and suggest activities
- to tell time
- to talk about the way you or someone else feels

¿Qué ves?

- Where are the people in the photo at left?
- What kind of store do you think is in the photo at left?
- What public buildings do you see in the photos on this page?

CAPÍTULO 7

¿Adónde vamos?

Primera etapa: Los edificios públicos
Segunda etapa: ¿Quieres ir al cine?
Tercera etapa: Las tiendas

CAPÍTULO 8

¿Dónde está... ?

Primera etapa: ¿Está lejos de aquí?
Segunda etapa: ¿Cómo llego a... ?

CAPÍTULO 9

¡La fiesta del pueblo!

Primera etapa: ¿A qué hora son los bailes folklóricos?
Segunda etapa: ¿Cómo están Uds.?

CAPÍTULO 7

¿Adónde vamos?

José Rivas va a la farmacia.

Objectives

- identifying places in a city
- identifying public buildings

Preparación

- What are some buildings that can be found in most cities or towns?
- What does the word **plaza** make you think of?
- Where are most of the public buildings located in your city or town?
- Which public buildings are within walking distance from where you live?

Los edificios públicos

*En nuestra ciudad hay muchos **edificios públicos*** (public buildings).

un aeropuerto
una estación de trenes
un banco
un hospital
una biblioteca *a library*
una iglesia *a church*
una catedral
un mercado *a market*
un colegio *a school*
una oficina de correos *a post office*
una escuela secundaria *a high school*
una plaza *a town, city square*
una estación de autobuses *a bus station*
una universidad
una estación de policía

Comentarios CULTURALES

La ciudad típica

Many cities in the Spanish-speaking world are built based on the same pattern. There is usually a **plaza** in the middle of town with several important buildings facing it: the cathedral or main church at one end; the main government building and a police station at the other; and shops, banks, hotels, and cafés on the two sides in between. Families and young people gather at the central plaza on weekends and summer evenings to take a walk, see their friends, and have a drink or a meal. Walking around a city and its plaza is considered one of life's pleasures by many different people in Spanish-speaking societies. The streets are full of life, movement, and music.

¡Te toca a ti!

A. ¿Qué es? Identify each building or place in the drawings that follow. Follow the model.

> **MODELO**   *Es una catedral.*

1.

2.

3.

4.

5.

6.   7.   8.   9.

B. ¿Dónde está...? (Where is . . . ?) You have just arrived in town and are looking at a map. Using the appropriate form of the definite article (el, la), ask where each building or place is located. Follow the model.

MODELO   oficina de correos
                ¿Dónde está la oficina de correos?

1. estación de trenes
2. aeropuerto
3. iglesia
4. estación de autobuses
5. universidad
6. plaza
7. escuela secundaria

8. biblioteca
9. catedral
10. oficina de correos
11. estación de policía
12. hospital
13. mercado
14. colegio

C. ¡Aquí está! (Here it is!) Now that you are familiar with the map of the town, a tourist asks you where certain buildings and places are. A classmate will play the role of the tourist. Using the expression **Aquí está,** indicate the various locations on the map. Follow the model.

MODELO   la plaza
          Turista: *¿Dónde está la plaza?*
              Tú: *¿La plaza? Aquí está.*

1. la catedral
2. la oficina de correos
3. la universidad
4. la biblioteca
5. la estación de trenes
6. la escuela secundaria

7. el aeropuerto
8. la estación de policía
9. la iglesia
10. el hospital
11. la estación de autobuses
12. el colegio

PRONUNCIACIÓN THE CONSONANT g

In Spanish, **g** is pronounced like the *g* in the English word *goal* when it is before the vowels **a, o,** and **u,** as in **gato, gota,** and **gusta** or before the consonants **l** and **r** as in **globo** or **grupo.** It has this sound before **ue** and **ui** as in **guerra** and **guitarra,** in which cases the **u** is silent. The letter **g** is also pronounced this way when it is the first letter of a word or follows the consonant **n.**

Práctica

D. Listen and repeat as your teacher models the following words.

1. gato	4. ganas	7. Gustavo	9. un gato
2. grupo	5. gracias	8. tengo	10. un globo
3. gordo	6. globo		

ESTRUCTURA

The verb ir and the contraction al

¿Adónde **van** Uds.?   *Where are you going?*
Yo **voy** a Nueva York.   *I am going to New York.*

Alicia **va** a la plaza.   *Alicia is going to the (town) square.*

Vamos al mercado.   *We are going to the market.*

ir *(to go)*			
yo	**voy**	nosotros(as)	**vamos**
tú	**vas**	vosotros(as)	**vais**
él		ellos	
ella	**va**	ellas	**van**
Ud.		Uds.	

1. The verb **ir** is irregular, so you need to memorize its forms.

2. When the preposition **a** is followed by the definite article **el,** they contract to form one word, **al.**

Aquí practicamos

E. ¿Adónde vas? Pick an activity from the first column, and then choose the place associated with it from the second column. Form a sentence, following the model.

> **MODELO** Me gusta viajar.   el aeropuerto
> *Me gusta viajar; por eso (because of that) voy al aeropuerto.*

A	B
1. Tienes que ver al médico.	la biblioteca
2. Necesitamos más libros.	el banco
3. Quisieran comprar fruta.	el museo
4. Me gusta caminar (*walking*).	la oficina de correos
5. Usted necesita dinero.	la estación de policía
6. Ellos tienen que aprender.	el hospital
7. Me gusta el arte moderno.	la iglesia
8. Tengo que mandar una carta.	la escuela
9. Quiero hablar con un policía.	el mercado
10. Desean escuchar música religiosa.	el aeropuerto
	el parque

F. En la estación de trenes You are at the railroad station with a group of friends who are all leaving to visit different Spanish cities. Each time you ask a friend if someone is going to a certain city, he (she) tells you that you are wrong. Ask and answer questions with a partner, following the model.

> **MODELO** Raquel / Salamanca / Cádiz
> **Tú:** *¿Va Raquel a Salamanca?*
> **Amigo(a):** *No, Raquel no va a Salamanca. Ella va a Cádiz.*

1. Teresita / León / Burgos
2. Carlos / Valencia / Granada
3. Antonio / Málaga / Córdoba
4. Carmencita / Sevilla / Toledo
5. Miguel / Pamplona / Ávila
6. Mari / Barcelona / Valencia
7. Juan / Córdoba / Segovia

PALABRAS ÚTILES

Expressing frequency

Following are some more phrases used in Spanish to say how often you do something.

rara vez rarely		**a menudo**	frequently, often
nunca never		**de vez en cuando**	from time to time

Nunca usually precedes the verb. The other adverbs may be placed at the beginning or end of a sentence.

Nunca vamos a la estación de policía.

We never go to the police station.

Rara vez voy al hospital.

I rarely go to the hospital.

Andrés va a la biblioteca **a menudo**.

Andrés goes to the library often.

Aquí practicamos

G. Una encuesta (A survey) Ask three other students the following questions and write down their answers. They do not need to answer with complete sentences. Your classmates should use a variety of expressions of frequency in the answers, including **siempre, todos los días, a veces,** and those learned in Chapter 1. Follow the model.

> MODELO
>
> Tú: ¿Vas al aeropuerto a menudo?
> Compañero(a): *Muy rara vez.* o: *Sí, a menudo.* o: *No, nunca.*

1. ¿Vas a la iglesia a menudo?
2. ¿Vas a la catedral a menudo?
3. ¿Vas a la plaza a menudo?
4. ¿Vas al mercado a menudo?
5. ¿Vas a la biblioteca a menudo?
6. ¿Vas al hospital a menudo?

H. Los resultados *Using complete sentences, report your findings from Activity G to your classmates. Follow the model.*

> MODELO
>
> *Josh nunca va a la biblioteca. Linda va a la biblioteca de vez en cuando y Denise va a menudo.*

Aquí escuchamos

El autobús *An announcement describes the route that a city bus takes on a typical day and the stops it makes.*

 Antes de escuchar To prepare for the announcement you will hear, review the vocabulary you have learned for buildings and places.

 A escuchar Listen to the announcement twice before marking the order of the stops on your activity master.

Después de escuchar Based on what you just heard, write numbers next to the stops mentioned to indicate their order along the route.

__ el aeropuerto	__ la estación de auto- buses	__ el mercado
__ la biblioteca		__ la oficina de correos
__ la catedral	__ la estación de policía	__ la plaza
__ la escuela secundaria	__ el hospital	__ la universidad

¡ADELANTE!

 En la calle (On the street) You run into a classmate on the street. 1) Greet each other. 2) Then ask where he (she) is going, 3) what he (she) is going to do there, and 4) whether he (she) goes there often. Follow the model.

MODELO

Estudiante 1:	*¡Hola! ¿Qué tal?*
Estudiante 2:	*Muy bien, ¿y tú?*
Estudiante 1:	*Bien, gracias. ¿Adónde vas?*
Estudiante 2:	*Voy a la biblioteca.*
Estudiante 1:	*¿Qué vas a hacer?*
Estudiante 2:	*Voy a estudiar.*
Estudiante 1:	*¿Vas a menudo a la biblioteca?*
Estudiante 2:	*Sí, todos los días.* o: *No, voy de vez en cuando.*

¿Cuándo? Write a list of sentences using each of the following expressions to indicate how frequently you go to different public buildings in your town or city.

a menudo	nunca	siempre
a veces	rara vez	todos los días
de vez en cuando		

SEGUNDA ETAPA

¿Quieres ir al cine?

Una conversación telefónica:

Isabel: ¡Hola! ¿Celia?
Celia: Sí. ¿Quién habla?
Isabel: Habla Isabel.
Celia: Hola, Isabel. ¿Qué tal?
Isabel: Muy bien. Delia y yo vamos al cine esta **tarde**. **¿Quieres venir** con nosotras?
Celia: Mm…, **lo siento,** pero no es posible porque voy al museo con Marcos, y esta noche vamos a la discoteca.
Isabel: Bueno, **en otra oportunidad.**
Celia: Gracias, Isabel. Hasta luego.
Isabel: De nada. Adiós.

• •

Otros lugares *(places)* **en la ciudad:**

un cine *a movie theater*	un parque	**un estadio** *a stadium*
un museo *a museum*	una discoteca	un teatro
un club	**una piscina** *a swimming pool*	

• •

tarde *afternoon*   **Quieres venir** *Do you want to come*   **lo siento** *I'm sorry*   **esta noche** *tonight*
en otra oportunidad *some other time*

Comentarios CULTURALES

El teléfono

There are different ways of answering the phone in Spanish, depending on the country. **Bueno** is used in Mexico, **hola** and **aló** are used in several South and Central American countries, and **diga** or **dígame** is used in Spain.

¡Te toca a ti!

A. ¿Qué lugares son? Identify each building or place that follows.

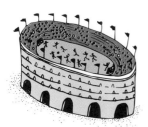
1.

2.

3.

4.

5.

6.

B. ¿Hay un(a)... en el barrio (neighborhood)? Ask a passerby if the places listed are in the neighborhood. The passerby will answer affirmatively and tell you the street where each can be found. Act this out with a partner, alternating roles.

> **MODELO**
> restaurante / en la calle (street) San Martín
> Tú: *Perdón, señor (señorita). ¿Hay un restaurante en el barrio?*
> Compañero(a): *Sí, hay un restaurante en la calle San Martín.*

1. parque / en la calle Libertad
2. discoteca / en la calle Tucumán
3. teatro / en la avenida 9 de Julio
4. museo / en la calle Cervantes
5. cine / en la avenida Lavalle
6. piscina / en la calle Bolívar
7. oficina de correos / en la calle Independencia

C. ¿Qué hay en Nerja? Following are examples of public buildings that are found in many cities and towns. Using the map of Nerja and its legend, make two lists, indicating what there is and what there is not in this small beach town. Use the headings **Hay...** and **No hay...** Then, with a partner, decide on the three additional public buildings that you think the town most needs to add.

| estación de trenes | museo | parque | restaurante | hospital | oficina de correos | cine | estadio |

| hotel | discoteca | aeropuerto | café | biblioteca | iglesia | plaza |

PRONUNCIACIÓN THE CONSONANT **g**

When the letter **g** (in the same combinations you studied in the previous **etapa**) follows a vowel or any consonant except **n,** it is pronounced like the *g* in the English word *sugar* when it is said very quickly.

Práctica

D. Listen and repeat as your teacher models the following words.

1. lago
2. amigo
3. llego
4. nos gusta
5. conmigo

6. Ortega
7. regular
8. lugar
9. hasta luego
10. jugar

Repaso ♻

E. ¿Adónde van? Félix and his family are visiting Medellín, Colombia, for the day. Because they all want to go to different places, they decide to split up. Based on the drawings, give Félix's explanation of where each person is headed. Follow the model.

MODELO
mi tío
Mi tío va a la catedral.

1. mis padres

2. mi prima y yo

3. mi tía

4. mi hermana

5. mi hermano

6. mis primas

F. **¿Adónde quisiera ir...?** You are talking to a friend about where other friends want to go this weekend. Ask him (her) about each of the following people and he (she) will answer using the places suggested. Follow the model.

> **MODELO**   Miguel / el club
>
> **Tú:** *¿Adónde quisiera ir Miguel?*
> **Amigo(a):** *Miguel quisiera ir al club.*

1. Elsa / la piscina
2. Isabel / el parque
3. Roberto / la discoteca
4. Mónica / el cine
5. Manuel / el museo
6. Pilar / el teatro
7. Luis / el estadio
8. Lidia / el café

ESTRUCTURA

The verbs querer and preferir

querer (to want, to love)			
yo	**quiero**	nosotros(as)	**queremos**
tú	**quieres**	vosotros(as)	**queréis**
él ella Ud.	**quiere**	ellos ellas Uds.	**quieren**

preferir (ie) (to prefer)			
yo	**prefiero**	nosotros(as)	**preferimos**
tú	**prefieres**	vosotros(as)	**preferís**
él ella Ud.	**prefiere**	ellos ellas Uds.	**prefieren**

1. The verb **querer** is used to express desire. It is more commonly used than the verb **desear** (*to wish, to want*).

2. In Spanish, some verbs are called stem-changing verbs because they have irregular stems (infinitives minus the -**ar**, -**er**, or -**ir** ending) that change when the verbs are conjugated. **Querer** and **preferir** are examples of verbs in which the final vowel in the stems changes from e to ie in all forms except **nosotros(as)** and **vosotros(as)**. The Spanish-English and English-Spanish glossaries at the end of your textbook, as well as many dictionaries, list stem-changing verbs with their vowel change in parentheses, as done here in the charts for **querer (ie)** and **preferir (ie)**.

3. **Querer** and **preferir** may be followed by a noun or an infinitive. To make these constructions negative, place **no** before the conjugated forms of **querer** and **preferir**.

Tú quieres un taco.	*You want a taco.*
Rosa quiere comer algo también.	*Rosa wants to eat something too.*
Javier no quiere comer.	*Javier doesn't want to eat.*
Ellos prefieren el tren.	*They prefer the train.*
Yo no prefiero el tren.	*I don't prefer the train.*
Yo prefiero viajar en autobús.	*I prefer to travel by bus.*

Aquí practicamos

G. Preferencias Create original sentences using words from each column to indicate what the following people want or prefer to do.

A	B	C
Mario	querer	ir a la discoteca
ellos	preferir	un coche
yo	ir al parque	
nosotros	leer este libro	
tú	viajar en tren	
Uds.		

H. ¿Adónde quieres ir? You and a friend are visiting a town in Mexico. Each of you wants to see something different. Find out what she (he) wants to see by asking specific questions. Follow the model.

> **MODELO** la plaza / la iglesia
> **Tú:** *¿Quieres ir a la plaza?*
> **Amiga(o):** *No, quiero ir a la iglesia.*

1. la biblioteca / la piscina
2. el club / el teatro
3. el museo / la oficina de correos
4. la plaza / el parque
5. la estación de trenes / la estación de autobuses
6. la escuela secundaria / el mercado

I. ¿Qué quieres hacer? You and your friend are making plans for the afternoon. Your friend makes a suggestion. Tell him (her) if you agree with the suggestion. If you don't agree, express your own preference. Follow the model.

> **MODELO** ir al teatro
> **Amigo(a):** *¿Quieres ir al teatro?*
> **Tú:** *Sí, quiero ir al teatro.* o: *Mm... no, prefiero ir al cine.*

1. comer en un café
2. ir a la piscina
3. bailar en la discoteca
4. visitar un museo
5. estudiar toda la mañana
6. correr por el parque
7. escuchar música
8. tomar algo

J. Decisiones You and a friend need to decide what you want to do after school. In pairs, decide what you want to do, alternating roles in asking and answering questions. Then give your answer to the class. Follow the model.

> **MODELO**   ¿ir en bicicleta o caminar?
>
>   **Tú:**   *¿Quieres ir en bicicleta o caminar?*
>   **Amigo(a):**   *Yo prefiero caminar.*
>   **Tú:**   *Nosotros preferimos caminar.*

1. ¿jugar *(to play)* al tenis o al vólibol?
2. ¿ir a mi casa o al café?
3. ¿visitar a nuestros amigos o estudiar?
4. ¿ir a la plaza o al parque?
5. ¿comer o tomar un refresco?

Aquí escuchamos

En el centro *Gloria and Marilú have a conversation on their way downtown to run some errands.*

Antes de escuchar Based on the information you have learned in this chapter, answer the following questions.

1. What are some of the places where Gloria and Marilú might go to on a trip downtown?
2. How do you say in Spanish that you have to do something?

 A escuchar Listen twice to the conversation between Gloria and Marilú, paying attention to the places where they plan to go.

Después de escuchar On your activity master, list as many of the places that Gloria and Marilú mention as you can.

En la calle While heading for a place of your choice in town, you bump into a friend.

1. Greet your friend.
2. Find out how he (she) is.
3. Ask where he (she) is going.
4. He (she) will ask you where you are going.
5. If you are going to the same place, suggest that you go there together. (**¡Vamos juntos/juntas!**)
6. If not, say good-bye and continue on your way.

 Una invitación Write a note to a Spanish-speaking friend.

1. Invite him (her) to go to the movies with you.
2. Say what movie you want to see.
3. Ask if he (she) prefers to see a different one.
4. Mention where you can meet downtown.
5. Ask if he (she) wants to eat dinner before the movie.
6. Close by asking him (her) to call you on the phone with an answer.

TERCERA ETAPA

- What is the difference between a department store and a mall?

- How would you describe a specialty shop?

- Make a list of five different kinds of specialty shops that you can think of.

- On your list, mark the shops where you like to go. Be prepared to discuss whether you prefer them to a department store or a large discount center and why.

Las tiendas

*En nuestra ciudad hay muchas **tiendas** (stores).*

una carnicería *a butcher shop*   **una librería** *a book store*

una farmacia *a drugstore*   **una panadería** *a bakery*

una florería *a flower shop*

Comentarios CULTURALES

Las tiendas

In many parts of the Spanish-speaking world, small stores are more common than large supermarkets. Each one of these stores sells only one type of article or food. The name of the shop is taken from the products sold; for example, **pan** *(bread)* is sold at the **panadería; flores** *(flowers)* are sold at the **florería.**

¡Te toca a ti!

A. ¿Qué es? Identify each of the following buildings or places.

1.

2.

3.

4.

5.

6.

B. Cerca de aquí (Near here)

You ask a passerby whether certain stores and places are nearby. A classmate will play the role of the passerby. He (she) will answer affirmatively and indicate the street where you can find each building. Follow the model.

> **MODELO**   banco / en la calle Alcalá
> **Tú:**   *Perdón, señorita (señor). ¿Hay un banco cerca de aquí?*
> **Compañero(a):**   *Sí, hay un banco en la calle Alcalá.*

1. farmacia / en la avenida Libertad
2. hotel / en la calle Perú
3. librería / en la calle Mayor
4. banco / en la calle San Marco
5. panadería / en la avenida Independencia
6. florería / en la avenida Colón

C. ¿Adónde vamos primero (first)?

Whenever you run errands with your friend, you like to know where you are headed first. However, each time you suggest a place, your friend has another idea. Follow the model.

> **MODELO**   banco / librería
> **Tú:**   *¿Adónde vamos primero? ¿Al banco?*
> **Amigo(a):**   *No, primero vamos a la librería. Luego (Then) vamos al banco.*

1. carnicería / mercado
2. librería / florería
3. museo / banco
4. farmacia / panadería
5. hotel / oficina de correos
6. biblioteca / colegio

PRONUNCIACIÓN   THE SOUND OF SPANISH j

The Spanish **jota** is similar to the sound of the *h* in the English word *hot*. This sound is spelled with .g when it is followed by the vowels e or i. The consonant *j* (**j**) ia always pronounced in this way.

Práctica

D. Listen and repeat as your teacher models the following words.

1. Juan
2. trabajo
3. julio
4. jueves
5. jugar
6. tarjeta
7. geografía
8. biología
9. general
10. Jorge

E. Los padres de tus amigos Your parents are curious about your friends. Tell them where your friends' parents work and where they often go when they're not working. Follow the model.

> MODELO   el padre de Cristina (hospital / biblioteca)
> *El padre de Cristina trabaja en el hospital. Va a la biblioteca a menudo.*

1. el padre de Roberto (estación de trenes / cine)
2. la madre de Isabel (universidad / parque)
3. el padre de Vicente (oficina de correos / museo)
4. la madre de Marilú (restaurante / mercado)
5. el padre de Josefina (biblioteca / librería)

Comentarios CULTURALES

Las direcciones y los teléfonos

Usually when an address **(una dirección)** is given in Spanish, the name of the street is followed by the number. Also, when the numbers of addresses go over a hundred, they are usually grouped in sets of two. Thus, the number in **Avenida Bolívar, número 1827** would be said as **dieciocho, veintisiete.** Phone numbers **(los números de teléfono)** are also usually grouped in sets of two. For example, the number 925–6534 would be read as **nueve, veinticinco, sesenta y cinco, treinta y cuatro.**

PALABRAS ÚTILES

Numbers from 20 to 100

20 veinte	24 veinticuatro	28 veintiocho	32 treinta y dos	70 setenta
21 veintiuno	25 veinticinco	29 veintinueve	40 cuarenta	80 ochenta
22 veintidós	26 veintiséis	30 treinta	50 cincuenta	90 noventa
23 veintitrés	27 veintisiete	31 treinta y uno	60 sesenta	100 cien

Aquí practicamos

F. Cuenta tú

1. Cuenta *(Count)* del 0 al 30, y luego del 30 al 0.
2. Cuenta del 20 al 100 de cinco en cinco.
3. Cuenta los números pares *(even)* del 0 al 100.
4. Cuenta los números impares *(odd)* del 1 al 99.
5. Cuenta de diez en diez del 0 al 100.

G. ¿Cuántos hay en la ciudad?
While working for the tourist bureau during the summer, you have to research the number of hotels, movie theaters, etc., that the city has. Interview the city's leading statistician in order to collect this information. Work in pairs and take turns playing the role of the statistician. Remember to use **¿Cuántos?** or **¿Cuántas?** according to the noun that follows. Follow the models.

MODELOS

hoteles / 15

Tú: *¿Cuántos hoteles hay?*
Compañero(a): *Hay quince hoteles.*

piscinas / 17

Compañero(a): *¿Cuántas piscinas hay?*
Tú: *Hay diecisiete.*

1. librerías / 11
2. panaderías / 18
3. clubes / 13
4. mercados / 26
5. farmacias / 16

6. carnicerías / 27
7. teatros / 14
8. cines / 12
9. florerías / 20
10. cafés / 22

H. ¡Diga!
You want to make several telephone calls from a small town where you need to talk to the operator to get connected. Tell him (her) the number that you want. Follow the model.

MODELO

730–89–70
Siete, treinta, ochenta y nueve, setenta, por favor.

1. 825–5978
2. 654–6783
3. 222–5160
4. 382–6791

5. 943–5690
6. 537–4087
7. 795–4670
8. 497–5530

? **¿Qué crees?**

You are traveling in Uruguay and the schedule says that your bus leaves at 22:00 hrs. When will it go?

a) It's a misprint; you don't know when the bus leaves.
b) at 2 o'clock
c) at 10:00 p.m.

respuesta 🖙

PALABRAS ÚTILES

Expressions with tener

1. To ask someone's age in Spanish, use **tener**.

—¿Cuántos años tienes?   *How old are you?*
—Tengo catorce años   *I am fourteen years old.*

—¿Cuántos años tiene   *How old is your sister?*
   tu hermana?
—Tiene cuatro.   *She's four.*

2. Other expressions with **tener** are **tener hambre** *(to be hungry)* and **tener sed** *(to be thirsty)*.

—Tengo hambre. ¿Y tú?   *I'm hungry. And you?*
—No, yo no tengo hambre, *No, I'm not hungry, but I am*
   pero sí tengo mucha sed. *very thirsty.*

Aquí practicamos

☞ C

I. **¿Cuántos años tienes?** You want to find out how old the people you know are. Working with a classmate, take turns asking and telling how old the following people are. Use the verb **tener** and the word **años.** Follow the model.

> **MODELO** **Tú:** ¿Cuántos años tiene Felipe? (13)
> **Compañero(a):** *Felipe tiene trece años.*

1. ¿Cuántos años tiene Carmelita? (17)
2. Y el señor Ramos, ¿cuántos años tiene? (64)
3. ¿Cuántos años tiene Ana María? (20)
4. ¿Cuántos años tiene Roberto? (12)
5. ¿Cuántos años tiene don Alberto? (82)
6. Y doña Ester, ¿cuántos años tiene ella? (55)

J. **¿Tienen hambre?** You are hosting a picnic and you want to know if your guests are hungry or thirsty and what they would like to have. Ask five classmates what they want. Follow the model.

> **MODELO** **Tú:** *¿Tienes hambre? ¿Tienes sed?*
> **Compañero(a) 1:** *Sí, tengo mucha hambre. No tengo sed.*
> **Tú:** *¿Qué quieres comer?*
> **Compañero(a) 1:** *Un taco, por favor.*

Aquí escuchamos

Números *Several people give their names, addresses, and telephone numbers.*

Antes de escuchar Review the numbers 1–100 in Spanish before listening to the information that follows.

A escuchar Each person on the recording will give a phone number, name, and address. Listen to each person repeat himself (herself), paying particular attention to the telephone numbers and the cities mentioned. On your activity master, write down as many of the phone numbers as you can.

Después de escuchar On your activity master, put a check mark next to the cities that were mentioned in the information you just heard. Next to the cities that you mark, write down the nationality of a person from that city.

__Bogotá, Colombia

__Buenos Aires, Argentina

__Caracas, Venezuela

__Ciudad de México, México

__Lima, Perú

__Madrid, España

__San Juan, Puerto Rico

__Santiago, Chile

```
                                CALLE 25 N
··  23-0662  VARGAS CANTO NESTOR MANUEL
                CALLE 100 N° 120 CP 97240 ············  21-5451
··  26-5072  VARGAS CASTILLO MANUEL AUGUSTO
                CALLE 55 N° 417 CP 97160 ············   24-4442
··  26-5852  VARGAS CASTRO GRACIA IRMA
                CALLE 75 N° 561-D ZP 97 ············    21-2513
··  24-6827  VARGAS CECILIA CAMPOS DE
                CALLE 51 N° 287 CP 97119 ············   26-1624
··  23-5894  VARGAS CELIA AGUILAR DE
                CALLE 23 N° 222 ············            21-0965
··  24-8169  VARGAS CERVERA ALBERTO
                CALLE 26 N° 299-A CP 97148 ············  26-3349
··  24-9655  VARGAS CERVERA AMADO-CALLE 30 N° 501 M    21-8303
··  24-1515     CALLE 54 N° 521 B 1 ············        21-6829
                CALLE 65 N° 429 ZP 97 ············      24-2920
··  23-4418  VARGAS CERVERA JORGE-CALLE 49 N° 558-C    23-6529
                CALLE 9 N° 226 ············             25-1682
··  25-6829  VARGAS CETINA ELSA-CALLE 7 A N° 281 ····  27-0748
             VARGAS CETINA RAUL M PROF
··  24-6358     CALLE 63 B N° 224 ············          21-5753
··  25-6206  VARGAS CHACON ADELA-CALLE 48 N° 517 ····  23-8658
··  21-2058  VARGAS CLARA ELENA DIAZ DE
                CALLE 25 N° 496 B ············          27-1435
             VARGAS CORREA ANDRES DR
··  27-3503     CALLE 109 N° 349 CP 97270 ············  24-1253
             VARGAS CORREA JORGE BERNARDO DR
··  24-0449     CALLE 25 N° 212 CP 97140 ············   26-0366
             VARGAS CRUZ RAYMUNDO
··  27-7773     CALLE 39 N° 325 CP 97119 ············   26-3449
             VARGAS DE LA PEÑA FERNANDO DR
··  23-9413     CALLE 36 N° 428 ············            27-8225
                COLON 203-A ············                25-5899
··  21-4050  VARGAS DIAZ RAYMUNDO
                CALLE 21 N° 12 CP 97070 ············    25-8927
··  24-2776  VARGAS DOMITILA DIAZ DE
                CALLE 40 N° 440 A ············          27-6069
          ···GAS DURAN HUMBERTO
              ···203 ZP 97                     ··1277
```

```
CALLE 30 N° 334
VARGAS MENDEZ JO
   CALLE 65 N° 570
VARGAS MIRIAM SO
   CALLE 8 N° 128-
VARGAS MONZON E
VARGAS NIDIA AVI
   CALLE 57 A N°
VARGAS NIDIA CRI
VARGAS OLGA EST
   CALLE 29-A N°
VARGAS PACHECO
VARGAS PATRON
VARGAS PERAZA
   CALLE 11 PTE
VARGAS PERAZA
   CALLE 95 N° 5
VARGAS PERERA
   CALLE 88 N° 4
VARGAS PINZON
VARGAS QUIJANO
   CALLE 61 N°
VARGAS QUINTA
   CALLE 83 N° 4
VARGAS QUINTA
   CALLE 46 N° 5
VARGAS RAMIRE
   CALLE 18 N° 1
   CALLE 64 N° 5
VARGAS RAMIRE
   CALLE 15 N° 1
VARGAS RAMOS
VARGAS RIVERO
   CALLE 30 N° 9
VARGAS ROSA EL
   CALLE 44 N° 5
VARGAS ROSA PA
```

En la oficina de correos While standing in line at the post office, you strike up a conversation with the person standing next to you.

1. Greet him or her.
2. Find out how many brothers and sisters he (she) has.
3. Ask what their ages are.
4. When you leave, find out where your new friend is going.
5. Tell him (her) where you are going.
6. Ask if you can walk together (**¡Vamos juntos/juntas!**).
7. If not, say good-bye.

 Más números You want to find out the "vital statistics" of some of your classmates. On the chart in your activity master, record the appropriate information (name, age, address, and phone number) for yourself and three of your classmates. Write out the numbers in Spanish and be prepared to tell them to your classmates when asked. Follow the model.

MODELO

Nombre de mi amigo(a)	Su edad	Su dirección	Su teléfono
Carlos	16 (dieciséis) años	Calle Central 2586 (veinticinco, ochenta y seis)	845-3370 (ocho, cuarenta y cinco, treinta y tres, setenta)

Connect with the Spanish-speaking world! Access the **¡Ya verás!** *Gold* home page for Internet activities related to this chapter.

http://yaveras.heinle.com

VOCABULARIO

Para charlar

Para contestar el teléfono
¡Bueno!
¡Diga! / ¡Dígame!
¡Hola!

Para preguntar la edad
¿Cuántos años tienes?

Para contar
veinte
veintiuno
veintidós
veintitrés
veinticuatro
veinticinco
veintiséis
veintisiete
veintiocho
veintinueve
treinta
treinta y uno
treinta y dos
cuarenta
cincuenta
sesenta
setenta
ochenta
noventa
cien

Temas y contextos

Los edificios y los lugares públicos
un aeropuerto
un banco
una biblioteca
una catedral
un cine
un club
un colegio
una discoteca
una escuela secundaria
una estación de autobuses
una estación de policía
una estación de trenes
un estadio
un hospital
un hotel
una iglesia
un museo
una oficina de correos
un parque
una piscina
una plaza
un teatro
una universidad

Las tiendas
una carnicería
una farmacia
una florería
una librería
un mercado
una panadería

Vocabulario general

Verbos
ir
querer (ie)
preferir (ie)

Expressions of frequency
a menudo
de vez en cuando
rara vez
nunca

Otras palabras y expresiones
¿Adónde vamos?
al
cerca de aquí
una dirección
en otra oportunidad
esta noche
llamar a
Lo siento.
primero
¿Quieres venir?
la tarde
tener hambre
tener sed

La Pequeña Habana

Antes de leer

1. In which cities in the United States are there large numbers of Spanish-speaking people?

2. Have you visited some of these cities? If so, what do you remember about them?

3. Briefly scan the reading. What part of the United States is this reading about?

La Pequeña Habana es un barrio de la ciudad de Miami. Aquí se reúnen muchos de los cubanos que llegaron de Cuba porque no quisieron vivir bajo el sistema político impuesto en la isla por Fidel Castro en 1959. Hoy en día, este sector de la ciudad es un centro social importante, no sólo para los cubanos sino también para numerosas personas de otros países de habla hispana. Para ellos, la Pequeña Habana es como un segundo hogar.

Para los norteamericanos y los turistas extranjeros que la visitan, el área es uno de los sectores más atractivos del sur de la Florida. Los vistantes disfrutan enormemente de la cultura cubana: de su comida, sus fiestas y su artesanía. En todas partes de la Pequeña Habana—en los cafetines, en las calles, en el sonido de los dominós, la música y las radios—el corazón cubano y la imagen de Cuba siguen vivos.

En la Pequeña Habana, la gente se reúne en los cafetines del barrio para charlar y jugar al dominó.

Guía para la lectura

Here are some words and expressions to keep in mind as you read.

se reúnen	*get together*
cafetines	*small coffee shops*
impuesto	*imposed*
hogar	*home*
disfrutan	*enjoy*
corazón	*heart*
siguen vivos	*live on*

Después de leer

1. Where is la Pequeña Habana located?

2. **La Habana** is the capital of Cuba. Why is this area of Miami called **La Pequeña Habana**?

3. Do you know of any other American cities, towns, or neighborhoods that maintain especially strong links with the culture of another country? In what ways do these communities express their ties to other cultures?

CAPÍTULO 8

¿Dónde está...?

—¿Dónde está el museo de arte?
—Está al final de la Avenida Libertad.

Objectives

- asking for directions
- giving directions
- telling people to do something

Preparación

- How would you find your way around a city if you had never been there before?

- When you ask for directions, what do you usually want to find out?

- When someone asks you how to get to a particular place in town, what information do you give?

¿Está lejos de aquí?

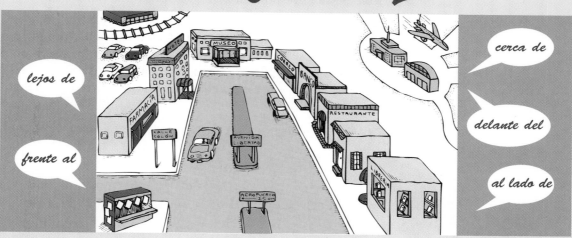

¿*Dónde están* (where are) *los edificios públicos de la ciudad?*

¿Dónde **está** el aeropuerto?	Está **lejos de** la ciudad.
¿Dónde está la estación de trenes?	Está **cerca del** hotel.
¿Dónde está la oficina de correos?	Está **frente al** hotel
¿Dónde está la farmacia?	Está **al lado del** hotel.
¿Dónde está el museo?	Está **al final de** la avenida Libertad.
¿Dónde está el **quiosco de periódicos**?	Está **en la esquina de** la calle Colón y la avenida Libertad.
¿Dónde está el coche de Mario?	Está en un **estacionamiento detrás del** hotel.
¿Dónde está el coche de Teresa?	Está en la avenida **delante del** banco.
¿Dónde está el banco?	Está **entre** el restaurante y la oficina de correos.

está *is (located)* **lejos de** *far from* **cerca de** *near* **frente a** *across from, facing* **al lado de** *next to* **al final de** *at the end of* **quiosco de periódicos** *newspaper kiosk* **en la esquina de** *at the corner of* **estacionamiento** *parking lot* **detrás de** *behind* **delante de** *in front of* **entre** *between*

¡Te toca a ti!

A. Mi ciudad When a tourist asks you about the town pictured on page 185, you answer using the suggested expressions. Follow the model.

> **MODELO**
>
> **Turista:** ¿Dónde está la estación de trenes? (cerca del hotel)
>
> **Tú:** *Está cerca del hotel.*

1. ¿Dónde está el hotel? (al lado de la farmacia)
2. ¿Dónde está el banco? (frente a la iglesia)
3. ¿Dónde está el aeropuerto? (lejos de la ciudad)
4. ¿Dónde está la oficina de correos? (cerca del restaurante)
5. ¿Dónde está la farmacia? (en la esquina de la calle Colón y la avenida Libertad)
6. ¿Dónde está la estación de trenes? (al lado del museo)
7. ¿Dónde está el restaurante? (entre la florería y el banco)

B. No, te equivocas (you're wrong)... A young man (woman) asks you for information about the town pictured on page 185. He (she) is not quite right about the locations. You politely tell the person he (she) is wrong and point out the correct information. Follow the model.

> **MODELO**
>
> **Muchacho(a):** El aeropuerto está cerca de la ciudad, ¿no? (lejos de)
>
> **Tú:** *No, te equivocas; está lejos de la ciudad.*

1. El restaurante está al lado de la iglesia, ¿verdad? (frente a)
2. La estación de trenes está lejos del museo, ¿no? (cerca de)
3. La florería está frente a la librería, ¿verdad? (al lado de)
4. El quiosco de periódicos está al final de la avenida Libertad, ¿verdad? (en la esquina de la avenida Libertad y la calle Colón)
5. El museo está al lado del banco, ¿no? (al final de la avenida Libertad)
6. El coche de Teresa está detrás de la iglesia, ¿verdad? (delante del banco)
7. La florería está frente a la librería y el restaurante, ¿no? (entre)

C. En la cola (In line)

While waiting to get into the movies, you point out some of your friends to your brother. Tell him where each person is located in the line. Use the drawing that follows to give your answers. Follow the model.

MODELO   Estela / detrás
¿Estela? Ella está detrás de
Alejandro.

1. Amanda / delante
2. Pablo / detrás
3. Marcos / entre

4. Antonio / detrás
5. Alejandro / delante
6. Estela / entre

Antonio   Amanda   Marcos   Pablo   Estela   Alejandro

PRONUNCIACIÓN   THE SOUND OF /s/

The sound of Spanish /s/ is spelled with the consonants **s** or **z**. Usually, these are pronounced in the same way as *s* in the English word *say*. Note that **z** is never pronounced as the *z* in the English words *zoo, zebra,* and *zero.*

Práctica

D. Listen and repeat as your teacher models the following words.

1. siempre
2. salsa
3. sábado
4. zapato
5. plaza

6. señor
7. semana
8. López
9. arroz
10. lápiz

E. ¿Vas a... a menudo? Find out how often your partner goes to the places listed. Take turns interviewing each other. Keep track of his (her) answers and make a list of places ranging from most to least frequently visited. When you have completed your lists, compare them to see which places you go to with the same frequency. Follow the model.

> **MODELO**   la panadería
> **Tú:** *¿Vas a la panadería a menudo?*
> **Compañera(o):** *No, nunca voy a la panadería.* o:
> *Voy a la panadería todos los días.*

1. la farmacia
2. el banco
3. la librería

4. la panadería
5. la florería
6. la piscina

7. la oficina de correos
8. la carnicería

F. ¿Qué cuarto tienes? Your class has just arrived at a hotel in Panama City where you are going to spend a week. You want to find out your friends' room numbers. Ask a partner where each person is staying. Follow the model.

> **MODELO**   Anita / 23
> **Tú:** *¿Qué cuarto tiene Anita?*
> **Compañero(a):** *Anita tiene el cuarto número veintitrés.*

1. Claudia / 68
2. Bill / 20
3. Betty y Rosa / 15
4. Paul / 36
5. Martha y Ann / 72
6. Antonio / 89
7. Sue y Clara / 47
8. John y Tom / 11

NOTA GRAMATICAL

The preposition de and the definite article el

Es el portafolio **del** profesor.   *It's the teacher's briefcase.*

El coche de Teresa está al lado **del** hotel.   *Teresa's car is next to the hotel.*

1. When the preposition **de** is followed by the definite article **el**, they contract to form one word, **del**.

2. Many of the phrases used to indicate location that have been presented in this **etapa** include **de**. When they are followed by the definite article **el**, the same rule for contraction applies.

   al final **del** estacionamiento   cerca **del** aeropuerto   detrás **del** museo

   al lado **del** banco   delante **del** quiosco   lejos **del** estadio

Aquí practicamos

G. ¿Dónde está? Replace the words in italics with the words in parentheses and make the necessary changes.

1. El banco está *cerca de* la estación. (al lado de / detrás de / lejos de)

2. Nosotros vivimos *al lado del* restaurante. (detrás de / delante de / frente a)

3. ¿Hay una farmacia frente a *la iglesia?* (museo / estadio / cine / casa)

4. Hay un café lejos de *la panadería.* (carnicería / hotel / oficina de correos / florería)

5. —¿De quién es el coche nuevo?
   —Es *de la señorita Galdós.* (profesor / Sr. Álvarez / Sra. Ruiz / muchacho)

H. Direcciones Using the drawing on page 185, answer these questions that different people ask about the city. Be as precise as possible. Follow the model.

> **MODELO**   Señora: Perdón. ¿Dónde está el quiosco de periódicos, por favor?
> Tú: *¿El quiosco? Está en la esquina de la calle Colón y la avenida Libertad, cerca de la farmacia.*

1. Perdón, ¿el restaurante, por favor?

2. Perdón, ¿Dónde está el hotel, por favor?

3. Perdón, ¿el museo, por favor?

4. Por favor, ¿la farmacia?

5. ¿Dónde está la oficina de correos, por favor?

6. ¿Hay una librería cerca de aquí?

ESTRUCTURA

The verb estar

Yo **estoy** en el hotel Trinidad.

I am at the Hotel Trinidad.

Ana y Raúl **están** en el coche.

Ana and Raúl are in the car.

estar (to be)			
yo	**estoy**	nosotros(as)	**estamos**
tú	**estás**	vosotros(as)	**estáis**
él ella Ud.	**está**	ellos ellas Uds.	**están**

1. The **yo** form of the verb **estar** is irregular, and all second and third person forms have a written accent on the **a** of the verb endings.

2. Spanish has two verbs that mean *to be:* **estar** and **ser.** Each verb has its own specific uses. In Chapter 1, you learned to use **estar** to ask and talk about health as in **¿Cómo estás? Estar** is also used to express the location of people and things.

Aquí practicamos

I. ¿Cómo y dónde? Taking information from each column, use different forms of the verb **estar** to create complete sentences. Follow the model.

MODELO Mario / Madrid
Mario está en Madrid.

A	B	C
Graciela y Ana		en Buenos Aires
el (la) profesor(a)		en el banco
mi amigo(a)		cerca de la iglesia
la biblioteca	estar	con José
tú		mal
los abogados		en la calle Alameda
nosotros		cerca de la iglesia
la panadería		bastante bien
yo		al lado del hotel
Esteban		

J. ¿Dónde están? When you get home, your sister is the only person there. Ask her where everybody is. Follow the model.

> **MODELO**   la abuela / mercado
>   **Tú:** *¿Dónde está la abuela?*
>   **Tu hermana:** *Está en el mercado.*

1. tía Ana / piscina
2. papá y mamá / banco
3. Lourdes / café de la esquina
4. Ángel / cine
5. las primas / estadio
6. mi perro / tu cuarto

¿Dónde estamos?

Aquí escuchamos

No está lejos *A woman asks a man for the location of a building.*

Antes de escuchar Review the phrases used to indicate place (page 185). Then, answer the following questions.

1. What is the opposite of **lejos de?**
2. What verb is used in Spanish to indicate location of people, animals, places, or things?

 A escuchar Listen twice to the conversation and write down the four public places that are mentioned.

Después de escuchar Based on the conversation you just heard, decide whether the following statements are true or false. If a statement is false, provide the correct information in English.

1. The woman wants to go to the bank.
2. The man indicates that the place the woman is looking for is nearby.
3. The woman finds out that the bank and the post office are on the same street.
4. The man says there is a university right in the downtown area of the city.
5. The woman discovers that there are two libraries she can visit.

¡ADELANTE!

 Intercambio Ask a classmate the following questions.

1. ¿Vas al aeropuerto de vez en cuando? ¿Está cerca de la ciudad? ¿Cerca de tu casa?
2. ¿Vas al cine a menudo? ¿Hay un cine cerca de tu casa? ¿Qué hay al lado del cine?
3. ¿Hay una panadería cerca de tu casa? ¿Qué hay frente a la panadería?
4. ¿Qué hay entre tu casa y la escuela? ¿Casas? ¿Edificios de apartamentos? ¿Una biblioteca? ¿Tiendas?
5. ¿Qué hay delante de la escuela? ¿Y detrás de la escuela?

 Por favor, ¿dónde está...? You are walking down the street in your town when a Spanish-speaking person stops you and asks where a certain place (movie theater, bank, train station, drugstore, etc.) is located. You indicate the street or avenue and then try to describe the area (such as what the building is near to, next to, across from, behind, between).

 Para ir a mi escuela Write out in Spanish directions for some out-of-town guests from Honduras. Tell them how to get from your school to the downtown area of your city or town, where you will meet them at a restaurant for lunch. Refer to specific buildings as well as streets in your description.

SEGUNDA ETAPA

- What do you say when you stop somebody on the street to ask for directions?

- What sorts of things do you say when you give someone directions?

- Is it easy for you to understand directions? Why or why not?

- What helps you to remember directions?

¿Cómo llego a... ?

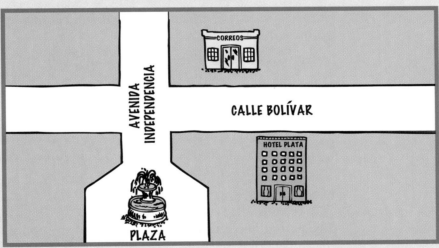

Una señora quiere ir a la oficina de correos, pero necesita **ayuda** (help).

Señora:	Perdón, señor. ¿Hay una oficina de correos cerca de aquí?
Señor:	Sí, señora. En la calle Bolívar.
Señora:	**¿Cómo llego a** la calle Bolívar, por favor?
Señor:	Mm..., **cruce** la plaza y **tome** la avenida Independencia, **siga derecho por** Independencia **hasta** llegar a la calle Bolívar. **Doble a la derecha.** La oficina de correos está **a la izquierda,** frente al Hotel Plata.
Señora:	Muchas gracias.
Señor:	De nada.

¿Cómo llego a...? *How do I get to...?*   **cruce** *cross*   **tome** *take*   **siga derecho por** *go, continue straight along*
hasta *until*   **Doble a la derecha.** *Turn right.*   **a la izquierda** *on the left*

Comentarios CULTURALES

El español en el mundo

Spanish is the fourth most widely spoken language in the world after Chinese, Hindi, and English. It is spoken by more than 400 million people in Spain, the Americas, and in other areas of the world that were once Spanish possessions. Today, after English, Spanish is by far the most widely spoken and studied language in the United States.

¡Te toca a ti!

A. Cómo llegar Give the following directions by replacing the words in italics.

1. Cruce *la calle*. (la plaza / la avenida / el parque)
2. Siga derecho hasta *la avenida de las Américas*. (la plaza San Martín / la calle Corrientes / la catedral)
3. Doble a la derecha *en la esquina*. (al llegar al río *[river]* / en la calle Córdoba / al llegar a la avenida Libertad)
4. Doble a la izquierda en *la avenida 9 de Julio*. (la calle Santa Fe / la calle Florida / la calle Esmeralda)

B. Perdón, señorita. ¿Cómo llego a...? Work with a partner and take turns playing the role of the police officer at **la Puerta del Sol** (circled in red on the following map). Explain how to get to the places that follow. Follow the model.

MODELO	la estación de metro Antón Martín

Señor(ita): *Perdón, señor (señorita). ¿Cómo llego a la estación de metro Antón Martín?*

Policía: *Tome la calle Carretas hasta llegar a la Plaza Benavente. Tome la calle Atocha a la izquierda de la plaza. Siga derecho. La estación de metro Antón Martín está a la izquierda.*

1. la Plaza Mayor
2. la Capilla del Obispo
3. la Plaza de la Villa
4. el Teatro Real
5. la Telefónica en la Gran Vía

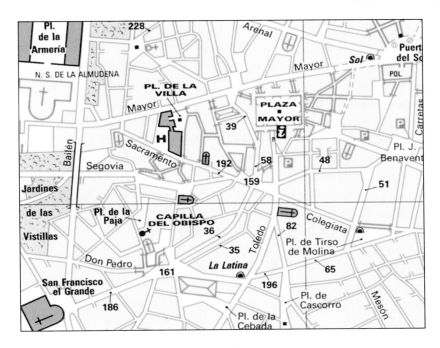

?¿Qué crees?

In which Latin American city were many archaeological findings discovered while building a subway system? One of the stations is decorated by an excavated pyramid.

a) Buenos Aires, Argentina
b) Mexico City, Mexico
c) Caracas, Venezuela

respuesta 🖘

PRONUNCIACIÓN   THE SOUND OF **/s/**

The sound of /s/ can also be spelled with the consonant **c** when it is before the vowels **e** and **i** as in **cena** and **cine**.

Práctica

C. Listen and repeat as your teacher models the following words.

1. cena
2. centro
3. cerca
4. dulce

5. a veces
6. cine
7. cinta
8. cita

9. cien
10. gracias

Repaso ♻

D. ¿Por favor...?   Some tourists stop you in the Zócalo to ask where certain places are located. Work in a group. Using the map that follows, tell the tourist as precisely as possible the location of each of the places that they are looking for. Follow the model.

| MODELO | Escuela Normal Preparatoria |

Turista: *¿La Escuela Normal Preparatoria, por favor?*

Tú: *La Escuela Normal Preparatoria está frente al Templo Mayor.*

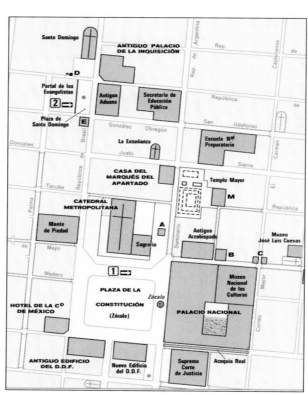

1. Casa del Marqués del Apartado
2. Monte de Piedad
3. Suprema Corte de Justicia
4. Hotel de la Ciudad de México
5. Antiguo Arzobispado
6. Nuevo Edificio del D.D.F.

☞ **b**

ESTRUCTURA

The imperative with **Ud.** and **Uds.**: Regular second-person commands

Tome la avenida Atocha.	*Take Atocha Avenue.*
¡**Escuchen** bien!	*Listen well!*
¡No **doble** por esa calle!	*Don't turn onto that street!*

Regular Second-person Commands

	Singular	Plural
-ar verbs	Cant**e**.	Cant**en**
-er verbs	Com**a**.	Com**an**
-ir verbs	Escrib**a**.	Escrib**an**

1. Command forms of a verb are used to tell someone to do something, as when giving orders, directions, or suggestions.

2. To form the **Ud.** commands, drop the -o from the **yo** form of the present tense and add -e for regular -**ar** verbs and -a for regular -**er** and -**ir** verbs. To form the **Uds.** commands, do the same, but add -**en** for regular -**ar** verbs and -**an** for regular -**er** and -**ir** verbs.

ESTRUCTURA (CONTINUED)

hablar			
yo **hablo**	**habl-**	**hable** (Ud.)	**hablen** (Uds.)
beber			
yo **bebo**	**beb-**	**beba** (Ud.)	**beban** (Uds.)
escribir			
yo **escribo**	**escrib-**	**escriba** (Ud.)	**escriban** (Uds.)
tener			
yo **tengo**	**teng-**	**tenga** (Ud.)	**tengan** (Uds.)

3. Commands are made negative by placing **no** in front of the verb forms: ¡No baile! ¡No canten!

Aquí practicamos

E. Hablen español Use the **Ud.** and **Uds.** command forms of the following verbs. Follow the model.

> **MODELO**   doblar a la derecha
> *Doble a la derecha.*
> *Doblen a la derecha.*

1. estudiar
2. no beber mucho
3. aprender español
4. tener paciencia
5. no comer mucho
6. leer todos los días

F. A mi profesor(a) Use the **Ud.** command to tell your teacher to do the following. Follow the model.

> **MODELO**   *no bailar en clase*
> *No baile en clase.*

1. tener paciencia
2. no trabajar mucho
3. escribir las instrucciones
4. leer en la biblioteca
5. viajar mucho
6. no hablar tan despacio (*so slowly*)

G. ¡Vamos! Using the suggested verbs, tell two of your classmates to do something. Use the suggested verbs. Follow the models.

bailar   correr   escuchar   trabajar
cantar   escribir   mirar   usar

> **MODELOS**   *Luisa y Marta, ¡canten bien!*
> *Antonio y Marta, ¡bailen mucho!*

ESTRUCTURA

1. Note the spelling changes that verbs ending in -car, -gar, and -zar have in the **Ud.** and **Uds.** commands. Another -car verb you should learn is **buscar** *(to look for)*.

2. The verbs **ir** and **ser** have irregular command forms: **Vaya** (Ud.) and **vayan** (Uds.) for **ir**; **sea** (Ud.) and **sean** (Uds.) for **ser**.

Aquí practicamos

H. Lleguen temprano Use the **Ud.** and the **Uds.** command forms of these verbs. Follow the model.

> **MODELO**   ir de vacaciones
> *Vaya de vacaciones.*
> *Vayan de vacaciones.*

1. ser bueno
2. ir a bailar
3. no ser antipático
4. ir a clase
5. practicar el piano
6. no llegar tarde *(late)*
7. cruzar la calle
8. buscar las llaves

Aquí escuchamos

Está cerca de aquí *A man is looking for the Museo Nacional.*

Antes de escuchar Review the command forms that you just learned about (pages 196-198). Then, answer the following questions.

1. How do you tell someone to turn to the left in Spanish?
2. What is the difference between **derecho** and **derecha?**

A escuchar Listen twice to the conversation, and pay special attention to the name of the street the man is looking for. Write the name of the street on your activity master, as well as any other street names you hear.

Después de escuchar On your activity master, put a check mark next to the phrases that you heard in the conversation.

__ ahí está	__ ¿Dónde está?	__ frente al banco
__ doble a la derecha	__ está cerca	__ siga cinco cuadras
__ doble a la izquierda	__ está lejos	__ siga tres cuadras

¡ADELANTE!

 Vamos a la escuela Explain to one of your classmates how you get from where you live to your school.

1. Give specific directions, including street names and turns.
2. Name at least three buildings that you pass on the way.
3. Include in your explanation the verbs **ir, cruzar,** and **doblar.**

 Para ir a la Plaza Mayor You and a Peruvian pen pal have just arrived in Madrid. While having lunch at **la Puerta del Sol,** you look at a map similar to the one on page 195 and find the red circle marking where you are. You are headed to **la Plaza Mayor** and your friend is meeting his (her) family in front of **el Teatro Real.** Discuss the best way to get to your destinations. Together, write down specific directions in Spanish from your current location to each destination.

VOCABULARIO

Para charlar

Para dar (to give) direcciones

Cruce la calle.
Doble a la derecha.
Doble a la izquierda.
Está a la derecha.
Está a la izquierda.
Está al final de…
Está al lado de…
Está cerca de…
Está delante de…
Está detrás de…
Está en la esquina de…
Está entre…
Está frente a…
Está lejos de…
Tome la calle, la avenida…
Siga derecho por… hasta…

Para pedir (to ask for) direcciones

¿Cómo llego a…?
¿Dónde está…?
¿Está cerca de aquí?
¿Está lejos de aquí?

Vocabulario general

Sustantivos

un estacionamiento
un quiosco de periódicos

Verbos

buscar
cruzar
doblar
estar
llegar

Otras palabras y expresiones

ayuda
del
Sea Ud…
Sean Uds…
Vaya Ud…
Vayan Uds…

El centro colonial de Quito

Antes de leer

1. According to the title, what will this reading be about?

2. Are you familiar with any historic sites or tourist attractions in your city or town?

3. In what kind of document might you find this text?

Si vas a Quito, Ecuador, visita el viejo centro colonial. Coge un taxi o un autobús hasta la Plaza de la Independencia. Al lado oeste de la Plaza está el Palacio de Gobierno original. Hoy es en parte un museo. Al lado sur está La Companía; la catedral original y una joya artística. Al lado norte, en la esquina, hay un hotel con un buen café. En la misma vecindad hay una serie de tiendas y restaurantes. Al lado este, hay más tiendas y restaurantes.

Cerca de la Plaza vas a encontrar muchos museos, iglesias llenas de arte y calles angostas de piedra. Allí hay arquitectura con más de 500 años. Esta área ha sido restaurada. Visita el viejo centro quiteño y camina por uno de los Monumentos de la Humanidad. Las Naciones Unidas designan así al viejo centro colonial de Quito.

Guía para la lectura

Here are some words and expressions to keep in mind as you read.

coge	*take*
joya	*jewel*
vecindad	*vicinity*
angostas	*narrow*
de piedra	*stone, cobbled*
restaurada	*restored*

Después de leer

1. If you visited Quito, which aspects of the city would interest you most—the old colonial section described here, or the Avenida Amazonas, a modern area with nightlife and shopping?

2. Do you prefer modern architecture or older architecure? Why?

3. Choose an historical site or tourist attraction in your town or city. With a classmate, take turns explaining why she or he might want to visit your chosen site, and give him or her directions for getting there.

CAPÍTULO 9

¡La fiesta del pueblo!

¡Bienvenidos a la fiesta del pueblo!

Objectives

- talking about leisure-time activities
- making plans
- telling and asking for the time

- What are some of the holidays that are important to the people who live in your town or city? What kinds of events or activities does your town or city hold to celebrate national holidays, such as the Fourth of July?

- Have you ever celebrated a special holiday in another country? Where did this happen and what was it like?

- Do you think it is a good idea for people to get together to celebrate a holiday? Why or why not?

¿A qué hora son los bailes folklóricos?

En Guatemala la gente se prepara para (people are getting ready for) *la fiesta del Día de la Independencia.*

Octavio García vive en Guatemala. Como en **la mayoría de las ciudades** y **pueblos hispanos**, la Ciudad de Guatemala tiene una **gran fiesta una vez al año**. En Guatemala celebran el Día de la Independencia el 15 de septiembre. Octavio mira el póster que **anuncia** los programas **para** el festival.

Día de la Independencia
Ciudad de Guatemala

10:30	**Misa** de **Acción de Gracias** en la Catedral
12:00	Feria de la comida
13:30	Bailes folklóricos en la Plaza Mayor
14:45	**Concurso de poesía—Premio al mejor poema**
16:30	**Desfile** de las escuelas
19:00	Banquete en el Club Independencia
21:00	**Fuegos artificiales** en el Parque Nacional
22:00	Baile popular (Parque Nacional)

la mayoría de *most*   pueblos *towns*   hispanos *Hispanic*   gran fiesta *large party, festival*   una vez al año *once a year*   anuncia *announces*   para *for*   Misa *Mass*   Acción de Gracias *Thanksgiving*   Concurso de poesía *Poetry contest*   Premio *Prize*   el mejor *the best*   poema *poem*   Desfile *Parade*   Fuegos artificiales *Fireworks*

Comentarios CULTURALES

La fiesta del pueblo

Many towns in the Hispanic world have at least one big celebration each year. There are religious festivals in honor of the patron saints of the towns, celebrations for the coming of spring and harvest, grape-pressing festivals, and more. The whole town participates in these celebrations. The festivals often begin with a religious ceremony and prayers said in the local churches. In the evening there are parties with dancing, eating, and sometimes fireworks.

¡Te toca a ti!

A. El Día de la Independencia Elena is planning her activities for the day of the festival. Complete the following paragraph according to the information found on the poster on page 204.

Primero voy a la catedral para escuchar la Misa de _____ __

_____. Luego voy a comer en la casa de Adela. Después de comer,

Adela y yo vamos a ver los bailes _____ en la _____ Mayor.

Adela va a leer su poema en el _____ de _____. No vamos a

ver el _____ de las escuelas porque va a ser muy largo.

Tampoco vamos a ir al _____ en el _____ Independencia,

porque es muy caro (*expensive*). Por la noche, vamos a ver los

_____ _____ en el Parque Nacional, y luego vamos al

_____ popular. Va a ser (*It's going to be*) un día divertido.

B. ¿Qué quisieran hacer durante la fiesta? Look at the schedule on page 204 and list the three events that you would most like to attend. Then, ask several classmates what they would like to do at the **fiesta**. Find out whose itineraries are most similar to yours. Follow the model.

> **MODELO** **Tú:** *¿Qué quisieras hacer tú, Jaime?*
> **Jaime:** *Yo quisiera ver el desfile.*

PRONUNCIACIÓN THE CONSONANTS **m** AND **n**

When the consonants **m** and **n** are the first letters of a word or syllable, they are pronounced exactly like *m* and *n* in English.

Práctica

C. Listen and repeat as your teacher models the following words.

1. mamá	4. merienda	7. una	10. bueno
2. mal	5. mermelada	8. nada	
3. más	6. tener	9. noche	

Repaso ♻

D. ¿Dónde hay un (una)...? You are a tourist in Lima and want to find out where various places are, so you ask the clerk at the Hotel Bolívar. Among the places you can ask directions for are **el estadio, el Museo de Arte, la oficina de correos, la catedral,** etc. Enact the conversation with a partner, following the model.

MODELO

Tú: *¿Dónde está la Plaza Grau, por favor?*
Compañero(a): *Está en la esquina del Paseo de la República y la avenida Grau.*

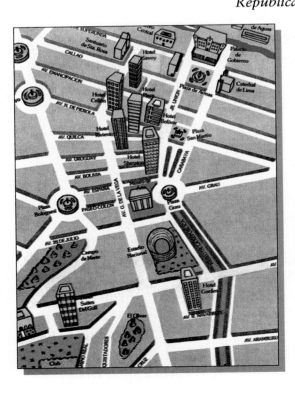

ESTRUCTURA

Telling time

¿Qué hora es?   *What time is it?*

Es la una.

Son las dos.

Son las dos y diez.

Son las dos
y cuarto.

Son las dos
y media.

Son las tres
menos veinte.

Son las tres
menos cuarto.

Es **medianoche**
(*midnight*).

Es **mediodía**
(*noon*).

1. To distinguish between A.M. and P.M., use the expressions **de la mañana** (*in the morning*), **de la tarde** (*in the afternoon*), or **de la noche** (*in the evening*).
2. Notice that in Spanish **es la** is used for one o'clock and **son las** is used for all other hours.

Aquí practicamos

E. La hora Give the time for every five minutes between 9:00 and 10:00.

F. ¿Qué hora es? Find out the time from a classmate. He (She) should indicate whether it is morning (**de la mañana**), afternoon (**de la tarde**), or evening (**de la noche**). Take turns telling the time. Follow the model.

> **MODELO**   2:20 A.M.
>
>   Tú: ¿Qué hora es?
> Compañera(o):   Son las dos y veinte de la mañana.

1. 8:20 A.M.	6. 11:45 P.M.
2. 1:00 P.M.	7. 4:15 P.M.
3. 1:30 A.M.	8. 5:35 A.M.
4. 3:10 P.M.	9. 7:45 A.M.
5. 10:55 A.M.	10. 10:25 P.M.

PALABRAS ÚTILES

Questions about time

1. To ask someone what time something happens, use **¿A qué hora...?** The response to this question requires the preposition **a.**

—¿**A qué hora** comes?	¿*At what time do you eat?*
—**A las 6:15.**	*At 6:15.*

2. To ask someone when something occurs, use **¿cuándo?** To indicate that something happens between two times, use either **entre las... y las...** or **desde las... hasta las... .**

—¿**Cuándo** corres?	*When do you run?*
—**Entre las 5:00 y las 6:00.**	*Between 5:00 and 6:00.*
—¿**Cuándo** trabaja tu madre?	*When does your mother work?*
—**Desde las 9:00 hasta las 5:00.**	*From 9:00 to 5:00.*

Aquí practicamos

G. ¿A qué hora? Your friend asks you at what time you do each of the following activities. Tell him (her) between what times you do them. Follow the model.

> **MODELO**   mirar la TV
>
>   Amigo(a):   ¿A qué hora miras la TV?
>   Tú: Miro la TV entre las 7:00 y las 9:00 de la noche.

1. preparar la tarea *(to prepare homework)* de español
2. usar el laboratorio de lenguas
3. comer
4. practicar el tenis
5. trabajar
6. leer

ESTRUCTURA

The verb venir

¿A qué hora **viene** Mónica?
Nosotros **venimos** a las tres.

What time is Mónica coming?
We are coming at three.

venir *(to come)*			
yo	**vengo**	nosotros(as)	**venimos**
tú	**vienes**	vosotros(as)	**venís**
él		ellos	
ella	**viene**	ellas	**vienen**
Ud.		Uds.	

The irregular verb **venir** follows a pattern similar to the verb **tener,** with variations in the **nosotros** and **vosotros** forms.

Aquí practicamos

H. ¿Quién viene? Create original sentences using words from each column.

A	B	C
Laura	venir	a la fiesta
Cristina y yo		de Acapulco
Uds.		a mi casa
tus amigos		del supermercado
la profesora		
tú		

I. ¿Quién viene al baile con nosotros? You and your boyfriend (girlfriend) are going to the dance for **el Día de la Independencia.** You talk about who else is coming with you. Follow the model.

> **MODELO** Ana / sí
> *Ana viene al baile.*

1. Elena y su hermano / no
2. Elvira / no
3. tú / sí

4. mis abuelos / sí
5. David y Juliana / sí
6. Uds / no

J. ¿Quieres venir a mi fiesta esta noche? You are giving a party tonight and you are inviting people in your class. Ask five people whether they want to come. If they cannot come, they give you an excuse. Follow the model.

> **MODELO** **Tú:** *Rob, ¿quieres venir a mi fiesta esta noche?*
> **Rob:** *Sí, ¡cómo no!* o: *No, lo siento, pero tengo que estudiar.*

Aquí escuchamos

La hora *Some people are talking about time: class times, time zones, plans for an evening's activity, and bus schedules.*

Antes de escuchar Review the different ways of telling time (pages 207 and 208).

 A escuchar Listen twice to the conversations and pay special attention to the times given. On your activity master, write down as many of the times as you can.

Después de escuchar On your activity master, answer the following questions, based on what you heard.

Conversación 1	Conversación 2	Conversación 3	Conversación 4
1. ¿Cuándo empieza *(begins)* la clase de inglés? 2. ¿Hasta qué hora es la clase?	3. ¿Qué hora es en Nueva York cuando son las 7:00 en Madrid? 4. ¿Qué hora es en Los Ángeles cuando son las 7:00 en Madrid?	5. ¿A qué hora van a ir a un restaurante el muchacho y la muchacha? 6. ¿A qué hora es la película que van a ver?	7. ¿A qué hora va el autobús a Santa Fe? 8. ¿A qué hora llega el autobús a Santa Fe?

En la fiesta del pueblo Imagine that your class is in Guatemala for the annual **Día de la Independencia.** Consult the poster on page 204.

1. Decide on three events that you would like to attend.

2. Working with two classmates, reach an agreement on one event on each person's list that you will attend together.

3. Finally, create a schedule, indicating at what time each event begins and how long you will be at the **fiesta**. Be prepared to report on your choices and your schedule.

 Un programa Work with a classmate and prepare a poster in Spanish announcing a celebration in your town or city for the Fourth of July, or for some other holiday of your choice. Write down the events for an entire day and evening as well as the times they will take place. If you wish, you can use the program on page 204 as a model.

Preparación

- What kinds of special events does your town or city plan for special holidays?

- If you could help plan events for a public holiday celebration, what suggestions would you make?

¿Cómo están Uds.?

*Hay muchas actividades **para ver** (to see) durante la fiesta del pueblo.*

Ana:	**Entonces,** ¿adónde vamos **ahora**? ¿Hay más actividades?
Julia:	**Por supuesto,** pero estoy muy **cansada.** Quisiera **descansar** por una hora.
Miguel:	Pues, yo estoy muy bien. Estoy **listo** para continuar la fiesta.
Consuelo:	Ahora es el concurso de poesía. Yo quiero ver quién gana el premio.
Julia:	Bueno, vayan Uds.
Ana:	Muy bien. ¿Dónde **nos encontramos?**
Miguel:	Delante del cine Odeón en la avenida Los Andes.
Julia:	**De acuerdo.** ¡Hasta luego!

Entonces *Then* **ahora** *now* **Por supuesto** *Of course* **cansada** *tired* **descansar** *rest* **listo** *ready*
nos encontramos *we meet* **De acuerdo.** *O.K., Agreed.*

¡Te toca a ti!

A. De acuerdo

You and a classmate are planning to attend the **fiesta del pueblo** in Guatemala City. Ask your classmate what he (she) wants to do at the festival. When your classmate suggests an activity, indicate your agreement or disagreement by saying **De acuerdo. ¡Buena idea!** or **No, prefiero….** Agree on three of the activities listed. Follow the model.

> **MODELO**   ir a ver el desfile
> **Tú:**   *Entonces, ¿adónde vamos?*
> **Compañero(a):**   *Vamos a ver el desfile.*
> **Tú:**   *De acuerdo. ¡Buena idea!*

1. ir a la feria de las comidas regionales`
2. ir a mirar los fuegos artificiales
3. ir a ver los bailes folklóricos
4. ir al banquete
5. ir al baile popular

B. ¿A qué hora nos encontramos? ¿Y dónde?

You and your classmate have decided where you want to go. Now you need to arrange a time and place to meet. Follow the model.

> **MODELO**   10:00 / delante del cine Odeón
> **Compañero(a):**   *¿A qué hora nos encontramos?*
> **Tú:**   *A las 10:00.*
> **Compañero(a):**   *¿Dónde?*
> **Tú:**   *Delante del cine Odeón.*
> **Compañero(a):**   *De acuerdo, a las 10:00, delante del cine Odeón.*

1. 11:00 / delante de la catedral
2. 3:00 / delante del Club San Martín
3. 4:00 / en la avenida Los Andes, esquina de la calle Corrientes
4. 9:00 / en el Parque Nacional

? ¿Qué crees?

One of the shows that is common in town festivals in Spain is the **Toros de Fuego** *(Bulls of Fire)*. Do you think they are:

a) bullfights
b) bulls set on fire
c) people dressed as bulls carrying fireworks on their backs

respuesta ☞

PRONUNCIACIÓN THE CONSONANT ñ

The consonant **ñ** is pronounced like the *ni* in the English word *onions*.

Práctica

C. Listen and repeat as your teacher models the following words.

1. año
2. mañana
3. señorita
4. baño
5. señor
6. español

D. ¿Qué hora es? A friend asks what time it is. Answer according to the cues, following the model.

> **MODELO**   2:30
> Amigo(a):   *¿Qué hora es?*
> Tú: *Son las dos y media.*

1. 7:25
2. 11:52
3. 10:15

4. 3:30
5. 8:10
6. 1:45

7. 4:40
8. 12:05
9. 9:16

ESTRUCTURA

Estar + adjectives of condition

Yo **estoy** muy **cansada**.   *I am very tired.*

Yo **estoy listo** para   *I am ready to continue with the*
  continuar la lección.   *lesson.*

1. **Estar** is used with adjectives that describe physical or emotional conditions.

aburrido	*bored*	enojado	*angry*
cansado	*tired*	listo	*ready*
contento	*happy*	tarde	*late*
enfermo	*sick*	triste	*sad*

2. Like all adjectives, these agree in gender and number with the person they describe.

Ella está **cansada**.   **Ellas** están **cansadas**.

Él está **cansado**.   **Ellos** están **cansados**.

☞ C

Aquí practicamos

E. ¿Qué hacen? (What are they doing?) Complete the following sentences with an adjective from the above **Estructura**. Tell how you and the people mentioned feel when they do each activity. Follow the model.

> **MODELO**   Voy al cine cuando...
> *Voy al cine cuando estoy aburrido(a).*

1. Voy al hospital cuando...

2. Tomamos una siesta cuando...

3. Ustedes necesitan correr cuando...

4. Mis amigos comen cuando...

5. Mi hermana va de compras cuando...

6. Escuchamos música cuando...

7. Llamo a mi mejor amigo(a) cuando...

8. Raquel y Pablo no hablan cuando...

9. Tomas el examen cuando...

10. Voy al centro cuando...

F. ¿Estás bien? Look at the pictures and describe how these people feel today.

1. Marisol

2. Graciela

3. Santiago

4. Diego y Fernando

5. Julia

6. Benjamín y Laura

G. ¿Cómo están Uds.? Ask five of your classmates how they are feeling today. Then report to the class. Follow the model.

MODELO	
Tú:	*¿Cómo estás?*
Compañero(a) 1:	*Estoy muy contento(a).*

ESTRUCTURA

Possessive adjectives: Third person

—¿Es la bicicleta de Vicente?   *Is it Vicente's bike?*
—Sí, es **su** bicicleta.   *Yes, it's his bike.*

Possessive Adjectives

		Singular		Plural
él, ella	**su**	his, her, its	**sus**	his, her, its
ellos, ellas	**su**	their	**sus**	their

1. Like other possessive adjectives, **su** and **sus** agree in gender and number with the noun they modify.

2. **Su** and **sus** have several English equivalents: **your** (formal; singular and plural), **his, her, its,** and **their.** To clarify who the possessor is, the phrases **de él (ella), de Ud., de Uds.,** and **de ellos (ellas)** can be used instead of **su** and **sus.**

—Es **su** coche?   *Is it her car?*
—Sí, es **el coche de ella.**   *Yes, it's her car.*

Aquí practicamos

H. Sí, es su... Answer the questions affirmatively, following the model.

> **MODELO**   ¿Es el cuaderno de Pedro?
> *Sí, es su cuaderno.*

1. ¿Es el libro de Ana María?   2. ¿Son las llaves de Antonio?   3. ¿Son las amigas de Raquel y Susana?

4. ¿Es el perro de Pilar?

5. ¿Es el gato de Mariano y Adela?

6. ¿Son las hijas de Marcos y Carmen?

7. ¿Es la hermana de Raúl?

8. ¿Es la casa de Benito?

Aquí escuchamos

¿Cómo están? *A man asks five people how they are. They answer and say why they feel this way.*

Antes de escuchar Review the adjectives of condition or mood (page 214). Then, answer the following questions.

1. What verb is used in Spanish with the adjectives listed to describe how a person feels?

2. What ending does the adjective usually have if referring to a male? to a female?

 A escuchar Listen twice to the conversation. On your activity master, write next to each name mentioned the adjective that the person uses to describe how she (he) feels.

	Adjective
Alejandra	
Beatriz	
Patricia	
Mónica	
Raimundo	
Ramón	
Raquel	
Roberto	

Después de escuchar On your activity master, answer the following questions in English, based on what you heard. Use the notes that you took while listening.

1. How does Raquel feel and why does she feel this way?
2. Which person is happy and what is the reason?
3. What does Patricia say about the mood she is in?
4. What does Raimundo want and how is he?
5. What about Alejandra? How does she feel?

¡ADELANTE!

 ¿Cómo estás? Tell a partner how you feel when you carry out the following activities. Then he (she) tells you about his (her) feelings. Follow the model.

> **MODELO** Cuando voy a un concierto…
> *Cuando voy a un concierto, estoy contento(a).*

1. Cuando corro…
2. Cuando voy a clase…
3. Cuando escucho música…
4. Cuando estudio…
5. Cuando hablo con mis amigos…
6. Cuando recibo una F…

 Una encuesta Take a poll of four classmates.

1. Write down a sentence or two about how each of your classmates feels today.
2. Include the reason each person gives for feeling that way.
3. Then, organize a chart based on your findings, grouping the names of your classmates by the feeling they expressed. Be prepared to report back to the class.

EN LÍNEA

Connect with the Spanish-speaking world! Access the *¡Ya verás! Gold* home page for Internet activities related to this chapter.

http://yaveras.heinle.com

VOCABULARIO

Para charlar

Para pedir la hora
¿Qué hora es?
¿A qué hora?
¿Cuándo?

Para dar la hora
a la medianoche
a las cinco de la
  mañana
a las nueve de la noche
a la una de la tarde
al mediodía
desde la(s)... hasta
  la(s)...
entre la(s)... y la(s)...
Es la una y media.
Son las dos y cuarto.
Son las tres menos
  veinte.

Temas y contextos

La fiesta del pueblo
un baile popular
unos bailes folklóricos
un concurso de poesía
un desfile
el Día de la Independencia
una feria
unos fuegos artificiales
una gran fiesta
la misa de Acción de
  Gracias
un premio

Vocabulario general

Verbos
anunciar
celebrar
descansar
estar
preparar
venir

Adjetivos
aburrido(a)
cansado(a)
contento(a)
enfermo(a)
enojado(a)
hispano(a)
listo(a)
tarde
triste

Otras expresiones
ahora
¡Buena idea!
De acuerdo.
¿Dónde nos encontramos?
entonces
la mayoría de
el mejor
por supuesto
su
sus
la tarea
todo(a)
una vez al año

Los muchos colores del júbilo

Antes de leer

1. Look at the title. Can you guess the meaning of the word *júbilo*? Look at the photos, what do you think the reading will be about?

2. Scan the reading and take note of the different festivals mentioned. Are you familiar with any of them?

3. What festivals are held in your area? What is the purpose of these festivals?

Públicas o privadas, religiosas o seculares, las fiestas de un pueblo dicen mucho sobre su historia y temperamento. Tanto España como los países en Latinoamérica celebran muchísimas fiestas y carnavales, que simbolizan tanto la gran imaginación de sus ciudadanos como la complicada historia de sus tradiciones.

Entre las más hermosas festividades hispanas están las celebraciones del Día de los Muertos. En Guatemala, en la provincia de Santiago de Sadatepeques, el pueblo eleva gigantescas cometas para recordar a sus muertos. Estas "mensajeras" suben al cielo llevando en sus colas mensajes a los muertos de la familia. En México, es tradicional preparar golosinas que se ofrecen al espíritu del muerto para complacerlo durante esta celebración.

Varios países latinos celebran el carnaval en febrero; otra celebración llena de colorido, música y diversión. La gente—niños, adolescentes y adultos—se disfrazan. Participan en desfiles y concursos de disfraces. También hay muchas fiestas de disfraces en casas privadas y en clubes.

Otro festival muy divertido se celebra en Valencia, España. Hace algún tiempo, los habitantes del pueblo de Buñol decidieron abandonar su tradicional corrida de toros, por considerarla muy cruel. En su lugar, Buñol comenzó a celebrar su anual Tomatina, en la que cantidades de tomates se llevan a la plaza del pueblo y más de 20.000 personas participan en la batalla de comida más grande del mundo.

Guía para la lectura

recuerda	*remembers*
eleva	*flies*
cometas	*kites*
colas	*tails*
mensajeras	*messengers*
golosinas	*sweets, candy*
complacerlo	*to please (him/her)*
llena de colorido	*full of color, colorful*
diversión	*fun*
se disfrazan	*dress in costumes, disguises*
disfraces	*costumes, disguises*
concursos	*competitions*
corrida de toros	*bullfight*

Después de leer

1. Did you know anything about these festivals? Did you have any previous opinions about them? Have your opinions changed? If so, how?

2. Think about holidays or festivals celebrated in the United States. Make lists of differences and similarities between the festivals mentioned in the reading and those you're familiar with.

3. How did Buñol's *tomatina* begin? Would you enjoy participating in the *tomatina*? Why or why not?

Conversemos un rato

A. Un día en la vida de... Role-play the following situations with another classmate.

1. You and your partner have decided to switch lives for an afternoon. You will take over your partner's classes, afternoon activities, and you will eat dinner at your partner's home. Your partner will take over your day. Give each other the information needed to complete your routine.

   a. Tell your partner the rest of your class schedule. Don't forget to tell him/her where and when the classes are.

   b. Give your partner your after-school routine and explain where and when each activity occurs.

   c. Give your partner the directions to your house so he/she can eat dinner there tonight. Be sure to tell him/her what time to be there.

   d. Give your partner any other information you think he/she might need.

2. Now switch partners with another pair of classmates and tell your new partner about a day in your first partner's life. Which daily routine do you prefer; your day or your partner's day?

B. El festival You and two of your classmates are in Guatemala for the annual festival. Using the poster on page 204, plan your activities for the day.

1. Decide on at least two different activities to do together.

2. Choose one activity that each of you will do alone.

3. Make plans to meet later in the day. Set a time and a place where you will meet.

Taller de escritores

Writing a persuasive description

Create a short description of your city or town aimed at Spanish speakers who might be considering vacationing or working there.

Writing Strategy
• Group brainstorming using clusters

¡Bienvenidos a mi pueblo!

Cuando estás en mi pueblo estás en casa. Las personas son simpáticas. Es pequeño pero tiene de todo: en el centro, por ejemplo, hay una oficina de correos, dos bancos, restaurantes, librerías, y la estación de policia. También hay hoteles, dos hospitales, bibliotecas y supermercados. Tiene un aeropuerto, una estacíon de trenes y de autobuses. Mi pueblo está cerca de la playa.

A. Reflexión In a small group as assigned by your teacher, brainstorm the topic; that is, think about all the points you would like to include and share them with your group. Then, working in the same group, form clusters by relating the topics to the major points you wish to cover.

B. Primer borrador Write a first draft of the description.

C. Revisión con un(a) compañero(a) Exchange descriptions with a classmate. Read each other's work and comment on it, based on these questions. What aspect of the description is the most interesting? What aspect of the town/city can you most easily visualize? Is the writing appropriate for its audience? Does the writing reflect the task assigned? What aspect of the writing would you like to have clarified or made more complete?

D. Versión final Revise your first draft at home, based on the feedback you received. Check grammar, spelling, punctuation, and accent marks. Bring your final draft to class.

E. Carpeta Your teacher may choose to place your work in your portfolio, display it on a bulletin board, or use it to evaluate your progress.

Conexión con la geografía

Los husos horarios

Para empezar Nuestro planeta tiene veinticuatro husos horarios (zonas de tiempo) porque hay veinticuatro horas en el día. Mientras el planeta **da vueltas**, las horas del día pasan de un huso horario a otro. Por ejemplo, en el **dibujo** siguiente, la hora "mediodía" pasa de Nueva York a Chicago, y luego de Chicago a Denver. Cuando es mediodía en Denver, es la una en Chicago y son las dos en Nueva York.

El mapa tiene todos los husos horarios del mundo. Siempre es la misma hora en las ciudades que están en el mismo huso horario. Con este mapa, es posible contar la diferencia de horas entre dos ciudades que están muy lejos.

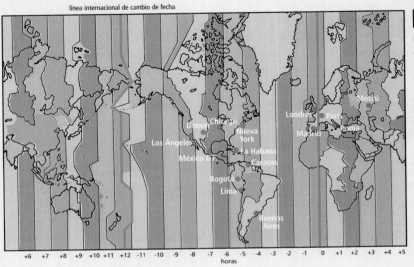

Países que tienen diferencias de media hora con los husos horarios al lado, o que no participan en el sistema de husos horarios.

da vueltas *rotates*   dibujo *drawing*

A. Cuando es la una...
Answer the following questions based on the drawings and the reading passage.

1. Cuando es la una en Nueva York, ¿qué hora es en Denver?
2. Cuando es la una en Nueva York, ¿qué hora es en Los Ángeles?
3. Cuando es mediodía en Denver, ¿dónde es la una?
4. Cuando es mediodía en Denver, ¿dónde son las once?

B. Los horarios de las ciudades

1. ¿Cuáles ciudades latinoamericanas están en el mismo huso horario que Nueva York?
2. ¿Hay otras ciudades europeas que están en el mismo huso horario que Madrid? ¿Cómo se llaman?
3. ¿En qué huso horario está tu ciudad?
4. ¿Cuántos husos horarios hay entre Nueva York y Madrid? ¿entre Nueva York y Los Ángeles? ¿entre Los Ángeles y Madrid? ¿entre Londres y Madrid?

C. ¿A qué hora...?
Work with a partner and find out at what time he or she performs the following daily activities. Make a list of the activities and the time your partner does each activity. Use your knowledge of time zones to imagine what people in other parts of the world do at that hour.

MODELO   comer el desayuno

Estudiante 1:   ¿A qué hora comes el desayuno?
Estudiante 2:   Desayuno a las siete de la mañana.
Estudiante 1:   Cuando tú desayunas, la gente en París...

1. estudiar
2. ir a la escuela
3. llegar a casa
4. estar cansado(a)
5. descansar en la cama
6. mirar la televisión
7. comer en la cafetería
8. pasar el tiempo con amigos

Vistas

de los países hispanos

Costa Rica

Capital: San José

Ciudades principales: Alajuela, Cartago, Heredia

Población: 2.800.000

Idiomas: español

Área territorial: 50.700 km^2

Clima: cálido y húmedo, temperatura media anual de 25° a 27°

Moneda: colón

cálido *warm*

EXPLORA

Find out more about Costa Rica! Access the **Nuestros vecinos** page on the *¡Ya verás! Gold* web site for a list of URLs.

http://yaveras.heinle.com/vecinos.htm

En la comunidad

Paul Kearney: **En caso de una emergencia**

"After being burned in a fire as a child, you would think the last career I would choose would be that of firefighter. However, later in life I knew that's what I wanted to be because I wanted to help people who were in trouble.

My desire to help people suits my profession: I know a lot about fires, a lot about rescue procedures, and a lot about how to talk to both English- and Spanish-speaking people during emergencies. My Spanish isn't polished, but it's still very useful when I need to know things like: Who's in the building? Are there any pets to rescue? How did the fire start? What else is flammable in the building? And, even, what's on the other side of a particular window or door, in case there's a danger I'm unaware of."

¡Ahora te toca a ti!

With a partner, find out who the "emergency specialists" are in your city or town. Research who is in charge and how to reach them. Find the phone number for the fire department, the police department, a local hospital, or other emergency specialists in your community. Give the phone numbers in Spanish and give simple directions for how a Spanish-speaking person might contact each emergency specialist in the case of an emergency.

UNIDAD 4

Vamos al centro

Objectives

In this unit you will learn:

- to make plans for various activities in town
- to talk about the future
- to use the Madrid subway
- to give directions for using the Madrid subway

¿Qué ves?

- Who are these people in the photographs?
- Where are they going? How?
- Where do you think they are?

229

CAPÍTULO 10

¿Quieres ir al centro?

—¿Quieres ir al centro conmigo?
—Sí, tengo que comprar algo.

Objectives

- making plans to go downtown
- identifying what to do in town
- talking about when and how to go downtown

PRIMERA ETAPA

- What do you do when you go downtown?
- Why do you go there?
- How do you invite someone to go with you?

¿Para qué?

Estas personas tienen planes en el centro.

Miguel: Voy al centro para ver a mis amigos.
Sandra: Ah, tienes una **cita** con tus amigos.

Andrés: Voy al centro para **ir de compras.**
Adela: Ah, quieres comprar algo.

Cristina: Voy al centro para ir al cine.
Javier: Ah, **tienes ganas de** ver una película.

Natalia: Voy al centro para **hacer un mandado** para mi madre.
Pedro: Ah, **debes** hacer un mandado.

¿Para qué? *For what reason?* **cita** *date* **ir de compras** *to go shopping* **tienes ganas de** *you feel like*
hacer un mandado *do an errand* **debes** *you must*

| Daniel: | ¿Para qué vas al centro? |
| Noemí: | Voy al centro para **dar un paseo.** |

Una situación

Elena:	¿Francisco, quieres ir al centro conmigo?
Francisco:	¿Para qué?
Elena:	Para hacer un mandado para mi padre. Tengo que ir a la farmacia.
Francisco:	Mm, bueno, quiero comprar un disco compacto. ¡Vamos!
Elena:	De acuerdo. ¡Vamos!

dar un paseo *take a walk*

¡Te toca a ti!

A. ¿Para qué va al centro? Your teacher wants to know why the following students are going downtown. On the basis of the following drawings, explain why. Follow the model.

> **MODELO**
> ¿Para qué va María al centro?
> *Ella va al centro para ver a una amiga.*

1. ¿Para qué va Vicente al centro?

2. ¿Para qué va Anita al centro?

3. ¿Para qué va José al centro?

4. ¿Para qué va Laura al centro?

5. ¿Para qué van Patricio y Julia al centro?

6. ¿Para qué van Mario y Luis al centro?

B. **¿Quieres ir al centro conmigo?** You are going downtown and invite a friend to go along. When you explain the reason for going, your friend decides to accompany you. Use the following drawings to explain your reasons for going. Follow the model.

MODELO

Tú: *¿Quieres ir al centro conmigo?*

Amigo(a): *¿Para qué?*

Tú: *Tengo que ir a la oficina de correos.*

Amigo(a): *Bueno. Vamos.*

1.

2.

3.

4.

5.

PRONUNCIACIÓN THE CONSONANT **h**

In Spanish, unlike English, the letter **h** is always silent.

Práctica

C. Listen and repeat as your teacher models the following words.

1. hay
2. hospital
3. hola
4. hoy
5. hace

6. hotel
7. hablar
8. hispano
9. ahora
10. hora

En el centro de Madrid, España

ESTRUCTURA

The immediate future: Ir a + infinitive

Voy a comer.	*I am going to eat.*
Vamos a estudiar.	*We are going to study.*
Vas a dar un paseo.	*You are going to take a walk.*
¿Qué van a hacer esta tarde?	*What are they going to do this afternoon?*

1. One way to express a future action, especially one that will occur in the near future, is to use a present tense form of **ir + a** + infinitive. This structure is equivalent to the English *to be going to* + verb.

2. To make a sentence or question that uses **ir a** + infinitive negative, place **no** before the conjugated form of **ir**.

No voy a comer en el centro.	*I'm not going to eat downtown.*
Ellos no van a estudiar.	*They're not going to study.*

Aquí practicamos

D. ¿Qué van a hacer? Use words from each column to form sentences expressing future plans.

A	B	C
yo	ir a	dar un paseo
Susana		comer en un restaurante
Marcos		estudiar en la biblioteca
nosotros		comprar un disco compacto
Juan y su novia		mirar un programa de televisión
Uds.		
tú		
Ud.		

E. ¿Qué vas a hacer el sábado por la tarde (Saturday afternoon)? You are trying to find out what your friends are going to do Saturday afternoon. Ask your classmates these questions, and they will use the expressions in parentheses to answer. Follow the model.

> **MODELO** **Tú:** Marcos, ¿qué vas a hacer el sábado por la tarde? (comer en un restaurante)
> **Compañero(a):** *Voy a comer en un restaurante.*

1. Carlos, ¿qué vas a hacer el sábado por la tarde? (estudiar en la biblioteca)
2. ¿Y qué va a hacer Juan? (ver a una amiga en el centro)
3. ¿Y Fernando y su amigo? (dar un paseo)
4. ¿Y Bárbara y Julián? (ir de compras)
5. Marcos, ¿qué vas a hacer? (comprar un disco compacto)

F. ¿Qué vas a hacer este fin de semana (this weekend)? Answer the following questions about your weekend plans.

1. ¿Vas a estudiar español?
2. ¿Vas a leer un libro? ¿Qué libro?
3. ¿Vas a comprar algo?
4. ¿Vas a mirar un programa de televisión? ¿Qué programa?
5. ¿Vas a bailar en una fiesta?
6. ¿Vas a hablar por teléfono con un(a) amigo(a)? ¿Con qué amigo(a)?

PALABRAS ÚTILES

Tener ganas de + infinitive

Tengo ganas de estudiar.	*I feel like studying.*
Tienes ganas de comer una hamburguesa con queso.	*You feel like eating a cheeseburger.*
Tenemos ganas de bailar.	*We feel like dancing.*
Tienen ganas de escuchar la radio.	*They feel like listening to the radio.*

In Spanish, when you want to say you feel like doing something, use the expression **tener ganas de** + infinitive. Simply conjugate **tener** and use the infinitive form of the verb that expresses what you feel like doing.

G. Tienen ganas de... Create original sentences, using words from each column.

A	B	C
Esteban yo nosotros tú Marta y Julia Uds.	tener ganas de	comer en un restaurante estudiar bailar mirar la televisión ir a un museo dar un paseo ir al centro

H. ¿Qué tiene ganas de hacer...? Tell what the people in the following drawings feel like doing. Follow the model.

> **MODELO** ¿Qué tienen ganas de hacer Isabel y Juan?
> *Isabel y Juan tienen ganas de bailar.*

¿Qué tienen ganas de hacer Isabel y Juan?

1. ¿Qué tiene ganas de hacer Irma?

2. ¿Qué tienen ganas de hacer Julián y Javier?

3. ¿Qué tiene ganas de hacer Eva?

4. ¿Qué tienen ganas de hacer tus amigos?

5. ¿Qué tiene ganas de hacer Esteban?

6. ¿Qué tienen ganas de hacer Bárbara y Carolina?

I. Tengo ganas de... pero debo... A friend invites you to do something. You say that you want to but cannot because you ought to do something else. Give him (her) a good excuse. Follow the model.

MODELO
ir al centro
Amigo(a): *¿Tienes ganas de ir al centro conmigo?*
Tú: *Sí, pero debo estudiar español.*

1. comprar un disco compacto
2. ver una película
3. caminar al centro
4. ir a la librería
5. comer en un restaurante
6. dar un paseo

Aquí escuchamos

¿Quieres ir al centro? *Elena invites Francisco to go downtown with her.*

Antes de escuchar Think about how you would invite someone to go downtown with you in Spanish.

 A escuchar Listen twice to the conversation between Elena and Francisco before answering the questions about it that follow.

Después de escuchar Answer the following questions based on what you heard.

1. Why is Elena going downtown?
2. Where is she going?
3. Why does Francisco want to go downtown?
4. What else does Elena invite Francisco to do?
5. What phrase does Francisco use to agree to accompany Elena?

—¿Quieres ir al cine conmigo?
—Sí, pero no hay un cine por aquí.
—¿Entonces quieres ir al centro?
—¡Vamos!

¿Quieres ir al centro conmigo?   Make a list of things you want or need to do in town. Then interview several classmates to find someone who would like to go downtown for some of the same reasons. When you find someone who wants to join you, try to arrange a time that will be convenient for both of you. Use **no puedo** to say *I can't*. Follow the model.

MODELO	Tú:	*¡Hola, Catalina! ¿Qué vas a hacer en el centro?*
	Catalina:	*Debo ir a la farmacia. Y tengo ganas de ir de compras.*
	Tú:	*Yo quiero ir de compras también. ¿Quieres ir conmigo?*
	Catalina:	*Sí, cómo no. ¿A qué hora?*
	Tú:	*¿A las once?*
	Catalina:	*No, no puedo a las once, porque tengo una cita con mi abuela a mediodía. Nosotras vamos a comer juntas.*
	Catalina:	*Entonces, vamos al centro a las tres.*
	Tú:	*De acuerdo.*

Este fin de semana tengo ganas de...   Write a note to a friend in which you tell what you feel like doing this weekend. Mention four different activities. For each one, write when, where, or with whom you want to do these things. Name a fifth activity that you are not going to do because of a previous commitment.

SEGUNDA ETAPA

- In this **etapa** you will be talking about various activities that you do on certain days and at specific times of the day. What are some ways of dividing a day into different parts?

- Do you know the names of the days of the week in Spanish?

- How do you ask someone what he (she) is going to do on a specific day or during a specific part of a day?

¿Cuándo vamos?

Voy a hacer muchas cosas hoy y mañana.

Hoy

Mañana

1. **Esta mañana,** yo voy a la escuela.

2. **Mañana por la mañana,** voy a dormir tarde.

3. **Esta tarde,** yo voy a estudiar.

4. **Mañana por la tarde,** voy a ir de compras.

hoy *today*   **mañana** *tomorrow*   **viernes** *Friday*   **Esta mañana** *This morning*   **sábado** *Saturday*   **Mañana por la mañana** *Tomorrow morning*   **Esta tarde** *This afternoon*   **Mañana por la tarde** *Tomorrow afternoon*

Hoy	Mañana

5. **Esta noche,** yo voy a mirar la televisión en casa.

6. **Mañana por la noche,** voy a ver a mis amigos en el cine.

Una situación

Liliana: ¿Quieres ir al centro **conmigo?** Tengo que ir a la oficina de correos.

Guillermo: Sí, yo también. Tengo que hacer un mandado para mi padre. ¿Cuándo quieres ir? ¿Esta mañana?

Liliana: No, es imposible. **No puedo ir** esta mañana. Tengo que estudiar hasta las 12:00. ¿Esta tarde? **¿Está bien?**

Guillermo: Sí, está bien. Vamos al centro esta tarde.

Esta noche *Tonight*   **Mañana por la noche** *Tomorrow night*   **conmigo** *with me*   **No puedo ir** *I can't go*
¿Está bien? *Is that O.K.?*

¡Te toca a ti!

A. ¿Cuándo vas al centro? Based on the drawings that follow, indicate when the following activities take place. Pretend that today's date is the fifth of March. Follow the model.

la mañana

la tarde

la noche

MODELO   ¿Cuándo va Anita al centro?
Ella va al centro esta noche.

el 5 de marzo

el 5 de marzo

el 6 de marzo

el 5 de marzo

1. ¿Cuándo van a ir al cine tus padres?

2. ¿Cuándo va Enrique al centro?

3. ¿Cuándo va a estudiar tu hermana?

el 6 de marzo

el 6 de marzo

el 5 de marzo

4. ¿Cuándo va a comprar Julián el disco compacto?

5. ¿Cuándo vas a ver a tus amigos?

6. ¿Cuándo van a hacer el mandado tus hermanos?

B. ¿Cuándo quieres ir? Make plans with a friend. Using the information provided, imitate each of the model conversations.

> **MODELO**   ir al cine, esta noche / sí
>   **Tú:**   *¿Quieres ir al cine conmigo?*
>   **Amiga(o):**   *Sí. ¿Cuándo quieres ir?*
>   **Tú:**   *Esta noche. ¿Está bien?*
>   **Amiga(o):**   *Sí, por supuesto. Vamos al cine esta noche.*

1. ir al centro, esta noche / sí

2. ir a la biblioteca, mañana por la tarde / sí

3. ir a la piscina, mañana por la tarde / sí

> **MODELO**   ir al centro, esta tarde / no (trabajar) / mañana por la tarde / sí
>   **Amiga(o):**   *¿Quieres ir al centro conmigo?*
>   **Tú:**   *Sí, ¿cuándo quieres ir?*
>   **Amiga(o):**   *Esta tarde. ¿Está bien?*
>   **Tú:**   *No, es imposible. Tengo que trabajar. ¿Mañana por la tarde?*
>   **Amiga(o):**   *Claro que sí. Vamos al centro mañana por la tarde.*

4. ir al museo, esta tarde / no (hacer un mandado) / mañana por la tarde / sí

5. dar un paseo, esta mañana / no (dormir) / esta tarde / sí

6. ir al cine, esta noche / no (estudiar) / mañana por la noche / sí

Repaso ♻

C. Preguntas Your partner will play the role of an exchange student who has just arrived at your school. He (she) wants to get to know you. Answer his (her) questions, paying close attention to whether each question is general and therefore requires the present tense, or whether it deals with a specific future time and thus calls for **ir a** + infinitive.

1. ¿Estudias mucho? ¿Vas a estudiar esta noche?

2. Usualmente, ¿qué haces por la noche? ¿Qué vas a hacer esta noche?

3. ¿Vas frecuentemente al centro? ¿Qué haces en el centro? ¿Vas al centro mañana?

4. ¿Estudias español? ¿ruso? ¿chino? ¿francés? ¿Vas a estudiar otra lengua?

5. ¿Te gusta dar un paseo? ¿Vas a dar un paseo esta noche?

ESTRUCTURA

The days of the week

El jueves yo voy al cine.	*On Thursday I'm going to the movies.*
El domingo vamos a dar un paseo.	*On Sunday we're going to take a walk.*
Los domingos vamos a la iglesia.	*On Sundays we go to church.*
Los sábados no vamos a la escuela.	*On Saturdays we don't go to school.*

1. In Spanish the days of the week (**los días de la semana**) are as follows:

lunes	*Monday*	**jueves**	*Thursday*	**sábado**	*Saturday*
martes	*Tuesday*	**viernes**	*Friday*	**domingo**	*Sunday*
miércoles	*Wednesday*				

2. Spanish speakers consider the week to begin on Monday and end on Sunday. The names of the days are masculine and are not capitalized.

3. To express the idea of *on a certain day* or *days*, use the definite article **el** or **los** with the day of the week. When you are simply telling what day it is, however, the article is omitted.

—**¿Qué día es hoy?**	*What day is it today?*
—**Es miércoles.**	*It is Wednesday.*

Aquí practicamos

D. Hoy es... Form questions using the day indicated. Then, answer each question negatively using the next day in your response. Follow the model.

> MODELO   lunes
> *¿Es lunes hoy?*
> *No, hoy no es lunes. Hoy es martes.*

1. jueves	3. miércoles	5. viernes
2. sábado	4. domingo	6. martes

E. Ellos llegan el jueves Some students from Bolivia are going to visit your school. They come from different cities and will arrive on different dates. Using the following calendar, indicate on what day of the week each student will arrive. Follow the model.

> **MODELO** Miguel va a llegar el 18.
> *Ah, él llega el jueves.*

1. Enrique va a llegar el 15.
2. Mario y Jaime van a llegar el 17.
3. María y Anita van a llegar el 20.
4. Francisco va a llegar el 21.
5. Roberto va a llegar el 16.
6. Todos los demás *(All the rest)* van a llegar el 19.

Enero

L	M	M	J	V	S	D
15	16	17	18	19	20	21

ESTRUCTURA

The verb *hacer*

1. In the present tense, the **yo** form of the verb **hacer** (**hago**) is irregular, but all other forms are conjugated in the same way as regular **-er** verbs.

hacer *(to do, to make)*			
yo	**hago**	nosotros(as)	**hacemos**
tú	**haces**	vosotros(as)	**hacéis**
él ella Ud.	**hace**	ellos ellas Uds.	**hacen**

2. When asked a question that includes **hacer** or one of its forms, you normally answer with the verb that expresses what it is you do.

—¿Qué **haces** los lunes?	*What do you do on Mondays?*
—**Voy** a la escuela.	*I go to school.*
—¿Qué **vas a hacer** el viernes?	*What are you going to do on Friday?*
—**Voy a estudiar.**	*I'm going to study.*

Aquí practicamos

F. ¿Qué hacen? Replace the words in italics with each of the words in parentheses, making all necessary changes.

1. ¿Qué hace *Juan* los sábados? (Anita / tú / Uds. / Susana y Enrique / yo / Ud.)

2. ¿Qué van a hacer *ellos* el domingo por la tarde? (tú / Uds. / Alberto / yo / Linda y Mario / nosotros)

G. ¿Qué hace Juan...? Your sister asks you what your friends usually do on a certain day of the week. Respond with the activities in parentheses. Follow the model.

> MODELO   Tu hermana: ¿Qué hace Martín los lunes por la noche? (estudiar)
>
> Tú: *Martín estudia.*

1. ¿Qué hace Martín los martes por la noche? (mirar la televisión)
2. ¿Qué hace Lucía los viernes? (comer en un restaurante)
3. ¿Qué hacen Elisa y Jaime los sábados por la noche? (ir al cine)
4. ¿Qué hace Marina los jueves en el centro? (ir de compras)
5. ¿Qué hacen Mario y Susana los domingos? (dar un paseo)

H. ¿Qué va a hacer Timoteo... ? Your teacher asks you what your friends are going to do on a certain day. Respond with the activities in parentheses. Follow the model.

> MODELO   Tu profesora: ¿Qué va a hacer Timoteo esta noche? (leer)
>
> Tú: *Timoteo va a leer esta noche.*

1. ¿Qué va a hacer José esta noche? (escuchar discos compactos)
2. ¿Qué va a hacer Ernestina el viernes? (estudiar)
3. ¿Qué van a hacer Antonio y Catarina mañana? (ir al museo)
4. ¿Qué va a hacer Pepita en el centro el martes? (ver a una amiga)
5. ¿Qué van a hacer Teodoro y Alicia el sábado? (hacer un mandado)

Aquí escuchamos

¿Cuándo vamos? *Elena and Francisco discuss their plans to go downtown.*

Antes de escuchar Think about how Elena might invite Francisco to do something, how he might agree or disagree, and how they could settle on a time of day.

A escuchar Listen twice to the conversation before answering the questions about it that follow.

Después de escuchar Answer the following questions, based on what you heard.

1. What does Elena have to do downtown?
2. Why does Francisco have to go downtown?
3. Why can't Francisco go in the morning?
4. When do they decide to go?

¡ADELANTE!

 ¿Qué haces los fines de semana? Ask several of your classmates what they do on the weekends. Keep track of your findings and be ready to report back to the class. Ask as many class-mates as you can in the time allotted.

 Este fin de semana Write a note to a friend, explaining what you are going to do this weekend. Include at least five activi-ties. Ask your friend what he (she) is going to do.

Este fin de semana, voy a la feria con Jorge.

¿Cómo prefieres ir, en coche o a pie?

*Hay muchas **maneras** (ways) de ir al centro.*

El Sr. Valdés va en metro.

La Sra. Candelaria va en coche.

La Sra. López va en autobús.

El Sr. Cano va en taxi.

Pedro va en bicicleta.

Fernando va a pie *(on foot)*.

Una situación

Andrés: ¿Quieres ir al Museo del Prado hoy?
Gabriela: Sí. Me gustan las pinturas de Velázquez. ¿Vamos a pie?
Andrés: No. Está muy lejos. Vamos en metro.
Gabriela: Bien, de acuerdo. Vamos a **tomar** *(take)* el metro.

Museo del Prado: *Located in Madrid, the Prado is considered one of the most important art museums in the word. It contains over 6,000 works by Spanish artists such as Velázquez, Goya, and El Greco, as well as masterpieces by other artists such as Bosch, Rubens, and Raphael.*

¡Te toca a ti!

A. ¿Cómo van? Based on the drawings that follow, tell how each person gets downtown. Follow the model.

MODELO Jorge va...
Jorge va en bicicleta.

1. Francisco va...

2. La Sra. Fernández va...

3. Carlos va...

4. Marta va...

5. El Sr. González va...

6. Santiago y su hermana van...

7. El Sr. López va...

B. ¿Tú quieres ir...? You invite a friend to go somewhere with you. He (she) responds affirmatively, saying **Claro que sí.** Your friend then suggests a way of going there, but you have a different idea. Follow the model.

MODELO   museo / metro / a pie
                Tú: *¿Quieres ir al museo?*
         Amigo(a): *Claro que sí. ¿Vamos en metro?*
                Tú: *No. ¡Vamos a pie!*
         Amigo(a): *De acuerdo. Vamos a pie.*

1. cine / a pie / autobús
2. centro / autobús / coche
3. biblioteca / taxi / metro
4. parque / coche / a pie
5. restaurante / metro / autobús
6. farmacia / autobús / metro /
7. estadio / bicicleta / a pie
8. mercado / a pie / coche

Repaso ♻

C. Intercambio Ask the following questions of a classmate, who will answer them.

1. ¿Qué tienes ganas de hacer el sábado próximo *(next)*?
2. ¿Qué haces los domingos por la mañana?
3. ¿Qué haces los lunes por la mañana? ¿Por la tarde?
4. ¿Cuándo estudias? ¿Cómo vas a la escuela? ¿Cuándo vas al centro? ¿Para qué? ¿Cuándo vas al cine?

ESTRUCTURA

The present tense of the verb poder

poder (ue) *(to be able)*			
yo	puede	nosotros(as)	**podemos**
tú	puedes	vosotros(as)	**podéis**
él ella Ud.	puede	ellos ellas Uds.	pueden

1. The verb **poder** is a stem-changing verb in which the vowel in the stem (**pod-**) changes from **o** to **ue** in all forms except **nosotros(as)** and **vosotros(as)**. The verb **contar** *(to count, to tell a story)* follows this same pattern: **yo cuento**, but **nosotras contamos**.

2. **Poder** is followed directly by an infinitive. To make this construction negative, place **no** before the conjugated form of the verb **poder**.

—¿**Puede hablar** francés Marcos?   *Can Marcos speak French?*

—No, **no puede hablar** francés.   *No, he cannot speak French.*

Aquí practicamos

D. Podemos... Tell what the following people can do, using words from each column.

A	B	C
Linda yo tú Gregorio y Verónica Uds. nosotros	poder	ir al centro ir a un restaurante ir al concierto ir al museo ir al cine

E. Hoy no puedo... A classmate invites you to do something. You cannot do it at the time he (she) suggests, but you suggest another time when you can. Follow the model.

> **MODELO**   ir al cine, hoy / sábado por la noche
> **Compañero(a):** *¿Puedes ir al cine hoy?*
> **Tú:** *No, hoy no puedo, pero puedo ir el sábado por la noche.*

1. ir al centro, ahora / viernes por la tarde

2. ir a un restaurante, esta noche / mañana por la noche

3. ir al museo, esta tarde / domingo por la tarde

4. ir al concierto, esta semana / la semana próxima

5. ir de compras, esta mañana / sábado por la mañana

F. No, no puedo You suggest an activity to a friend. He (she) is interested, but cannot do it on the day you have proposed and gives you a reason why not. You then suggest a different day, which is fine with your friend. Follow the model.

> **MODELO**   dar un paseo, mañana / trabajar / sábado
> **Tú:** *¿Puedes dar un paseo mañana?*
> **Amigo(a):** *No, no puedo. Tengo que trabajar.*
> **Tú:** *¿El sábado? ¿Está bien?*
> **Amigo(a):** *Sí. Vamos a dar un paseo el sábado.*

1. ir al centro, esta noche / ir al cine con mis padres / mañana por la noche

2. hacer un mandado, el sábado / trabajar / domingo

3. ir al museo, esta tarde / estudiar / sábado

4. ir a tomar un café, el sábado / ir de compras con mi madre / domingo

5. ir al cine, mañana / hacer un mandado / viernes

6. ir a la biblioteca, hoy / ver a un amigo / martes

Aquí escuchamos

¿Puedes ir conmigo? *Elena invites Francisco to accompany her to a building downtown.*

Antes de escuchar Think about how you invite someone in Spanish to accompany you to do something. Try to predict how Elena might invite Francisco to do something, how he could agree or disagree, and how they could settle on a means of transportation.

 A escuchar Listen twice to the conversation before answering the questions about it that follow.

Después de escuchar Answer the following questions, based on what you heard.

1. Where does Elena invite Francisco to go?
2. When does she want to go?
3. When does Francisco suggest they go?
4. How do they decide to go?
5. What phrase does Elena use to agree when Francisco suggests a new time?

¡ADELANTE!

 ¿Puedes ir conmigo? Ask a classmate if she (he) can do something with you. When you get an affirmative response, arrange a day, a time, and a place to meet. Then agree on a means of transportation.

 El sábado... Write a short note to a classmate.

1. Ask if he (she) can accompany you to do something on Saturday.
2. Mention where you want to go.
3. Tell him (her) what you plan to do when you get there.
4. Mention how you expect to get there.
5. Be sure to suggest a time of day.

EN LÍNEA

Connect with the Spanish-speaking world!
Access the *¡Ya verás! Gold* home page for
Internet activities related to this chapter.

http://yaveras.heinle.com

VOCABULARIO

Para charlar

Para hablar de los planes

¿Está bien?
ir + a + *infinitive*
poder + *infinitive*
tener ganas + de +
 infinitive

Para decir adónde vas

Voy a dar un paseo.
Voy a hacer un
 mandado.
Voy a ir de compras.
Voy a ver a un
 amigo.

Para decir cuándo

Vamos esta mañana.
…esta tarde.
…hoy.
…mañana.
…mañana por la
 mañana.
…mañana por la
 tarde.
…mañana por la
 noche.

Para decir sí o no

¡Claro que sí!
Es imposible.
No, no puedo.
No puedo ir.
Sí, puedo.
Sí, tengo ganas de…

Para ir al centro

Voy en autobús.
…a pie.
…en bicicleta.
…en coche.
…en metro.
…en taxi.

Para preguntar qué día es

¿Qué día es hoy?

Temas y contextos

Los días de la semana

el lunes
el martes
el miércoles
el jueves
el viernes
el sábado
el domingo
el fin de semana

Vocabulario general

Verbos

deber
hacer
poder
tomar

Otras palabras y expresiones

una cita
conmigo
¿Para qué?
próximo(a)
usualmente

Estrellas de la música latina

Antes de leer

1. Look at the photos to see if you recognize these people. What do they do?

2. Do you know the names of any other Spanish-speakers within this profession? Where are they from?

Si se va a una tienda de discos en una de las grandes ciudades de los Estados Unidos o de Europa, es posible encontrar una gran variedad de música latina. Dos de los ritmos musicales más populares en Latinoamérica son la salsa y el merengue. A pesar de que la salsa se originó en Puerto Rico y el merengue en la República Dominicana, hoy en día esta música se baila en toda Latinoamérica y en muchas de las ciudades de los Estados Unidos y el mundo.

Rubén Blades

Rubén Blades, abogado panameño graduado de la universidad de Harvard, trae una dimensión social y panamericana a la salsa. Escribe muchas de sus propias canciones y cuenta historias mejor que nadie. Canciones como "Decisiones" y "Buscando América" reflejan la vida y la realidad latinoamericana.

Celia Cruz

Celia Cruz, "la reina de la salsa", es cubana y tiene una voz potente, con toda la gracia y el color de los trópicos. Embajadora de la música del Caribe, viaja constantemente por el mundo, actuando en compañía de Tito Puente, otro salsero legendario. Muchas personas que van a los conciertos de Celia Cruz se ponen a bailar porque es imposible resistir el ritmo de su música.

Juan Luis Guerra

Juan Luis Guerra, de la República Dominicana, canta sobre los problemas sociales y económicos de su gente mientras los invita a desahogarse de la mejor manera que saben: bailando. Con canciones como "Ojalá que llueva café" y "Burbujas de amor", este cantante dinámico le da al merengue una nueva popularidad.

Guía para la lectura

1. Here are some words and expressions to keep in mind as you read.

voz	*voice*
Embajadora	*Ambassador (female)*
se ponen a	*begin to*
propias	*own*
mientras	*while*
desahogarse	*unburden themselves*
Burbujas	*Bubbles*

2. **"Ojalá que llueva café"** ("Oh how I wish it would rain coffee") In this song Guerra describes a landscape so abundant with food that it rains coffee, the plains sprout sweet potatoes and strawberries, and there are hills of wheat and rice. Here everyone is happy and the children sing. Although Guerra is dealing with a serious subject, the catchy rhythm and playful lyrics have made the song extremely popular.

Después de leer

1. According to the reading, which singer has given salsa a more Pan-American flavor? What does this mean? Do you think it's good for this artist's music to have a Pan-American dimension? Why or why not?

2. According to the reading, which singer's music calls to people to release their frustrations by dancing? How might dancing help people express themselves? Do you think dancing is a good way to express emotions? Why or why not?

3. The music of these three Hispanic musicians is popular in the United States and in other countries around the world. What other Hispanic musicians are you familiar with? What kinds of music do they create?

4. Are you a musician? If so, what kinds of music do you play? Do you believe your music helps you to express yourself? If so, how?

CAPÍTULO 11

Vamos a tomar el metro

—¿Tomamos un autobús?
—No, vamos a tomar el metro.

Objectives

● talking about taking the Madrid subway
● buying subway tickets
● making and accepting invitations

PRIMERA ETAPA

> **Preparación**
>
> - Have you ever ridden a subway?
>
> - What cities in the U.S. have subways? Have you heard of the "L" in Chicago; the "T" in Boston; "BART" in San Francisco; "MARTA" in Atlanta; or the Metro in Washington, DC?

¿En qué dirección?

¿Cómo van a llegar Elena y Clara al Museo del Prado?

Elena y su prima Clara van a tomar el metro al Museo del Prado. Están cerca de la Plaza de España, donde hay una estación de metro. Las dos **jóvenes** miran el **plano** del metro en la **entrada** de la estación.

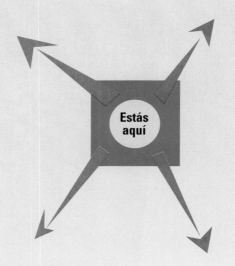

Elena:	Bueno. Estamos aquí, en la Plaza de España.
Clara:	¿Dónde está el Museo del Prado?
Elena:	Está cerca de la Estación Atocha. Allí.
Clara:	Entonces, ¿qué hacemos?
Elena:	Es fácil. Tomamos la dirección de Legazpi.
Clara:	¿Es necesario **cambiar** de trenes?
Elena:	Sí. Cambiamos en Sol, dirección de Portazgo.
Clara:	Y debemos **bajar** en Atocha, ¿verdad?
Elena:	Exacto, allí en Atocha bajamos.

jóvenes *young people*   **plano** *map*   **entrada** *entrance*   **cambiar** *to change*   **bajar** *to get off*

¡Te toca a ti!

A. Cambiamos en... Bajamos en... A friend asks you questions about where to change lines and where to get off the subway in order to get to his (her) destination. Based on the cues, answer his (her) questions. The place to change lines is listed first and the destination is second. Follow the model.

> **MODELO**   Sol / la Plaza de España
> > **Amigo(a):**   *¿Es necesario cambiar de trenes?*
> > **Tú:**   *Sí, tienes que cambiar en Sol.*

Amigo(a): *¿Dónde bajo del tren?*
Tú: *Debes bajar en la Plaza de España.*

1. Pacífico / Manuel Becerra
2. Callao / Lavapiés
3. Bilbao / Goya

4. Ópera / Cuatro Caminos
5. Ventas / Banco de España
6. Goya / Sol

B. ¡Vamos a tomar el metro! Use the metro map that follows to explain how to use the subway. The metro line number (shown in parentheses after the name of each station mentioned) will help you locate the stations. Follow the model.

MODELO   Juan / la Plaza de España (3, 10) → Ventas (2)
Juan, para ir a Ventas desde la Plaza de España, es necesario tomar la dirección Legazpi. Tienes que cambiar de tren en Callao, dirección de Canillejas, y debes bajar en Ventas.

1. Marcos / Argüelles (4) → Rubén Darío (5)
2. Pilar / Nueva Numancia (1) → Embajadores (3)
3. Felipe / Delicias (3) → Atocha (1)
4. Nilda / Manuel Becerra (6) → Plaza de Castilla (1)

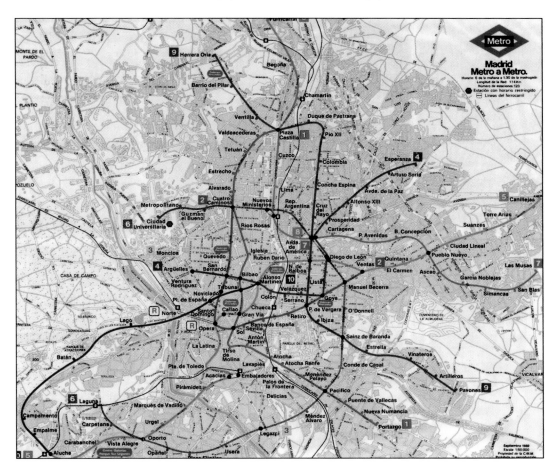

PRONUNCIACIÓN THE CONSONANT ch

The sound of **ch** in Spanish is like the *ch* in the English word *church*.

Práctica

C. Listen and repeat as your teacher models the following words.

1. chocolate
2. Chile
3. mucho
4. muchacho
5. coche

6. ocho
7. leche
8. noche
9. ochenta
10. mochila

Comentarios CULTURALES

El metro

The **metro** is one of the most popular means of transportation in Madrid. The rate for each trip on the subway is fixed. Booklets of tickets are available, and buying tickets by the booklet is cheaper than buying individual tickets. To get around on the **metro** you must first find the **línea** on which you want to travel. Then look for the direction you want to go on that line and find the name of the last station. Follow the signs for that station.

Repaso

D. Como de costumbre (As usual) Some members of your family follow a regular routine. On a certain day of the week, they always do the same thing. Describe where they go and how they get there, based on the following drawings. Follow the model.

MODELO

tu madre
Los lunes mi madre va al centro.
Usualmente ella va a pie.

SÁBADO

1. tu abuelo

SÁBADO

2. tu primo

MARTES

3. tu hermana

VIERNES

4. tu tío y tu tía

JUEVES

5. tus primas

DOMINGO

6. tus padres

ESTRUCTURA

Adverbs for the present and the future

Mi mamá trabaja **hoy.**	*My mother is working today.*
Mañana ella no va a trabajar.	*Tomorrow she's not going to work.*
¿Dónde están **ahora?**	*Where are they now?*

1. You have already learned several adverbs that express present or future time.

hoy	**mañana**
esta mañana	**mañana por la mañana**
esta tarde	**mañana por la tarde**
esta noche	**mañana por la noche**

2. Here are some additional expressions you should learn.

ahora *now*	**la semana próxima** *next week*
esta semana *this week*	**el mes próximo** *next month*
este mes *this month*	**el año próximo** *next year*
este año *this year*	

ESTRUCTURA (continued)

3. The expressions **por la mañana, por la tarde, por la noche**, and **próximo(a)** can be combined with the days of the week: **el lunes por la mañana, el sábado por la tarde, el domingo por la noche, el lunes próximo**, etc. Time expressions are usually placed at the very beginning or end of a sentence.

El domingo por la noche
   voy a mirar la televisión.

*On Sunday night, I am
   going to watch television.*

Aquí practicamos

E. ¿Cuándo van? Create original sentences using words from each column.

A	B	C	D
Yo	ir	al cine	hoy
Roberto		a Madrid	esta tarde
Nosotros		al museo	el viernes por la noche
mi hermana		al banco	el domingo por la mañana
Uds.		a la iglesia	la semana próxima
Tú		a la escuela	el jueves por la noche
			ahora

F. Esta noche no... Your mother asks you about people's activities, but she has them confused. Correct her statements, using the information given. Follow the model.

> **MODELO**   ¿Van al cine tú y Luis esta noche? (mañana por la noche)
> *Esta noche no podemos ir al cine. Vamos al cine mañana por la noche.*

1. ¿Van tú y Felipe al centro el miércoles por la noche? (miércoles por la tarde)
2. ¿Vas a hacer un mandado mañana por la mañana? (el sábado por la mañana)
3. ¿Va a comer Mario en un restaurante esta semana? (la semana próxima)
4. ¿Va a estudiar español tu hermano este año? (el año próximo)
5. ¿Van al cine tú y Yolanda esta noche? (el viernes por la noche)
6. ¿Va a usar el coche tu hermana esta tarde? (el domingo por la tarde)
7. ¿Van a llegar tus abuelos hoy? (el jueves próximo)
8. ¿Vas a estudiar ahora? (esta noche)

G. El horario (schedule) de los González

Answer the questions about what the González family did during the month of February. Choose the appropriate time expressions, assuming that today is the morning of February 15. Follow the models.

lunes	martes	miércoles	jueves	viernes	sábado	domingo
1	2	3	4	5 *restaurante*	6	7 *iglesia*
8	9	10	11	12 *restaurante*	13	14 *iglesia*
15 *Sr y Sra. teatro en el centro (noche)*	16 *Sr. jugar al tenis*	17 *Sr. trabajo (noche)*	18 *Sra. museo*	19 *Sra. trabajo (mañana) restaurante*	20 *Sra. curso de francés (tarde)*	21 *iglesia*
22 *catedral*	23 *los Martínez*	24	25	26 *restaurante*	27	28 *iglesia*

FEBRERO

MODELO   ¿Cuándo va a visitar el museo la Sra. González?
El jueves.

1. ¿Qué noche va a trabajar el Sr. González?
2. ¿Cuándo van a visitar los González la catedral?
3. ¿Cuándo van a comer en un restaurante?
4. ¿Cuándo van a llegar los Martínez?
5. ¿Cuándo va a jugar al tenis el Sr. González?
6. ¿Qué mañana va a trabajar la Sra. González?

MODELO   ¿Qué va a hacer el Sr. González el miércoles por la noche?
Él va a trabajar.

7. ¿Qué van a hacer los González esta noche?
8. ¿Qué van a hacer el Sr. y la Sra. González el domingo?
9. ¿Qué va a hacer la Sra. González el sábado por la tarde?
10. ¿Qué van a hacer los González el viernes próximo?

Aquí escuchamos

¿Tomamos el metro? *Elena and Francisco are making plans to go downtown.*

Antes de escuchar Based on what you've learned in this **etapa,** what do you expect Elena and Francisco might say about why they have to go downtown and about how they will get there?

 A escuchar Listen twice to the conversation between Elena and Francisco. Pay special attention to what they plan to do and how they plan to get there.

Después de escuchar Answer the following questions based on what you heard.

1. Why does Elena want to go downtown?
2. What does Francisco want to do?
3. How does Francisco suggest they go?
4. Where will they get on the subway?
5. Where do they change trains?

¿Qué dirección tomamos?   You and your family are staying in Madrid at a hotel near the Plaza de Castilla (line 1). You need to go to the American Express office near Banco de España (line 2). You have just arrived in Madrid and do not understand the subway system yet, so you ask the desk clerk for help. Have a classmate play the role of the desk clerk. After he (she) explains how to get there, you repeat the instructions to make sure you have understood. Use the metro map on page 259.

Muchas cosas que hacer   A foreign exchange student from Caracas will arrive at your school next week. You and two partners want to introduce the student to some of your favorite places and activities. You will have a week of vacation left before classes, so you can plan your schedule over several days.

1. Begin by brainstorming on places to go (favorite restaurants, museums, parks) and things to do (concerts, movies, parties, sports).
2. Narrow your list down so that you have time to do it all during your vacation.
3. Then write out a schedule, beginning when your guest arrives (**llega**). Decide on which days and at what time of day you will do each item on your list (**el sábado próximo por la tarde, el martes entre el mediodía y las tres,** etc.).

Mis actividades este mes   Make a calendar for the current month and indicate what you will be doing on various days of the month. Use the calendar in activity G on page 263 as an example.

DICIEMBRE

lunes	martes	miércoles	jueves	viernes	sábado	domingo
1	2	3	4	5	6	7
8	9	10	11	12	13	14
15	16	17	18	19	20	21
22	23	24	25	26	27	28

- What does it cost to ride public transportation in your town or city?
- Do you pay with currency or can you use tokens?
- Can you use a pass?
- What do you do if you do not have exact change?

En la taquilla

*Elena y Clara entran en la estación del metro y van a la **taquilla** (ticket booth).*

Elena: ¿Vas a comprar un **billete sencillo**?

Clara: No, voy a comprar un **billete de diez viajes**. Es más **barato**. Un billete sencillo **cuesta** 125 pesetas y un billete de diez viajes cuesta 625. ¿Y tú, vas a comprar un billete?

Elena: No, yo tengo una **tarjeta de abon transportes**. Con esta tarjeta puedo tomar el metro o el autobús **sin** límite por **un mes entero**.

Clara: ¡Qué bien! Por favor, señorita, un billete de diez viajes.

La empleada: Seiscientas veinticinco pesetas, señorita.

billete sencillo *single ticket*   billete de diez viajes *ten-ride ticket*   barato *cheap*   cuesta *costs*
tarjeta de abono transportes *commuter pass*   sin *without*   un mes entero *a whole month*

¡Te toca a ti!

A. En la taquilla

At the ticket booth, ask for the indicated metro tickets. Follow the model.

MODELO
1 ticket
Un billete sencillo, por favor.

1. 2 tickets
2. 1 book of ten tickets
3. 2 books of ten tickets
4. 1 ticket that allows you to travel for a month

B. En el metro

Explain to the people described in the following activity how to take the subway to get where they need to go. Specify the kind of ticket they need to buy. Consult the **metro** map on page 259. **Metro** line numbers are given in parentheses. Follow the model.

MODELO
Your friend Andrea is with you near Menéndez Pelayo (1). She wants to go to Estrecho (1).
Tú vas a la estación Menéndez Pelayo. Compras un billete sencillo, tomas la dirección de Plaza de Castilla y bajas en Estrecho.

1. Gina, your Italian friend, is in Madrid for a couple of days. Her hotel is near Cuatro Caminos (2). She wants to go see a church that is near Atocha (1).

2. Mr. and Mrs. Dumond, French friends of your family, are spending three weeks in Madrid. Their hotel is near the Cruz del Rayo station (9) and they want to go to the bullfights. The Madrid Plaza de Toros *(bullring)* is near the Ventas station (2).

3. Near the Delicias station (3), you meet a disoriented tourist who wants to get to the American Express office near the Banco de España station (2).

—**Un billete sencillo, por favor.**

Comentarios CULTURALES

Billetes para el transporte público

Metro tickets in Spain can be bought singly **(un billete sencillo)** or in groups of ten **(un billete de diez viajes).** Also available are three-day or five-day tourist tickets **(un metrotour de tres días** or **de cinco días).** You can also buy a full-month commuter pass **(una tarjeta de abono transportes),** which allows unlimited use of the buses as well as the subway for the specific month.

Repaso

C. ¿Qué haces? Using the adverbs of time that you learned on page 261, tell your classmates about your usual activities (**los sábados, los lunes por la mañana,** etc.) and then about your upcoming plans (**el sábado próximo, el lunes próximo,** etc.). Follow the model.

MODELO
los lunes / el lunes próximo
Usualmente, los lunes voy a la escuela.
Pero el lunes próximo voy a visitar a mis abuelos.

1. los sábados por la tarde / el sábado próximo
2. los viernes por la noche / el viernes próximo
3. los domingos por la mañana / el domingo próximo
4. los lunes por la mañana / el lunes próximo
5. los jueves por la tarde / el jueves próximo
6. los sábados / el sábado próximo por la noche

ESTRUCTURA

The verb **pensar** and **pensar + infinitive**

pensar (ie) *(to think, to plan)*			
yo	**pie**nso	nosotros(as)	pensamos
tú	**pie**nsas	vosotros(as)	pensáis
él ella Ud.	**pie**nsa	ellos ellas Uds.	**pie**nsan

1. Like **querer** and **preferir**, **pensar** is a stem-changing, **e** to **ie** verb.

2. When **pensar** is followed by an infinitive, it means *to plan (to do something)*. This construction is useful for talking or writing about your future plans.

—¿Qué **piensas hacer** mañana?	*What do you plan to do tomorrow?*
—**Pienso ir** al centro.	*I plan to go downtown.*
—¿Qué **piensa hacer** Juan esta noche?	*What does Juan plan to do tonight?*
—**Piensa estudiar** en la biblioteca.	*He plans to study at the library.*

Aquí practicamos

D. ¿Qué piensan hacer? Using words from each column, create sentences that express future plans.

A	B	C	D
Julia	pensar	ir al cine	mañana por la tarde
Enrique y yo		comer en un restaurante	el sábado por la noche
tú		hacer un mandado	el viernes por la tarde
yo		estudiar	mañana
Uds.		dar un paseo	

¿Qué crees?

What city does not have a subway system?

a) Barcelona, Spain
b) Buenos Aires, Argentina
c) Bogotá, Colombia
d) Mexico City, Mexico

respuesta ☞

E. Piensan hacer otra cosa (something else) Your father asks if you plan to go to the movies with your friends. Explain to him that your friends all seem to have other plans. Follow the model.

> **MODELO**   Susana / ir a un concierto
> **Tu padre:**   *¿Piensas ir al cine con Susana?*
> **Tú:**   *No, ella piensa ir a un concierto.*

1. Esteban / ver a un amigo en el centro
2. tus hermanos / comer en un restaurante
3. Linda / ir a la biblioteca
4. tus primos / dar un paseo
5. José y Catarina / mirar la televisión en casa
6. Anita / ir de compras con su madre

Aquí escuchamos

¿Qué piensan hacer? *Elena and Francisco are talking about their plans for the weekend.*

Antes de escuchar Based on what you have learned in this **etapa,** what words and expressions do you expect Elena and Francisco to use to ask each other about their plans and to say what they might do?

 A escuchar Listen twice to the conversation between Francisco and Elena. Pay particular attention to what they say they will do each day.

Después de escuchar Answer the following questions based on what you heard.

1. What does Elena plan to do on Friday?
2. What does Francisco plan to do on Friday?
3. What does Elena plan to do on Saturday?
4. What does Francisco plan to do on Saturday?
5. What will they do on Saturday night?

Hoy pensamos ir al cine.

c

Por favor... You have now become an expert on the Madrid **metro.** While you are waiting at the Plaza de Colón station (4) for a bus to take you to the airport for your trip home, a group of Japanese tourists, just arriving in Madrid, ask you for help in getting to their hotel near the Puerta del Sol station (1). Give them directions, referring to the map on page 259. Have one of your classmates play the role of the group leader for the tourists.

¿Qué piensas hacer la semana próxima? Write a note to a friend indicating at least one thing you plan to do each day next week. Specify when you will do each thing by using **por la mañana, por la tarde,** and **por la noche.** Add a sentence in which you say that you *want* to do one of the activities and that you *have* to do another one.

EN LÍNEA

Connect with the Spanish-speaking world! Access the **¡Ya verás!** Gold home page for Internet activities related to this chapter.

http://yaveras.heinle.com

VOCABULARIO

Para charlar	Temas y contextos	Vocabulario general

Para tomar el metro

Bajamos en Plaza de España.
bajar
Cambiamos en Sol.
cambiar
¿En qué dirección?

Para hablar del futuro

pensar + *infinitive*
esta semana
este mes
este año
la semana entera
el mes entero
el año entero
la semana próxima
el mes próximo
el año próximo
el domingo por la noche

El metro

un billete sencillo
un billete de diez viajes
una entrada
una estación de metro
una línea
un metrotour de tres días
un metrotour de cinco días
un plano del metro
una taquilla
una tarjeta de abono transportes

Otras palabras y expresiones

barato
cuesta
un horario
jóvenes
jugar (al tenis)
sin

Viaje por *Latinoamérica*

Antes de leer

1. Skim the first paragraph. What is this reading going to be about?

2. What means of transportation are available where you live?

3. Do you know of any places where people get around differently? What forms of transportation are used there?

Reading Strategies
• Skimming for the gist
• Activating back-ground knowledge

El transporte en América Latina varía de país en país. Hay aviones, trenes, metros, autobuses, taxis, y coches particulares y otras formas de transporte modernas en todos los países. También hay formas de transporte más interesantes para los aventureros. Todo depende de la geografía o la cultura del país y dónde quieres ir.

Colombia fue el primer país en Sudamérica en tener una línea aérea. Se estableció como ACADTA en 1919 y ahora se llama Avianca. Las líneas aéreas colombianas tienen aviones enormes y avionetas pequeñas que vuelan entre las ciudades de Sudamérica y por el resto del mundo. Dentro de Colombia, otras formas de transporte incluyen las chivas— antiguos auto-buses de madera usados en áreas rurales— y los colectivos, entre un autobús y un taxi de tamaño.

También hay muchos trenes y metros. Ciudades como Caracas y la Ciudad de México disfru-tan de unos sistemas de trenes subterráneos rápidos y baratos. El metro de la Ciudad de México es uno de los sistemas más extensos del mundo. Al contraste, Paraguay tiene trenes anticuados de vapor, a base de leña. No son caros y ofrecen la oportunidad de viajar tranquilamente.

Si prefieres viajar en barco, hay muchos cruceros de lujo que viajan entre las ciudades latinoaméricanas y las islas del Caribe. También hay partes de la costa nicaragüense del Caribe y en el Lago de Nicaragua que sólo tienen acceso por barco. En Panamá los barcos son el medio principal de transporte en varias zonas.

Algunos sitios son bellos pero pocos accesibles. Venezuela, por ejemplo, tiene unos 40 parques nacionales que ofrecen una gran variedad de excursiones. Hay caminos bien marca-dos y caminos en la jungla que requieren un guía y machete. Para viajar al Salto Aponguao, una de las cataratas más espectaculares, tienes que salir de la carretera, viajar 40 kilómetros por caminos pequeños al pueblo indio de Iboribó, pagarle a un residente para que te lleve por canoa por el Río Aponguao, y caminar media hora hasta llegar a la catarata. Pero vale la pena porque se puede ver una catarata bellísima y nadar en las piscinas naturales debajo.

Guía para la lectura

Here are some words and expressions to keep in mind as you read.

línea aérea	*airline*
vuelan	*fly*
avionetas	*small, 2-engine planes*
madera	*wood*
tamaño	*size*
disfrutan	*enjoy*
vapor	*steam*
leña	*firewood*
barco	*ship, boat*
cruceros de lujo	*luxury cruise ships*
caminos	*paths*
cataratas	*waterfalls*
carretera	*highway*
para que te lleve	*to take you*

Después de leer

1. The reading mentioned various types of transportation in Latin America. Which types of transportation did you find particularly interesting? Explain your choices.

2. Do you enjoy challenges in getting places, or do you prefer to use quick and easy forms of transportation? Why?

3. Technology is gradually changing the face of transportation around the world. Do you think the more colorful forms of transportation in Latin America, such as wooden buses, canoes and steam-powered trains, will survive through the 21st century? Why or why not?

4. In your opinion, what kinds of transportation will be available around the world in 20 years? In 50 years?

CAPÍTULO 12

¿Cómo vamos?

—¿Cómo vamos? ¿A pie o en el coche de tu padre?
—Vamos en autobús.

Objectives

- taking a taxi
- expressing wishes and desires

Preparación

- Have you ever taken a taxi?
- What information must you give to the taxi driver?
- What information can you expect him or her to give you?
- What do you know about payment?
- Are you expected to give a tip?

¡Vamos a tomar un taxi!

*Linda y Julia van a una **agencia de viajes** (travel agency) pero **antes** (before), van a **almorzar** (eat lunch) en un restaurante que está cerca de la agencia. Piensan tomar un taxi.*

Linda:	¡Taxi! ¡Taxi!
El chófer:	¿Señoritas? ¿Adónde van? *Ellas suben* (get in) *al taxi.*
Linda:	Queremos ir al Restaurante Julián Rojo, avenida Ventura de la Vega 5, por favor. **¿Cuánto tarda** para llegar?
El chófer:	Diez minutos... quince **como máximo.**

*Ellas llegan al restaurante. Julia baja del taxi y Linda va a **pagar.***

Linda:	¿Cuánto es, señor?
El chófer:	**Trescientas ochenta** pesetas, señorita.
Linda:	Aquí tiene **quinientas** pesetas, señor.
El chófer:	Aquí tiene Ud. el **cambio, ciento veinte** pesetas.

*Linda le **da** 70 pesetas al chófer como **propina.***

Linda:	Y **esto es para Ud.**, señor.
El chófer:	Muchas gracias, señorita. Hasta luego.

Cuánto tarda *How long does it take* **como máximo** *at most* **pagar** *to pay* **trescientas ochenta** *Three hundred eighty* **quinientas** *five hundred* **cambio** *change* **ciento veinte** *one hundred twenty* **da** *gives* **propina** *tip* **esto es para Ud.** *this is for you*

¡Te toca a ti!

A. ¿Adónde van?
A taxi driver asks you where you and a friend are going. Have a classmate play the driver. Tell him (her) the name of the place and the address. Follow the model.

> **MODELO** Restaurante Capri / calle Barco 27
> **Compañera(o):** ¿Adónde van?
> **Tú:** *Queremos ir al Restaurante Capri, Calle Barco 27.*

1. Hotel Praga / calle Antonio López 65
2. Restaurante Trafalgar / calle Trafalgar 35
3. Hotel Don Diego / calle Velázquez 45
4. Café Elche / calle Vilá-Vilá 71
5. Hotel Ramón de la Cruz / calle Don Ramón de la Cruz 91

B. ¿Cuánto tarda para llegar?
As you make plans with a friend, you discuss how long it will take to get to your destination. The answer will depend on the means of transportation you choose. Remember that in Spanish the preposition **en** is used in the expressions **en coche, en autobús, en metro, en taxi,** and **en bicicleta,** but **a** is used in **a pie.** Follow the model.

> **MODELO** al parque / en autobús (10 minutos) / a pie (30 o 35 minutos)
> **Tú:** *¿Cuánto tardas para ir al parque?*
> **Amigo(a):** *Para ir al parque en autobús, tardo diez minutos.*
> **Tú:** *¿Y para llegar a pie?*
> **Amigo(a):** *¿A pie? Tardo treinta o (or) treinta y cinco minutos.*

1. a la biblioteca / a pie (25 minutos) / en bicicleta (10 minutos)
2. a la catedral / en metro (20 minutos) / en autobús (25 o 30 minutos)
3. al aeropuerto / en taxi (45 minutos) / en metro (30 o 35 minutos)
4. a la estación de trenes / en coche (20 minutos) / en metro (10 minutos)
5. al centro / a pie (35 minutos) / en autobús (15 minutos)

PRONUNCIACIÓN THE CONSONANT ll

You will recall when you learned the alphabet in **Capítulo 1** that the letters **ll** represent a sound in Spanish that is similar to the *y* in the English word *yes*.

Práctica

C. Listen as your teacher models the following words.

1. llamar	4. tortilla	7. ella	9. maravilla
2. calle	5. ellos	8. Sevilla	10. pollo
3. milla	6. llegar		

Repaso ♻

D. Pensamos hacer... Think of four different things that you plan to do during the coming week and write them down. Then ask several classmates about their plans. When you find someone who plans to do something that is on your list, try to arrange a day and time that you can do it together. Follow the model.

MODELO		
	Estudiante 1:	*¡Hola! ¿Qué piensas hacer esta semana?*
	Estudiante 2:	*Pienso ver una película el sábado próximo por la tarde.*
	Estudiante 1:	*Bueno, yo quiero ir al cine también. Vamos juntos.*
	Estudiante 2:	*Buena idea. ¿A qué hora quieres ir?*
	Estudiante 1:	*¿A la una?*
	Estudiante 2:	*De acuerdo.* o: *No puedo a la una porque tengo que hacer mandados con mi madre. ¿Puedes ir a las cuatro?*

Comentarios CULTURALES

La Puerta del Sol en Madrid

La Puerta del Sol is one of the most lively and popular **plazas** in Madrid. Several **metro** lines intersect there, and it is the location of **kilómetro 0,** the point from which official distances from Madrid to other cities in Spain and Portugal are measured. Below are the official distances from the capital to some major Spanish and Portuguese cities. Note that distances in Spain, as well as in most Spanish-speaking countries, are measured in kilometers **(kilómetros),** the metric equivalent of about 5/8 of a mile **(milla).**

Segovia	99 km	Granada	423 km
Salamanca	209 km	Málaga	532 km
Burgos	237 km	Porto	561 km
Valencia	351 km	Barcelona	617 km
Córdoba	389 km	Cádiz	624 km
Pamplona	401 km	Lisboa	632 km

¿Qué crees?

The distance between Madrid, Spain, and Paris, France is approximately equal to the distance between:

a) Detroit, MI and Atlanta, GA
b) Boston, MA and Washington DC
c) Chicago, IL and New Orleans, LA
d) Albuquerque, NM and Oklahoma, OK.

respuesta ☞

PALABRAS ÚTILES

Numbers from 100 to 1,000,000

100	cien	1.000	mil
101	ciento uno	2.000	dos mil
102	ciento dos	4.576	cuatro mil quinientos setenta y seis
200	doscientos(as)	25.489	veinticinco mil cuatrocientos ochenta y nueve
300	trescientos(as)	1.000.000	un millón
400	cuatrocientos(as)	2.000.000	dos millones
500	quinientos(as)		
600	seiscientos(as)		
700	setecientos(as)		
800	ochocientos(as)		
900	novecientos(as)		

PALABRAS ÚTILES (continued)

1. The word **cien** is used before a noun: **cien** discos compactos.

2. **Ciento** is used with numbers from 101 to 199. There is no **y** following the word **ciento**: 120 = **ciento veinte.**

3. **Cientos** changes to **cientas** before a feminine noun: **doscientos hombres, doscientas mujeres.**

4. Spanish uses a period where English uses a comma: **3.400** = 3,400 (three thousand four hundred).

5. **Millón/millones** is followed by **de** when it accompanies a noun: **un millón de dólares, tres millones de habitantes.**

Aquí practicamos

☞ a

E. **Los números**   Read the following numbers out loud.

1.	2.	3.	4.	5.
278	1.800	11.297	225.489	1.500.000
546	5.575	35.578	369.765	2.800.000
156	7.902	49.795	569.432	56.250.000
480	3.721	67.752	789.528	76.450.000
610	6.134	87.972	852.289	
817		98.386		
729				

F. **¿Cuál es la distancia entre Madrid y...?**   Take turns with a partner asking and answering questions about the distance between Madrid and each of the following cities. Consult the chart that follows to find the information you will need for your answers. Take notes and together create a list of the cities in the order of their distance from Madrid. Start your list with the city that is closest. Follow the model.

> **MODELO**   Segovia / Lisboa
>
> **Estudiante 1:**   *¿Cuál es la distancia entre Madrid y Segovia?*
> **Estudiante 2:**   *Noventa y nueve kilómetros.*
> **Estudiante 1:**   *¿Está más lejos que Lisboa?*
> **Estudiante 2:**   *No, Lisboa está a seiscientos treinta y dos kilómetros de Madrid.*

1. Valencia / Lisboa
2. Granada / Porto
3. Pamplona / Barcelona
4. Burgos / Málaga

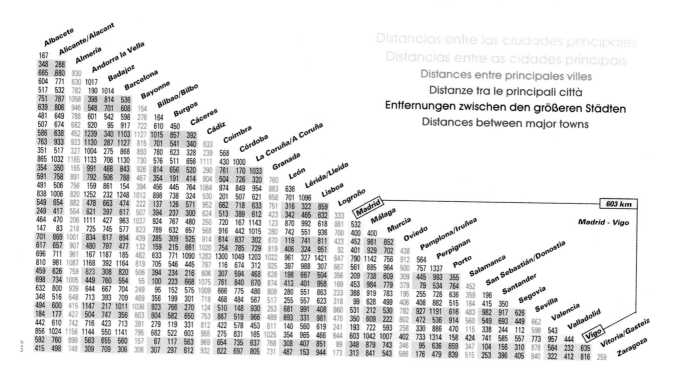

Aquí escuchamos

¡Taxi, taxi! *Elena and Francisco are going to take a taxi to a museum in the city.*

Antes de escuchar Based on what you've learned in this **etapa,** what do you expect Elena and Francisco 1) to ask the taxi driver, 2) to tell the taxi driver, and 3) to be told by the taxi driver?

A escuchar Listen twice to the conversation and pay special attention to the numbers mentioned.

Después de escuchar Answer the following questions based on what you heard.

1. Where do Elena and Francisco want to go?
2. What is the name of the street?
3. What is the street number?
4. How long will it take to get there?
5. How much did the taxi ride cost?

Tenemos que tomar un taxi. You are in Madrid with your parents, who don't speak Spanish. They want to go from their hotel (the Euro Building) to the Plaza Mayor. They ask you to go with them in a taxi. A classmate will play the role of the taxi driver.

1. Hail the taxi.
2. Tell the driver where you want to go.
3. Ask if your destination is nearby.
4. Ask how long the trip will take.
5. On arriving at your destination, ask how much the ride costs.
6. Give the driver a tip.

 ¿Cuál es la distancia entre Washington, DC, y...? In Washington, DC, there is also a point from which distances are measured. It is on the Ellipse, between the White House and the Washington Monument. A friend from Spain writes to you and is curious about distances between Washington, DC, and some other major cities, including where you live. Choose two cities in addition to your own and find out what the distances are. Write a letter giving your friend the information.

Preparación

- Have you ever been to a travel agency?
- When would you go to one?
- Where would you want to go on a trip?

En la agencia de viajes

Linda y Julia visitan la
agencia de viajes.

Agente:	**¿En qué puedo servirles?**
Linda:	Queremos planear un **viaje.**
Agente:	¿Adónde piensan ir?
Linda:	**Esperamos** viajar a París. ¿Cuánto cuesta viajar a París **en avión?**
Agente:	Muchísimo. Un **viaje de ida y vuelta** cuesta 31.000 pesetas.
Julia:	¿Y en tren?
Agente:	En tren es más barato. Un billete de ida y vuelta **sólo** cuesta 15.000 pesetas.
Linda:	**Es mucho. Sólo tengo** 10.000 pesetas y mi amiga tiene 9.000.
Agente:	Entonces, por 7.000 pesetas pueden ir a Barcelona o a Málaga.
Julia:	¡Mm, Málaga tiene unas **playas hermosas!**
Linda:	¡Buena idea! Pero primero tenemos que discutir los planes con nuestros padres.
Agente:	Muy bien. **Aquí estoy para servirles.**
Linda:	Muchísimas gracias.
Julia:	Hasta luego.

¿En qué puedo servirles? *How may I help you?*   **viaje** *trip*   **Esperamos** *We hope*   **en avión** *by plane*
viaje de ida y vuelta *round trip*   **en tren** *by train*   **sólo** *only*   **Es mucho.** *That's a lot.*   **Sólo tengo** *I only have*
playas hermosas *gorgeous beaches*   **Aquí estoy para servirles.** *I'm here to help you.*

¡Te toca a ti!

A. ¿Adónde esperas viajar?
Tell where you hope to travel, using the cities listed. Follow the model.

MODELO   San Juan
Espero viajar a San Juan.

1. San José
2. Lisboa
3. París
4. Nueva York
5. Quito

6. San Antonio
7. Seattle
8. Buenos Aires
9. Miami
10. Bogotá

B. ¿Adónde quiere viajar?
Tell where each of the people in the drawings below want to travel based on what it says on their luggage.

1. Sr. y Sra. Cano

2. Raúl

3. Bárbara

4. los estudiantes

5. tú

6. yo

C. Una encuesta
Ask as many classmates as possible where they hope to travel.

Repaso ♻

D. ¿Cuánto es? You and a friend are going over how much money you have paid for certain things. Each time you say a price, your friend asks for confirmation so you repeat more clearly. Follow the model.

> **MODELO** 320
>
> **Tú:** *Trescientos veinte.*
> **Amiga(o):** *¿Cuánto?*
> **Tú:** *Trescientas veinte pesetas.*

1. 430
2. 350
3. 1.250
4. 790

5. 940
6. 7.500
7. 860
8. 670

9. 30.750
10. 570
11. 760
12. 2.400.000

ESTRUCTURA

Esperar + infinitive and a summary of expressions for discussing plans

Espero comprar un coche nuevo el año próximo.	*I hope to buy a new car next year.*
Esperamos ir al cine el viernes próximo.	*We hope to go to the movies next Friday.*

1. **Esperar** *(to hope)* is a regular **-ar** verb. Like the other constructions you have learned for expressing future plans (**querer, pensar, ir a**), it is followed by an infinitive.

2. Note how the meanings of the four constructions you have learned for expressing future actions progress from uncertain to certain.

Quiero comprar un coche nuevo.	*I want to buy a new car.*
Espero comprar un coche nuevo.	*I hope to buy a new car.*
Pienso comprar un coche nuevo.	*I plan to buy a new car.*
Voy a comprar un coche nuevo.	*I am going to buy a new car.*

Aquí practicamos

E. En el futuro Using words from each column of the following table, form sentences to discuss future plans.

A	B	C	D
yo Uds. nosotros Esteban Linda y su amiga tú	(no)	esperar pensar ir a querer	viajar a Argentina algún día visitar a un(a) amigo(a) en Boston el mes próximo cenar con un(a) amigo(a) el sábado por la noche vivir en Colombia el año próximo

F. Algún día Indicate how each person in parentheses feels about doing the following activities. Use the verbs **esperar, pensar, querer,** and **ir a.** Follow the model.

> **MODELO** ir a Panamá (tu padre / tus amigos / tú)
> *Mi padre no quiere ir a Panamá.*
> *Mis amigos esperan ir a Panamá algún día.*
> *Yo pienso ir a Panamá el año próximo.*

1. ir a Lima (tu madre / tus hermanos [hermanas, amigos] / tú)
2. ser presidente (tú y tus amigos / tu padre / tu hermana [amigo])
3. tener un Rolls Royce (tu padre / tus amigos / tú)
4. vivir en Alaska (tu madre / tu hermana [hermano, amigo] / tú)

G. Intercambio Ask the following questions of a classmate, who will answer them.

1. ¿Qué piensas hacer esta noche?
2. ¿Qué vas a hacer el sábado por la tarde?
3. ¿Qué tienes ganas de hacer el sábado?
4. ¿Qué quieres hacer el domingo?
5. ¿Qué piensas hacer el año próximo?
6. ¿Qué esperas hacer algún día?

Aquí escuchamos

Vamos de viaje *Elena and Francisco are going to a travel agent to talk about plans for a trip.*

> **Antes de escuchar** Based on what you've learned in this **etapa,** what information do you expect Elena and Francisco to find out from the travel agent?

 A escuchar Listen twice to the conversation before answering the questions about it that follow.

Después de escuchar Answer the following questions based on what you heard.

1. Where do Elena and Francisco want to go at the beginning of the conversation?
2. What is the price if they go by train?
3. What is the price if they fly?
4. Where do they decide to go?
5. How will they get there?

¡ADELANTE!

 ¿Qué planes tienes para el verano próximo?
You and a partner are making plans to spend part of next summer together.

1. Agree to take a trip to at least three major destinations. **(Pensamos viajar a…)**
2. Determine at least one good reason to go to each place that you plan to visit. **(Quiero… Deseo ver… Me gusta ir de compras.)**
3. Decide on how long you will stay at each place. **(Pensamos estar allí cinco días.)**
4. Determine a means of transportation to use while at each destination. **(en taxi, en autobús, a pie)**
5. Decide how to get there and back. **(en avión, en tren)**
6. Estimate how much the transportation and lodging portions of your trip will cost. **(Un viaje de ida y vuelta cuesta…)**

 La semana próxima Write a note to a friend indicating your plans for each day of next week. Use each of the expressions for making plans that you've learned in this **etapa.**

 **EN LÍNEA**

Connect with the Spanish-speaking world!
Access the **¡Ya verás!** *Gold* home page for
Internet activities related to this chapter.

http://yaveras.heinle.com

VOCABULARIO

Para charlar

Para ir al centro

¿Cuánto tarda en
  llegar a…?
Tarda diez minutos,
  como máximo.
Esto es para Ud., señor
  (señora, señorita).

Para viajar

Aquí estoy para servirles.
¿En qué puedo servirles?
Queremos planear un viaje.
¿Cuánto cuesta un viaje
  de ida y vuelta en avión?
Es mucho. Sólo tengo
  2.500 pesetas.

Los planes

esperar + *infinitive*

Para contar

cien
ciento
ciento veinte
doscientos(as)
trescientos(as)
cuatrocientos(as)
quinientos(as)
seiscientos(as)
setecientos(as)
ochocientos(as)
novecientos(as)
mil
un millón

Temas y contextos

Los viajes

una agencia de viajes
billete de ida y vuelta
en avión
en taxi
en tren
kilómetro
milla
propina

Vocabulario general

Sustantivos

el cambio
la playa

Verbos

almorzar
discutir
pagar

Adjetivos

famoso(a)
hermoso(a)
nuevo(a)

Otras palabras y expresiones

algún día
antes
o
si
sólo

Explora el "Agua Grande"

Antes de leer

1. The title indicates that the reading is about a scenic attraction that some call *Agua Grande*. Why might a place be called *Agua Grande*?

2. What kinds of brochures would you expect to pick up at the information center in a national park? What information would such brochures usually contain?

3. Briefly scan the brochures about the Parque Nacional de Iguazú. Where are the Iguazú falls located?

Parque Nacional del Iguazú

**Horas: 7:30 A.M.-12:00 A.M. lunes a domingo
*Estación de primeros auxilios, Cuartos de baño, Cafetería***

Datos importantes:

- Las cataratas del Iguazú (que significa "Agua grande" en el idioma guaraní) están localizadas en la frontera entre Brasil y Argentina, y son las cataratas más espectaculares de Sudamérica.

- El sistema de cataratas tiene forma de herradura y tiene aproximadamente dos y media millas de ancho.

- Numerosas islas dividen las aguas en 275 cascadas, con un altitud de entre 200 y 269 pies.

Algunos puntos de interés:

- Puerto Peligro e Isla de San Martín
- Catarata principal: Garganta del diablo
- Cataratas mayores: Arrechea, San Martín, Tres mosqueteros
- Recorridos por la selva: camino Yacaretea y camino Macuco

Iguazú desde un helicóptero

Guía para la lectura

Here are some words and expressions to keep in mind as you read.

Recorrido	*tour*
Estación de primeros auxilios	*First aid station*
herradura	*horseshoe*
selva	*jungle*
estadía	*stay, sojourn*
nocturnos	*nighttime*

Agencia turística Del Salto:
Iguazú

Guía de excursiones: Costos y medios de transporte (pesos argentinos)

Excursión para acampar . . . . Duración: 3 días
Costo: 87,00 por día.

Recorrido de las cataratas . . . . Duración: 3 horas
Costo: 4,00 por persona.

Excursión en helicóptero . . . . Duración: 7 minutos
Costo: 52,00 por persona.

Safari fotográfico (con guía) . . . . . . Duración: 2 horas
Costo: 25,00 por grupo.

Paseos nocturnos por las cataratas.
Costo: 38,00 por persona.

Excursiones Yusumí:. . . . . Duración: 3 días
- Boleto de avión incluido
- Estadía en el Hotel Nacional (cuartos para dos personas)
- Guía turístico especializado
  Costo: 460,00 por persona.

Aventuras en la selva:
- Recorrido en jeep, caballo, bote o canoa . . . . *Costo:* 5,00-25,00 por persona.
- Alquiler de bicicletas de montaña
  Costo: 10,00 por día.
- Alquiler de canoas
  Costo: 10,00 por 30 minutos.

Despúes de leer

1. Mention at least 3 different means of transportation you can use at the park. Which ones would you use to explore the park? Explain your choices.

2. Indicate whether the following statements are true or false. Please correct the false statements.

   a. The falls have a rectangular shape.

   b. There are few means of transportation available to explore the Falls.

   c. Iguazú means *Fast Water*.

   d. You can rent a mountain bike at the falls.

   e. You need to get your own guide if you participate in one of the *Excursiones Yusumí*.

   f. You can see the waterfalls during the nighttime.

3. Would you enjoy visiting this park? Why or why not? What other scenic areas would you like to visit? Why?

Conversemos un rato

A. Explorando Quito Role-play the following situations.

1. You have just met a young traveler in Quito, Ecuador and the two of you decide to travel together for a few days. First you must get acquainted with each other. Some places to go to in Quito include many cathedrals and churches, museums (the Museo Aqueológico and Casa de la Cultura), El Jido park, the Colonial City, and shopping in outdoor markets or La Avenida Amazonas.

   a. Greet your new friend and invite him/her to join you for a drink at a café.

   b. Tell each other where you are from and what types of activities you like to do.

   c. Discuss three things you each would like to do in Quito, Ecuador.

   d. Then decide on one thing to do together and make plans to get together.

2. You and your new friend are making plans to spend Saturday in downtown Quito.

   a. Decide when and where you will meet.

   b. Agree on four places to visit or activities to do together.

   c. Decide on the best means of transportation to get downtown and back home.

   d. Finally describe your itinerary to two other classmates and invite them to go with you. Make any necessary changes to your plans to convince them to accompany you.

Taller de escritores

Writing a letter

In this unit you will write a letter describing a place you'd like to visit. A sample letter follows.

21 de septiembre de 19__

Querida Estela,

¡Estoy muy contenta! Mis padres me van a llevar a México. Vamos a pasar la semana de vacaciones en Manzanillo en el Hotel Las Hadas. Mi padre va hoy a la agencia de viajes para comprar los **boletos de avión**. Pensamos salir de aquí el 26 de diciembre y volver el 2 de enero. ¡Qué bueno, ¿verdad?!

Dicen mis padres que vamos a pasar un día en Colima donde hay un museo arqueológico muy interesante. Interesante para ellos. No me interesa mucho. Yo tengo ganas de pasar todo el tiempo en la playa. Mi madre dice que puedo comprar un **traje de baño** nuevo antes de ir. Voy a ir de compras mañana. ¡No puedo esperar!

Te escribo con más detalles.

Miles de besos y abrazos de

Carolina

Querida *Dear*   boletos de avión *airline tickets*   traje de baño *bathing suit*
Miles de besos y abrazos de *lots of hugs and kisses from*

A. Reflexión First think of a place you would like to go, then write down as many ideas about that place as possible. Create two major ideas and relate other minor points to each of them. Each cluster then forms the basis for a paragraph.

B. Primer borrador Write the first draft of your letter to your pen pal. To organize your thoughts, use the clusters you created.

C. Revisión con un(a) compañero(a) Exchange letters with a classmate. Read each other's work and comment on it, based on these questions.

1. What aspect of the letter do you like the best?
2. In which activities mentioned would you like to participate?
3. Is the letter appropriate for its audience?
4. Does the letter reflect the task assigned?
5. What aspect of the letter would you like to have clarified or made more complete?

D. Versión final At home revise your first draft, incorporating changes based on the feedback from your classmate. Revise content and check your grammar, spelling, punctuation, and accent marks. Bring your final draft to class.

E. Carpeta After you turn in your letter, your teacher may choose to place it in your portfolio, display it on a bulletin board, or use it to evaluate your progress.

Conexión con la biblioteconomía

Para empezar Most libraries now use computers to store information regarding book location. In fact, many libraries now offer access to books located in other libraries. Nevertheless, most libraries still need to use one of two systems of classification to organize their collection by subject; the Dewey Decimal system or the Library of Congress (LC) system. Do you know which system your school library uses? Which system does your local public library use?

Below is an abridged version of the LC subject headings in Spanish. Single letters indicate the major subject headings and the double letters indicate subcategories within each subject.

Clasificación de la Biblioteca del Congreso

A   *Obras generales*
     AE   Enciclopedias generales
     AG   Diccionarios

B   *Filosofía-religión*
     B   Filosofía general
     BF   Psicología
     BL   Religiones, mitología

D   *Historia y topografía (excepto continentes de América)*
     DP   España y Portugal

E y F   *Historia (los continentes de América)*

G   *Geografía y antropología*
     G   Mapas, átlases
     GR   Folklore
     GV   Recreación y tiempo libre

J   *Ciencia política*
     JK   Historia constitucional (Estados Unidos)
     JV   Colonias y colonización

M   *Música*

N   *Bellas artes y artes visuales*
     NA   Arquitectura
     NC   Dibujo, diseño
     ND   Pintura

P   *Lenguaje y literatura*
     PQ   Literatura romance
     PR   Literatura inglesa
     PS   Literatura de los Estados Unidos

Q   *Ciencias puras*
     QA   Matemáticas
     QB   Astronomía
     QC   Física
     QD   Química
     QE   Geología
     QK   Botánica

S   *Agricultura*

T   *Tecnología*

A. ¿Verdadero o falso?

A classmate has written down call numbers and topics to help you find some books. Decide which of the following are correct (*verdadero*) or incorrect (*falso*), based on the chart above. Then correct the topics and letters that are wrong.

MODELO	Tema	Cifra de clasificación
Ludwig von Beethoven	música	M
1. El Greco	mapas, atlases	G
2. William Shakespeare	literatura inglesa	PR
3. Sigmund Freud	Agricultura	S
4. Stephen Hawkings	Física	QC
5. Albert Einstein	Historia y topografía	D
6. Mikhail Barysnikov	Bellas artes y artes visuales	N

B. En la biblioteca

You are a student library assistant at a school in Bogotá. Today library patrons have been forgetting to write down the first letters of the call numbers. Supply the missing portions of the call numbers for the titles below.

MODELO	*Enciclopedia universal ilustrada*	AE 61.E56 1994
1. *Como agua para chocolate*		__6323.A5A6 1989
2. *El estilo de Frank Lloyd Wright*		__813.G7Z8 1993
3. *Mitología griega y romana*		__725.S62 1998
4. *Música y músicos en Panamá*		__L106.M6T3 1991
5. *Plantas de Costa Rica*		__217.P57 1985
6. *Planetas y satélites*		__501.S3 1997
7. *Historia de Paraguay*		__66.H5572 1995
8. *Atlas geográfico de la República Argentina*		__1755.A77 1992

C. Pair up with a classmate.

Each of you is to write down three topics that interest you, and give them to your partner. Your partner will write the Library of Congress letters which correspond to each topic.

MODELO Uso de las bicicletas de montaña en los Estados Unidos
GV

Vistas

de los países hispanos

México

Capital: Ciudad de México

Ciudades principales: Guadalajara, Monterrey, Puebla, León, Ciudad Juárez

Población: 86.200.000

Idiomas: español

Área territorial: 1.972.547 km^2

Clima: tiene una zona tropical y otra árida; mantiene una variedad climática muy grande.

Moneda: peso

árida *arid*

EXPLORA

Find out more about México! Access the **Nuestros vecinos** page on the *¡Ya verás!* *Gold* web site for a list of URLs.

http://yaveras.heinle.com/vecinos.htm

En la comunidad

"*My father jokes that his daughter works in transportation just as he did. The difference between us, he says, is that he sat still so others could travel, whereas I've always traveled so others didn't have to. My father was an air traffic controller; I'm a regional director for an international company that sells telecommunication equipment and I travel throughout Latin America. When my company wanted to send customer representatives to Central America, where we were selling ever-greater quantities of equipment, I decided I would be that person. I started taking classes in business administration, and set out to refresh my high school Spanish. I took an intensive, day-long class every Saturday, plus I listened to Spanish language-learning tapes in the car as I commuted to work. At the end of two years, my company sent me to Bogotá!*

Now, as the Latin American regional director, I manage eight employees in Bogotá as well as offices in Venezuela, Chile, Argentina, and Costa Rica. I'm the youngest such manager I know, and I spend all day speaking Spanish—to negotiate, to talk to employees and clients, or when I travel."

¡Ahora te toca a ti!

Make your information travel, so you don't have to! Look through classified ads in Spanish to see if there is a job overseas that might interest you. You can use a computer with Internet access, or go to a local library and look at foreign or Spanish edition newspapers (e.g. The Miami Herald). Use the computer or the newspaper to locate the classified (*los clasificados*) section of a Spanish language newspaper. Use a dictionary as necessary to find your dream job. Then write out in Spanish the corresponding information for the list below.

Job Title:

Company:

Newspaper/Source:

Date:

Responsibilities:

Experience needed:

Salary:

UNIDAD 5

Tu tiempo libre

Objectives

In this unit you will learn:

- to understand short readings about various aspects of the Spanish-speaking world
- to find out information about various activities in the Spanish-speaking world
- to talk about past, present, and future activities and events

¿Qué ves?

- Where are the people in the photographs?
- What are they doing?
- What do you see in the photos that is similar to what you would do in the United States?
- What do you see that is different?

Los pasatiempos

Actividades deportivas

Dos deportes populares

CAPÍTULO 13

Los pasatiempos

—Me encanta jugar al tenis.

Objectives

- talking about events and activities that took place in the past
- situating activities in the past

Preparación

- What do you like to do in your free time? Make a list of your favorite activities.

- What don't you like to do? Make a list of these activities.

¿Qué te gusta hacer?

A estas personas les gusta hacer cosas diferentes.

Me gusta ir de compras.

Me gusta leer.

Me gusta hablar por teléfono.

Me gusta escuchar música.

Me gusta alquilar vídeos.

Nos gusta montar en bicicleta.

Me gusta escribir cartas.

Nos gusta ir al cine.

Me gusta nadar.

Me gusta hacer ejercicio.

Nos gusta correr.

Nos gusta bailar.

¡Te toca a ti!

A. Me gusta... Imagine you are the person in the drawings that follow. Respond accordingly when one of your classmates asks you what you like to do. Follow the model.

MODELO ¿Qué te gusta hacer?
Me gusta nadar.

1.   2.   3.   4.

5.   6.   7.   8.

B. **¿Qué te gusta hacer?** Survey your classmates to find out what they like to do and what they don't like to do in their free time. Following the model, interview six classmates in Spanish. They can use the suggested activities or come up with their own. As you interview people, write down their likes and dislikes in the appropriate column on the chart on your activity master.

aprender	charlar	hacer ejercicio
bailar	comer	ir de compras
caminar	correr	mirar
cantar	descansar	trabajar

MODELO

Tú: *¿Qué te gusta hacer en tu tiempo libre?*

Compañero(a): *Me gusta estudiar, pero no me gusta escribir cartas.*

Nos gusta hacer estas actividades	No nos gusta hacer estas actividades
estudiar	*escribir cartas*

When you finish your survey, work in Spanish with a partner to study the results. 1) Compare your lists. Did you both get similar responses? 2) Count the number of times each activity occurs in the "like-to-do" column and how many times each occurs in the "don't-like-to-do" column. 3) Based on your tallies, what are the three most popular leisure activities among your classmates? What are the three least popular? 4) Did any activities come up in both columns?

ESTRUCTURA

Preterite tense of -ar verbs

Yo **hablé** con Juan ayer.

Él **bailó** mucho anoche.

I talked with Juan yesterday.

He danced a lot last night.

Preterite of -ar Verbs		
Subject Pronoun	Verb Ending	Conjugated Form of the Verb **cantar**
yo	**-é**	**canté**
tú	**-aste**	**cantaste**
él ella Ud.	**-ó**	**cantó**
nosotros(as)	**-amos**	**cantamos**
vosotros(as)	**-asteis**	**cantasteis**
ellos ellas Uds.	**-aron**	**cantaron**

1. In Spanish, the preterite is a verb tense used to talk about actions that happened in the past. To conjugate **-ar** verbs in the preterite, drop the **-ar** to find the stem (**cant-** for **cantar**) and add the verb ending that corresponds to the subject. Note that there is a written accent on the endings of the **yo** and the **él, ella, Ud.** forms.

2. You already know several **-ar** verbs such as **alquilar** and **preparar**. Here are some new verbs you should learn:

andar	*to walk*
cenar	*to eat dinner*
cocinar	*to cook*
contestar	*to answer*
desayunar	*to eat breakfast*
invitar	*to invite*
pasar	*to pass, to occur, to spend (time)*
preguntar	*to ask*
terminar	*to finish*
usar	*to use*

Aquí practicamos

C. Anoche (Last night) Di (say) lo que (what) tú y tus amigos hicieron (did) anoche. Sigue (Follow) el modelo.

> **MODELO** Yo compré un disco compacto nuevo.
> Roberto no compró un disco compacto nuevo.

A	B	C	D
yo	(no)	comprar	un programa de televisión
tú		mirar	para un examen
Roberto		estudiar	por teléfono
nosotros		hablar	un disco compacto nuevo
Uds.		escuchar	música rock
Elena y Juan			

D. Por supuesto... Your parents went out to dinner and returned late at night. They ask what you did while they were out. As they ask you questions, answer in the affirmative. Follow the model.

> **MODELO** ¿Terminaste tu tarea?
> Sí, por supuesto, terminé mi tarea.

1. ¿Hablaste por teléfono con tu amigo?
2. ¿Cenaste aquí?
3. ¿Estudiaste para el examen de español?
4. ¿Miraste un programa de televisión?
5. ¿Tomaste algo (something)?

E. El sábado pasado (Last Saturday) Pregúntales (Ask) a tus compañeros(as) lo que hicieron el sábado pasado. Usa preguntas (questions) de tipo **sí/no** con las actividades que siguen (that follow). Sigue el modelo.

> **MODELO** Tú: ¿Estudiaste el sábado pasado?
> Compañero(a): No, no estudié el sábado pasado. o:
> Sí, estudié para mi examen
> de matemáticas.

alquilar un vídeo

caminar al centro

cenar con un(a) amigo(a)

comprar un disco compacto

desayunar en un restaurante

escuchar tu estéreo

hablar por teléfono

mirar televisión

pasar tiempo con tu familia

visitar a un(a) amigo(a)

The preterite of the verb hacer

—¿Qué **hizo** Tomás ayer?
—Tomás habló con el profesor.

What did Tomás do yesterday?
Tomás talked to the teacher.

—¿Qué **hicieron** ellos anoche?
—Ellos estudiaron mucho.

What did they do last night?
They studied a lot.

—¿Qué **hiciste** tú anoche?
—No **hice** nada.
—**Hice** mi tarea de español.

What did you do last night?
I didn't do anything.
I did my Spanish homework.

hacer *(to do, to make)*			
yo	**hice**	nosotros(as)	**hicimos**
tú	**hiciste**	vosotros(as)	**hicisteis**
él ella Ud.	**hizo**	ellos ellas Uds.	**hicieron**

1. The verb **hacer** is used in the preterite to talk about what was done in the past.

2. When you are asked a question about the past with the verb **hacer**, you often respond with a different verb that expresses what was done.

3. Here are some common expressions with **hacer.**

hacer un viaje	*to take a trip*
hacer la cama	*to make the bed*
hacer las maletas	*to pack*
hacer ejercicio	*to exercise*
hacer un mandado	*to run an errand*

Ellos **hicieron un viaje** a Bogotá, Colombia el año pasado.

They took a trip to Bogotá, Colombia last year.

Ernestito **hizo la cama** ayer.

Ernestito made the bed yesterday.

¿**Hiciste las maletas** para tu viaje a Honduras?

Did you pack for your trip to Honduras?

Aquí practicamos

F. Lo que hice Sustituye las palabras en cursiva *(italics)* con las palabras que están entre paréntesis y haz *(make)* los cambios *(changes)* necesarios.

1. *Yo* no hice nada anoche. (nosotros / ella / ellos / tú / Ud. / Elena y yo)
2. ¿Qué hizo *Ud.* ayer? (tú / él / yo / Uds. / ellos / nosotras)
3. *Julio* hizo las maletas ayer. (yo / tú / María / nosotros / ellas)

G. ¿Qué hicieron anoche? Un(a) compañero(a) quiere saber lo que tú y tus amigos hicieron anoche. Tu compañero(a) te hace las preguntas. Responde según *(according to)* el modelo y los dibujos *(drawings)*.

MODELO	
Compañero(a):	*¿Qué hizo Roberto anoche?*
Tú:	*Roberto habló con María.*

Roberto

1. José

2. Marta y Ana

3. Melisa

4. Luis y Elena

5. Esteban

6. Sara

H. ¿Qué hiciste en casa de tu prima? Your parents
were out of town, so you spent the day yesterday at your cousin
Anita's house. Today, a friend wants to know how you spent the day.
Work with a partner and follow the model.

> **MODELO**   hablar con María, Linda
> **Amiga(o):**   *¿Hablaste con María?*
> **Tú:**   *No hablé con María, pero hablé
> con Linda.*

1. visitar a Julián, Alicia
2. estudiar con Teresa, Julia
3. hablar con los padres de Miguel, su hermana
4. tomar café, jugo de naranja
5. escuchar la radio, una cinta de Janet Jackson

Aquí escuchamos

¿Qué te gusta hacer? *Various students talk about what they like and don't like to do in their free time.*

Antes de escuchar What activities do you think the students
might mention? On your activity master, make a list based on the
leisure-time activities you have learned to discuss in Spanish.

 A escuchar Listen twice to what the students say and pay attention to what they like and do not like to do.

Después de escuchar On the chart in your activity master, indicate what each person likes to do and doesn't like to do by checking
off the appropriate column.

	Sí	No
Juan		
Eva		
Esteban		
Elena		

¿Qué hiciste tú durante el fin de semana?

It's Monday morning, and you and your friend are telling each other what you did and did not do over the weekend. Working in pairs, interview your partner to find out how he (she) spent last weekend. Record your partner's responses on your activity master. When you are asking questions, use expressions like **¿Qué hiciste el viernes pasado por la tarde?** When you are answering questions, choose from the suggestions provided, using the preterite. Possible activities are **trabajar mucho, mirar la televisión, bailar mucho, hablar por teléfono, estudiar,** etc.

viernes por la noche	
sábado por la mañana	
sábado por la noche	
domingo por la tarde	
domingo por la noche	

La semana pasada
Make a list of five things you did last week.

1. For each activity on your list, tell on which day and at what time of day you did it.
2. When you have completed your list, work with a partner to fill out the chart on your activity master.
3. For the activities that you both did, find out if you had a similar schedule (**¿Cuándo estudiaste para el examen de inglés?**).

Mis actividades	Las actividades de nosotros(as) dos	Las actividades de mi compañero(a)

Preparación

- Where do you go in your free time?
- What are some of the events you attend?

¿Adónde fuiste?

Un muchacho y una muchacha hablan de lo que hicieron anoche.

Olga: ¿Adónde fuiste anoche?
Daniel: A un **partido** de fútbol. ¿Y tú?
Olga: Fui a un concierto.

It's Monday morning and before class begins, Carmen and her friend, Cristina, are talking about where they and some of their friends went last Saturday afternoon.

Carmen: Hola, Cristina, ¿cómo estás?
Cristina: Bien, y tú, ¿qué tal?
Carmen: Muy, muy bien. ¿Qué hiciste el sábado pasado? **¿Fuiste** al cine?
Cristina: No, no. No **fui** al cine. Roberto y yo **fuimos** al concierto. ¿Y tú?
Carmen: Yo fui a la biblioteca.
Cristina: ¿Fuiste con tu novio?
Carmen: No, él **fue** al gimnasio.
Cristina: Y tu hermano, ¿qué hizo? ¿Fue al gimnasio, también?
Carmen: No, mi hermano y su novia **fueron** al partido de fútbol.

partido *game, match*   **fuiste** *you went*   **fui** *I went*   **fuimos** *we went*   **fue** *he, she went*   **fueron** *they went*

a la biblioteca

a casa de un(a) amigo(a)

al centro

al cine

de compras

a una fiesta

al gimnasio

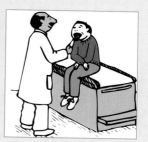

al médico

a un museo

al parque

al parque zoológico

a la playa

a un restaurante

a la piscina

ESTRUCTURA

The preterite of the verb ir

Yo **fui** al cine anoche.

Ellos **fueron** a un concierto
el sábado pasado.

Nosotros **fuimos** al centro ayer.

—¿**Fuiste** tú a la fiesta de Julia el
viernes pasado?
—No, no **fui** a la fiesta.

I went to the movies last night.

They went to a concert last Saturday.

We went downtown yesterday.

Did you go to Julia's party last Friday?

No, I didn't go to the party.

ir *(to go)*			
yo	**fui**	nosotros(as)	**fuimos**
tú	**fuiste**	vosotros(as)	**fuisteis**
él ella Ud.	**fue**	ellos ellas Uds.	**fueron**

¡Te toca a ti!

A. ¿Adónde fue...? Un(a) compañero(a) pregunta adónde fueron todos *(everyone)* ayer *(yesterday)* por la tarde. Sigue el modelo.

> **MODELO** David / cine
> **Compañera(o):** *¿Adónde fue David?*
> **Tú:** *Fue al cine.*

1. Carmen / concierto
2. tu hermana / museo
3. tú / biblioteca
4. Jorge y Hernando / banco
5. Victoria y Claudia / restaurante
6. la profesora / médico
7. tus padres / centro
8. Mario / parque zoológico

B. ¿Adónde fuiste? Ahora pregúntale a un compañero(a) adónde fue ayer. Sigue el modelo.

> **MODELO**   biblioteca /cine
>
> Tú: *¿Adónde fuiste ayer? ¿A la biblioteca?*
> **Compañero(a):**   *No, fui al cine.*

1. a la playa / a la piscina
2. a un restaurante / a casa de un(a) amigo(a)
3. al parque / al gimnasio
4. al partido de básquetbol / al concierto
5. a la biblioteca / de compras
6. a la piscina / a una fiesta

C. ¿Adónde fuiste anoche? Ask eight of your classmates where they went last night. Record their responses on the chart on your activity master, showing who went where. Be prepared to report your findings to the class.

	Nombre	Nombre	Nombre	Nombre
a un restaurante	Luis	Carla		
al parque				
al cine	David			
a una fiesta				
a casa de un(a) amigo(a)				
a un partido de básquetbol				
al trabajo				
…				
…				

D. No, no me gusta..., prefiero... You are discussing what you like and do not like to do. When your partner asks you if you like to do something, you respond negatively and indicate what you prefer to do instead. Follow the model.

> **MODELO** estudiar
> **Compañera(o):** *¿Te gusta estudiar?*
> **Tú:** *No, no me gusta estudiar. Prefiero ir al cine.*

1. estudiar
2. leer
3. hacer ejercicio

4. ir al cine
5. caminar por el parque
6. mirar la televisión

7. correr
8. alquilar vídeos
9. ir de compras

ESTRUCTURA

Preterite tense of -er and -ir verbs

Yo **comí** en un restaurante anoche.	*I ate in a restaurant last night.*
Nosotros **escribimos** una carta ayer.	*We wrote a letter yesterday*
Susana **no comprendió** la lección.	*Susana did not understand the lesson.*
¿**Recibieron** Uds. una invitación a la fiesta?	*Did you receive an invitation to the party?*
Ella **salió** de casa temprano ayer.	*She left home early yesterday.*

<table>
<tr><td colspan="10" align="center">comer (to eat), vivir (to live)</td></tr>
<tr><td>yo</td><td>-í</td><td>comí</td><td>viví</td><td>nosotros(as)</td><td>-imos</td><td>comimos</td><td>vivimos</td></tr>
<tr><td>tú</td><td>-iste</td><td>comiste</td><td>viviste</td><td>vosotros(as)</td><td>-isteis</td><td>comisteis</td><td>vivisteis</td></tr>
<tr><td>él
ella
Ud.</td><td>-ió</td><td>comió</td><td>vivió</td><td>ellos
ellas
Uds.</td><td>-ieron</td><td>comieron</td><td>vivieron</td></tr>
</table>

1. Note that the preterite endings for -er and -ir verbs are identical, and that the **yo** and the **él, ella, Ud.** forms have a written accent.

2. You already know several -er and -ir verbs such as **correr** and **discutir**. Here are some new verbs you should learn:

perder	*to lose*	**asistir a**	*to attend*
vender	*to sell*	**salir con**	*to go out with*
volver	*to return*	**salir de**	*to leave*
repetir	*to repeat*	**servir**	*to serve*

Aquí practicamos

E. Ayer después de la escuela Di lo que tú y tus amigos hicieron ayer después de la escuela. Usa las palabras *(words)* de cada *(each)* columna.

A	B	C	D
yo	(no)	comer	pizza
Miguel		escribir	dos cartas
tú		recibir	un(a) amigo(a)
Pedro y yo		salir con	un partido
Linda y Fernando		asistir a	un libro
Ud.		correr	dos millas
		perder	los ejercicios del libro

F. El fin de semana Compare notes with your partner about what you did over the weekend. Use the following expressions to begin your questions, alternating turns. Find at least one activity that you both did. Follow the model.

> **MODELO**   comer en un restaurante
> **Tú:**   *¿Comiste en un restaurante?*
> **Compañero(a):**   *Sí, comí en un restaurante.* o: *No, no comí en un restaurante.*

1. aprender información interesante
2. asistir a un concierto
3. perder la cartera
4. escribir una carta a tu amigo(a)
5. discutir un problema
6. recibir un regalo *(gift)*
7. correr un poco
8. comer en un restaurante
9. salir con un(a) amigo(a)
10. volver a casa tarde con un(a) amigo(a)

G. Una tarde típica

Using the drawings and verbs that follow as guides, explain to your parents how you and your boyfriend (girlfriend) spent the afternoon. Follow the model.

MODELO   salir
Salimos de la escuela.

1. tomar

2. estudiar

3. caminar

4. escuchar

5. salir

6. comprar

7. comer

8. mirar

9. escribir

10. beber

Aquí escuchamos

¿Qué hiciste anoche? *Olga and Esteban talk about what they did last night.*

Antes de escuchar Based on what you have been studying in this **etapa,** what do you think Olga and Esteban might say they did?

 A escuchar Listen twice to the conversation and pay special attention to the activities mentioned by each speaker.

Después de escuchar On your activity master, check off what each person did last night, based on what you heard.

	Olga	Esteban
caminar		
correr		
cenar con amigos		
escribir cartas		
estudiar		
hablar por teléfono		
leer		
mirar televisión		

¡ADELANTE!

 ¿Adónde fuiste y qué hiciste el verano pasado? Talk to five of your classmates. 1) Find out one place they went and one activity that they did last summer. 2) Make a list of their responses. 3) Select the most interesting place and the most interesting activity and report them to the class.

 La semana pasada Your pen pal in Argentina has reminded you that it is your turn to write. Write a note telling what you did and where you went last week. Indicate at least five things that you did and include at least two places that you went.

Preparación

As you begin this **etapa**, think about what your routine was last week.

- Did you go to school every day?
- Did you participate in any extracurricular activities?
- Did you study?
- Did you go out? Where?

Una semana típica

Elisabeth habla de lo que hizo la semana pasada.

El lunes, miércoles y viernes asistí a mi clase de ejercicio aeróbico. El martes y jueves fui a la piscina y nadé por una hora. El jueves por la noche estudié para un examen por dos horas. El viernes después de mi clase de ejercicio aeróbico, cené con mi novio Jay. Comimos pizza en un restaurante italiano. Después fuimos a un partido de fútbol del **equipo** de nuestra escuela. Nuestro equipo perdió.

El sábado a la una fui de compras con mi amiga Amy. Por la noche, alquilé un vídeo. Invité a mis amigos a mi casa y miramos el vídeo. El domingo fui al centro con mi amigo Billy. Compré dos discos compactos nuevos. Volví a casa a las 5:30 y cené con mis padres.

equipo *team*

¡Te toca a ti!

A. ¿Qué hizo Elisabeth?
Con un(a) compañero(a) di lo que hizo Elisabeth cada día de la semana pasada. Empieza *(Begin)* con el lunes pasado: ¿Qué hizo Elisabeth el lunes pasado?

1. lunes
2. martes
3. jueves
4. viernes
5. domingo

B. ¿Qué hizo Marta la semana pasada?
Di lo que hizo Marta la semana pasada. Basa *(Base)* tus respuestas *(answers)* en los dibujos. Sigue el modelo.

MODELO   sábado
El sábado pasado
Marta alquiló un vídeo.

1. viernes

2. miércoles

3. sábado

4. domingo

5. lunes

6. jueves

7. martes

8. domingo

C. ¿Qué hicieron? Basándote en los dibujos, di lo que hicieron las personas y cuándo lo hicieron. Sigue el modelo.

MODELO Martín y Catarina / el domingo por la tarde
*Martín y Catarina corrieron
el domingo por la tarde.*

1. Marisol y su hermano / el lunes por la mañana

2. Marirrosa y Juanita / el viernes por la noche

3. Juan / el miércoles por la tarde

ESTRUCTURA

Adverbs, prepositions, and other expressions used to designate the past

La semana pasada compré un disco compacto | *Last week I bought a CD.*

El viernes pasado comimos en un restaurante. | *Last Friday we ate at a restaurant.*

1. Here are some expressions used to talk about an action or a condition in the past.

ayer	*yesterday*	**anteayer**	*the day before yesterday*
ayer por la mañana	*yesterday morning*	**la semana pasada**	*last week*
ayer por la tarde	*yesterday afternoon*	**el fin de semana pasado**	*last weekend*
anoche	*last night*	**el mes pasado**	*last month*
el jueves (sábado, etc.) pasado	*last Thursday (Saturday, etc.)*	**el año pasado**	*last year*

2. The preposition **por** will enable you to express how long you did something.

Estudié **por** dos horas. | *I studied for two hours.*

Corrió **por** veinte minutos. | *She ran for twenty minutes.*

Aquí practicamos

D. ¿Qué hicieron recientemente (recently)? Di lo que tú y tus amigos hicieron recientemente. Usa palabras de cada columna.

A	B	C	D
nosotros	(no)	cenar en un restaurante	la semana pasada
tú		correr dos millas	ayer por la tarde
Margarita y Alicia		no asistir a clase	el viernes pasado
Julián		alquilar un vídeo	anteayer
yo		hacer ejercicio	ayer por la mañana
Marta y yo		caminar por el parque	el miércoles pasado

E. ¿Cuándo? Usa las expresiones que están entre paréntesis para decir cuándo hiciste las actividades que siguen. Sigue el modelo.

MODELO ¿Cuándo hablaste con María? (ayer por la mañana)
Hablé con María ayer por la mañana.

1. ¿Cuándo estudiaste francés? (el año pasado)
2. ¿Cuándo corriste? (ayer por la tarde)
3. ¿Cuándo hablaste con tu novia(o)? (el viernes pasado)
4. ¿Cuándo compraste tu bicicleta? (el mes pasado)
5. ¿Cuándo recibiste la carta de Julia? (el jueves pasado)
6. ¿Cuándo comiste pizza? (el domingo pasado)

ESTRUCTURA

Preterite of the verbs andar, estar, and tener

Yo **estuve** en casa de Pablo anteayer.

—¿**Anduviste** tú por el parque ayer?
—Sí, yo **anduve** con mi amiga Paula.

Nosotros no **tuvimos** que estudiar anoche.

I was at Paul's house the day before yesterday.

Did you walk in the park yesterday?
Yes, I walked with my friend Paula.

We did not have to study last night.

The verbs **andar**, **estar**, and **tener** are irregular in the preterite, but they are conjugated similarly.

Pronoun	andar *(to walk)*	estar *(to be)*	tener *(to have)*
yo	anduve	estuve	tuve
tú	anduviste	estuviste	tuviste
él ella Ud.	anduvo	estuvo	tuvo
nosotros(as)	anduvimos	estuvimos	tuvimos
vosotros(as)	anduvisteis	estuvisteis	tuvisteis
ellos ellas Uds.	anduvieron	estuvieron	tuvieron

Aquí practicamos

F. **¿Qué hicieron?** Sustituye las palabras en cursiva con las palabras que están entre paréntesis y haz los cambios necesarios.

1. *Catarina* tuvo que estudiar mucho anoche. (tú / Ud. / Ana y su novio / yo / nosotros)

2. *Juan y Roberto* no estuvieron en la fiesta de Sofía. (Uds. / Diego / yo / tú / nosotras)

3. ¿Anduvieron *Uds.* a la escuela ayer? (Ud. / Santiago y Enrique / Alicia / tú)

G. La semana pasada Ask several classmates the following questions. Have them 1) name three places where they were last week, 2) indicate three places they walked to, and 3) tell three things they had to do. Follow the model.

> **MODELO**
>
> ¿Dónde estuviste la semana pasada?
> *Estuve en la piscina el viernes por la tarde.*
> *Estuve en el parque el domingo por la mañana.*
> *Estuve en casa el martes por la noche.*

1. ¿Dónde estuviste la semana pasada?
2. ¿Adónde anduviste la semana pasada?
3. ¿Qué tuviste que hacer la semana pasada?

Aquí escuchamos

¿Qué hiciste este fin de semana? *Olga and Juan talk about what they did over the weekend.*

Antes de escuchar Think about what you did last weekend. Based on what you've learned in this **etapa**, what are some of the things you think that Olga and Juan might mention doing over the weekend?

 a escuchar Listen twice to the conversation between Olga and Juan before checking off on your activity master the activities that each of them did.

Después de escuchar On the chart on your activity master, check off each person's activities based on what you heard.

	Olga	Juan
fue al parque		
fue a la piscina		
fue a la biblioteca		
fue a cenar en un restaurante		
fue a un concierto		
fue a una fiesta		
fue al gimnasio		
fue de compras		
fue al cine		
estudió		
descansó		

¡ADELANTE!

 Intercambio Work with a partner and discuss what you did last week and for how long. Possible activities include: **estudiar, comprar, hablar con amigos, comer, asistir a un concierto, andar, tener que hacer algo,** etc.

 El fin de semana pasado Make a list of six things that you did last weekend. Write a postcard to a friend in Costa Rica, telling her (him) what you did.

EN LÍNEA

Connect with the Spanish-speaking world! Access the **¡Ya verás!** Gold home page for Internet activities related to this chapter.

http://yaveras.heinle.com

VOCABULARIO

Para charlar

Para hablar de una acción en el pasado

anoche
anteayer
el año pasado
ayer
ayer por la mañana
ayer por la tarde
el fin de semana
  pasado
el jueves (sábado,
  etc.) pasado
la semana pasada
el mes pasado
por una hora (un
  día, tres años, cua-
  tro meses, quince
  minutos, etc.)

Para hablar de las actividades

alquilar un vídeo
desayunar en un
  restaurante
montar en bicicleta
nadar

Lugares adónde vamos

el concierto
el gimnasio
el parque zoológico

Vocabulario general

Verbos

andar
asistir a
caminar
cenar
cocinar
comprar
contestar
invitar
pasar
perder
pregunatar
repetir
salir con
salir de
servir
terminar
usar
visitar
vender
volver

Otras palabras y expresiones

un equipo
hacer la cama
hacer ejercicio
hacer las maletas
hacer un viaje
nada
no hacer nada
un partido

Tu tiempo libre

Antes de leer

1. Read the title of the reading. What do you think the reading will be about?

2. Look at the photos. Describe the people you see in Spanish. What do you think they might do during their free time?

3. What do you like to do during your free time? Try to name at least three activities in Spanish that you enjoy.

"Me llamo Nora Nieves y vivo en Puerto Rico. Soy estudiante en el colegio y no tengo mucho tiempo libre. Cuando no estoy en clase, me gusta salir con mis amigas. Vamos de compras al centro comercial. También tomo una clase de escultura. El arte me fascina.

En mi clase de escultura

Hola, me llamo Marta Barrios y soy de San Antonio, Texas. Me gustan los fines de semana porque no tengo que levantarme temprano. Por ejemplo, este sábado me levanté a las diez de la mañana y fui a correr. Por la tarde fui a la casa de una amiga y escuchamos música. El domingo mi familia y yo visitamos a mis abuelos y fui de pesca con mi abuelo. Por la noche miré la tele-visión antes de acostarme."

¡Mi abuelo con un pescado grandísimo!

"Soy Andrés. Vivo en Buenos Aires, capital de la Argentina. Durante los fines de semana tengo mucho tiempo libre y a veces mis amigos y yo vamos al parque a jugar al fútbol o a montar en bicicleta. Por la tarde nos reunimos para ir al cine o a alguna fiesta en casa de unos amigos."

En bicicleta con mis amigos

Guía para la lectura

Here are some words and expressions to keep in mind as you read.

centro comercial	*shopping mall*
jugar al fútbol	*to play soccer*
nos reunimos	*we get together*
levantarme temprano	*get up early*
fui de pesca	*I went fishing*
antes de acostarme	*before going to bed*

Después de leer

1. Based on the information given by Nora, Andrés and Marta, determine which of them is involved in the following activities during his or her free time.

   a. montar en bicicleta   e. jugar básquetbol

   b. ir de pesca   f. mirar le televisión

   c. escuchar música   g. ir al cine

   d. hacer escultura   h. estar con los(as) amigos(as)

2. Based on the activities they mention, with which of the teens do you have the most in common?

3. Who would you prefer to spend your free time with, your friends or your family? Explain your answer.

4. Do you think young people today have too much free time or too little free time? How would you change your weekly schedule?

CAPÍTULO 14

Actividades deportivas

El baloncesto es un deporte muy popular en América Latina. Es muy divertido para todos.

Objectives

- talking about and situating activities and events in the past
- talking about sports and leisure time activities

As you begin this **etapa**, think about the sports you play.

- Do you play sports just for fun? For exercise?
- Are you on a sports team?

Los deportes

Esteban y Alberto hablan de los deportes que practican.

Esteban: ¡Hola! ¿Adónde vas?

Alberto: Voy a jugar al fútbol.

Esteban: ¿Estás en algún **equipo**?

Alberto: Sí, estoy en el equipo de nuestra escuela.

Esteban: ¿Vas a practicar?

Alberto: Sí, tengo que practicar los lunes, martes, miércoles y jueves.

Esteban: ¿Cuándo son los partidos?

Alberto: Los partidos son los viernes por la noche. Y tú, ¿estás en algún equipo?

Esteban: No. Me gusta mucho jugar al baloncesto, pero no estoy en un equipo. Sólo juego para hacer ejercicio.

hacer ejercicios aeróbicos

jugar al baloncesto

jugar al béisbol

equipo *team*

jugar al fútbol

jugar al fútbol americano

jugar al golf

jugar al hockey

jugar al hockey sobre hierba

jugar al tenis

jugar al vólibol

levantar pesas

montar en bicicleta

patinar

patinar sobre hielo

¡Te toca a ti!

A. ¿Qué deporte prefieres?
Pregúntale a un(a) compañero(a) qué deportes prefiere. Sigue el modelo.

MODELO
montar en bicicleta / jugar al vólibol
Tú: *¿Te gusta montar en bicicleta?*
Compañero(a): *No, no me gusta montar en bicicleta; prefiero jugar al vólibol.*

1. correr / levantar pesas
2. patinar sobre hielo / jugar al vólibol
3. jugar al golf / jugar al tenis
4. nadar / hacer ejercicio aeróbico
5. jugar al baloncesto / jugar al béisbol
6. jugar al fútbol americano / jugar al fútbol
7. jugar al hockey / esquiar
8. montar en bicicleta / patinar

B. ¿Qué deporte te gusta más?
1) Choosing from the sports you have learned to say in Spanish, list your three favorites. 2) When you have your list, circulate among your classmates, looking for people who share your interests. 3) When you find someone with whom you have an activity in common, try to arrange a time that you can practice it together.

MODELO
Tú: *¿Qué deporte te gusta, Juana?*
Juana: *Me gusta jugar al vólibol.*
Tú: *¿No te gusta nadar?*
Juana: *Sí, me gusta mucho nadar. ¿Y a ti?*
Tú: *¡Claro que sí! ¿Quieres ir a la piscina con mi hermana y yo?*
Juana: *¿Cuándo van Uds.?*
Tú: *El sábado próximo por la tarde.*
Juana: *¡Qué buena idea! o: No, no puedo ir el sábado. ¿Pueden Uds. ir el domingo?*
Tú: *Sí, cómo no.*

C. ¡Preguntas y más preguntas! Quieres saber lo que hizo tu amigo(a) el fin de semana pasado. Hazle las preguntas que siguen a un(a) compañero(a).

1. ¿Qué hiciste el viernes pasado?
2. ¿Estuviste en la escuela el sábado pasado?
3. ¿Miraste un programa de televisión el sábado por la noche?
4. ¿Hablaste por teléfono con alguien? ¿Con quién? ¿Cuándo?
5. ¿Tuviste que hacer algo el domingo pasado?
6. ¿Anduviste al centro con tus amigos?
7. ¿Tuviste que estudiar el domingo?
8. ¿Comiste en un restaurante? ¿Cuándo?

ESTRUCTURA

Hace and hace que for expressing how long ago something occurred

—¿**Cuánto hace que** Raúl **compró** el disco compacto?

How long ago did Raúl buy the CD?

—**Hace dos semanas que** Raúl **compró** el disco compacto.

Two weeks ago, Raúl bought the CD.

—Raúl **compró** el disco compacto **hace dos semanas.**

Raúl bought the CD two weeks ago.

1. To express how long ago something happened, Spanish uses the following two constructions:

> **Hace** + *length of time* + **que** + *verb in the preterite*
>
> *Verb in the preterite* + **hace** + *length of time*

2. To ask how long ago something occurred, Spanish uses the following construction:

> ¿**Cuánto** + **hace** + **que** + *verb in the preterite* ?

Aquí practicamos

D. ¿Cuánto hace? Sustituye las palabras en cursiva con las palabras que están entre paréntesis y haz los cambios necesarios.

1. Hace 2 *días* que Juan habló con su novia. (5 horas / 4 meses / 6 días / 1 mes / 3 semanas)

2. Marirrosa vendió su bicicleta hace *3 meses*. (8 días / 1 año / 6 semanas / 2 horas / 3 meses)

E. Hablé con ella hace... Un(a) amigo(a) quiere saber *(wants to know)* cuánto tiempo hace que hiciste algo *(how long ago you did something)*. Habla con un(a) compañero(a) y sigue el modelo.

> **MODELO** hablar con ella / 2 horas
>
> Compañera(o): *¿Cuánto hace que hablaste con ella?*
> Tú: *Hablé con ella hace 2 horas.*

1. vivir en Indiana / 10 años
2. estudiar francés / 2 años
2. comprar la bicicleta / 3 meses
4. recibir la carta de Ana / 5 días
5. comer en un restaurante / 2 semanas
6. ir al cine / 3 semanas

F. Hace... Now ask your partner the questions she (he) asked you in Exercise E. She (he) will answer, using the alternate construction below. Follow the model.

> **MODELO** hablar con ella / 2 horas
>
> Tú: *¿Cuánto hace que hablaste con ella?*
> Compañera(o): *Hace 2 horas que hablé con ella.*

G. ¿Cuánto hace que...?

Basándote en los dibujos, hazle preguntas a un(a) compañero(a). Empieza cada pregunta con la expresión ¿Cuánto hace que...?

1.

2.

3.

4.

5.

6.

7.

8.

ESTRUCTURA

The preterite of verbs ending in -gar

—A qué hora **llegaste** a la escuela ayer?   *What time did you arrive at school yesterday?*
—**Llegué** a las ocho de la mañana.   *I arrived at eight o'clock in the morning.*

—¿**Jugaron al** tenis tú y Julián el   *Did you and Julián play tennis last Sunday?*
  domingo pasado?
—Yo **jugué**, pero Julián no **jugó**.   *I played, but Julián did not play.*

—¿Cuánto **pagaste** tú por la bicicleta?   *How much did you pay for the bicycle?*
—Yo **pagué** 150 dolares.   *I paid 150 dollars.*

The Preterite of Verbs Ending in -gar

llegar (to arrive)			
yo	**llegué**	nosotros(as)	**llegamos**
tú	**llegaste**	vosotros(as)	**llegasteis**
él ella Ud.	**llegó**	ellos ellas Uds.	**llegaron**

1. In the **yo** form of verbs ending in **-gar,** the **g** of the stem (**lleg-** for **llegar**) changes to **gu** before the ending **-é**. The other forms of the verb are conjugated exactly like those you learned in Chapter 13 for **-ar** verbs in the preterite.

2. You already saw the verb **jugar,** which means *to play (a game or sport),* in Chapter 11. **Pagar** *(to pay)* is another verb ending in **-gar** that follows this pattern in the preterite.

Aquí practicamos

H. Pagamos, jugamos, llegamos
Sustituye las palabras en cursiva con las palabras que están entre paréntesis y haz los cambios necesarios.

1. El año pasado, *nosotros* pagamos 150 dólares por la bicicleta. (Marisol / yo / Ud. / Ángela y su mamá / él)

2. *Julián* no jugó al tenis ayer por la tarde. (nosotros / Uds. / yo / tú / Mario y David)

3. ¿Llegaste *tú* tarde *(late)* a la clase ayer? (Juan / yo / Bárbara y yo / Linda y Clara / Ud.)

I. **¿Cuánto pagaste por...?** Ask several classmates how much they paid for something they bought recently. Suggestions include: **una mochila, un disco compacto, una pizza,** etc.

J. **¿Cuándo llegaste a...?** Ask several classmates when they arrived at some place they went to recently. Suggestions include: **el partido, la escuela, a casa,** etc.

K. **¿A qué deporte jugaste y cuándo?** Ask several classmates what sport they played recently and when.

Aquí escuchamos

Los deportes *Sonia and Mari run into each other after school and they talk briefly.*

Antes de escuchar Think about the sports activities that you and/or your classmates participate in after school. Then answer the following questions.

1. What do you think Sonia and Mari might talk about?
2. Where do you think they might be going after school?

 A escuchar Listen twice to the conversation before answering the questions about it that follow.

Después de escuchar Answer the following questions based on what you heard.

1. What team is Sonia on?
2. Why is she tired?
3. When is the big game?
4. Where is Mari going?
5. Is she going there early or late?

¿Qué pasó? Work in pairs within groups of four. Ask your partner when the last time was he (she) went to a store (**tienda**), what he (she) bought, and how much he (she) paid for it. Ask your teacher to provide words you don't know, or use the dictionary. As a group, compile your responses. Your teacher will then record all the groups' responses on the board to determine the most popular purchases and their price ranges.

Querido... A friend from Argentina wants to know what sorts of sports are popular in the United States and which ones you like. Write a note to him (her).

1. Name some popular sports.
2. Tell which ones you prefer.
3. Mention whether you like to attend the games, watch them on television, or participate.
4. In a second paragraph, tell whether you are on a team, if you participate in competitions (**competiciones**), or if you prefer to do sports for exercise.
5. Tell some details about a sport that you play, when you last participated in it, and where.

Preparación

As you begin this **etapa**, think about sports or activities you like to do in the summer.

- Are you close to the beach?
- Do you go to a pool?
- Do you go camping?
- Do you go fishing?

Deportes de verano

Durante el **verano** (summer), *puedes practicar muchos deportes divertidos.*

practicar el esquí acuático

practicar el surfing

tomar el sol

practicar el windsurf

practicar la vela

ir de camping

la natación / nadar

practicar el alpinismo

la pesca / ir de pesca

practicar el ciclismo

el buceo / bucear

caminar en la playa

¡Te toca a ti!

A. ¿Qué actividad prefieres? Pregúntale a un(a) compañero(a) qué actividades de verano prefiere. Sigue el modelo.

> **MODELO** el ciclismo / el alpinismo
> **Tú:** *¿Te gusta practicar el ciclismo?*
> **Compañera(o):** *No, no me gusta practicar el ciclismo.*
> *Prefiero practicar el alpinismo.*

1. ir de pesca / nadar
2. la vela / el windsurf
3. el esquí acuático / el buceo
4. el alpinismo / ir de camping
5. el ciclismo / tomar el sol
6. el surfing / caminar en la playa

B. ¿Qué hacen? Basándote en los dibujos, di lo que hace cada persona. Sigue el modelo

MODELO Julián
Julián practica el esquí acuático.

1. Isabel

2. Juan

3. Mario y Julia

4. Elena

5. Pedro

6. Esteban y Roberto

7. Tomás y Laura

8. Regina

C. ¿Qué actividad de verano te gusta?

Compare your opinions about summer sports and activities with those of your partner. 1) On your activity master, indicate your opinion of each activity in the left column, using the numbers on the following scale to indicate how much you like each one. 2) Then, interview your partner, writing the appropriate number to indicate his (her) preferences in the right column. 3) Go over your results as explained below.

no = 0, poco = 1, bastante = 2, mucho = 3, muchísimo = 4

No tengo experiencia con esta actividad = X

MODELO

Tú:	*¿Te gusta practicar el surfing?*
Compañero(a):	*No, no me gusta practicar el surfing, pero me gusta mucho caminar en la playa.*

Yo	Actividad	Mi amigo(a)
3	**practicar el surfing**	0
2	**tomar el sol**	3
	caminar en la playa	
	practicar el esquí acuático	
	ir de pesca	
4	**nadar**	3
	practicar la vela	
	ir de camping	
	practicar el ciclismo	
x	**practicar el windsurf**	x
	bucear	
	jugar al golf	
	jugar al tenis	

Go over the results with your partner. Name the activities about which your attitudes are the same and those about which your opinions are the most different.

MODELO

A los (las) dos nos gusta tomar el sol y nadar.
No nos gusta ir de pesca.
Tenemos opiniones diferentes sobre (about) practicar el surfing.
No tenemos experiencia con el windsurf.

D. **¿Qué hizo Esteban ayer?** Basándote en los dibujos, di lo que Esteban hizo ayer.

1. andar

2. llegar

3. jugar

4. comprar

5. pagar

6. volver

E. **¿Qué hiciste tú ayer?** Ahora imagina que eres Esteban. Di lo que hiciste ayer usando los dibujos de la Actividad D.

F. **¿Cuánto hace que...?** Ask several classmates when they last did a specific activity. For example, ask when they played tennis, when they ate at a restaurant, walked in the park, etc. Take notes on their responses and be prepared to report back to the class.

ESTRUCTURA

The preterite of verbs ending in -car

—¿Quién **buscó** el libro?   *Who looked for the book?*
—Yo **busqué** el libro.   *I looked for the book.*

—**Tocó** Julián la guitarra en la   *Did Julián play the guitar at the party last*
   fiesta anoche?   *night?*
—No, yo **toqué** la guitarra anoche.   *No, I played the guitar last night.*

The Preterite of Verbs Ending in -car

buscar (to look for)			
yo	**busqué**	nosotros(as)	**buscamos**
tú	**buscaste**	vosotros(as)	**buscasteis**
él ella Ud.	**buscó**	ellos ellas Uds.	**buscaron**

1. In the **yo** form of verbs ending in -**car,** the **c** of the stem (**busc-** for **buscar**) changes to **qu** before the ending -**é.** The other forms of the verb are conjugated exactly like those you learned in Chapter 13 for -**ar** verbs in the preterite.

2. You already know the verbs **practicar** and **tocar.** The verb **sacar,** which means *to take out, to remove,* or *to obtain (a grade),* is another verb ending in -**car** that follows this pattern in the preterite.

Aquí practicamos

G. Todos buscan Sustituye las palabras en cursiva con las palabras que están entre paréntesis y haz los cambios necesarios.

1. *Elena* buscó la casa de Raúl. (tú / Ud. / Lilia y su novio / yo / Uds.)

2. *Olga* no tocó el piano anoche. (Uds. / Diego / yo / tú / nosotras)

3. ¿Practicaron *Uds.* ayer por la tarde? (nosotros / Santiago y Enrique / tú / yo / ella)

H. ¿Qué deporte practicaste el verano pasado?

Un(a) compañero(a) quiere saber qué deportes practicaste el verano pasado. Responde según el modelo.

MODELO

el windsurf

Compañera(o): *¿Practicaste el windsurf el verano pasado?*

Tú: No, *no practiqué el windsurf, practiqué el buceo.*

1. el buceo	3. el esquí acuático	5. el alpinismo
2. el surfing	4. la vela	6. el ciclismo

PALABRAS ÚTILES

Expressions used to talk about a series of actions

Primero, yo estudié en la biblioteca. **Entonces,** caminé al parque y visité a un amigo. **Por fin,** volví a casa.

1. When talking about a series of actions in the past, you will find the following expressions useful.

primero	*first*
entonces, luego	*then*
por fin, finalmente	*finally*

2. These expressions are also useful when talking about future actions.

Primero, voy a estudiar en la biblioteca. **Entonces,** voy a caminar al parque y voy a visitar a un amigo. **Por fin,** voy a volver a casa.

3. You can also use them to talk about daily routines.

Todos los días después de la escuela, llego a casa a las 4:00. **Primero,** como un sándwich y bebo un vaso de leche. **Entonces,** saco la basura. **Por fin,** estudio por unas horas.

Aquí practicamos

I. **¿Qué hizo Felipe?** Use the expressions in parentheses to tell what Felipe did in the past and in what order. Follow the model.

MODELO

Felipe tomó el autobús al centro.
(el domingo pasado)
El domingo pasado, Felipe tomó el autobús al centro.

1. Comió en un restaurante. (primero)
2. Compró un disco compacto. (entonces)
3. Visitó a una amiga en el parque. (luego)
4. Volvió a su casa a las 5:00 de la tarde. (finalmente)

Now tell what Felipe did last Saturday.

> **MODELO** Felipe fue a la playa. (el sábado pasado)
> *El sábado pasado, Felipe fue a la playa.*

5. Practicó el windsurf. (primero)
6. Nadó en el mar. (entonces)
7. Tomó el sol. (luego)
8. Caminó a casa. (finalmente)

Now tell what Felipe is going to do at some point in the future.

9. Felipe va a viajar a Ecuador. (el mes próximo)
10. Va a ir a Quito. (primero)
11. Va a visitar la ciudad de Guayaquil. (entonces)
12. Va a volver el 5 de junio. (por fin)

J. Primero... entonces... finalmente... Describe the order of each set of three activities. Choose logical verbs to go with the words provided. Follow the model.

> **MODELO** nosotros / piscina / en casa / programa de televisión
> *Primero, nosotros fuimos a la piscina. Entonces, estudiamos en casa. Finalmente, miramos un programa de televisión.*

1. ellos / escuela / sándwich / televisión
2. yo / biblioteca / centro / disco compacto
3. nosotros / casa / jugo de naranja / estéreo
4. ella / café y pan tostado / autobús / un amigo
5. él / sándwich de jamón y queso / metro / centro
6. ellas / parque / refresco / casa

Aquí escuchamos

¡Qué bien lo pasaste! *Roberto tells Felipe about his weekend at the beach.*

Antes de escuchar Have you been to the beach before? Based on what you have learned in this **etapa**, what activities do you think Felipe might have done there?

 A escuchar Listen twice to the conversation between Roberto and Felipe. Pay attention to the order of Roberto's activities and indicate the order on your activity master.

Después de escuchar On your activity master, write numbers next to the activities Roberto mentions to indicate the order in which he did them.

___bucear	___nadar
___caminar en la playa	___practicar el windsurf
___cenar	___tomar el sol

¡ADELANTE!

 El verano pasado Both you and your partner were very busy last summer, participating in many summer sports and activities. To report your activities to each other, organize them in the order in which you did them. Use time expressions to list them in order. Include at least five activities each. Find at least one activity in which you both participated.

 Durante las vacaciones... You've just come back to school from summer vacation and want to tell your pen pal in Chile what you did during the summer. Write your friend a note and indicate what you did, including at least five activities that you were involved in. Use time expressions to tell the order in which you did your summer activities.

EN LÍNEA

Connect with the Spanish-speaking world! Access the **¡Ya verás!** *Gold* home page for Internet activities related to this chapter.

http://yaveras.heinle.com

VOCABULARIO

Para charlar	Temas y contextos	Vocabulario general

Para hablar de una serie de acciones

primero
entonces
luego
finalmente
por fin

Para hablar del tiempo

un minuto
una hora
un día
una semana
un mes
un año

Deportes

hacer ejercicio aeróbico
jugar…
  al baloncesto
  al golf
  al hockey
  al hockey sobre hierba
levantar pesas
patinar
patinar sobre hielo

Deportes de verano

el buceo / bucear
caminar en la playa
ir de camping
la natación / nadar
la pesca / ir de pesca
practicar…
  el alpinismo
  el ciclismo
  el esquí acuático
  el surfing
  la vela
  el windsurf
tomar el sol

Verbos

sacar

Sustantivos

una guitarra

Otras expresiones

¿Cuánto hace que + *verb in the preterite*?
Hace + *length of time* + que + *subject* + *verb in the preterite.*
Subject + *verb in the preterite* + hace + *length of time.*

Una página de "surfing" latinoamericano

Antes de leer

1. Can you identify the format of this reading? What word in the title refers to this kind of format?

2. Scan the whole text. Find the names of at least four different countries that are mentioned in relation to surfing activities.

3. What do you know about surfing?

4. Where does surfing usually take place?

Netsite: http:// www.the grid.net/fleming/sites.html/

El Salvador: "punto" desconocido

Otros dos puntos para visitar son **Costa del Sol** y **El Cuco**

¡Atención! Recuerda viajar durante la temporada de lluvias, que es entre junio y noviembre, si quieres disfrutar del mejor oleaje.

Muchos saben que las <u>playas de Costa Rica</u> son un excelente lugar para "surfear," pero pocos saben que en El Salvador también hay estupendos lugares para practicar este deporte. Hay varios lugares muy buenos para "surfear" a lo largo de la costa, pero el mejor oleaje lo ofrece <u>La Libertad</u>, una popular área turística al sur de San Salvador. Allí vas a encontrar un estupendo rompeolas cerca del muelle, además de muchos restaurantes y hoteles. Recomendamos también que visites <u>Los Cobanos</u>, en el sur, que tiene un estupendo oleaje y un hotel muy económico.

Médanos + tablas = felicidad

Como todo amante del "surfeo" sabe, los brasileños de la ciudad de Florianópolis inventaron, en 1986, el deporte del "sandboarding", o deslizamiento en tablas sobre arena. Este deporte ha alcanzado gran popularidad en el mundo. Los médanos de Valizas en Uruguay son los más grandes de Sudámerica y alcanzan los 30 metros de altura. ¡Diversión—y algunos moretones—garantizados! <u>Presiona aquí</u> si quieres ver fotos de los mejores médanos del Uruguay.

Muncoarena: "Surfea" en el Uruguay
¡¡¡Disfruta tu estadía!!!

Todo el mundo ha oído hablar de Australia y Hawaii, pero pocos saben que el Uruguay ofrece algunos de los mejores puntos para "surfear" en el mundo. Aquí, algunas sugerencias para un viaje de "surfeo" uruguayo: <u>Punta del Este</u>/<u>José Ignacio</u>/<u>Santa Teresa</u>

Algunas recomendaciones para tu viaje de "surfing" a Punta del Este:

a. El aereopuerto principal se llama Aereopuerto Internacional Carrasco. Punta del Este está situada a 100 millas del aereopuerto. Para llegar, puedes tomar el bus o alquilar un automóvil.

b. Si necesitas comprar equipo para "surfear," visita la playa de <u>La Olla</u>, donde está la tienda de equipo de "surfing" más grande de Sur América, la tienda "Valle del Sol" de artículos deportivos.

c. En muchas áreas hay disponible alquiler de bicicletas y motoras.

d. Por último: ¡asegúrate de viajar durante la temporada de invierno—de octubre a diciembre—cuando el océano es más agresivo!

Guía para la lectura

1. Here are some words and expressions to keep in mind as you read.

"punto"	*spot, point—here it refers to a good surfing location*
oleaje	*surf, breaking waves*
muelle	*pier*
temporada de lluvias	*rainy season*
Médanos	*Sand dunes*
tablas	*boards (for surfing or sandboarding)*
deslizamiento	*sliding*
arena	*sand*
moretones	*bruises*
motoras	*motorboats*

2. Notice the different versions of the borrowed English word *surfing*: "surfear," "surfing," "surfeo."

Después de leer

1. This reading mentions two varieties of surfing. What are they? How are the two types of surfing similar, and how are they different?

2. If you wanted to go surfing, which of the sites mentioned in the reading would you visit? Explain your response.

3. Browsing the World Wide Web is commonly known as "surfing". Can you explain why?

CAPÍTULO 15

Dos deportes populares

Es muy divertido mirar el tenis, pero es aún mejor practicarlo.

Objectives

- talking about actions in the past, present, and future
- talking about sports

Preparación

- Think about the importance given to sports in the United States. When you think about sports in Latin America, what do you think of? This **etapa** begins with a short reading about a sport that is very popular in several Latin American countries.

El béisbol

El béisbol es un deporte muy popular en el Caribe.

Raúl Mondesi

Juan González

Roberto Alomar

Andrés Galarraga

El béisbol es el deporte nacional de los Estados Unidos. También es muy popular en varios países del mundo hispano, principalmente Cuba y la República Dominicana. En Canadá no es tan popular, pero hay dos equipos en las **ligas** mayores—un equipo en Montreal y otro en Toronto. El deporte también es muy popular en México, Puerto Rico, las naciones de Centroamérica, Venezuela y Colombia. También se juega en el Japón, Taiwan y en Corea del Sur.

Hay muchos beisbolistas de origen hispano que juegan en las ligas mayores. Por ejemplo, Juan González de los Texas Rangers, Andrés Galarraga de los Colorado Rockies, Raúl Mondesi de los Los Angeles Dodgers y Sandy Alomar de los Toronto Blue Jays. Hay ciertas **cualidades** que todos estos beisbolistas tienen en común: fuerza física, rapidez, **reflejos** rápidos. **Lanzar** la pelota y **golpearla** con el bate son actividades que requieren mucha práctica y preparación. ¿Te gusta el béisbol? ¿Cuál es tu equipo favorito?

¡Te toca a ti!

A. Estudio de palabras ¿Qué crees que significan las siguientes palabras que están en negrita en la lectura? *(What do you think the following words in boldface in the reading mean?)*

1. ligas
2. cualidades
3. reflejos
4. lanzar
5. golpear

B. Comprensión Responde a las siguientes preguntas sobre la lectura *(about the reading)*.

1. In what Latin American countries is baseball popular?
2. Is it popular in Canada?
3. Where else, besides the Americas, is baseball played?
4. What are some of the characteristics of good baseball players?
5. Why are the players mentioned in the reading significant?

C. ¿Qué hizo Alicia ayer? Basándote en los dibujos que siguen, di lo que hizo Alicia por la tarde.

1. salir de
2. practicar
3. llegar
4. primero / sacar

5. entonces / practicar
6. luego / cenar
7. finalmente / mirar

D. ¿Qué hiciste tú ayer? Ahora imagina que tú eres la persona que está en los dibujos. Di lo que hiciste ayer.

ESTRUCTURA

The present progressive

—¿Qué **están haciendo** Uds. ahora mismo?

What are you doing right now?

—**Estamos estudiando.**

We are studying.

Mi madre **está escribiendo** una carta.

My mother is writing a letter.

1. In Spanish, the present progressive is formed with the present tense form of the verb **estar** plus the **-ndo** form of another verb. The **-ndo** form of the verb is known as the present participle. In English, the present progressive consists of the present tense form of the verb *to be* plus the present participle (the *-ing* form) of another verb *(Charlie is playing tennis. We are resting.)*.

ESTRUCTURA (continued)

2. To form the present participle of **-ar** verbs, drop the **-ar** and add **-ando**. For **-er** and **-ir** verbs, drop the **-er** or the **-ir** and add **-iendo**. Note that the present participles of **leer** *(to read)* and **dormir** *(to sleep)* are irregular.

nadar	nad-	nad**ando**
correr	corr-	corr**iendo**
salir	sal-	sal**iendo**
dormir	durm- (irregular)	durm**iendo**
leer	ley- (irregular)	ley**endo**

3. In Spanish, the use of the present progressive is limited solely to expressing an action that is in progress at that very moment. In English, the -ing form of the verb can be used to express several different verb tenses. In Spanish, however, separate tenses are required: the present progressive, the present tense, and **ir a** + infinitive.

Juan **busca** las llaves.	*Juan is looking for the keys.*
Ellas **vienen** a la una.	*They are coming at one o'clock.*
Voy a dar un paseo.	*I am going to take a walk.*

Aquí practicamos

E. Ahora mismo Di lo que tú y tus amigos están haciendo ahora mismo *(are doing right now)*. Usa palabras de cada columna.

A	B	C	D
ahora mismo	yo	estar	estudiar
	[nombre de un(a) amigo(a)] y yo		comer
	[nombre de un(a) amigo(a)]		escribir
	tú		dormir
	[un(a) amigo(a)] y [otro(a) amigo(a)]		leer

F. ¿Qué están haciendo en este momento? Di lo
que están haciendo en este momento las personas de los dibujos.

1. Jaime

2. Julia

3. Marirrosa y Juan

4. Alberto

5. Carmen y Cristina

6. Juanito

Aquí escuchamos

¿Vienes a la fiesta? *Marta calls Luis to tell him that she can't
come to a party that Luis is hosting.*

Antes de escuchar How do you think Marta might ask Luis
about what her friends are doing? How might he describe what
everyone is doing?

 A escuchar Listen twice to the phone conversation between
Marta and Luis. Pay special attention to the activities that Luis says
each person is doing.

Después de escuchar On your activity master, indicate who is doing what by writing the name of the person next to the appropriate activity on the list.

_____está bailando.	_____está mirando el televisor.
_____está cantando.	_____está preparando.
_____está comiendo.	_____está tocanda la guitarra.
_____está leyendo.	_____está trabajando.

¡ADELANTE!

En este momento Think about various people in your life whose daily schedules are familiar to you. Make a list of four people who have different schedules, such as parents, brothers, sisters, boy/girl friends, best friends. Discuss with a partner what the people you each know are doing right now.

¿Qué está(n) haciendo? Look at the drawing that follows of people enjoying a weekend afternoon in the park. 1) Write at least six sentences telling what they are doing. Identify a different activity in each of your sentences. 2) Then, working with a partner, create a combined list of activities from which the two of you can write a brief composition describing how the people in the park are spending their afternoon. 3) Give your composition an introductory sentence and a closing sentence that briefly summarizes the point of the composition. Take care to organize the sentences between the beginning and end so that you guide your readers smoothly from one activity to the next.

(first sentence) *Hoy es domingo y hay muchas personas en el parque. Ellos están haciendo muchas cosas. Por ejemplo, hay una mujer que...*
(last sentence) *Siempre hay mucho para hacer en el parque durante el fin de semana.*

SEGUNDA ETAPA

- Have you ever played tennis?
- Have you ever watched a match on television?
- Who are some of the great players that you know about?
- What are some of the major tournaments that are played around the world?

El tenis

Hay muchas tenistas hispanas de mucho talento.

Mary Joe Fernández

Gabriela Sabatini

Conchita Martínez

Arantxa Sánchez Vicario

El tenis requiere **agilidad** y control del cuerpo, pero no gran fuerza. Por eso es un deporte que pueden jugar personas de **diversas** edades y condiciones físicas. Al nivel profesional, se necesita una combinación de **habilidad,** buena técnica y una excelente condición física.

Entre las mejores tenistas femeninas del mundo, hay un grupo de hispanas: Gabriela Sabatini de Argentina, Mary Joe Fernández de los Estados Unidos, Arantxa Sánchez Vicario y Conchita Martínez de España. Todas juegan en los grandes **torneos** que se juegan en Inglaterra, en Francia y en los Estados Unidos. En 1994, Conchita ganó el prestigioso torneo en Wimbledon y Arantxa ganó el U.S. Open y el French Open. Arantxa es tan popular en España que tiene que vivir en Andorra, un pequeño país entre Francia y España, para **evitar** a los **admiradores** y periodistas. ¿Te gusta el tenis? ¿Te gusta jugarlo o mirarlo? ¿Quién es tu tenista favorito?

¡Te toca a ti!

A. Estudio de palabras
¿Qué crees que significan las siguientes palabras que están en negrita en la lectura?

1. agilidad
2. diversas
3. habilidad
4. torneos
5. evitar
6. admiradores

B. Comprensión
Responde a las siguientes preguntas sobre la lectura.

1. What characteristics are required of a tennis player?
2. Where are the tennis players featured in the reading from?
3. What did Martínez do in 1994?
4. What did Sánchez Vicario do in 1994?
5. Why does Sánchez Vicario live in Andorra?

C. En este momento... Di lo que está haciendo en este momento cada persona de los dibujos que siguen.

1. Roberto

2. Esteban y Carmen

3. Marirrosa y su amigo

4. Carlos

5. Cristina

6. José y Patricio

7. mi papá

ESTRUCTURA

Past, present, and future time: A review

Pasado: Ayer **hablé** por teléfono con mi abuelo.
Presente: Hoy **hablo** con mis amigos en la escuela.
Progresivo: Ahora mismo **estoy hablando** con mi amigo.
Futuro: Más tarde **voy a hablar** con mi profesor.

Pasado: Esta tarde el estudiante **comió** en la cafetería.
Presente: **Come** en el Café Hermoso los viernes por la tarde.
Progresivo: **Está comiendo** en casa ahora mismo.
Futuro: **Tiene ganas de comer** en un restaurante mañana.

Pasado: La semana pasada **salimos** con nuestros primos.
Presente: Cada mes, **salimos** con nuestra madre.
Progresivo: En este momento **estamos saliendo** con toda la familia.
Futuro: La semana próxima **esperamos salir** con nuestros amigos.

In Units 1–5, you learned how to express past, present, and future events using various verb tenses and constructions, as well as several expressions that situate events in the past, present, and future. Reviewing these materials will help you keep your communication skills sharp.

1. Past time: preterite tense

—¿Qué **hiciste** anoche? — *What did you do last night?*
—**Cené** en un restaurante y **fui** al cine. — *I ate dinner in a restaurant and went to the movies.*

2. Present time for routine activities: present tense

—¿Qué **haces** tú después de la escuela todos los días? — *What do you do after school every day?*
—**Visito** a mis amigas. — *I visit my girlfriends.*

3. Present time for actions occurring at that very moment: present progressive

—¿Qué **estás haciendo** ahora? — *What are you doing now?*
—**Estoy buscando** mis libros. — *I am looking for my books.*

4. Future time: **esperar** + infinitive, **ir a** + infinitive, **pensar** + infinitive, **querer** + infinitive, **quisiera** + infinitive, **tener ganas de** + infinitive

—¿Qué **van a hacer** Uds. durante las vacaciones? — *What are you going to do during vacation?*
—Yo **voy a visitar** a amigos en Nueva York. — *I am going to visit friends in New York.*
—Yo **quiero ir** a Nuevo México. — *I want to go to New Mexico.*
—Y yo **quisiera viajar** a Colombia. — *And I would like to travel to Colombia.*
—Pablo **espera volver** a la Argentina. — *Pablo hopes to return to Argentina.*
—La profesora **piensa viajar** a Bolivia. — *The teacher plans to travel to Bolivia.*
—Mis padres **tienen ganas de ir** a la playa. — *My parents feel like going to the beach.*

Aquí practicamos

D. Hoy, ayer y mañana Di lo que tú y tus amigos están haciendo, hacen, hicieron y van a hacer.

A	B	C
ayer	yo	hablar por teléfono con sus amigos
ahora mismo	tú y ?	mirar un programa de televisión
todos los días	? y yo	estudiar para un examen
anoche	? y ?	comer en un restaurante
el fin de semana próximo	?	salir con sus amigos

E. Quisiera saber... Hazle las siguientes preguntas a un(a) compañero(a).

1. ¿Estás en la escuela todos los días? ¿Estuviste en la escuela el sábado pasado? ¿Vas a estar en la escuela el verano próximo?

2. ¿Haces un viaje todos los veranos? ¿Hiciste un viaje el año pasado? ¿Vas a hacer un viaje el año próximo?

3. ¿Desayunas todos los días? ¿Desayunaste ayer por la mañana? ¿Vas a desayunar mañana por la mañana?

4. ¿Miras algún programa de televisión los viernes? ¿Miraste un programa de televisión el domingo por la noche? ¿Vas a mirar un programa de televisión mañana por la noche?

5. ¿Hablas por teléfono con alguien cada noche? ¿Hablaste por teléfono con alguien anoche? ¿Vas a hablar por teléfono con alguien esta noche?

F. De costumbre... For each of the drawings that follow, explain what the people do normally (**de costumbre**), what they did in the past, and what they will do in the future. Begin each explanation with **De costumbre...**, continue it with **Pero...**, and finish it with **Y....** Follow the model.

> **MODELO** ¿Qué hace José Luis durante las vacaciones de verano?
> *De costumbre él escucha música. Pero el año pasado estuvo en la playa. Y el año próximo piensa viajar a México.*

de costumbre

el año pasado

el año próximo

1. ¿Qué hace Vera durante el fin de semana?

| de costumbre | el fin de semana pasado | el fin de semana próximo |

2. ¿A qué hora llega Marcos a la escuela?

| de costumbre | anteayer | el viernes próximo |

3. ¿Qué comen Sabrina y Carolina cuando van al centro?

| de costumbre | el sábado pasado | el sábado próximo |

4. ¿Qué hace Óscar los viernes?

| de costumbre | el viernes pasado | el viernes próximo |

G. Una entrevista

You are being interviewed by a reporter from your school newspaper about your many travels. Answer the questions using the cues given in parentheses. Follow the models.

MODELOS
¿Esperas viajar a España este año? (no, el año próximo)
No, voy a viajar a España el año próximo.

¿Piensas ir a México? (no, el año pasado)
No, fui a México el año pasado.

1. ¿Piensas ir de vacaciones mañana? (no, hoy)
2. ¿Viajaste a Costa Rica el verano pasado? (no, el mes próximo)
3. ¿Esperas viajar a Bogotá? (no, el año pasado)
4. ¿Quisieras visitar la Ciudad de Guatemala? (sí, el año próximo)
5. ¿Piensas ir a Santa Fe este año? (no, el año pasado)
6. ¿Quieres viajar a Europa el año próximo? (no, el verano pasado)

Aquí escuchamos

¿Para qué vas al centro? *Isabel invites Pedro to go downtown.*

Antes de escuchar How do you think Isabel might invite Pedro to go downtown? How might Pedro say he can or can't accompany her?

 A escuchar Listen twice to the conversation between Isabel and Pedro before answering the questions about it that follow.

Después de escuchar Answer the following questions based on what you heard.

1. Why does Isabel want to go downtown?
2. When does Isabel want to go?
3. Why can't Pedro go tomorrow afternoon?
4. When do they decide to go?

Intercambio Using the verbs indicated, ask a partner questions to obtain the listed information. When asking questions about the future, be sure to use some of the following expressions: **pensar, esperar, ir a, quisiera, querer, tener ganas de.** Find one activity that you have in common and one in which you differ.

1. **estudiar:** Find out where your friend usually studies; whether he (she) studied there last night; whether he (she) is planning to study there tonight.

2. **ir al cine:** Find out if your friend goes to the movies a lot; if he (she) went to the movies last week; whether he (she) is going to the movies soon.

3. **viajar:** Find out if your friend travels a lot; if he (she) traveled last year, and if so, where he (she) went; whether he (she) hopes to travel next year, and if so, where he (she) intends to go.

4. **ir / tomar / andar:** Find out how your friend usually gets to school; if he (she) got to school the same way this morning; whether he (she) will get to school the same way next year.

 Los fines de semana You have just received a note from a friend in El Salvador in which she asks about how students your age in the United States spend their weekends. Write a note to her in which you tell three things that you do in a typical weekend, three things that you did last weekend, and three activities that you plan to do next weekend.

Connect with the Spanish-speaking world!
Access the *¡Ya verás! Gold* home page for
Internet activities related to this chapter.

http://yaveras.heinle.com

VOCABULARIO

Para charlar

Para hablar de acciones en el futuro

esperar + *infinitive*
ir a + *infinitive*
pensar + *infinitive*
querer + *infinitive*
quisiera + *infinitive*
tener ganas de + *infinitive*

Para hablar de acciones que están pasando ahora

ahora
ahora mismo
en este momento
estar + *verb in present participle*

Vocabulario general

Otras palabras y expresiones

de costumbre
dormir
durante las vacaciones

Un héroe de Puerto Rico

Antes de leer

1. Look at the pictures that accompany the reading. What sport does this person play?

2. Look at the title. Where is this athlete from? Do you think he is held in great esteem in his country? Why?

3. Scan the second paragraph of the reading. Find two cognates or familiar terms related to baseball playing, then find the names of two baseball teams from the United States.

Muchos jugadores en la historia del béisbol son famosos no sólo por sus logros atléticos, sino por su interés en ayudar a sus comunidades. Babe Ruth enseñó a batear a muchos niños y Cal Ripken, Jr. hoy en día promueve los programas de educación para adultos. Roberto Clemente, formidable atleta puertorriqueño, ha sido tal vez el único jugador que ha dado su vida por ayudar a otros.

Roberto Clemente nació en Carolina, Puerto Rico, en 1934. A los 20 años firmó su primer contrato para jugar al béisbol profesional con los Dodgers de Brooklyn. Un año más tarde, en 1955, firmó un contrato para jugar con los Piratas de Pittsburgh. Allí tuvo una brillante carrera y muchos todavía consideran a Clemente como uno de los mejores jugadores de la historia del béisbol. En octubre de 1971, los Piratas ganaron la Serie Mundial y Clemente fue el factor principal de ese triunfo. Clemente, nombrado el jugador más valioso (MVP) de esa serie, bateó en 1972 su hit número 3,000—algo que muy pocos jugadores logran.

Ese año, después de terminar la temporada de béisbol, Clemente volvió a Puerto Rico para pasar el invierno. A finales de diciembre, hubo un terremoto catastrófico en Nicaragua, que dejó a muchas personas sin casa y sin comida. Clemente, cuando oyó que se estaban robando las provisiones y medicinas de las víctimas del terremoto, decidió ir en persona a hacer la entrega.

El 31 de diciembre de 1972, un sobrecargado DC-7 despegó del Aeropuerto de Isla Verde hacia Nicaragua. Roberto Clemente era uno de los pasajeros. Minutos después, el avión explotó en el aire y desapareció para siempre en el fondo del océano. El verano después de su muerte, Clemente fue elegido para formar parte del Pabellón de la Fama en Cooperstown, Nueva York. Hoy lo recordamos con un monumento colocado frente al estadio de Pittsburgh y con un premio que celebra los logros de los jugadores de béisbol tanto en el estadio como en la comunidad.

Guía para la lectura

logros	*achievements, feats*
batear	*to hit (baseball)*
promueve	*promotes*
programas de educación	*literacy programs*
ha dado su vida	*has given his life*
firmó	*he signed*
Serie Mundial	*World Series*
terremoto	*earthquake*
se estaban robando	*(supplies) were being stolen*
hacer la entrega	*make the delivery*
sobrecargado	*overloaded*
despegó	*took off*
explotó	*exploded*
premio	*award*

Después de leer

1. Explain in your own words the meaning of the last sentence of the first paragraph. What makes Roberto Clemente special?

2. Some vocabulary words in the reading have not been defined for you. Try to glean meaning from context and from the recognition of cognates.

   What is the meaning of these phrases in italics?

   a. firmó *un contrato*

   b. nombrado el *jugador más valioso*

   c. *ganaron* la serie mundial

   d. decidió ir *en persona* a hacer la entrega

3. Who are the public figures you admire? What is it about them that you find admirable? Do you think it's important to have "heroes?" Why or why not?

Conversemos un rato

A. La semana pasada In groups of three or four students, role-play the following discussion about what you each did last week. Try to decide who had the busiest week.

1. Each member of the group will take turns describing his or her past week by listing the events or activities in the order they occurred. Be sure to use a variety of verbs in the past and use appropriate time indicators.

2. The other members of the group will ask for clarification.

3. Reach an agreement about who had the busiest week in the group.

B. ¡Vivan las vacaciones! Imagine that your Spanish class has just won an all-expense-paid trip to the Spanish-speaking countries of your choice. There will be a competition to decide the itinerary for the class trip. The team with the winning itinerary will get to travel in first class.

1. In teams of three or four students, role-play the following discussion in order to plan an itinerary for the big trip.

    a. Each member of the team must suggest a country to visit. Decide on two.

    b. Each member must suggest an interesting activity to do and organize them into an itinerary.

    c. As a team, decide on the kind of transportation you will use and how you will travel from place to place.

2. Then, meet with another team to compare itineraries.

    a. Each team will describe their itinerary to the other team.

    b. Both teams will then combine their itineraries to create one travel plan, taking the most interesting ideas from each team.

    c. Finally, present your travel plan to the entire class and try to persuade them to adopt your itinerary. Remember, the winning team gets to travel in first class!

Taller de escritores

Writing a report

You will practice your writing in Spanish by writing a two- or three-para-graph report on a trip you took or an exciting leisure-time experience you have had. Your audience will be the readers of the Spanish Club Newsletter.

Un viaje a la playa

El mes pasado fuí de vacaciones con mis padres a Manzanillo, en la costa de México. Pasamos una semana en el Hotel Las Hadas. Hicimos el viaje en avión y salimos el 26 de diciembre y volvimos el 2 de enero. Tuvimos un viaje muy divertido.

Manzanillo tiene un clima muy bueno en el invierno. Pasamos mucho tiempo en la playa del hotel donde nadamos mucho. También nos acostamos cerca de la piscina grande del hotel. Un día fuimos a otra playa donde practicamos el esquí acuático y el buceo deportivo. Tomamos el sol todos los días, menos un día cuando no hizo sol.

Un día fuimos a Colima, la capital del estado. Allí vimos un museo de arqueología muy grande. También fuimos a comer a muchos restaurantes buenos. Nos sirvieron comidas muy variadas. Hicimos muchas cosas durante los siete días. Para unas vacaciones magníficas les recomiendo Manzanillo.

A. Reflexión After choosing the trip you will describe, select the main point of each paragraph and write an outline. Add subheadings to each major heading to increase the detail.

B. Primer borrador Write a first draft of your description. Remember you are writing for a student newsletter.

C. Revisión con un(a) compañero(a) Exchange papers with a classmate. Read each other's work and comment on it, based on the questions below.

1. What do you like best about your classmate's first draft?
2. What part do you find the clearest?
3. What part do you find the most interesting?
4. Does the first draft keep the audience in mind?
5. Does the writing reflect the task assigned?
6. Does the first draft raise questions that, if answered, you think would make the writing clearer, more interesting, or more complete?

D. Versión final At home, revise your first draft, incorporating changes based on the feedback from your classmate. Revise content and check your grammar, spelling, punctuation and accent marks. Bring your final draft to class.

E. Carpeta After you turn in your report, your teacher may choose to place it in your portfolio, display it on a bulletin board, or use it to evaluate your progress.

Conexión con las ciencias

Para empezar The following passage discusses aerobic exercises and the amount of energy we use (how many calories we burn) when we do certain activities.

El término aeróbico significa "vivir en la presencia del oxígeno". Los ejercicios aeróbicos, la natación, el ciclismo y el correr, por ejemplo, estimulan el corazón y los pulmones con el objetivo de aumentar la cantidad de oxígeno que el cuerpo pueda utilizar dentro de un período de tiempo. Los ejercicios aeróbicos también son ideales para quemar calorías y bajar de peso, ya que el coeficiente de utilización de energía (CUE) de estas actividades es muy alto. Esto quiere decir que utilizamos mucha energía cuando las practicamos.

Cuanto más tiempo se pasa haciendo ejercicios aeróbicos, más energía se utiliza. Las personas de mayor peso suelen utilizar más energía que las de menor peso haciendo la misma actividad.

La primera columna del siguiente esquema nos da el CUE de varias actividades, algunas aeróbicas y otras no. Se multiplica el CUE por el peso de una persona—en kilogramos—para determinar el número de calorías que se queman haciendo una actividad. ¿Cuánto pesas tú en kilogramos? La fórmula para convertir las libras en kilogramos no es muy complicada.

Fórmula:	libras X 0,45 =	kilogramos
Ana pesa 100 lbs	X 0,45 =	Ana pesa 45 kilogramos
Pedro pesa 150 lbs	X 0,45 =	Pedro pesa 68 kilogramos

Ya mencionamos que las personas de mayor peso queman más calorías que las de menor peso haciendo la misma actividad. ¿Quién utiliza más energía haciendo las actividades de la lista, Pedro o Ana?

corazón *heart*   pulmones *lungs*   cuerpo *body*   bajar de peso *lose weight*   el coeficiente de utilización de energía *energy use coefficient*   esquema *chart*   libras *pounds*

Actividad	CUE(se multiplica por)	X		El peso		Calorías por minuto
El boliche	0,0471	X	(Ana)	45kg	=	2,1
			(Pedro)	68kg	=	3,2
Caminar 1 milla en 17 minutos	0,0794	X	(Ana)	45kg	=	3,5
			(Pedro)	68kg	=	5,4
El ciclismo 1 milla en 6,4 minutos	0,0985	X	(Ana)	45kg	=	4,4
			(Pedro)	68kg	=	6,7
La natación	0,1333	X	(Ana)	45kg	=	6,0
			(Pedro)	68kg	=	9,1
Correr 1 milla en 10 minutos	0,1471	X	(Ana)	45kg	=	6,6
			(Pedro)	68kg	=	10,0

meta final

A. Vocabulario Work with a partner to match the term in the first column with its definition in the second column. Record your choices on a separate sheet of paper. Prepare for class discussion!

_____1. el kilogramo   A. unidad de energía

_____2. la caloría   B. la actividad de montar en bicicleta

_____3. el ciclismo   C. la actividad de nadar

_____4. aeróbico   D. gas que respiramos

_____5. los pulmones   E. unidad de peso del sistema métrico

_____6. el oxígeno   F. en la presencia del oxígeno

_____7. la natación   G. dos órganos que usamos para respirar

B. Taller Refer to the chart to answer the following questions.

1. Ana caminó por 30 minutos ayer por la tarde (velocidad = 1 milla en 17 minutos). ¿Cuántas calorías quemó ella?

2. Pedro comió una pizza que contenía unas 500 calorías el viernes por la noche. ¿Cuántos minutos tiene que nadar para quemar esas calorías?

3. Cuántos minutos tiene que jugar al boliche para quemar las 500 calorías?

4. Cuántos minutos tiene que montar en bicicleta para quemar las mismas 500 calorías?

5. Una persona misteriosa corrió en el parque por 45 minutos. Sabemos que la persona quemó 450 calorías. ¿Quién fue al parque, Pedro o Ana?

Vistas de los hispanos en los Estados Unidos

California

Capital: Sacramento

Ciudades principales: Los Angeles, San Francisco, San Diego, San José

Población: 29.839.225

Idiomas: inglés y español

Área territorial: 411.047 km²

Clima: muy variado, temperatura se mantiene de 32° C para bajo

Florida

Capital: Tallahassee

Ciudades principales: Miami, Jacksonville, Tampa, St. Petersburg, Orlando

Población: 12.937.926

Idiomas: inglés y español

Área territorial: 151.939 km²

Clima: tropical, húmedo

EXPLORA

Find out more about California and Florida! Access the **Nuestros vecinos** page on the *¡Ya verás! Gold* web site for a list of URLs.

http://yaveras.heinle.com/vecinos.htm

En la comunidad

¡Se buscan estrellas de béisbol!

"*My name is Anita Lopez-Jenkins. My father is a quiet man who was born in Detroit. He always wanted a child he could play baseball with. My mother is a gregarious Dominican-American who always wanted a child she could speak Spanish with. My father dreamed I'd be a famous female ball player. My mother thought I'd make a great Spanish teacher.*

Fortunately, I've always liked Spanish and I've always liked sports. In high school, I took Spanish all four years and played hockey, track, and girl's basketball. In college, I double-majored in Spanish and physical education, while I continued playing basketball, plus took up tennis and swimming. Once I graduated, however, I wasn't sure how I could combine sports and Spanish. I thought about teaching, social work with kids, or working at a luxury resort as an activities director, but nothing seemed quite right for me. Then I saw an article in a sports magazine about sports recruiters, and a light went on. I wrote to the managers of major and minor league baseball teams all over the country. I described my background and my knowledge of sports and Spanish. On my third interview, I got a job! Nowadays, I spend most of the year traveling to Puerto Rico, the Dominican Republic, and other Spanish-speaking countries where baseball is an important sport. I help evaluate talent during professional try-outs and interview potential players in Spanish. It's a lot of fun; I love my job!"

¡Ahora te toca a ti!

Choose a well-known, Spanish-speaking actor, singer, writer, or athlete to research. Use the resources at your local library to locate an interview, a review, or an article with information on your subject. Consider your subject's hobbies, country of origin, occupation and contribution to his or her field. Then write a short paragraph in Spanish (at least five sentences), describing the person you have chosen. List your source(s). You may wish to share your research with the class.

UNIDAD 6

Vamos de compras

Objectives

In this unit you will learn:

- to express what you and other like or dislike
- to give informal commands
- to ask for and understand information about making purchases
- to make purchases in stores
- to indicate quantities
- to point out people, places, and objects
- to compare prices, objects, and prople

¿Qué ves?

- What is the girl in these photographs doing?
- Where is she?
- Why is she there?

CAPÍTULO 16

Vamos al centro comercial

—Quiero comprar un disco
 compacto nuevo.
—Yo también. ¡Vamos!

Objectives

- making purchases and choices
- expressing quantity
- asking for prices

PRIMERA ETAPA

- Do you like to go shopping? Why, or why not?

- Where do you usually go to buy the things you need?

- What kinds of questions do you normally need to ask when you are shopping?

- Do you do your grocery shopping at the same place where you buy such items as records, clothes, shoes, and sporting goods?

En la tienda de música

Beatriz y Mónica van de compras.

Anoche Beatriz y Mónica **fueron** a un concierto de rock en el Parque Luna. **A ellas les encantó** escuchar a su grupo favorito, Juan Luis Guerra y los 440. Hoy Mónica quiere comprar uno de sus discos compactos. **Por eso,** van a la tienda de música "La Nueva Onda". Beatriz quiere comprar un disco compacto de Jon Secada, pero es muy **caro**.

Beatriz: ¡Qué pena! No tengo **suficiente dinero** para comprar el disco compacto.

Mónica: Mira, yo encontré la cinta de Juan Luis Guerra y los 440 que me gusta y es muy barata.

Beatriz: **A ver.** ¿Dónde están las cintas?

Mónica: Allí, al lado de los vídeos.

Beatriz: ¡Super! Aquí está la cinta que me gusta a mí.

fueron *went* **A ellas les encantó** *They loved* **Por eso** *That is why* **caro** *expensive* **¡Qué pena!** *What a shame* **suficiente** *enough* **dinero** *money* **A ver.** *Let's see.*

¡Te toca a ti!

A. Para mi cumpleaños... Make up a "wish list" for your next birthday by completing the following sentences.

1. Yo quiero…

2. Quisiera…

3. Necesito…

4. Por favor, compra…

5. ¿Tienes suficiente dinero para comprar…?

B. Los regalos You are at "La Nueva Onda," buying presents for your family and friends. 1) Decide which tapes or CDs you will get for whom. 2) Develop a list of at least four people and gifts as you make your decisions. When you have made your choices, 3) discuss them with a partner. As you go through your list, 4) make a comment explaining each choice. Follow the model.

MODELO	**Tú:**	*Pienso comprar este disco compacto para mi prima. [X] es su cantante favorito. Y esta cinta es para papá. Escucha siempre la música de [X].*
	Compañero(a):	*Buena idea. Yo voy a comprar esta cinta para mi hermano. Le gusta mucho el jazz latino. Quisiera comprar el disco compacto pero es muy caro.*

PRONUNCIACIÓN THE CONSONANT r

A single **r** within a word is pronounced like the *dd* in the English words *daddy* and *ladder,* that is, with a single tap of the tip of the tongue against the gum ridge behind the upper front teeth.

Práctica

C. Escucha a tu maestro(a) cuando lee las siguientes palabras y repítelas después para practicar la pronunciación.

1. cámara
2. pájaro
3. farmacia
4. cuatro
5. pintura
6. estéreo
7. libro
8. hermano
9. parque
10. serio

ESTRUCTURA

The verbs **gustar** and **encantar**

Le gusta tocar la guitarra.	*You (formal) like to play the guitar.*
Les gusta el concierto.	*You (plural) like the concert.* *They like the concert.*
No nos gustan las películas de horror.	*We don't like horror movies.*

1. To express what someone else likes or dislikes, Spanish uses the pronouns **le** (singular) and **les** (plural). The pronoun **nos** is used for **nosotros(as)**. Remember to use **gusta** if what is liked is a singular noun or an infinitive and to use **gustan** if what is liked is a plural noun.

2. The verb **encantar** (*to like very much, to really like, to love*) follows the same pattern as the verb **gustar**.

Nos encanta el helado.   *We love ice cream.*

3. To clarify or emphasize who likes or dislikes something, use the preposition **a** plus the pronoun(s) or noun(s) that identify the person(s).

A mí me encantan los deportes.   *I really like sports.*

A ti no te gusta ir de camping.   *You don't like to go camping.*

A Ud. le gusta el jazz.   *You* (formal) *like jazz.*

A mi hermana le encanta la música latina.   *My sister loves Latin music.*

A Lucy y a mí nos gusta bailar.   *Lucy and I like to dance.*

A Uds. les encantan los vídeos.   *You* (plural) *love the videos.*

A Ana y Javier no les gusta la cinta.   *Ana and Javier don't like the tape.*

Aquí practicamos

D. Los gustos Ask two classmates what items or activities they like most. After they answer, indicate the ones that both of them like. If they do not like the same things, indicate what each of your classmates likes. Follow the model.

> MODELO
>
> **Tú:** ¿*Les gusta más la radio o la grabadora?*
> **Estudiante 1:** *Me gusta más la grabadora.*
> **Estudiante 2:** *Me gusta más la grabadora.* o:
> *Me gusta la radio.*
> **Tú:** *Ah, a los dos les gusta la grabadora.* o:
> *Ah, a él (ella) le gusta la grabadora y a ella (él) le gusta la radio.*

1. los discos compactos o las cintas
2. el concierto o la película
3. ir de compras o hablar por teléfono
4. la computadora o la máquina de escribir
5. el jazz o la música clásica
6. las fotografías o los vídeos
7. la televisión o el cine
8. la radio o la grabadora
9. bailar o mirar la televisión

E. ¿Qué les gusta hacer?
Do you know your friends and family well? What is the one thing they most like to do? Tell what each person listed likes to do. Follow the model.

MODELO
mi hermana
A mi hermana le gusta estudiar.

1. mi mejor amigo(a)
2. mi madre
3. mis abuelos
4. mis compañeros de clase
5. mis primos
6. mi padre
7. mi hermano(a)
8. mis profesores

F. El concierto de rock
Tell who liked the concert a lot and who did not like it. Follow the models.

MODELOS
a mi hermano / sí
A mi hermano le encantó el concierto.

a mis padres / no
A mis padres no les gustó el concierto.

1. a Benito y a mí / sí
2. a Laura / no
3. a mi prima / no
4. a mí / sí
5. a ellos / no
6. a Ud. / sí
7. a nosotros / sí
8. a Uds. / sí
9. a ella / no
10. a Eduardo y a mí / sí

G. ¿Qué le encanta a tu compañero(a)?
Find out from a classmate the things that he (she) likes and loves to do and eat, the places that he (she) likes to go, and the music or group (**grupo**) that he (she) likes to listen to. Then report that information to the class. Work with a partner and follow the model.

MODELO

Tú:	¿Qué te gusta hacer?
Compañera(o):	*A mí me gusta… y me encanta…*
Tú:	*A Anita le gusta… y le encanta…*

Aquí escuchamos

Me gusta la música... *Isabel and Miguel give information about their likes and dislikes.*

Antes de escuchar Based on what you've learned in this **etapa,** what are some of the likes and dislikes you expect Isabel and Miguel to talk about?

 A escuchar On your activity master, make a list of some of the things that Isabel likes and another of the things that Miguel likes.

Después de escuchar Responde a las siguientes preguntas sobre la conversación entre Isabel y Miguel.

1. ¿A quién le gustan muchos tipos de música?
2. ¿Qué música le gusta más a Isabel? ¿Y a Miguel?
3. ¿Por qué le gustan más a Miguel las cintas que los discos compactos?
4. ¿A quién le gusta Jon Secada?
5. ¿Adónde van a ir Isabel y Miguel?

¡ADELANTE!

 ¿Qué te gusta hacer los fines de semana?
Work in pairs and 1) tell your partner the things that you like to do on weekends. 2) Find out if there are activities that you both like. 3) Then, report your likes and dislikes to the class. Follow the model.

MODELO		
	Compañera(o):	*¿Qué te gusta hacer los fines de semana?*
	Tú:	*A mí me gusta hablar por teléfono con mis amigos.*
	Compañera(o):	*A mí también me gusta hablar por teléfono con mis amigos.*
	Tú:	*A nosotros(as) nos gusta hablar por teléfono con nuestros amigos.*

 Un diálogo de contrarios Imagine that you and another student are completely opposite in every way. The two of you are friends, despite great differences in likes, dislikes, interests, and possessions. With a partner, make up some details about your two lives and write a dialogue together of about twelve sentences in length, that is, about six to eight comments from each of you.

Preparación

- What are some of the items that you will find at a stationery store or in the paper goods section of a department store?

- What are some of the questions that a person who works in a store usually asks a customer?

En la papelería

Mario y Andrés van de compras a la **papelería** (stationery store).

Señora:	Buenos días, muchachos. ¿En qué puedo servirles?
Mario:	Necesitamos **papel para escribir a máquina.** ¿Tiene?
Señora:	¡Cómo no! ¿Cuántas **hojas** quieren?
Mario:	Diez, por favor. ¿Y **papel de avión?**
Señora:	Aquí tienen. **¿Algo más?**
Andrés:	Sí, yo necesito tres **tarjetas de cumpleaños** y una tarjeta del Día de la Madre.
Señora:	Acabamos de recibir unas muy bonitas. Mira aquí.
Andrés:	Mm… Sí, son muy bonitas. ¿Vienen con **sobres?**
Señora:	¡Pues, claro!
Mario:	Bien. **Es todo por hoy.**

papel para escribir a máquina *typewriter paper*   **hojas** *sheets*   **papel de avión** *airmail paper*   **¿Algo más?** *Anything else?* **Tarjetas de cumpleaños** *birthday cards*   **sobres** *envelopes*   **Es todo por hoy.** *That's all for today.*

¡Te toca a ti!

A. ¿Qué compraron en la papelería?
Mira las fotos que siguen y di qué compró la persona indicada. Sigue el modelo.

MODELO   Estela
Estela compró una tarjeta de felicitación.

Estela

1. La Srta. Balboa

2. Ignacio

4. Cristina

3. Inés

6. Roberto

5. el Sr. Rodríguez

B. ¿Adónde vas para comprar... ? Mira los dibujos y di adónde vas para comprar cada cosa. Sigue el modelo.

> **MODELO** Voy a la tienda de música
> para comprar discos compactos.

1.

2.

3.

4.

5.

6.

7.

Repaso

C. En la tienda de música You are shopping for presents for three of your friends at "La Nueva Onda." Together with another student, 1) alternate playing the roles of the clerk and the customer at a record store. 2) Tell the clerk the music your friends like. The clerk will make suggestions for each gift. 3) Buy two CDs and a tape. 4) Pay and leave. Follow the model.

> **MODELO** **Tú:** ¿En qué puedo servirle?
> **Compañero(a):** A mi amiga Claudia le gusta la música clásica. Quiero comprar un disco compacto para ella. ¿Qué tiene Ud.?

PRONUNCIACIÓN THE CONSONANT **rr**

An **rr** (called a trilled *r*), within a word is pronounced by flapping or trilling the tip of the tongue against the gum ridge behind the upper front teeth. When an **r** is the first letter of a Spanish word, it also has this sound.

Práctica

D. Escucha a tu maestro(a) cuando lee las siguientes palabras. Después repítelas para practicar la pronunciación.

1. borrador
2. perro
3. correo
4. barrio
5. aburrido
6. radio
7. Roberto
8. rubio
9. río
10. música rock

ESTRUCTURA

The imperative with tú: Affirmative familiar commands

—Raquel, **mira** las tarjetas de cumpleaños.   *Raquel, look at the birthday cards.*

—Son muy bonitas. **Compra** dos.   *They are very pretty. Buy two.*

1. Regular affirmative **tú** commands have the same form as the present-tense form for **él, ella,** and **usted.**

El **escucha** el disco compacto.	*He is listening to the CD.*
¡Escucha!	*Listen!*
Ella **corre** todos los días.	*She runs every day.*
¡Corre!	*Run!*
Usted **escribe** muy bien.	*You write very well.*
¡Escribe la carta ahora!	*Write the letter now!*

2. The verbs **decir** *(to say, tell),* **hacer, ir, poner** *(to put, place),* **salir, ser, tener,** and **venir** *(to come, to go)* have irregular affirmative **tú** commands.

decir	**di**	ir	**ve**	salir	**sal**	tener	**ten**
hacer	**haz**	poner	**pon**	ser	**sé**	venir	**ven**

Aquí practicamos

E. Tú lo debes... Da la forma del mandato *(command)* con **tú,** de los siguientes verbos.

1. hablar
2. comer
3. hacer
4. mirar
5. leer
6. salir
7. doblar
8. comprar
9. decir
10. correr
11. descansar
12. ser
13. escuchar
14. escribir
15. tener

F. A tu hermano
Use the command form to get your younger brother to do what you want. Follow the model.

MODELO   caminar al quiosco de la esquina
Camina al quiosco de la esquina.

1. venir aquí
2. ser bueno
3. hacer la tarea
4. poner la radio
5. salir de mi cuarto

6. ir al quiosco de periódicos
7. comprar mi revista favorita
8. usar tu dinero
9. tener paciencia
10. decir la verdad

G. Consejos
Your best friend has problems at school. Give him (her) some advice on what to do to improve the situation. Use these verbs in the **tú** command form in complete sentences. Follow the models.

MODELOS   *Haz la tarea todos los días.*
Llega a clase temprano.

decir	escuchar	hablar	ir	llegar	salir	venir
escribir	estudiar	hacer	leer	practicar	trabajar	

Aquí escuchamos

Para mi computadora... *A clerk helps a customer in a store.*

Antes de escuchar Think about some of the items you might buy to use with a computer. Some of the same vocabulary that you already know in Spanish applies. Can you think of examples?

 A escuchar Listen twice to the conversation between the clerk and the customer before answering the questions about it that follow.

Después de escuchar Responde a las siguientes preguntas sobre la conversación entre la empleada y el señor.

1. ¿Qué necesita el señor que va a la papelería?
2. ¿En paquetes de cuántos se venden los disquetes para la computadora?
3. ¿Qúe le pregunta la empleada si necesita el señor?
4. ¿Qué dice él cuando ella le pregunta eso?
5. ¿Qué recuerda el señor que necesita comprar para su esposa?

Ve a la papelería You need computer disks from the stationery store, but you have to stay home to prepare for a major test.

1. Call your friend and explain the situation.
3. Tell him (her) one other thing that you need from the stationery store.
4. After your friend agrees to do this errand, tell him (her) when and where to meet you to deliver the purchases.
5. Thank your friend for the help.

Use informal commands as needed to make your requests. Follow the model for the beginning of your conversation. Work with a partner and finish the conversation

MODELO		
Tú:	*¡Hola, Estela!*	
Estela:	*¡Hola! ¿Qué tal?*	
Tú:	*Bien, pero tengo mucho que hacer.*	
Estela:	*¿Qué tienes que hacer?*	
Tú:	*…*	

Consejos One of your friends has some problems with school work. He (she) has asked you what to do in order to be more successful. Try to help by writing a list of eight suggestions for improving the situation. Use the informal command forms of the following verbs in the sentences you write: **estudiar, trabajar, hablar, hacer, practicar, escribir, decir, tener, salir, ver.** Then arrange your sentences in order of priority, starting with the three most useful suggestions for ensuring your friend's success.

Preparación

- Where do you go to shop for sports equipment?
- What are some examples of sports equipment?
- What items do you usually buy when you go to a sporting goods store?
- Which sports require the most expensive equipment, and which require the least expensive?

La tienda de deportes

Elsa y Norma **entran** *(enter) en una tienda de deportes.*

Empleado:	Sí, señoritas, ¿qué necesitan?
Elsa:	Quisiera saber cuánto **cuesta** la **raqueta** en el **escaparate.**
Empleado:	¡Ah! **Buen ojo.** Es una raqueta muy buena y cuesta 120 dólares.
Elsa:	¿Cómo? ¿No está **en oferta?**
Empleado:	No, señorita. La oferta **terminó** ayer.
Elsa:	¡Qué pena! Bueno. Y las **pelotas de tenis, ¿qué precio tienen?**
Empleado:	Mm… tres dólares.
Elsa:	Bueno, **voy a llevar** tres. ¿Puedo ver los **zapatos de tenis** también, por favor?
Empleado:	Por supuesto. ¿Algo más?
Norma:	Sí. ¿Venden **esquíes?**
Empleado:	Sí, pero no hay más. Vendimos todos los esquíes en la oferta.
Norma:	Mm… bueno. Gracias.
Empleado:	**A sus órdenes.**

cuesta *costs* **raqueta** *racket* **escaparate** *display window* **Buen ojo.** *Good eye.* **en oferta** *on sale* **terminó** *ended* **pelotas de tenis** *tennis balls* **¿qué precio tienen?** *What do they cost?* **Voy a llevar** *I'll take* **zapatos de tenis** *tennis shoes* **esquíes** *skis* **A sus órdenes.** *At your service.*

¡Te toca a ti!

A. Necesito comprar...
You are in a sporting goods store and you want to examine the following items before you buy. Ask to see them. Follow the model.

MODELO
pelotas de tenis
Quisiera ver las pelotas de tenis, por favor.

1.

2.

3.

4.

5.

6.

B. ¿Cuánto cuesta...?
You want to know the price of different items in the sporting goods store. Ask the clerk. In pairs, play the roles of the customer and clerk. The person playing the clerk should make up reasonable prices for each item from Activity A. Follow the model.

MODELO
(pelotas de tenis)

Tú: *Buenos días. ¿Cuánto cuestan las pelotas de tenis en el escaparate?*
Compañera(o): *Cuestan 3 dólares por tres.*
Tú: *Mm... bien. Voy a llevar seis. Aquí tiene 6 dólares.*

? ¿Qué crees?

The site of the 1992 Olympic summer Games was:

a) Spain
b) Korea
c) Mexico
d) U.S.A.

respuesta ☞

Repaso ♻

C. Mis libros favoritos
You need to buy a present for a friend. You have decided to get something from a bookstore, but you need some advice. Ask a classmate to suggest three books that you could buy as a present. He (she) should use the **tú** command to make the suggestions.

ESTRUCTURA

The imperative with tú: Negative familiar commands

¡**No lleves** tus esquíes!	*Don't take your skis!*
¡**No vendas** tu raqueta!	*Don't sell your racket!*
¡**No compartas** tu comida con el perro!	*Don't share your food with the dog!*

1. To form regular negative **tú** commands, drop the **-o** from the **yo** form of the present tense and add **-es** for **-ar** verbs and **-as** for **-er** and **-ir** verbs.

bailar	yo	bailo	bail-	**no bailes**
beber	yo	bebo	beb-	**no bebas**
escribir	yo	escribo	escrib-	**no escribas**

2. Verbs ending in **-car**, **-gar**, and **-zar** have the same spelling change in the negative **tú** command as they do in the **Ud.** and **Uds.** commands. In verbs ending in **-car**, the **c** in the **-car** ending changes to **qu** (**no practiques**). Verbs that end in **-gar**, add a **u** after the **g** of the ending (**no llegues**). In verbs ending in **-zar**, the **z** of the ending changes to **c** (**no cruces**).

3. Here are the negative **tú** commands of the eight verbs with irregular affirmative **tú** commands you saw in the previous **etapa**:

decir	**no digas**	ir	**no vayas**
hacer	**no hagas**	poner	**no pongas**
salir	**no salgas**	tener	**no tengas**
ser	**no seas**	venir	**no vengas**

Aquí practicamos

D. ¡No hagas eso (that)! Da la forma negativa del mandato con **tú** de los siguientes verbos.

1. esquiar aquí
2. llevar los libros
3. ir al parque
4. comer en tu casa
5. ser antipático
6. vender tus pelotas de tenis
7. comprar los zapatos allí
8. salir de la tienda
9. cruzar la calle
10. tener miedo *(to be afraid)*

E. Consejos

Tell your friend not to do these things. Work in pairs. Then reverse roles and repeat.

1. ser malo
2. llegar tarde
3. tener problemas
4. doblar a la derecha
5. escribir en el libro
6. buscar tus cuadernos
7. mirar mucho la TV
8. venir solo(a) a la fiesta
9. poner la radio en clase
10. decir malas palabras

F. Recomendaciones

You are new in the neighborhood and don't know where to go for the best buys. Your friend will direct you to various shops in town to get good prices and good quality. Work with a partner and follow the model.

> **MODELO**
>
> Tú: *Compro carne en la Carnicería Montoya.*
> Compañero: *No compres allí. Compra en la Carnicería Martín. Es mejor* (better).

1. Como en el restaurante La Estancia.
2. Hago compras en la Frutería la Sevillana.
3. Voy a la Panadería López.
4. Escucho discos compactos en la tienda de música Cantar y Bailar.
5. Busco lápices y borradores en la Papelería Mollar.
6. Miro las flores en la Florería La Rosa Roja.

Aquí escuchamos

El tenista *A customer is looking for a special item at a sporting goods store.*

Antes de escuchar Based on what you have learned in this **etapa**, what are some of the phrases and expressions that you expect the customer and the saleswoman to use in their conversation?

A escuchar Listen twice to the conversation between the saleswoman and the customer before answering the true-or-false questions about it on your activity master.

Después de escuchar On your activity master, indicate whether the following statements are true or false. If a statement is false, provide the correct information.

1. The customer wants to buy some tennis shoes.
2. The customer indicates that he already has a tennis racket.
3. The customer wants a larger tennis racket.
4. The saleswoman says that the large rackets are still on sale.
5. The price of the racket is $199.
6. The offer comes with a free can of tennis balls.
7. The man decides not to buy the racket because it is too expensive.

¡ADELANTE!

 ¿Qué deporte? Your friend wants to take up a new sport and asks you for advice because you are familiar with a number of sports.

1. Ask your friend about his (her) preferences for season, team, or individual sports.
2. Find out if your friend likes to play sports for competition or pleasure, and about any equipment to which she (he) has access.
3. Choose a sport and advise your friend to take it up.
4. Explain why, basing your decisions on your friend's talents and preferences.
5. Tell her (him) what to buy in order to start practicing.

 Mi deporte preferido Write six to eight sentences about your favorite sport, indicating why you like it, how often you participate in that sport, where, and with whom.

Connect with the Spanish-speaking world! Access the *¡Ya verás! Gold* home page for Internet activities related to this chapter.

http://yaveras.heinle.com

VOCABULARIO

Para charlar

Para expresar gustos

me / te / le / nos / les encanta(n)
me / te / le / nos / les gusta(n)

Lugares para comprar

una papelería
una tienda de deportes
una tienda de música

Expresiones para comprar o vender

¿En qué puedo servirle(s)?
¿Qué necesita(n)?
No hay más.
Voy a llevar...
Aquí tiene(n).
¿Algo más?
Es todo por hoy.
A sus órdenes.

Para preguntar el precio

¿Cuánto cuesta(n)?
¿Qué precio tiene(n)?
¿No está(n) en oferta?

Temas y contextos

En la tienda de música

una cinta
un disco compacto
un vídeo

En la papelería

una hoja
papel de avión
papel para escribir a máquina
un sobre
una tarjeta de cumpleaños

En la tienda de deportes

unos esquíes
una pelota de tenis
una raqueta
unos zapatos de tenis

Vocabulario general

Sustantivos

un centro comercial
un escaparate
la música latina
el precio

Verbos

decir
poner

Adjetivos

barato(a)
bonito(a)
caro(a)
favorito(a)
suficiente

Otras expresiones

A ver.
Buen ojo.
fueron
por eso
¡Qué pena!
¡Super!

Ritos importantes para los jóvenes hispanohablantes

Reading Strategies

- Activating background knowledge
- Recognizing cognates
- Scanning for specific information

Social rites of passage are important in every society because they can mark a transition from one stage of life to another. In the following reading you will learn about some rites of passage for 15-year-old girls and 13-year-old boys in some Spanish-speaking countries.

Antes de leer

1. Scan the first paragraph and find at least five cognates. Then, guess what kind of celebration is being described.

2. Scan the second paragraph and find three articles of clothing mentioned.

3. Can you describe a rite of passage that you, or someone you know, has experienced?

• •

La quinceañera es una fiesta que se celebra en diversas partes del mundo hispanohablante cuando una chica cumple los quince años. Este día la adolescente es presentada en sociedad. La joven, que también se llama quinceañera, lleva para la ocasión un elegante traje largo, zapatos de tacón y muchas veces aretes, anillo, pulsera y collar de perlas. Esta fiesta tradicional se celebra en un salón de uno de los mejores hoteles de la ciudad en compañía de otras quinceañeras. Para preparar la fiesta, la familia pasa mucho tiempo en las tiendas y los centros comerciales y, claro, gasta mucho dinero. Las familias con menos dinero tienen la fiesta en casa. Hoy en día, algunas quinceañeras prefieren no tener fiesta y gastar el dinero en un largo viaje al extranjero o en comprar un coche.

Los chicos en algunos lugares pasan por un rito cuando empiezan el colegio, a los doce o trece años. Tradicionalmente, el uniforme de la escuela incluye pantalones cortos. Al pasar al colegio, los chicos pueden llevar pantalones largos. Cuando llegan a los quince años, los chicos empiezan a asistir a las fiestas de quinceañeras, como acompañantes, donde generalmente llevan frac.

Guía para la lectura

1. Here are some words and expressions to keep in mind as you read.

cumple	*turns (a certain age)*
zapatos de tacón	*high heels*
aretes	*earrings*
anillo	*ring*
pulsera	*bracelet*
collar	*necklace*
al extranjero	*abroad*
frac	*coat and tails*

Después de leer

1. What are the rites of passage between childhood, the teenage years, and adulthood in your culture? How are the rites similar to those mentioned in the reading? How are they different?

2. What other social rites do you know about that may affect you directly or that may affect your friends?

3. Does clothing play an important role in rites of passage in your culture? Explain why or why not.

CAPÍTULO 17

¿Cuánto cuesta...?

—Quisiera medio kilo, por favor.
—Bueno. Son 500 pesos.

Objectives

- making purchases and choices
- expressing quantity
- asking for prices

Preparación

- Have you ever been to an open-air market? If so, where? when?

- What kinds of products can you buy in a market?

- How is the shopping experience in an outdoor market different from going to a regular grocery store?

Día de feria

La Sra. Fernández va de compras al **mercado** (market).

Ayer jueves fue **día de feria** en Oaxaca. La señora Fernández caminó **hasta** la plaza cerca de su casa donde cada semana hay un **mercado al aire libre**. A la señora Fernández le gusta comprar las **frutas** y los **vegetales** que **ofrecen** los **vendedores** porque son productos **frescos** y baratos. **Además** a ella le encanta **regatear**. Hoy, piensa comprar vegetales para una **ensalada**.

Sra. Fernández:	¿Cuánto cuesta el **atado** de zanahorias?
Vendedora:	1.300 pesos.
Sra. Fernández:	Bueno, 2.000 pesos por **estos** dos atados.
Vendedora:	Tenga, 2.100.
Sra. Fernández:	Está bien.

Unas frutas y unos vegetales:

 unas fresas

 unos limones

 unas manzanas

 una naranja

 unas peras

 unas uvas

 unas cebollas

 unos guisantes

 una lechuga

 el maíz

 unas papas

 unos tomates

 unas zanahorias

día de feria *market day*   hasta *as far as*   mercado al aire libre *open-air market*   frutas *fruit*   vegetales *vegetables*   ofrecen *offer*   vendedores *sellers*   frescos *fresh*   Además *Besides*   regatear *to bargain*   ensalada *salad*   atado *bunch*   estos *these*

Comentarios CULTURALES

Los mercados al aire libre

Open-air markets are characteristic of many Spanish-speaking countries. In rural areas, these markets are particularly important since they offer a place where people from the surrounding communities can meet to buy, sell, and socialize. Once a week, vendors and shoppers gather in a designated location, often the main **plaza** of a small town. Farmers come from all over the local countryside, bringing vegetables and fruit they have grown on small plots of land. One can also buy pots, pans, brooms, soap, and other household items at the markets, as well as regional handicrafts such as hand woven cloth, colorful shirts, embroidered dresses, musical instruments, and wooden carvings. More and more commonly, there are manufactured goods and high-tech equipment such as radios and televisions for sale.

¡Te toca a ti!

A. ¿Qué son? Identifica las frutas y los vegetales que siguen.

1.

2.

3.

4.

5.

6.

7.

8.

9.   10.   11.   12.

B. Preparar una ensalada You and a classmate are making a salad for a class party. Decide whether you will make a fruit salad or a green salad. Then, as you examine the contents of the refrigerator (shown in the following drawings), take turns identifying what you see. Together make a list of the items that you want for your salad and a list of those that you don't. Follow the model.

> MODELO   **Compañero(a):**   *Hay maíz. ¿Quieres maíz?*
>   **Tú:**   *Sí, quiero maíz. Me gusta el maíz.* o:
>   *No, no me gusta mucho el maíz.* o:
>   *¡Claro que no! ¡Es una ensalada de frutas!*

1.   2.   3.   4.

5.   6.   7.   8.

9.   10.

C. La oferta You and a friend have saved some money to shop for sporting goods at a flea market. One of you is interested in newer, more expensive items. The other is always looking for bargains. Take turns trying to persuade each other, following the model. The first item in each pair is the more expensive one.

> **MODELO** **Tú:** *Voy a comprar la pelota de fútbol.* o:
> *Mira la pelota de fútbol.* o: *¡Qué buena pelota de fútbol!*
> **Amiga(o):** *Pero no compres la pelota de fútbol. Compra las pelotas de tenis. Son más baratas.*
> **Tú:** *Tienes razón* (You're right). *Voy a llevar las pelotas de tenis.* o: *No, yo prefiero la pelota de fútbol.*

1. raqueta grande / pequeña
2. zapatos nuevos / usados
3. esquíes para la nieve / esquíes para el agua
4. fútbol nuevo / viejo
5. bicicleta Cinelli / Sprint
6. pelota de básquetbol / pelota de fútbol

PRONUNCIACIÓN THE CONSONANT f

The consonant f in Spanish is pronounced exactly like the *f* in English.

Práctica

D. Escucha a tu maestro(a) cuando lee las siguientes palabras. Después repítelas para practicar la pronunciación.

1. fútbol
2. flor
3. ficción
4. frente
5. final

6. farmacia
7. favorito
8. fresco
9. alfombra
10. suficiente

ESTRUCTURA

Demonstrative adjectives

—¿Quieres **estas** manzanas verdes o
 esas manzanas rojas?
—Quiero **aquellas** manzanas de allá.

Do you want **these** green apples
or **those** red apples?
I want **those** apples over there.

The Demonstrative Adjectives

	next to the speaker	near the speaker	far from the speaker
	this	*that*	*that*
Masc. sing.	**este** limón	**ese** limón	**aquel** limón
Fem. sing.	**esta** manzana	**esa** manzana	**aquella** manzana
	these	*those*	*those (over there)*
Masc. plural	**estos** limones	**esos** limones	**aquellos** limones
Fem. plural	**estas** uvas	**esas** uvas	**aquellas** uvas

1. Demonstrative adjectives are used to point out specific people or things. In Spanish, there are three sets of demonstrative adjectives. Each one specifies people or things in relation to their distance from the speaker.

2. Like all adjectives in Spanish, demonstrative adjectives agree in number and gender with the noun they modify. They are always placed before the noun.

Aquí practicamos

E. ¿Esta, esa o aquella? Replace each definite article with the correct demonstrative adjective, according to its column heading. Follow the models.

MODELOS la papa, *near the speaker:*
esta papa

el croissant, *near the listener:*
ese croissant

los bocadillos, *far from listener and speaker:*
aquellos bocadillos

next to the speaker
1. la manzana
2. el limón
3. los pasteles

near the speaker
4. el limón
5. los tomates
6. las fresas

far from the speaker
7. el maíz
8. las peras
9. el queso

F. ¿Prefiere estas manzanas o esos tomates? You are the checkout person at a grocery store. Your customer is undecided about what to buy. Offer him (her) choices according to the cues. Work with a partner and follow the model.

> | MODELO | fresas / uvas |
> |---|---|
> | Tú: | ¿Prefiere Ud. estas fresas o esas uvas? |
> | Compañero(a): | Prefiero estas uvas, por favor. |

1. naranjas / manzanas
2. banana / pera
3. limón / papas
4. maíz / guisantes

5. tomates / lechuga
6. cebollas / bananas
7. uvas / fresas
8. zanahorias / naranjas

PALABRAS ÚTILES

Expressions of specific quantity

¿Cuánto cuesta un litro de leche?
Quisiera medio kilo de uvas.

How much is a liter of milk?
I would like a half kilo of grapes.

The following expressions are used to indicate quantities.

un kilo de	a kilogram of
medio kilo de	a half kilogram of
una libra de	a pound of
50 gramos de	50 grams of
un litro de	a liter of
una botella de	a bottle of
una docena de	a dozen of
un pedazo de	a piece of
un atado de	a bunch of
un paquete de	a package of

Aquí practicamos

G. ¿En qué puedo servirle? Usa la información entre paréntesis para contestar las preguntas de los vendedores. Sigue el modelo.

> | MODELO | ¿Qué desea? (2 kilos de tomates / 1 kilo de uvas) |
> |---|---|
> | | Deseo dos kilos de tomates y un kilo de uvas. |

1. ¿Qué necesita hoy? (1/2 kilo de lechuga / un atado de zanahorias)
2. ¿Qué quisiera? (200 gramos de jamón / 2 docenas de peras)
3. ¿Qué desea? (1/2 litro de leche / 1 botella de agua mineral)
4. ¿En qué puedo servirle? (1/2 docena de naranjas / 2 kilos de uvas)
5. ¿Necesita algo? (3 botellas de limonada / 1 paquete de mantequilla)

H. ¿Cuánto compraron?
Mira los dibujos que siguen y di cuánto de cada cosa compró la persona indicada. Sigue el modelo.

MODELO
¿Qué compró Juanita?
Ella compró cincuenta gramos de queso.

1. ¿Qué compró Mercedes? 2. ¿Qué compró el señor González? 3. ¿Qué compró Antonio?

4. ¿Qué compró Maribel? 5. ¿Qué compró la señora Ruiz? 6. ¿Qué compró Francisco?

I. En el mercado
You are shopping in an open-air market in Caguas, Puerto Rico. Ask the seller the price of each item, and then say how much you want to buy. Work with a partner, alternating the roles of customer (**cliente**) and seller (**vendedor[a]**). Use the cues provided and follow the model.

MODELO   zanahorias: 2 dólares el atado / 2 atados
        Cliente: *Cuánto cuestan estas zanahorias?*
  Vendedor(a): *Dos dólares el atado.*
        Cliente: *Quiero dos atados, por favor.*
  Vendedor(a): *Aquí tiene. Cuatro dólares, por favor.*

1. leche: 2 dólares la botella / 3 botellas
2. naranjas: 3 dólares la docena / 1/2 docena
3. papas: 2 dólares el kilo / 500 gramos
4. cebollas: 1.50 dólares el kilo / 1/2 kilo
5. mantequilla: 2.50 dólares el paquete / 2 paquetes
6. pastel: 1 dólar el pedazo / 2 pedazos

Aquí escuchamos

De compras en el mercado
Mr. Estévez has a conversation with a vendor at the market.

Antes de escuchar Based on what you have learned in this **etapa,** what are some of the questions that you think Mr. Estévez and the vendor might ask each other?

 A escuchar Listen twice to the conversation between Mr. Estévez and the vendor. Pay special attention to the products that Mr. Estévez actually buys.

Después de escuchar En tu hoja reproducible, haz una marca junto a las cosas que compró el Sr. Estévez.

__aguacates	__lechuga	__melón	__zanahorias
__cebollas	__maíz	__papas	__plátanos
__fresas	__mangos	__tomates	
__guisantes	__manzanas	__uvas	

El postre (dessert) Your mother has put you in charge of buying some fruit for dessert. Work in pairs and follow the directions.

Salesperson	Customer
1. Greet the customer.	Greet the salesperson.
2. Ask what he (she) needs.	Say that you need some fruit to buy for dessert **(para el postre)**.
3. Offer a choice of fruits.	Decide what you are going to buy. Ask how much the fruit(s) cost(s).
4. Tell him (her) the price(s).	Bargain over the price.
5. Agree on the price. Ask if he (she) needs something else.	Answer.
6. Respond if necessary, then end the conversation.	End the conversation.

¿Te gusta más...? You and a friend have just won the lottery and you want to buy a number of things. 1) Bring to class pairs of magazine pictures of five objects (two different versions of each) whose names you know in Spanish and that you would like to own. Catalogs will be a good source for finding multiple pictures of objects. 2) Following the model, get each other's opinion about which items you each like better, using the appropriate forms of **este** and **ese**. 3) Make a list of the first five things you plan to buy together with your winnings. Follow the model.

MODELO

Tú: *¿Te gusta más esta bicicleta americana o esta bicicleta italiana?*

Amiga(o): *Prefiero esa bicicleta italiana. Y tú, ¿prefieres este viaje a Panamá o este viaje a Costa Rica?*

Tú: *A mí me gusta más ese viaje a Panamá.*

¿Qué comemos? Your family has invited an exchange student from Venezuela, who is your friend at school, to join you for dinner. His parents are in town and are also invited. Work with a classmate to write up a shopping list of eight food items that you need to buy for the dinner, indicating the quantity or amount of each. Consider drinks, salads, vegetables, meat, and desserts.

Preparación

- What are some of the differences between shopping at a supermarket and at an open-air market?

- What products can you find at a supermarket that you could not get at an open-air market?

- When you go shopping for food, where do you prefer to go? Why?

En el supermercado

Ricardo y Roberto van de compras al supermercado.

Una vez por semana Ricardo hace las compras en el supermercado **para** su mamá. Hoy Roberto también tiene que ir al supermercado para comprar **alimentos** para su familia. Los dos amigos van **juntos**. Primero, van a la sección de los **productos lácteos** porque Ricardo tiene que comprar mantequilla, leche, yogur, crema y queso.

También van a la sección de las **conservas** porque necesitan tres **latas** de **sopa** y una lata de **atún**, una botella de **aceite** y un paquete de **galletas**.

Una vez *Once* **para** *for* **alimentos** *food* **juntos** *together* **productos lácteos** *dairy products* **conservas** *packaged goods* **latas** *cans* **sopa** *soup* **atún** *tuna* **aceite** *oil* **galletas** *cookies*

Luego pasan por la sección de los productos congelados porque Roberto tiene que comprar pescado, una pizza, un pollo y también: ¡helado de chocolate, por supuesto! A Roberto le encanta el helado.

Para terminar, ellos compran pastas, harina, azúcar, sal, pimienta, arroz y mayonesa. El carrito de Roberto está muy lleno.

Luego pasan por *Then they go by*   congelados *frozen*   pescado *fish*   pollo *chicken*   helado *ice cream*   harina *flour*
sal *salt*   pimienta *pepper*   carrito *shopping cart*   lleno *full*

Comentarios CULTURALES

Las frutas y los vegetales tropicales

In the tropical parts of Central and South America, Mexico, and the Caribbean, many kinds of delicious vegetables and fruits are commonly available for everyday consumption. You may be familiar with the **aguacate** *(avocado)* and the chile. Fruits such as **papayas** (small melon-like fruit) and **mangos** (peach-like fruit) can be found fresh as well as in fruit juices in many supermarkets in the U.S. The **plátano** (a large green banana) is eaten frequently with meals in a number of Caribbean countries. It is generally served fried or boiled. The **mamey** (coconut-like fruit) and the **zapote** (fruit shaped like an apple with green skin and black pulp inside) can often be found on the Mexican table as a much-appreciated dessert. Another popular dessert is guava paste, served with fruit or cheese.

¡Te toca a ti!

A. En el carrito de Lidia hay...
Lidia's mother sent her to the store. But since Lidia forgot the shopping list, the supermarket employee helps her to remember by mentioning some items. Work with a partner, alternating the roles of the employee and Lidia. Look at the drawings that follow and indicate what Lidia is buying. Follow the model.

> **MODELO** Empleado(a): ¿Necesitas arroz?
> Lidia: *No, pero necesito pasta.*

1. ¿Necesitas harina?

2. ¿Necesitas pimienta?

3. ¿Necesitas pollo?

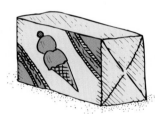
4. ¿Necesitas galletas?

5. ¿Necesitas yogur?

6. ¿Necesitas mayonesa?

B. Preferencias personales
Your father always likes to give you a choice when he prepares meals. He is preparing this week's menu. Tell him what you would like each day from the choices given. Then, with a partner, set up a different menu for the following week, agreeing on what to serve each day. Follow the model.

> **MODELO** ¿Quisieras carne o pescado hoy?
> *Quisiera carne, por favor.*

1. ¿Quisieras pollo o atún el lunes?
2. ¿Quisieras yogur o helado el martes?
3. ¿Quisieras pizza o pescado el miércoles?
4. ¿Quisieras pasta o papas el jueves?
5. ¿Quisieras pollo o sopa el viernes?
6. ¿Quisieras mayonesa o aceite en la ensalada el sábado?
7. ¿Quisieras fruta o helado el domingo?

C. ¿Preparamos una sopa de vegetales? Your favorite aunt and uncle are coming to your house for dinner tonight. They are strict vegetarians, so you have to plan the meal carefully. You have decided to serve vegetable soup and fruit salad. With a classmate, write a shopping list; one for fruits and one for vegetables. Include at least five items on each list. Then, since your budget may not allow you to purchase all the items, organize the fruits and vegetables in the order in which you would prefer to include them in the menu.

> **MODELO**
> *En la sopa podemos poner _____.*
> *En la ensalada de frutas podemos poner _____.*

ESTRUCTURA

The interrogative words cuál and cuáles

¿**Cuáles** prefieres, las manzanas verdes o las manzanas rojas?	*Which (ones) do you prefer, the green apples or the red apples?*

1. To express *which* or *which one(s)* in questions, the interrogative word ¿**cuál**? is used when asking about a singular noun. ¿**Cuáles**? is used when asking about a plural noun.

2. Like the interrogative word ¿**qué**?, ¿**cuál**? and ¿**cuáles**? can also mean *what*? ¿**Qué**? is used to ask for an explanation or a definition, while ¿**cuál**? and ¿**cuáles**? are used to indicate a choice within a group of nouns.

¿**Qué** es un plátano?	*What is a plantain?*
¿**Qué** hizo Marcos anoche?	*What did Marcos do last night?*
¿**Cuál** es tu dirección?	*What is your address?*
¿**Cuál** es tu número de teléfono?	*What is your phone number?*

Aquí practicamos

D. ¿Cuál quieres? You are babysitting for a young child who doesn't speak very clearly yet. You are trying to guess what he wants by offering him some choices. Follow the model.

> **MODELO**
> este libro grande / aquel libro pequeño
> *¿Cuál quieres; este libro grande o aquel libro pequeño?*

1. el vídeo de Mickey Mouse / el vídeo de Blanca Nieves (*Snow White*)
2. esta fruta / ese pan dulce
3. este sándwich de queso / aquél de jamón
4. este chocolate / ese jugo
5. estas uvas / esas fresas
6. este helado de chocolate / esa botella de leche

❓ ¿Qué crees?

Chocolate is a product that originally came from:

a) Switzerland
b) Europe
c) Mexico
d) South America

respuesta ☞

E. Preguntas personales When you are applying for a part-time job in the local grocery store, the manager asks you a series of personal questions. With a partner, role-play the interview, switching roles after completing the first interview. Use **cuál** and **cuáles** in your questions. Follow the model.

> MODELO   tu nombre
> *¿Cuál es tu nombre?*

1. tu nombre
2. tu dirección
3. tu número de teléfono

4. tus días preferidos para trabajar
5. tu modo de transporte

NOTA GRAMATICAL

Demonstrative pronouns

Ese yogur no es muy bueno.
Éste de es mejor.

That yogurt (there) is not very good.
This one (here) is better.

Estas manzanas son rojas, ésas amarillas
y **aquéllas** verdes.

These apples (here) are red, those (there) yellow,
and those (over there) green.

The Demonstrative Pronouns

	next to the speaker	near the speaker	far from the speaker
	this one	*that one*	*that one (over there)*
Masc. sing.	**éste**	**ése**	**aquél**
Fem. sing.	**ésta**	**ésa**	**aquélla**
Neuter. sing.	**esto**	**eso**	**aquello**
	these ones	*those ones (there)*	*those ones (over there)*
Masc. plural	**éstos**	**ésos**	**aquéllos**
Fem. plural	**éstas**	**ésas**	**aquéllas**

1. Used to point out specific people or things, demonstrative pronouns replace the nouns to which they refer. They have the same forms as the demonstrative adjectives, but they add a written accent in most forms to differentiate them from adjectives. They also reflect the number and gender of the nouns they replace.

2. The neuter singular form (**esto, eso, aquello**) is used to refer to ideas, situations, or objects in a general way. These are equivalent to the English *this, that*. These forms do not have an accent because there are no adjectives to differentiate them from.

Esto es muy interesante.
Eso pasa.
Aquello no me gustó.

This is very interesting.
That happens.
I didn't like that.

3. You can use adverbs of location with demonstrative pronouns to clarify or emphasize the distance of the nouns from the speaker. You already know **aquí,** and **allí.** The adverb **allá** means *over there*. Use the preposition **de** before the adverb when emphasizing a pronoun.

¿Quiere Ud. **esta** lechuga de **aquí,**   *Do you want this lettuce here, that one there,*
ésa de **allí** o **aquélla** de **allá?**   *or that one over there?*

Aquí practicamos

F. ¿Cuál?   You are doing some shopping with a friend. Because there are so many items to choose from, you have to explain which objects you are discussing. Use **éste(a), ése(a),** or **aquél(la)** in your answer, according to the cues in parentheses. Follow the model.

> **MODELO**   ¿Qué libros vas a comprar? *(those ones there)*
> *Voy a comprar ésos.*

1. ¿Qué calculadora vas a comprar? (this one)
2. ¿Qué frutas vas a comprar? (those ones over there)
3. ¿Qué galletas quieres? (those ones there)
4. ¿Qué paquete de arroz quieres? (this one)
5. ¿Qué pescado vas a comprar? (that one there)
6. ¿Qué jamón quieres? *(that one over there)*

G. ¿Cuál prefieres?   Use the cues that follow to tell what you prefer. Remember to make the pronoun agree with the noun provided. Work with a partner and follow the model.

> **MODELO**   queso / allí
> **Compañero(a):**   *¿Qué queso prefieres?*
> **Tú:**   *Prefiero ése de allí.*

1. paquete de mantequilla / allí
2. botella de aceite / allá
3. paquete de arroz / aquí
4. lata de sopa / allá
5. paquete de galletas / allí
6. lata de atún / allá
7. paquete de harina / aquí

Aquí escuchamos

Por favor, compra... *Teresa and her mother talk about the groceries they need.*

Antes de escuchar Based on what you have learned in this **etapa,** what types of food do you think Teresa and her mother might need for a dinner party?

A escuchar Listen twice to the conversation between Teresa and her mother before answering the questions about it on your activity master.

Después de escuchar On your activity master, complete the following sentences in English, based on what you heard.

1. The person who is going to do the shopping is . . .
2. The shopping will be done at . . .
3. Three of the items on the shopping list are . . .
4. Some of the fruit to be bought is . . .

¡ADELANTE!

Un picnic You and a friend are planning a picnic. At the delicatessen you have to decide what you want to buy, but you do not always agree with each other. For each suggestion you make, your friend disagrees and tells you to buy something else. Work with a partner. Use the cues provided and follow the model. Finally, decide on five items that you both are willing to take to the picnic.

MODELO	estos sándwiches de atún / esos sándwiches de pollo
Tú:	*¿Vamos a llevar estos sándwiches de atún?*
Compañero(a):	No, *no lleves ésos de atún. Lleva ésos de pollo.*

1. esa ensalada de frutas / aquella ensalada verde
2. esos tacos de carne / aquellos tacos de queso
3. estos licuados de banana / esos licuados de fresa
4. este helado de fresas / ese yogur de fresas
5. aquella tortilla de jamón / esa tortilla de papas
6. este pastel de fresas / aquel pastel de manzanas
7. esa salsa de tomate / esta salsa de chile
8. esa sopa de pollo / esta sopa de pescado

¿Cuánto cuesta todo esto? You and two friends are planning a dinner for some classmates. You are on a tight food budget. You have only $16 to spend—$3 for beverages, $3 for dessert, and $10 for the main course (**el plato principal**). Compare the prices on the lists and decide how much you can buy of each thing without going over the limit. After you decide, write down what you will buy and how much you will have spent. Work with two classmates and follow the model. Be prepared to report to the class your final menu and its cost.

MODELO		
	Tú:	*¿Qué vamos a servir?*
	Compañero(a) 1:	*Bueno, para el plato principal, ¿por qué no preparamos pollo con papas fritas y vegetales?*
	Compañero(a) 2:	*A ver. El pollo cuesta…*

PRODUCTOS CONGELADOS
Pescado . . . . . . .1 kilo/**$5**
Pizza **$5**
Papas fritas (fried) . .**$2**
Pollo . . . . .2/**$5**
Vegetales **$2**
Helado **$4**

PRODUCTOS LÁCTEOS
Yogur . . . . .3/**$2**
Leche . . . . .1 litro/**$1**
Mantequilla **$1**
Crema . . . . .2/**$1**
Queso **$2**

OTROS PRODUCTOS
Pan **$1**
Galletas **$2**
Arroz **$2**
Pastas **$2**
Lechuga **$1**
Tomates . . . . . . .1 kilo/**$2**

BEBIDAS
Café . . . . .1 kilo/**$5**
Refrescos . . . . . . .2 litros/**$2**
Agua mineral . . . . .1 litro/**$2**
Limonada . . . . . . .2 litros/**$3**

CONSERVAS
Sopa . . . . .2/**$1**
Atún . . . . .2/**$2.50**
Salsa de tomate . .2/**$1.50**
Aceitunas . . . . . . .2/**$1.50**

VOCABULARIO

Para charlar

Temas y contextos

Para preguntar sobre las preferencias

¿Cuál prefieres…?
¿Cuál quieres…?

Cantidades

un atado de
una botella de
una docena de
50 gramos de
un kilo de
una libra de
una lata de
un litro de
medio kilo de
un paquete de
un pedazo de

Conservas

el aceite
el atún
la sopa

Frutas

un aguacate
una ensalada de frutas
una fresa
un limón
una manzana
una naranja
una pera
un plátano
una uva

Productos congelados

el helado
el pescado
el pollo

Productos lácteos

la crema
un yogur

Productos varios

el azúcar
una galleta
el harina
la mayonesa
la pasta
la pimienta
la sal

Vegetales

una cebolla
una ensalada de vegetales
una ensalada (verde)
unos guisantes
una lechuga
el maíz
una papa
un tomate
una zanahoria

Vocabulario general

Sustantivos

los alimentos
un carrito
una feria
un(a) cliente
un mercado al
  aire libre
un(a) vendedor(a)

Verbos

ofrecer
pasar
regatear

Adjetivos

este(a) / estos(as)
ese(a) / esos(as)
aquel(la) / aquellos(as)
amarillo(a)
fresco(a)
lleno(a)
rojo(a)
verde

Otras palabras y expresiones

éste(a) / éstos(as)
ése(a) / ésos(as)
aquél(la) / aquéllos(as)
además
allá
allí
hasta
juntos
luego
una vez

ENCUENTROS CULTURALES

◆

El Centro Sambil

Antes de leer

1. **Centro Sambil**, in Caracas, Venezuela, is advertised as **el centro comercial más grande de Sudamérica.**

   a. Do you or any of your classmates know which shopping center is the largest in the United States? In the world?

   b. Talk about your "shopping center experience." Nowadays, the mall has become a kind of "home away from home" for many people. Why? What kinds of things are there to do in a mall? Do you spend a lot of time at the mall?

   c. What are the positive and negative aspects of large, multipurpose shopping malls?

2. What do you think **locales comerciales** means? Scan the five paragraphs and try to find how many **locales comerciales** there are in the entire **Centro Sambil**.

PRIMER NIVEL	SEGUNDO NIVEL	TERCER NIVEL	CUARTO NIVEL
### Autopista	### Acuario	### Libertador	### Feria
Este, nuestro primer nivel comercial, se encuentra al nivel de la autopista Francisco Fajardo. Está distribuido alrededor de cinco plazas o puntos de encuentro que facilita su recorrido. Las cinco plazas son Plaza Jardín, Plaza de la Fuente, Plaza Central, Plaza de la Música y Plaza del Arte. Disfrute aquí de más de 31 locales comerciales y de seis salas de cine.	En este segundo nivel puede usted disfrutar de un acuario marino de más de 120.000 litros de capacidad. Aquí puede usted ver una gran variedad de especies marinas del Océano Pacífico. Encuentre aquí además nuestra joyería, 31 minitiendas y una cafetería, junto a más de 131 diferentes locales comerciales.	Este nivel se encuentra a nivel de la avenida Libertador, a la que tiene acceso peatonal directo. En este nivel puede encontrar usted locales comerciales organizados alrededor de cuatro plazas. Visite aquí 92 diferentes locales comerciales o cualquiera de nuestros restaurantes y cafés al aire libre.	En este nivel puede disfrutar de muchas actividades variadas y servicios diferentes. Encuentre aquí la Feria, nuestro centro de comida rápida, donde hay trece diferentes puntos de venta y capacidad para aproximadamente 1.200 personas. Puede contar con acceso a las terrazas, para que pueda disfrutar de las más variadas vistas y espacios recreativos. Va a encontrar en este nivel 82 locales comerciales, tres plazas y cinco salas de cine.

Guía para la lectura

Here are some words and expressions to keep in mind as you read.

autopista	*highway*
nivel	*level*
puntos de venta	*points of sale*
facilita	*will make easier*
salón de festejos	*party and convention center*
recorrido	*stroll, journey*
patinaje sobre hielo	*ice-skating*
disfrute	*enjoy*
Parque de Diversiones	*Amusement Park*
acceso peatonal	*pedestrian access*
pies cuadrados	*square feet*
al aire libre	*outdoors*

QUINTO NIVEL

Diversión

En este, el quinto y más alto nivel comercial del Centro Sambil, hay toda clase de espectaculares atracciones. Aquí usted puede hacer uso de nuestros 20 diferentes locales comerciales, de nuestro salón de usos múltiples y de nuestro salón de festejos. Distrute junto a su familia de un día de patinaje sobre hielo o diviértanse en nuestro gigantesco Parque de Diversiones, que cubre un área de 7.989,59 metros cuadrados.

Después de leer

1. Where can you eat at the **Centro Sambil**? Where can you go to a café? To a fast-food restaurant?

2. There are **plazas** or "squares" on two different levels of the shopping center; which levels are they?

3. What is your opinion of having a skating rink, an aquarium and an amusement park in a shopping mall? Which of these areas would you go to the most?

4. Is this shopping center similar to ones you have been to in the United States? How is it different?

CAPÍTULO 18

¿Qué quieres comprar?

—Quiero comprar zapatos nuevos.
—Pues, éstos son bonitos y no son caros.

Objectives

- making purchases and choices
- comparing things

PRIMERA ETAPA

Preparación

- What do you think the name of the store below means?
- What are some of the clothing items that are missing in the drawings?
- Do you know how to say *hat* in Spanish?
- What kinds of things do you say when you make comparisons?

"La Alta Moda"

chaqueta camisa blusa vestido abrigo

pantalones suéter

impermeable

falda camiseta

Hay muchas tiendas en el centro comercial.

Hoy sábado Mercedes y Sarita van de compras al centro comercial en El Paso, Texas. Ellas necesitan comprar un **regalo** para el cumpleaños de Rosa. También a ellas les gusta **ir de escaparates.**

Mercedes: Aquí tienen **ropa** muy moderna.
Sarita: ¡Mira esta **falda azul**! ¡Qué linda!
Mercedes: A Rosa le va a gustar ese color. Con este **cinturón negro** es muy **bonita. Creo** que le va a gustar.

Sarita: Sí, **tienes razón.** Perfecto. Ahora yo necesito un **vestido** para mí.
Mercedes: Aquí al frente hay una boutique muy elegante.
Sarita: Mm... entonces, **seguro** que es cara.
Mercedes: Vamos a ir de escaparates.

regalo *gift* **ir de escaparates** *go window-shopping* **ropa** *clothes* **falda azul** *blue skirt* **cinturón negro** *black belt* **bonita** *pretty* **creo** *I think* **tienes razón** *you are right* **vestido** *dress* **seguro** *surely*

Los colores

una camisa roja

un suéter azul

una chaqueta verde

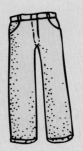

pantalones amarillos

una falda blanca

un impermeable negro

¡Te toca a ti!

A. ¿Qué llevan hoy? In your job as fashion reporter for the school newspaper, you need to know what everyone is wearing. Describe each person's outfit in the drawings that follow. Follow the model.

MODELO   Luis lleva una camisa roja con unos pantalones blancos.

Luis

1. Roberta

2. Nadia

3. Alfonso

4. Arturo

5. Olga

6. Esteban

B. ¿Dónde trabajas durante las vacaciones? You have decided to get a sales job this summer at a store in the local shopping center. Explain where you are going to work and what you are going to sell. Follow the model.

> MODELO tienda de música
> *Voy a trabajar en la tienda de música, y voy a vender discos compactos y cintas.*

1. papelería
2. tienda de deportes
3. tienda de música
4. tienda de ropa para mujeres *(women)*
5. tienda de ropa para hombres *(men)*
6. tienda de ropa para niños *(children)*

C. ¿Qué ropa llevas a la fiesta? You are trying to decide what to wear to a party tonight. Using the items of clothing on page 421 and your favorite colors, put together your outfit. Work with a partner and ask each other what you will be wearing. Be prepared to report back to the class. Follow the model.

> MODELO Compañero(a): *¿Qué vas a llevar a la fiesta?*
> Tú: *Voy a llevar unos pantalones negros y un suéter rojo.*

Repaso ♻

D. En el mercado For dinner, you need to get fruits and vegetables at the grocery store. In pairs, play the roles of the shopkeeper and the customer. Remember that all the produce is not available all year round. Before you begin, 1) make a list of what you want to buy. 2) Your partner will make a list of what is available. 3) Then make up your own conversation, following the model.

> MODELO Vendedor(a): *Buenos días, señorita (señor). ¿Qué desea?*
> Cliente: *¿Tiene fresas?*
> Vendedor(a): *Sí, ¿cuánto quiere?*
> Cliente: *Medio kilo, por favor.*
> Vendedor(a): *Aquí tiene. ¿Algo más?*

PRONUNCIACIÓN   The Consonant l

The consonant l in Spanish is pronounced like the *l* in the English word *leak*.

Práctica

E. Escucha a tu maestro(a) cuando lee las siguientes palabras. Después repítelas para practicar la pronunciación.

1. lápiz
2. leche
3. listo
4. inteligente
5. papel

6. libro
7. luego
8. malo
9. abuela
10. fútbol

ESTRUCTURA

Expressions of comparison

Estas cintas son **más** caras **que** ésas.	*These tapes are more expensive than those.*
Hoy hay **menos** clientes **que** ayer.	*Today there are fewer customers than yesterday.*

1. The following constructions are used in Spanish to express the comparisons *more than* and *less/fewer than,* respectively:

más + *noun or adjective* + **que**	**menos** + *noun or adjective* + **que**

2. A few adjectives have an irregular comparative form and do not make comparisons using **más** or **menos.**

bueno, buen	*good*	**mejor(es)**	*better*
malo, mal	*bad, sick*	**peor(es)**	*worse*
joven	*young*	**menor(es)**	*younger*
viejo	*old*	**mayor(es)**	*older*

Estos vestidos son **mejores que** esas blusas.	*These dresses are better than those blouses.*
Yo soy **menor que** mi hermano.	*I am younger than my brother.*

Aquí practicamos

F. ¿Qué tienes? You are in a bad mood today and disagree with everyone. Say the opposite of what you hear. Follow the model.

> **MODELO**   Pedro tiene más cintas que Juan.
> *No, Pedro tiene menos cintas que Juan.*

1. Rafael tiene más dinero que José.
2. Anita tiene menos amigas que Pilar.
3. Yo tengo más paciencia que tú.
4. Tomás tiene menos camisas que Alfonso.
5. Tú tienes más faldas que yo.
6. Mi familia tiene más niños que tu familia.

G. ¿Cuál es mejor? Express which one of the two items shown in the drawings would be a better addition to your wardrobe. Follow the model.

> **MODELO**   falda blanca / chaqueta verde
> *Para mí, una falda blanca es mejor que una chaqueta verde.*

1.   2.   3.   4.

5.   6.   7.   8.

H. Mis amigos y yo   Use the nouns provided to compare yourself to your friends. Use the expressions **más... que** and **menos... que.** Follow the model.

> **MODELO**   hermanas
> *Yo tengo menos hermanas que mi amiga Ana.*

1. hermanos
2. tíos
3. amigos
4. radios
5. cintas
6. libros
7. dinero
8. bicicletas

Aquí escuchamos

¿Más o menos?   *Elena and Patricia discuss several items of clothing at the store.*

Antes de escuchar   Based on what you have learned in this **etapa,** what clothing qualities do you think Elena and Patricia might compare?

 A escuchar   Listen twice to the conversation between Elena and Patricia before answering the true-or-false questions about it on your activity master.

Después de escuchar   On your activity master, indicate whether the following statements are true or false. If a statement is false, provide the correct information.

1. Patricia sees a blue blouse that costs $50.
2. The blue blouse is more expensive than the green one.
3. The green blouse is prettier than the blue one.
4. Patricia has a lot of money and doesn't care about the cost of the blouses.
5. Elena sees some blouses on sale that cost less than the other blouses.
6. Patricia doesn't like the white blouse.
7. Patricia says that she is going to buy a black skirt.

Mis parientes Using the vocabulary that you have learned in earlier chapters, tell your classmates how many grandparents, aunts, uncles, cousins, brothers, and sisters you have. As you mention the different numbers, a classmate says that he (she) has more or fewer than you. Follow the model.

MODELO

Tú: *Yo tengo tres hermanos.*
Compañero(a): *Yo tengo menos hermanos que tú.*
Tengo un hermano.

 La gente (people) famosa You are a reporter for the school paper and are responsible for this month's gossip column. Imagine that you have interviewed several celebrities and are comparing their lifestyles. Choose your own celebrities and write eight comparisons. Be prepared to read them back to the class. Follow the model.

MODELO

Jay Leno tiene más _____ que David Letterman.
Paula Abdul es menos _____ que Diana Ross.

—A mí me gustan estos pantalones. ¿Y a ti?
—Me gustan, pero no quiero comprarlos ahora.

SEGUNDA ETAPA

Zapatería "El Tacón"

¿Qué puedes comprar en una zapatería (shoe store)?

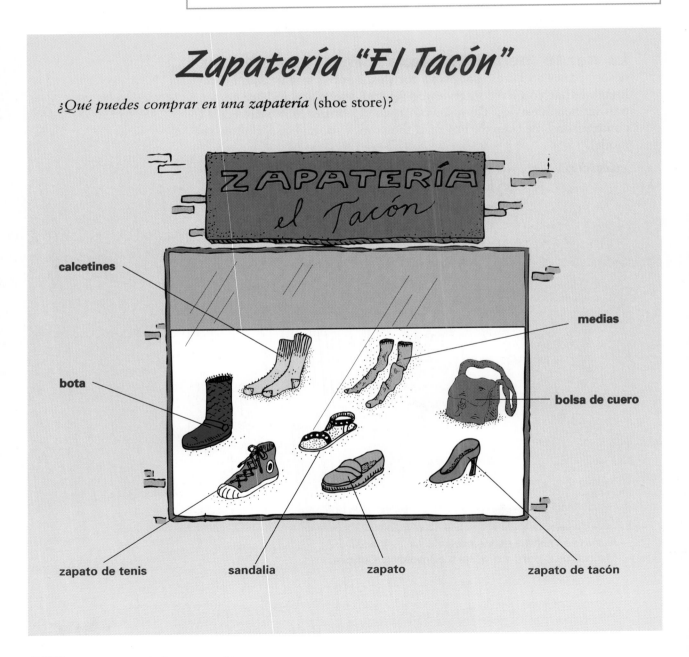

calcetines

medias

bota

bolsa de cuero

zapato de tenis

sandalia

zapato

zapato de tacón

¡Te toca a ti!

A. En la zapatería You need to get some new shoes. When the clerk asks you, tell him (her) what you want to see. Take turns with a partner in playing the role of the clerk. Follow the model.

> **MODELO**   Empleado(a):   *¿En qué puedo servirle?*
> Cliente: *Quisiera ver unos zapatos de tacón.*

B. ¿Qué número? Now repeat Activity A and give your shoe size to the clerk. Use your European size. Refer to the chart on page 431 for sizes. Follow the model.

> **MODELO**   Empleado(a):   *¿En qué puedo servirle?*
> Cliente: *Quisiera ver unos zapatos de tenis.*
> Empleado(a):   *¿Qué número?*
> Cliente: *Cuarenta y tres, por favor.*

Repaso ♻

C. La ropa de María y de Marta Use the information in the following chart to make comparisons between María's and Marta's clothes. Use the expressions for comparison **más... que** and **menos... que**. Follow the model.

> **MODELO**   *María tiene menos camisetas que Marta.*

	María	Marta
Camisetas	5	6
Faldas	2 faldas cortas 1 falda larga 2 faldas negras	1 falda azul 1 falda amarilla
Vestidos	1 vestido de fiesta 1 vestido rojo 1 vestido verde	1 vestido de fiesta 4 vestidos rojos 1 vestido verde
Suéteres	5	4
Cinturones	1	3
Pantalones	4	2

ESTRUCTURA

Expressing equality

El carrito de Roberto está **tan lleno** como el de Ricardo.	*Roberto's shopping cart is as full as Ricardo's.*
Margarita compra **tan frecuentemente** como Linda.	*Margarita shops as frequently as Linda.*
Este señor compró **tanta ropa** como esa señora.	*This man bought as much clothing as that woman.*
Laura alquiló **tantos vídeos** como Sonia.	*Laura rented as many videos as Sonia.*

1. To express equality in Spanish, you can use the phrase **tan... como** *(as...as)* with an adjective or an adverb.

tan	+	*adjective or adverb*	+	**como**

2. The phrase **tanto... como** *(as much/as many...as)* is used with nouns to express equality. Tanto agrees with the nouns to which it refers in gender and number.

tanto(a)	+	*noun*	+	**como**
tantos(as)	+	*noun*	+	**como**

Aquí practicamos

D. Los gemelos Because they are identical twins, Nicolás and Andrés are the same in almost every way. Compare them using the cues given. Follow the model.

> **MODELO** alto
> *Nicolás es tan alto como Andrés.*

1. inteligente
2. gordo
3. bueno
4. energético
5. interesante
6. simpático
7. guapo
8. divertido

E. Nicolás come tanta comida como Andrés The twins' mother is always careful to serve them exactly the same amount of food. Describe what they have on their plates, using the cues that follow. Make sure to use the correct form of **tanto**. Follow the model.

MODELO

helado

Nicolás tiene tanto helado como Andrés.

1. papas fritas
2. pescado
3. carne
4. galletas

5. queso
6. fruta
7. pastas
8. pollo

F. ¡Yo soy mejor que tú!

Some people always think that they are the best. With a classmate, have a bragging contest. Use the cues and your imagination. Follow the model.

MODELO

mi casa / bonita

Tú: *Mi casa es tan bonita como la casa del presidente.*

Compañera(o): *No importa. (That doesn't matter.) Mi casa es más bonita que la casa del presidente.*

1. mis notas / altas
2. mi madre / inteligente
3. mi hermana / bonita

4. mi padre / importante
5. mi tío / rico
6. mi hermano / divertido

¿Qué crees?

If you went shopping in Mexico City, in which place would you bargain?

a) supermarket
b) drug store
c) open-air market
d) department store

respuesta ☞

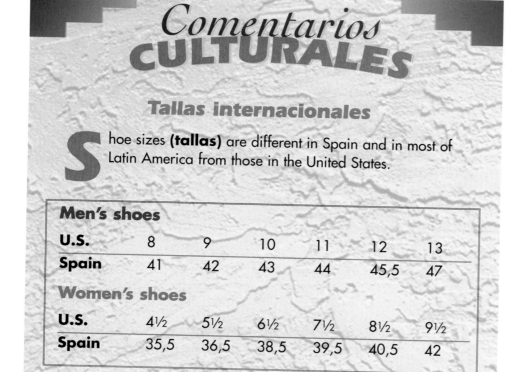

Comentarios CULTURALES

Tallas internacionales

Shoe sizes (**tallas**) are different in Spain and in most of Latin America from those in the United States.

Men's shoes

U.S.	8	9	10	11	12	13
Spain	41	42	43	44	45,5	47

Women's shoes

U.S.	4½	5½	6½	7½	8½	9½
Spain	35,5	36,5	38,5	39,5	40,5	42

Capítulo 18 ¿Qué quieres comprar? **431**

Aquí escuchamos

¿De qué talla? *Francisco goes to the shoe store, where a clerk helps him with his requests.*

Antes de escuchar Review the expressions of comparison that you learned in this **etapa.** What kinds of comparisons do you expect Francisco and the sales clerk might make when talking about different shoes?

 A escuchar Listen twice to the conversation between Francisco and the clerk. Pay special attention to the characteristics of the shoes they are discussing, including color, price, and size.

☞ C

Después de escuchar On your activity master, circle the letter of the correct statements, based on what you heard.

1. Francisco wants to buy . . .
 	
   a. a pair of brown shoes.
 	
   b. a pair of black shoes.
 	
   c. a pair of white shoes.
	4. The second pair of shoes costs . . .
	
	   a. more than the first pair.
	
	   b. the same as the first pair.
	
	   c. less than the first pair.

2. The price of the first pair of shoes that the salesman brings out is . . .
 	
   a. $85.
 	
   b. $65.
 	
   c. $75.
	5. Francisco is most concerned about . . .
	
	   a. the price of the shoes.
	
	   b. the style of the shoes.
	
	   c. the color of the shoes.

3. Francisco's shoe size is . . .
 	
   a. 10 to 10 1/2.
 	
   b. 9 to 9 1/2.
 	
   c. 11 to 11 1/2.	

¡ADELANTE!

¿Cuánto cuesta todo esto (all this)? Work with a partner. You need new shoes, socks, and a bag for this season. You have $40 to spend. Following are the ads for two different shoe stores. Compare their prices and decide where you can get the best deals and what you can buy without going over the limit. Follow the models.

MODELOS
    Los zapatos de tacón son más caros en
    "La Casa del Zapato".
    Los zapatos de fiesta cuestan tanto en
    "La Casa del Zapato" como en la zapatería
    "El Tacón".

¡"La Casa del Zapato" anuncia una gran oferta de zapatos!

zapatos de tacón	$50
zapatos negros	$25
zapatos de tenis	2 pares por $30
bolsas de cuero	desde $5 hasta $15
medias	5 pares por $10
calcetines	$2 el par
botas	$50
sandalias	$35
zapatos de fiesta	$75

Zapatería "El Tacón" tiene los mejores precios de la ciudad.

zapatos de tacón	$45
zapatos negros	$20
zapatos de tenis	$30 el par
bolsas de cuero	$25
medias	5 pares por $10
calcetines	$2 el par
botas	$50
sandalias	$35
zapatos de fiesta	$75

 Comparaciones With a partner, 1) discuss the differences between two quite different stores with which you are both familiar. Consider such factors as location (**la localización**), prices (**los precios**), service (**el servicio**), merchandise quality (**la calidad**), brand names (**las marcas**), sizes (**las tallas**), variety of departments or offerings (**la variedad disponible**), customers (**la clientela**), and background music (**la música de fondo**). 2) Make a list of at least four differences between the two stores. Use the expressions of comparison you have learned. 3) Then, decide on three items that you would prefer to purchase in each store.

VOCABULARIO

Para charlar

Para hacer comparaciones

más... que
menos... que
mayor
mejor
menor
peor

Para establecer igualdad

tan... como
tanto(a)... como
tantos(as)... como

Temas y contextos

Una tienda de ropa

un abrigo
una blusa
una camisa
una camiseta
una chaqueta
un cinturón
una falda
un impermeable
unos pantalones
un suéter
las tallas
un vestido

Una zapatería

una bolsa de cuero
una bota
unos calcetines
unas medias
unas sandalias
un zapato
un zapato de tacón
un zapato de tenis

Vocabulario general

Sustantivos

una boutique
la moda
un regalo
la ropa

Verbos

llevar

Adjetivos

azul
blanco(a)
moderno(a)
negro(a)
seguro(a)

Otras palabras y expresiones

ir de escaparates
No importa.

◆

Los trajes de Guatemala

Antes de leer

1. Look at the title and photos. Can you guess the meaning of the word
    traje? What do you notice immediately about Guatemalan weaving?

2. Skim the first paragraph of the reading to get its gist. What do you
    think the reading will be about?

En los Estados Unidos la mayoría de la gente va a la tienda para comprar su ropa, pero hay muchos lugares donde la gente hace su propia
ropa. Guatemala es uno de los pocos países donde la población indígena todavía usa su ropa tradicional—los típicos *trajes*—a diario. Los colores y diseños son espectaculares; representan los diferentes pueblos y
más de 21 grupos lingüísticos del país. Visitar la región es como caminar entre un arcoiris humano.

El *Popol-vuh*, el libro más importante de la cultura
maya, cuenta la historia de la creación de los indios
Maya-Quiché. Una de las leyendas dice que cuatro
dioses mantienen las esquinas del cielo. Cada
esquina está identificada con un color. Para los
descendientes de los antiguos Mayas los colores
tienen también gran importancia, como demuestran
los trajes típicos. Entre los más hermosos están los
trajes de las mujeres del Nebaj, que consisten de un
corte (o falda) roja y amarilla, una faja bordada, un
huipil—la tradicional blusa—y un colorido adorno
de cabeza.

A diferencia de la ropa masculina occidental, tradicionalmente de colores oscuros, los hombres
guatemaltecos todavía usan frecuentemente sus co-
loridos trajes típicos. A veces es más práctico para
ellos combinar los trajes con ropas modernas. Las
mujeres normalmente siguen la tradición; así,
podemos disfrutar de los huipiles de Santiago

Atitlán, blancos y púrpura, con hermosos diseños de flores y animales, o de los bonitos trajes, de color malva y dorado, de las mujeres de San Juan Sacatepéquez. Los indios Tzutuhil hacen diseños de perros y barcos sobre fondos azules. Los textiles verdes y rojos con franjas y diseños de plumas vienen de la región de Patzun. Los guatemaltecos crean un ambiente tan bello, con sus labores y tradiciones tan espléndidos, no es raro que el pájaro nacional de Guatemala es el quetzal—un pájaro con plumas brillantes de rojo y verde.

Guía para la lectura

Here are some words and expressions to keep in mind as you read.

diseños	*designs*
arcoiris humano	*human rainbow*
faja bordada	*embroidered sash*
adorno de cabeza	*headdress*
oscuros	*dark*
tejidas	*woven*
malva y dorado	*mauve and gold*
fondos	*backgrounds*
franjas	*fringes*
plumas	*feathers*
ambiente	*environment*
labores	*handiwork, needlework*

Después de leer

1. What is the *Popol-vuh*? Explain how it relates to the reading.

2. How do you decide what colors to wear, and what brand of clothing to buy? Does your taste vary, or do you dress the way you did a few years ago?

3. Do you agree that western male clothing tends to be conservative? Would you like to see men wear more colorful clothing? If you are a male, would you wear a more colorful clothing? Why or why not?

4. Think of ways that people identify themselves through clothing. In Guatemala, there has sometimes been pressure for the indigenous people to abandon their traditional dress. To what extent do you think clothing is a form of self-expression? Do you feel pressure to look or dress a certain way? Do you develop opinions about people you don't know based on their clothing?

Conversemos un rato

A. De compras Role-play the following shopping situations with another classmate. Work in pairs and take turns playing each role.

1. You and your mother go shopping for clothes but have very different opinions on what you should buy.

   a. Tell your mother what articles of clothing you hope to buy. Tell her the colors and combinations you like.

   b. Your mother will react to your choices and tell you what articles of clothing and colors she thinks you should buy.

   c. Reach an agreement about two articles of clothing you will buy.

2. You and a friend are in a music store and you start a discussion about your tastes in music.

   a. Tell your friend what type of music you like and the groups you like to hear, and then ask your friend for his/her favorite music and favorite groups.

   b. Your friend will tell you about his/her taste in music, then ask whether you prefer cassettes or CDs.

   c. Reach an agreement about two new cassettes or CDs you will buy.

B. ¡Celebramos con fiesta! In teams of three or four students, role-play the following discussion among a group of students who are organizing the Spanish Club party to celebrate the end of the school year. The school administrators will sponsor the party with the best plan and give free tickets to the winning team.

   a. Each member of the team must help decide the location of the party, the menu, the activities, and the music.

   b. Set a budget for each aspect of the party, then decide what each student should bring.

   c. Finally, present your party plan to the entire class and try to persuade them to have your party. Remember, the winning team gets free tickets!

Taller de escritores

Writing a composition

In this unit you will write two to three paragraphs about a purchase you have made (for yourself or as a gift), without revealing the name of the item. You will present your composition to your classmates who will try to guess the item.

La compra que hice para mi abuela

Mañana es el cumpleaños de mi abuela y tuve que comprar un regalo. Pensé mucho antes de decidir comprar esta cosa. A mi abuela le gustan muchas cosas pero es difícil saber exactamente lo que quiere. Hablé con ella y me dijo que tiene mucho tiempo libre. La mayoría de su familia vive lejos y lo más importante para ella es comunicarse con su familia y sus amigas. No le gusta hablar por teléfono pero le gusta recibir cartas. Por fin tuve una idea para un regalo para mi abuela. Tomé el autobús al centro comercial y fui a una papelería. ¿Sabes qué decidí comprarle?

Writing Strategy
- Asking who? what? why? when? where?

A. Reflexión Choose a purchase to describe, then ask yourself ¿quién? ¿qué? ¿por qué? ¿cuándo? ¿dónde? Try to answer these questions as you write.

B. Primer borrador Write a first draft of the composition.

C. Revisión con un(a) compañero(a) Exchange compositions with a classmate. Read each other's work and comment on it, based on these questions. What aspect of the description is the most interesting? What part is the clearest? Is the writing appropriate for its audience? Does the writing reflect the task assigned? What aspect of the composition would you like to have clarified or made more complete?

D. Versión final Revise your first draft at home, based on the feedback you received. Check grammar, spelling, punctuation, and accent marks. Bring your final draft to class.

E. Carpeta Your teacher may choose to place your work in your portfolio, display it on a bulletin board, or use it to evaluate your progress.

Conexión con la economía

El tipo de cambio

Para empezar Shopping in another country requires knowledge of that country's currency, or monetary system. The following passage discusses **el tipo de cambio,** or the exchange rate.

Before you read the passage and the accompanying chart, try to recall what you already know about exchange rates.

The basic monetary unit in the United States is the dollar. What is the basic monetary unit of England? Spain? France? Germany? Japan? For whom are exchange rates important? When do we need to know about exchange rates?

Cuando la gente quiere comprar algo en otros países es necesario cambiar la **moneda** de su país por la moneda del otro. El tipo de cambio determina el valor de la moneda de un país respecto a la moneda del otro, indicando la cantidad que se puede comprar. Por ejemplo, si se pueden cambiar 125 pesetas españolas (125 pp) por un dólar ($1) estadounidense, un español que viaja a Nueva York con 400 pesetas tiene tres dólares estadounidenses para **gastar** durante su visita. También el norteamericano que llega a Madrid con $3 sale de la casa de cambio con 400 pesetas.

El tipo de cambio varia de día en día, **basándose en** la demanda internacional de las monedas. El siguiente **esquema** indica el tipo de cambio en dólares estadounidenses del 15 de enero de 1998. Se multiplica la cantidad de moneda extranjera por el tipo de cambio del mismo país para determinar el valor en dólares (U.S.).

tipo de cambio *exchange rate*   moneda *money, currency*
gastar   *to spend*   basándose en *based on*   esquema *chart*

El tipo de cambio

País (moneda)	Cantidad		Tipo de cambio		Valor en dólares (U.S.)
Argentina (el peso):	100	X	1,002	=	$100,20
Canadá (el dólar):	100	X	0,696	=	$69,60
Chile (el peso):	100	X	0,0021	=	$00,21
Colombia (el peso):	100	X	0,000755	=	$00,075
Ecuador (el sucre):	100	X	0,000222	=	$00,02
España (la peseta):	100	X	0,00645	=	$00,64
Japón (el yen):	100	X	0,0076	=	$00,76
México (el peso):	100	X	0,1209	=	$12,09
Perú (el sol):	100	X	0,3675	=	$36,75
Venezuela (el bolívar):	100	X	0,0019	=	$00,19

A. La moneda Answer the following questions based on the reading.

1. ¿Cuándo es necesario cambiar la moneda de un país a otro?
2. ¿Qué determina el valor de la moneda de un país?
3. ¿Con cuánta frecuencia cambia el tipo de cambio?
4. ¿Cuál es el título del esquema?
5. ¿Cuáles son las monedas que están en más demanda?

B. ¿Cuánto valen? Reading a chart is not difficult if you approach the task in an organized way. Refer to the exchange rate chart to answer the questions.

1. ¿Qué hay en la primera columna de la izquierda del esquema? ¿la segunda? ¿la tercera? ¿la cuarta?
2. ¿Es importante el orden de las columnas del esquema? ¿Por qué?
3. ¿Cuánto valen 100 dólares canadienses en los Estados Unidos?
4. ¿Cuánto valen 100 soles peruanos en los Estados Unidos?
5. ¿Cuánto valen $12,09 (U.S.) en México?
6. ¿Cuánto valen 64 centavos (U.S.) en España?
7. Jaime tiene 200 bolívares. ¿En qué país puede gastarlos? ¿Qué monedas necesita si va a la Argentina? ¿a Chile? ¿a Colombia? ¿al Ecuador? ¿al Japón?

Vistas

de los países hispanos

Venezuela

Capital: Caracas

Ciudades principales: Maracay, Valencia, Maracaibo, Barquisimeto

Población: 21.051.000

Idiomas: español, dialectos indígenas

Área territorial: 912.050 km^2

Clima: El clima es variado, según la altitud; con zonas de tempatura caliente y fría, varia de 18º a 29ºC

Moneda: bolívar

El Salvador

Capital: San Salvador

Ciudades principales: Santa Ana, San Miguel

Población: 5.640.000

Idiomas: español

Área territorial: 20,752 km^2

Clima: En la meseta el clima es templado, en la costa, cálido. La temperatura media es de 24°C

Moneda: colón

meseta *plateau, tableland*

EXPLORA

Find out more about Venezuela and El Salvador! Access the **Nuestros vecinos** page on the *¡Ya verás! Gold* web site for a list of URLs.

http://yaveras.heinle.com/vecinos.htm

Vistas de los hispanos en los Estados Unidos

Arizona

Capital: Phoenix

Ciudades principales: Tucson, Mesa, Scottsdale

Población: 3.677.985

Idiomas: inglés y español

Área territorial: 295.260 km^2

Clima: árido, con una temperatura media anual de 21° C.

New Mexico

Capital: Santa Fe

Ciudades principales: Albuquerque, Las Cruces

Población: 1.515.069

Idiomas: inglés y español

Área territorial: 314.939 km^2

Clima: clima templado y semiárido, temperatura anual de 44° C (40° F) en las montañas, 18° C (64° F) en el sur.

EXPLORA

Find out more about Arizona and New Mexico! Access the **Nuestros vecinos** page on the *¡Ya verás! Gold* web site for a list of URLs.

http://yaveras.heinle.com/vecinos.htm

En la comunidad

Yolanda Miller: representante de tus derechos

"When you go into a department store or a supermarket, you're probably thinking about what you're about to buy rather than how it came to be in the store in the first place. In my job, however, I'm focused on what's behind the scenes—who worked to make the dress you're buying or who stocked the shelves in the grocery store. I'm a union lawyer for the National Labor Relations Board, or NLRB, and it's my job to protect people's rights.

I work out of Newark, New Jersey, where there's a large Spanish-speaking population. Because I speak Spanish, most of my caseload is Hispanic. My clients work in many different settings; from the clothing construction factories to the theater district of New York. It's my responsibility to enforce federal laws and help these workers be informed of their rights. That includes everything from the hours they work and the benefits they receive to their right to unionize. I also see to the environment in which they work. I ensure that their working conditions are safe and healthy.

My work is challenging and at times frustrating, but also deeply satisfying. Everything I studied in law school has now come to life in the faces of the people I represent."

¡Ahora te toca a ti!

Take a simple food or object you use on a daily basis. Try to trace its origins. For example, if you chose a loaf of bread, try to find out what went into getting that bread to your table. Who put the bread on the shelf in the store? Who delivered the bread to the store? Who made the bread? Where did the flour come from? Where did the other ingredients come from? Do as much research as you can on your one item, then draw a diagram showing sequence of events which resulted in your being able to use the product you chose. In Spanish, explain your diagram to the class.

Investigate volunteer organizations in your community. Write a brief paragraph in Spanish describing a volunteer activity that interests you. If you wish, do some volunteer work for the organization you have chosen.

Reading Strategies

The chapter references in parentheses indicate the **Encuentros culturales** sections in which the strategies are used.

Predicting/Previewing

When you predict, you draw on what you already know about a topic, person, or event. Using what you already know helps you make a logical prediction which, in turn, helps you to focus on the material you are reading. You make a prediction, and then you read to check if your prediction is correct. Previewing is looking over the whole reading before you start to read it. This will help you get a sense of what the reading may be about before you begin to read it. The following reading strategies covered in your textbook are related to predicting and previewing.

Activating background and/or prior knowledge

Recalling what you already know or have personally experienced about the reading's topic (Chapters 6-14, Chapters 16-18)

Examining format for content clues

Looking closely at the shape, size, general makeup, and organization of the reading to determine the kind of text it is (for example, an advertisement, a brochure, or a calendar or a description, a comparison, or a narration) and using that knowledge to predict the kinds of information it will include (Chapters 1 & 2, Chapter 8, Chapter 14, Chapter 18)

Scanning for specific information

Searching quickly for some particular piece(s) of information in the reading such as names, dates, and numbers (Chapters 1 & 2, Chapter 5, Chapter 7, Chapter 9, Chapter 12, Chapters 14-18)

Skimming for the gist

Rapidly running your eyes over the reading to see what the overall topic and ideas are and to determine what kind of text it is (Chapters 1-3, Chapter 11, Chapter 18)

Using photos, artwork, and/or illustrations to predict meaning and/or content

Examining the pictures and graphic elements that accompany or make up the reading and making logical guesses about what the text will be about (Chapters 4-6, Chapter 10, Chapter 13, Chapters 15 and 16)

Using the title and the photos, artwork, and/or illustrations to predict meaning and/or content

In combination with the title, examining the pictures and/or graphic elements that accompany or make up the reading to make logical guesses about what the text will be about (Chapter 3, Chapter 9, Chapter 18)

Using the title to predict meaning and/or content

Looking at the reading's title and making logical guesses about what the text will be about (Chapters 12 & 13, Chapter 15, Chapter 17)

Cognate Recognition

Cognates are words that are spelled similarly in two languages and share the same meaning. For example, the Spanish words **hospital, universidad,** and **moderno** are cognates of the English words hospital, university, and modern. There are cognates, however, whose meanings are not what they at first appear to be. For instance, **lectura** in Spanish means reading, not lecture. This type of word is called a false cognate. Looking for cognates and being aware of false cognates will help you understand more easily what you read.

Recognizing cognates

Purposely searching the reading for Spanish words that look like English words and using them to guess at meaning (Chapters 1 & 2, Chapter 5, Chapters 15 & 16)

Writing Strategies

The unit references in parentheses indicate the **Taller de escritores** *section in which the strategy is used.*

Asking who? what? why? *(Unit 6)*

Group brainstorming using clusters *(Unit 3)*

Individual brainstorming using clusters *(Unit 4)*

List writing *(Unit 1, Unit 2)*

Making an outline *(Unit 5)*

Glossary of functions

The numbers in parentheses refer to the chapter in which the word or phrase may be found.

Greeting / taking leave of someone

¡Hola! (1)
Buenos días. (1,2)
Buenas tardes. (1)
Buenas noches. (1)
¿Cómo estás? (1)
¿Cómo está(n) Ud(s).? (2)
¿Cómo te va? (1)
¿Qué tal? (1)
Muy bien, gracias. (1,2)
Bien gracias. ¿Y tú? (1)
(Estoy) bien, gracias. ¿Y Ud.? (2)
Más o menos. (1)
Adiós. (1)
Chao. (1)
Hasta luego. (1)
Saludos a tus padres. (2)

Introducing someone

Te presento a... (1)
Quisiera presentarle(les) a... (2)
Mucho gusto. (1)
Encantado(a). (2)
Me llamo... (4)
Se llama... (6)

Being polite

Por favor... (1)
(Muchas) gracias. (1)
De nada. (1)
Sea(n) Ud(s). ... (8)
Vaya(n) Ud(s). ... (8)

Talking about preferences

(No) me / te / le / les / nos gusta(n). (1,16)
Me / te / le / les / nos encanta(n). (16)
¿Cuál quieres? (17)
¿Cuál prefieres? (17)
¿Qué te gusta más? (5)
Me gusta más... (5)
Prefiero... (11)
Sí, tengo ganas de... (10,15)

Ordering / taking orders for food or drink

Vamos al café. (1)
Vamos a tomar algo. (1)
¿Qué van a pedir? (3)
¿Qué desea(n) tomar? (1)
¿Y Ud.? (1)
Yo quisiera... (1)
Voy a comer... (1)
Para mí... (1)
Aquí tiene(n). (1)
¡Un refresco, por favor! (1)

Commenting about food

¡Qué bueno(a)! (3)
¡Qué comida más rica! (3)
¡Qué picante! (3)
¡Es riquísimo(a)! (3)
¡Es delicioso(a)! (3)

Identifying personal possessions

¿De quién es / son? (4)
Es / Son de... (4)

Getting information about other people

¿De dónde eres / es? (3)
¿Dónde vive? (6)
¿Cuántos(as)... ? (6)
¿Por qué... ? (6)
¿Qué... ? (6)
¿Quién... ? (3,6)
¿Cómo es / son? (6)
Está casado(a) con... (6)
¿Cuántos años tienes? (7)
Tiene... años. (7)
Vive en... (4)
Es de... (3)
Pregúntales a los otros. (12)

Expressing frequency / time

a menudo (7)
de vez en cuando (7)
en otra oportunidad (7)

nunca *(7)*
rara vez *(7)*
una vez al año *(9)*
algún día *(12)*
como de costumbre *(11)*
una vez *(17)*
cada domingo *(6)*
todos los días *(6)*
la semana entera *(11)*
por unos minutos *(13)*
    una hora *(13)*
    un día *(13)*
    dos meses *(13)*
    tres años *(13)*

Telling time

¿Qué hora es? *(9)*
¿A qué hora? *(9)*
¿Cuándo? *(9)*
a las cinco de la mañana *(9)*
a la una de la tarde *(9)*
desde… hasta… *(9)*
entre… y… *(9)*
al mediodía *(9)*
a la medianoche *(9)*
ahora *(9)*

Asking for / giving directions

¿Cómo llego a… ? *(8)*
¿Dónde está… ? *(8)*
¿Está lejos / cerca de aquí? *(8)*
Allí está… *(3)*
Cruce la calle… *(8)*
Doble a la derecha. *(8)*
    a la izquierda. *(8)*
Está al final de… *(8)*
    al lado de… *(8)*
    cerca de… *(8)*
    delante de… *(8)*
    detrás de… *(8)*
    entre… y… *(8)*
    en la esquina de… *(8)*
    frente a… *(8)*
    lejos de… *(8)*
Tome la calle… *(8)*
Siga derecho por… *(8)*

Making plans to go out / to go into town

¿Quieres ir conmigo? *(10)*
¿Para qué? *(10)*
Tengo que… *(10)*
¿Cuándo vamos? *(10)*
¿Cómo vamos? *(12)*
¿Adónde vamos? *(7)*
Vamos a dar un paseo. *(10)*
    hacer un mandado. *(10)*
    ir de compras. *(10)*
    ver a un amigo. *(10)*
Vamos en autobús. *(10)*
    a pie. *(10)*
    en bicicleta. *(10)*
    en coche. *(10)*
    en metro. *(10)*
    en taxi. *(10)*
Vamos hoy. *(10)*
    esta mañana / tarde / noche. *(10)*
    mañana. *(10)*
    mañana por la mañana. *(10, 11)*
    el sábado por la noche. *(10, 11)*
¿Cuánto tarda en llegar a… ? *(12)*
Tarda diez minutos, como máximo. *(12)*

Taking the subway

Por favor, un billete sencillo. *(11)*
    un billete de diez viajes. *(11)*
    un metrotour de tres días. *(11)*
    un metrotour de cinco días. *(11)*
    una tarjeta de abono transportes. *(11)*
    un plano del metro. *(11)*
¿Dónde hay una estación de metro? *(11)*
¿Dónde bajamos del tren? *(11)*
Bajamos en… *(11)*
Cambiamos en… *(11)*
¿En qué dirección… ? *(11)*
¿Qué dirección tomamos? *(11)*
una línea *(11)*

Making travel plans

Quiero planear un viaje. *(12)*
Aquí estoy para servirles. *(12)*
¿En qué puedo servirles? *(12)*
¿Cuánto cuesta un viaje de ida y vuelta? *(12)*
    en avión? *(12)*
Es mucho—sólo tengo… pesetas. *(12)*
Tengo que hacer las maletas. *(13)*

Talking about the past

el año pasado   (13)
el mes pasado   (13)
la semana pasada   (13)
el fin de semana pasado   (13)
el jueves pasado   (13)
ayer por la mañana   (13)
    por la tarde   (13)
ayer   (13)
anoche   (13)
anteayer   (13)
¿Cuánto hace que (no te veo)?   (14)
Hace (5 años) que (no te veo).   (14)
(José,) (no te veo) hace (5 años).   (14)

Talking about the present

Nos vamos ahora.   (15)
    ahora mismo.   (15)
    en este momento.   (15)
Estoy comiendo (estudiando, etc.).   (15)

Talking about the future

Pienso ir a...   (11, 15)
Espero hacer un viaje a...   (13)
Quiero...   (15)
Quisiera...   (15)
Tengo ganas de...   (15)
Voy a...   (7)
Vamos a ir de viaje esta semana.   (11)
    este año.   (11)
    este mes.   (11)
    la semana próxima.   (11)
    el mes próximo.   (11)
    el año próximo.   (11)
    mañana por la tarde.   (10, 11)

Expressing wishes and desires

Quiero...   (11, 15)
Tengo ganas de...   (10, 15)
Espero...   (12, 15)
Quisiera...   (15)

Making purchases

¿Cuánto cuesta(n)?   (16)
¿Qué precio tiene(n)?   (16)
¿No está en oferta?   (16)
A ver.   (16)
¡Super!   (16)
A sus órdenes.   (16)
Aquí tiene(n).   (16)

¿Cuántos hay?   (4)
¿Dónde hay... ?   (4)
Aquí hay otro(a)...   (3)
No hay más.   (16)
¡Qué pena!   (16)
Voy a llevar...   (16)
(Tiene Ud.) buen ojo.   (17)
¿Qué necesita(n)?   (16)
Necesito(amos) un atado de...   (17)
    una botella de...   (17)
    una docena de...   (17)
    50 gramos de...   (17)
    un (medio) kilo de...   (17)
    una libra de...   (17)
    un litro de...   (17)
    un paquete de...   (17)
    un pedazo de...   (17)
¿Algo más?   (16)
Es todo por hoy.   (16)

Making comparisons

mayor que...   (18)
peor que...   (18)
mejor que...   (18)
menor que...   (18)
menos... que...   (18)
más... que...   (18)
tan / tanto... como...   (18)

Expressing disbelief

¿Verdad?   (2)
¿No?   (2)

Making plans to meet

¿Dónde nos encontramos?   (9)
¿A qué hora nos encontramos?   (9)
De acuerdo.   (9)
¡Claro (que sí)!   (5, 10)
Sí, puedo.   (10)
No, no puedo.   (10)
Lo siento.   (7)
Es imposible.   (10)

Answering the telephone

¡Bueno!   (7)
¡Hola!   (7)
¡Diga!   (7)
¡Dígame!   (7)

Verb Charts

Regular Verbs

SIMPLE TENSES

Infinitive	Present Indicative	Preterite	Commands
hablar	hablo	hablé	habla
to speak	hablas	hablaste	(no hables)
	habla	habló	hable
	hablamos	hablamos	hablen
	habláis	hablasteis	
	hablan	hablaron	
vivir	vivo	viví	vive
to live	vives	viviste	(no vivas)
	vive	vivió	viva
	vivimos	vivimos	vivan
	vivís	vivisteis	
	viven	vivieron	

Infinitive	Present Indicative	Preterite	Commands
aprender	aprendo	aprendí	aprende
to learn	aprendes	aprendiste	(no aprendas)
	aprende	aprendió	aprenda
	aprendemos	aprendimos	aprendan
	aprendéis	aprendisteis	
	aprenden	aprendieron	

COMPOUND TENSES

Present progressive	estoy	estamos	hablando aprendiendo viviendo
	estás	estáis	
	está	están	

Stem-Changing Verbs

SIMPLE TENSES

Infinitive Present Participle Past Participle	Present Indicative	Commands
pensar *to think* **e → ie** pensando pensado	**pienso** **piensas** **piensa** pensamos penséis **piensan**	**piensa** **no pienses** **piense** **no penséis** **piensen**

Change of Spelling Verbs

SIMPLE TENSES

Infinitive Present Participle Past Participle	Present Indicative	Preterite
comenzar (e → ie) *to begin* **z → c** **before e** comenzando comenzado	comienzo comienzas comienza comenzamos comenzáis comienzan	**comencé** comenzaste comenzó comenzamos comenzasteis comenzaron

Infinitive Present Participle Past Participle	Present Indicative	Preterite
pagar *to pay* **g → gu** **before e** pagando pagado	pago pagas paga pagamos pagáis pagan	**pagué** pagaste pagó pagamos pagasteis pagaron

Infinitive Present Participle Past Participle	Preterite
tocar *to play* **c → que** **before e** tocando tocado	**toqué** tocaste tocó tocamos tocasteis tocaron

SIMPLE TENSES

andar — to walk

Infinitive / Present Participle / Past Participle	Preterite
andar *to walk* andando andado	anduve anduviste anduvo anduvimos anduvisteis anduvieron

estar — to be

Infinitive / Present Participle / Past Participle	Present Indicative	Preterite	Commands
estar *to be* estando estado	estoy estás está estamos estáis están	estuve estuviste estuvo estuvimos estuvisteis estuvieron	está (no estés) esté estén

hacer — to make, do

Infinitive / Present Participle / Past Participle	Present Indicative	Preterite	Commands
hacer *to make, do* haciendo **hecho**	**hago** haces hace hacemos hacéis hacen	hice hiciste hizo hicimos hicisteis hicieron	haz (no hagas) haga hagan

ir — to go

Infinitive / Present Participle / Past Participle	Present Indicative	Preterite	Commands
ir *to go* yendo ido	voy vas va vamos vais van	fui fuiste fue fuimos fuisteis fueron	ve (no vayas) vaya id (no vayáis) vayan

poder — can, to be able

Infinitive / Present Participle / Past Participle	Present Indicative
poder *can, to be able* **pudiendo** podido	puedo puedes puede podemos podéis pueden

querer — to like

Infinitive / Present Participle / Past Participle	Present Indicative
querer *to like* queriendo querido	quiero quieres quiere queremos queréis quieren

ser — to be

Infinitive / Present Participle / Past Participle	Present Indicative	Commands
ser *to be* siendo sido	soy eres es somos sois son	sé (no seas) sea sean

tener — to have

Infinitive / Present Participle / Past Participle	Present Indicative	Preterite	Commands
tener *to have* teniendo tenido	tengo tienes tiene tenemos tenéis tienen	tuve tuviste tuvo tuvimos tuvisteis tuvieron	ten (no tengas) tenga tened (no tengáis) tengan

Glossary

Spanish-English

The numbers in parentheses refer to the chapters in which active words or phrases may be found.

A

a to (1)
  a menudo frequently, often (7)
  a pesar de in spite of
  a pie on foot, walking (10)
  ¿A qué hora? At what time? (9)
  a veces sometimes (1)
  A ver. Let's see. (16)
  al final de at the end of (8)
  al lado de beside, next to (8)
abrazo *m.* embrace, hug (1)
abrigo *m.* coat (18)
abogado(a) *m. (f.)* lawyer (3)
abuela *f.* grandmother (6)
abuelo *m.* grandfather (6)
aburrido(a) bored, boring (6)
acabar de... to have just . . . (2)
acción *f.* action (9)
aceite *m.* oil (17)
aceite de oliva *m.* olive oil
aceituna *f.* olive (2)
acontecimiento *m.* event
¡adelante! go ahead!
además besides (17)
adiós good-bye (1)
adivino(a) *m. (f.)* fortune-teller
¿adónde? where? (7)
adverbio *m.* adverb (1)
aeropuerto *m.* airport (7)
aficionado(a) *m. (f.)* (sports) fan
agua *f.* water (1)
aguacate *m.* avocado (17)
ahora now (9)
  ahora mismo right now (15)
al contraction of **a + el** (7)
alcanzar to reach
alemán (alemana) *m. (f.)* German (3)
Alemania Germany (3)
alfombra *f.* rug, carpet (4)
algo something (1)
alguno(a) some, any
  algún día someday (12)
alimento *m.* food (17)
almorzar to have lunch (12)
alpinismo *m.* mountain climbing; hiking (14)
alquilar un vídeo to rent a video (13)

alrededor around
alto(a) tall (6)
alumno(a) *m. (f.)* student (4)
allá over there (17)
allí there (4)
amarillo(a) yellow (17)
americano(a) *m. (f.)* American (3)
amigo(a) *m. (f.)* friend (1)
andar to go along, walk (13)
animal *m.* animal (5)
anoche last night (13)
anteayer the day before yesterday (13)
antes before (12)
antipático(a) disagreeable (6)
anunciar to announce (9)
anuncio *m.* advertisement
año *m.* year (11)
apartamento *m.* apartment (4)
apellido *m.* last name (6)
aprender to learn (5)
aquel(la) that (17)
aquél(la) *m. (f.)* that one (17)
aquí here (1)
  aquí hay here is/are (2)
Argentina Argentina (3)
argentino(a) *m. (f.)* Argentine (3)
arquitecto(a) *m. (f.)* architect (3)
arroz *m.* rice (3)
arte *m.* or *f.* art (5)
asistir a to attend (13)
atado *m.* bunch (17)
atún *m.* tuna (17)
aunque although
autobús *m.* bus (4)
  estación de autobuses *m.* bus terminal (7)
ave *f.* bird, fowl
avión *m.* plane (12)
ayer yesterday (13)
ayuda *f.* help (8)
ayudar to help
azúcar *m.* sugar (17)
azul blue (18)

B

bailar to dance (1)
baile *m.* dance (9)
  baile folklórico *m.* folk dance (9)

  baile popular *m.* popular dance (9)
bajar to go down, to lower, to get off a train (11)
bajo(a) short (6), *prep.* under
banana *f.* banana (11)
banco *m.* bank (7)
barato(a) cheap (11)
barco *m.* boat
barrio *m.* neighborhood (7)
barro *m.* clay
básquetbol *m.* basketball (5)
bastante enough (1)
  Bastante bien. Pretty good. (1)
batalla *f.* battle
beber to drink (5)
bebida *f.* drink (1)
béisbol *m.* baseball (5)
belleza *f.* beauty
beso *m.* kiss (5)
biblioteca *f.* library (7)
bicicleta *f.* bicycle (4)
bien well, fine; very (1)
bienvenido(a) welcome (3)
billete *m.* ticket (11)
  billete de diez viajes *m.* ten-trip ticket (11)
  billete de ida y vuelta *m.* round-trip ticket (12)
  billete sencillo *m.* one-way ticket (11)
biología *f.* biology (5)
blanco white (18)
blusa *f.* blouse (18)
bocadillo *m.* sandwich (French bread) (1)
bocina *f.* speaker (4)
bolígrafo *m.* ball-point pen (4)
Bolivia Bolivia (3)
boliviano(a) *m. (f.)* Bolivian (3)
bolsa *f.* purse (18)
bonito(a) pretty (6)
borrador *m.* eraser (4)
bota *f.* boot (18)
botella *f.* bottle (1)
boutique *f.* boutique (18)
bucear to snorkel, dive (14)
buceo *m.* snorkeling, diving (14)
bueno(a) good (3)
  Buenas noches. Good evening. / Good night. (1)
  Buenas tardes. Good afternoon. (1)

¡Bueno! Hello? (answering the phone) (7)

Buenos días. Good morning. (1)

burbuja *f.* bubble

buscar to look for (8)

C

caballo *m.* horse

cacahuete *m.* peanut (2)

cada each, every (6)

caer to fall

café *m.* café, coffee (1)

calamares *m.* squid (2)

calcetín *m.* sock (18)

calculadora *f.* calculator (4)

calidad *f.* quality

caliente hot (1)

calle *f.* street (8)

cama *f.* bed (4)

cámara *f.* camera (4)

camarero(a) *m. (f.)* waiter (waitress) (1)

cambiar to change (11)

cambio *m.* change, alteration (12)

caminar to walk (13)

    caminar en la playa to walk on the beach (14)

camisa *f.* shirt (18)

camiseta *f.* T-shirt (18)

campaña *f.* campaign

campo *m.* country (vs. city)

Canadá Canada (3)

canadiense *m. or f.* Canadian (3)

canción *f.* song

cansado(a) tired (9)

cantante *m. or f.* singer

cantar to sing (1)

cantidad *f.* quantity (17)

carne *f.* meat (3)

carnicería *f.* butcher shop (7)

caro(a) expensive (16)

carrera *f.* career

carrito *m.* shopping cart (17)

carta *f.* letter

cartera *f.* wallet (4)

casa *f.* house (4)

casado(a) married (6)

casi almost†

catedral *f.* cathedral (7)

catorce fourteen (4)

cazar to hunt

cebolla *f.* onion (17)

celebrar to celebrate (9)

cenar to have supper (13)

centro *m.* center, downtown (4)

    centro comercial shopping center (16)

cerca (de) near, close to (7)

cerrar to close

¡Chao! Bye! (1)

chaqueta *f.* jacket (18)

charlar to chat (1)

chico(a) *m. (f.)* boy (girl)

chile *m.* hot pepper (3)

Chile Chile (3)

chileno(a) *m. (f.)* Chilean (3)

China China (3)

chino(a) *m. (f.)* Chinese (3)

chocolate *m.* chocolate (1)

chorizo *m.* sausage (2)

ciclismo *m.* cycling (14)

cien one hundred (7)

ciencia *f.* science (5)

ciento one hundred (12)

cinco five (4)

cincuenta fifty (7)

cine *m.* movie theater (7)

cinta *f.* tape (cassette) (4)

cinturón *m.* belt (18)

cita *f.* date, appointment (10)

ciudad *f.* city (6)

¡Claro! Of course! (5)

    ¡Claro que sí! Of course! (reaffirmed) (10)

cliente *m.* customer (17)

club *m.* club (7)

coche *m.* car (4)

cola *f.* tail

colegio *m.* school (7)

Colombia Colombia (3)

colombiano(a) *m. (f.)* Colombian (3)

comedor *m.* dining room

comentar to comment (3)

comentario *m.* commentary

comer to eat (1)

comida *f.* food, meal (1)

    comida mexicana Mexican food (3)

como how, as, like (11)

    como de costumbre as usual (11)

¿cómo? how?, what? (3)

    ¿Cómo es? / son? How is it / are they? (6)

    ¿Cómo está Ud.? How are you? (formal) (2)

    ¿Cómo estás? How are you? (informal) (1)

    ¿Cómo te llamas? What's your name? (4)

    ¿Cómo te va? How is it going? (1)

cómoda *f.* dresser (4)

compañía *f.* company (3)

comparación *f.* comparison (18)

compartir to share (5)

comprar to buy (13)

comprender to understand (5)

computadora *f.* computer (4)

con with (1)

concierto *m.* concert (13)

concurso de poesía *m.* poetry contest (9)

congelado(a) frozen (17)

conmigo with me (10)

conserva *f.* preserve, canned good (17)

construir to build

contador(a) *m. (f.)* accountant (3)

contar to tell, to count (4)

contento(a) happy (9)

contestar to answer (1)

continuar to continue (9)

contra against

conversación telefónica *f.* telephone conversation (7)

corazón *m.* heart

correr to run (5)

corto short (in length)

cosa *f.* thing (4)

Costa Rica Costa Rica (3)

costarricense *m. or f.* Costa Rican (3)

costumbre *f.* custom

crema *f.* cream (17)

croissant *m.* croissant (1)

cruzar to cross (8)

cuaderno *m.* notebook (4)

cuadrado *m.* square

¿cuál? which? (17)

cualquier any (13)

¿cuándo? when? (9)

¿cuántos(as)? how many? (6)

    ¿Cuántos años tienes? How old are you? (7)

    ¿Cuánto cuesta(n)? How much is it (are they)? (16)

    ¿Cuántos hay? How many are there? (4)

cuarenta forty (7)

cuarto *m.* room (4)

cuatro four (4)

cuatrocientos(as) four hundred (12)

Cuba Cuba (3)

cubano(a) *m. (f.)* Cuban (3)

cuero *m.* leather (18)

cuerpo *m.* body

D

dar to give (8)
de of (3)
    de acuerdo OK (we are in agreement) (9)
    de costumbre usually (15)
    ¿De dónde es (eres)? Where are you from? (3)
    De nada You're welcome. (1)
    ¿De quién es... ? Whose is it? (4)
    de vez en cuando from time to time (7)
deber to owe, must, should (10)
decir to say (10)
dejar to leave, to relinquish
del contraction of **de + el** (8)
delante de in front of (8)
delgado(a) thin (6)
delicioso(a) delicious (3)
demás rest, remaining
dentista m. or f. dentist (3)
dentro inside
deporte m. sport (5)
deportista sportsman, sportswoman
derecha right (8)
derecho(a) straight (8)
desahogar to ease pain
desayunar to eat breakfast (13)
desayuno m. breakfast (1)
descansar to rest (9)
desconocido(a) unknown
desde from (9)
desear to want, wish for (1)
desempleo m. unemployment
desfile m. parade (9)
desierto m. desert
despacio slow (8)
despedirse to say good-bye (1)
después de after (1)
detrás de behind (8)
día m. day (10)
    Día de la Independencia m. Independence Day (9)
dibujo m. drawing
    dibujos animados animated film, cartoon
dieciseis sixteen (4)
diecisiete seventeen (4)
dieciocho eighteen (4)
diecinueve nineteen (4)
diez ten (4)
¡Diga! / ¡Dígame! Hello? (answering the phone) (7)

dinero m. money (2)
dirección f. direction, address (7)
disco compacto m. compact disc (4)
discoteca f. dance club (7)
disculparse to apologize (7)
discutir to argue (12)
disfrutar to enjoy
divertido(a) fun, amusing (6)
divorciado(a) divorced (6)
doblar to turn (8)
doce twelve (4)
docena f. dozen (17)
doctor(a) m. (f.) doctor (3)
domingo m. Sunday (10)
dominicano(a) m. (f.) Dominican (3)
¿dónde? where? (3)
    ¿Dónde está... ? Where is . . . ? (8)
    ¿Dónde hay... ? Where is / are there . . . ? (4)
dormir to sleep (15)
dos two (4)
doscientos(as) two hundred (12)
dueño(a) m. (f.) owner
durante during (15)

E

Ecuador Ecuador (3)
ecuatoriano(a) m. (f.) Ecuadoran (3)
edad f. age (7)
edificio m. building (7)
ejemplo m. example
    por ejemplo for example
el m. the (2)
él he (2)
El Salvador El Salvador (3)
ella she (2)
ellos(as) m. (f.) they (2)
embajador(a) m. (f.) ambassador, ambassadress
empezar to begin
en in (1)
    en este momento at this moment (15)
    en otra oportunidad at some other time (7)
    ¿En qué dirección? In which direction? (11)
    ¿En qué puedo servirle(s)? How can I help you (plural)? (12)
encantado(a) delighted (2)
enchilada f. soft, corn tortilla filled with cheese, meat, or chicken (3)
encontrar to find (9)

encontrarse (con) to meet (9)
encuesta f. survey (12)
enemigo(a) m. (f.) enemy
enfermero(a) m. (f.) nurse (3)
enfermo(a) sick (9)
enojado(a) angry, mad (9)
ensalada f. salad (17)
    ensalada de frutas f. fruit salad (17)
    ensalada de vegetales (verduras) f. vegetable salad (17)
entero whole (11)
entonces then (9)
entrada f. entrance ticket (11)
entre between (8)
equipo m. team (13)
escaparate m. shop window (16)
escribir to write (5)
escrito written
escritorio m. desk (4)
escuchar to listen (to) (1)
escuela f. school (4)
    escuela secundaria f. high school (7)
escultura f. sculpture (5)
ese(a) that (17)
ése(a) m. (f.) that one (17)
espacio m. space
España Spain (3)
español(a) m. (f.) Spaniard, Spanish (1)
especia f. spice
especial special (11)
especie f. species
esperar to hope, to wait (12)
espíritu m. spirit
esposa f. wife (6)
esposo m. husband (6)
esquema m. chart, diagram
esquí m. ski (16)
esquí acuático m. water ski (14)
esquina f. corner (8)
    en la esquina de on the corner of (8)
establecer to establish (18)
estación f. station (7)
estacionamiento m. parking lot (8)
estadio m. stadium (7)
Estados Unidos United States (3)
estadounidense m. or f. American, from the United States (3)
estante m. book shelf (4)
estar to be (8)
    Está al final de... It's at the end of . . . (8)
    estar en forma to be in shape
este(a) this (17)

éste(a) *m. (f.)* this one (17)
estéreo *m.* stereo (4)
estrella *f.* star
estudiante *m. or f.* student (3)
estudiar to study (1)
etapa *f.* stage, phase
éxito *m.* success
expresar to express (1)
expresión *f.* expression (1)

F

fácil easy
falda *f.* skirt (18)
familia *f.* family (6)
famoso(a) famous (12)
farmacia *f.* pharmacy, drugstore (7)
favorito(a) favorite (16)
feo(a) ugly, plain (6)
feria *f.* fair (9)
fiesta *f.* party (9)
    Fiesta del pueblo *f.* religious festival
    honoring a town's patron saint (9)
fin de semana *m.* weekend (13)
finalmente finally (14)
firmar to sign
flan *m.* caramel custard (3)
flecha *f.* arrow
florería *f.* flower shop (7)
francés (francesa) *m. (f.)* French (3)
Francia France (3)
frecuentemente frequently (10)
frente a across from, facing (8)
fresa *f.* strawberry (1)
fresco(a) cool (17)
frío(a) cold (1)
frijoles *m.* beans (3)
fruta *f.* fruit (17)
fuegos artificiales *m.* fireworks (9)
fuerza *f.* strength
fútbol *m.* soccer (5)
    fútbol americano *m.* football (5)
futuro *m.* future (15)

G

gafas *f. pl.* eyeglasses
galleta *f.* biscuit, cookie (17)
ganar to earn (2)
garaje *m.* garage (3)
gastar to spend, to waste
gato *m.* cat (5)
gente *f.* people
gimnasio *m.* gym (13)

globo *m.* globe, sphere, balloon (1)
gordo(a) fat (6)
grabadora *f.* tape recorder (4)
gracia *f.* grace
gracias thank you (1)
    la misa de Acción de Gracias *f.*
    Thanksgiving Day mass (9)
gramo *m.* gram (17)
granadina *f.* grenadine (1)
grande large, big (6)
gratis free
grupo *m.* group (1)
guapo(a) handsome (6)
Guatemala Guatemala (3)
guatemalteco(a) *m. (f.)* Guatemalan (3)
guisante *m.* pea (17)
guitarra *f.* guitar (14)
gustar to like (1)
gusto *m.* taste (5)

H

habilidad *f.* ability
hablar to talk (1)
hacer to do, to make (10)
    hacer la cama to make the bed (13)
    hacer ejercicio to exercise (13)
    hacer las maletas to pack (13)
    hacer un mandado to do an errand
    (10)
    hacer un viaje to take a trip (13)
hamburguesa *f.* hamburger (3)
harina *f.* flour (17)
hasta until (1)
    Hasta luego. See you later. (1)
hay there is / are (4)
helado *m.* ice cream (17)
hermana *f.* sister (6)
hermano *m.* brother (6)
hermoso(a) beautiful (12)
hija *f.* daughter (6)
hijo *m.* son (6)
hispano(a) *m. (f.)* Hispanic (9)
historia *f.* history, story
hoja *f.* leaf, piece of paper (16)
¡Hola! Hello! (1)
hombre *m.* man (3)
Honduras Honduras (3)
hondureño(a) *m. (f.)* Honduran (3)
hora *f.* hour (9)
horario *m.* schedule (11)
horrible horrible (3)
hospital *m.* hospital (7)
hotel *m.* hotel (7)
hoy today (10)

I

ida y vuelta round trip
idea *f.* idea (9)
iglesia *f.* church (7)
igual equal
igualdad *f.* equality (18)
Igualmente. Likewise. (2)
impermeable *m.* raincoat (18)
imposible impossible (10)
indígena native
ingeniero(a) *m. (f.)* engineer (3)
Inglaterra England (3)
inglés (inglesa) *m. (f.)* Englishman
    (Englishwoman), English (3)
inteligente intelligent (6)
intercambio *m.* exchange (3)
interesante interesting (6)
invierno *m.* winter
invitar to invite (13)
ir to go (7)
    ir a... to be going to . . . (10)
    ir de camping to go camping (14)
    ir de compras to go shopping (10)
    ir de pesca to go fishing (14)
    Vamos a... Let's (go) . . . (1)
Italia Italy (3)
italiano(a) *m. (f.)* Italian (3)
izquierda left (8)

J

jamón *m.* ham (1)
Japón Japan (3)
japonés (japonesa) *m. (f.)* Japanese (3)
jazz *m.* jazz (5)
joven young person (11)
joya *f.* jewel
jueves *m.* Thursday (10)
jugador(a) *m. (f.)* player
jugar to play (a sport or game) (11)
    jugar al baloncesto to play basketball
    (14)
    jugar al hockey to play hockey (14)
    jugar al hockey sobre hierba to play
    field hockey (14)
    jugar al golf to play golf (14)
jugo *m.* juice (1)
juguete *m.* toy
junto together (17)
juventud *f.* youth

K

kilo *m.* kilogram (17)
   medio kilo half kilo (17)
kilómetro *m.* kilometer (12)

L

la *f.* the (2)
lácteo(a) dairy (17)
   producto lácteo *m.* dairy product (17)
lápiz *m.* pencil (4)
largo long
las *f.* the (plural) (4)
lata *f.* can, tin (17)
leche *f.* milk (1)
lechuga *f.* lettuce (17)
leer to read (5)
lejos (de) far (from) (8)
lengua *f.* language; tongue (5)
levantar pesas to lift weights (14)
leyenda *f.* legend
libra *f.* pound (17)
librería *f.* bookstore (7)
libro *m.* book (4)
licuado *m.* milkshake (1)
limón *m.* lemon (1)
limonada *f.* lemonade (1)
línea *f.* line (11)
listo(a) ready (9)
litro *m.* liter (17)
llamar to call (7)
llamarse to be called (4)
   Me llamo... My name is ... (4)
   Se llama... His or her name is ... (6)
llave *f.* key (4)
llegar to arrive (8)
lleno(a) full (17)
llevar to take, carry (4)
llover to rain
los *m.* the (plural) (4)
luchar to fight
luego then, afterwards (14)
lugar *m.* place, location (7)
lunes *m.* Monday (10)
luz *f.* light

M

madre *f.* mother (6)
maíz *m.* corn (17)
mal poorly (1)

malo(a) bad (3)
mamá mother, mom (2)
mantener to maintain
mantequilla *f.* butter (1)
manzana *f.* apple (17)
mañana *f.* morning; tomorrow (10)
martes *m.* Tuesday (10)
máquina *f.* machine (4)
   máquina de escribir *f.* typewriter (4)
más more (2)
   más o menos so-so (1)
   más... que more ... than (18)
mayonesa *f.* mayonnaise (17)
mayor older (18)
mayoría *f.* majority
mecánico(a) *m. (f.)* mechanic (3)
media *f.* stocking (18)
medianoche *f.* midnight (9)
médico *m.* doctor (3)
medio(a) half (17)
medio *m.* middle, means (4)
   medio de transporte *m.* means of transportation (4)
mediodía *m.* midday, noon (9)
mejor better, best (9)
melocotón *m.* peach (1)
menor younger (18)
menos less; minus (4)
menos... que less ... than (18)
mercado *m.* market (7)
   mercado al aire libre *m.* open-air market (17)
merienda *f.* snack (1)
mermelada *f.* jelly (1)
mes *m.* month (11)
metro *m.* subway (10)
   estación de metro *f.* subway station (11)
mexicano(a) *m. (f.)* Mexican (3)
México Mexico (3)
mi(s) my (plural) (4)
mí me (1)
mientras in the meantime
miércoles *m.* Wednesday (10)
mil one thousand (12)
milla *f.* mile (12)
millón *m.* million (12)
minuto *m.* minute (14)
mirar to look at, to watch (2)
   ¡Mira! Look! (3)
mismo(a) same
mitad *f.* half
mochila *f.* knapsack (4)
moda *f.* style, fashion (18)

moderno(a) modern (18)
montar en bicicleta to ride a bicycle (13)
moreno(a) *m. (f.)* dark-haired, brunet(te) (6)
morir to die
motocicleta *f.* motorcycle (4)
muchacha *f.* young woman (4)
muchacho *m.* young man (4)
muchísimo very much (1)
mucho(a) a lot (1)
   Muchas gracias. Thank you very much. (1)
   Mucho gusto. Nice to meet you. (1)
muerte *f.* death
mujer *f.* woman (3)
mundo *m.* world
museo *m.* museum (7)
música *f.* music (1)
   música clásica *f.* classical music (5)
   música rock *f.* rock music (5)
muy very (1)
   Muy bien, gracias. Very well, thank you. (1)

N

nacer to be born
nacionalidad *f.* nationality (3)
nada nothing (13)
nadar to swim (13)
nadie nobody
naranja *f.* orange (1)
natación *f.* swimming (14)
naturaleza *f.* nature (5)
necesitar to need (2)
negocio *m. (f.)* business (3)
   hombre (mujer) de negocios *m. (f.)* businessman (businesswoman) (3)
negro black (18)
Nicaragua Nicaragua (3)
nicaragüense *m. or f.* Nicaraguan (3)
niña *f.* girl, baby
niño *m.* boy, baby
nivel *m.* level
no no; not (1)
noche *f.* night (9)
   esta noche tonight (7)
nombre *m.* name (6)
norte *m.* north
norteamericano(a) *m. (f.)* North American (3)
nosotros(as) *m. (f.)* we (1)
novecientos(as) nine hundred (12)

noventa ninety (7)
novia *f.* girlfriend (5)
novio *m.* boyfriend (5)
nuestro(a) our (4)
nueve nine (4)
nuevo(a) new (12)
número *m.* number (7)
nunca never (7)

O

o or (12)
ocho eight (4)
ochenta eighty (7)
ochocientos(as) eight hundred (12)
oferta *f.* sale (16)
   ¿No está(n) en oferta? It's not on sale? (16)
oficina de correos *f.* post office (7)
ofrecer to offer (17)
ojo *m.* eye
once eleven (4)
orden *m.* order (12)
   a sus órdenes at your service (12)
oreja *f.* ear
oro *m.* gold
otro(a) other, another (11)
   otra cosa *f.* another thing (11)

P

padre *m.* father (6)
   padres *m.* parents (2)
pagar to pay (12)
país *m.* country (8)
paisaje *m.* landscape
pájaro *m.* bird (5)
palabra *f.* word (1)
pan *m.* bread (1)
   pan dulce *m.* any kind of sweet roll (1)
   pan tostado *m.* toast (1)
panadería *f.* bakery (7)
Panamá Panama (3)
panameño(a) *m. (f.)* Panamanian (3)
pantalones *m.* trousers (18)
papa *f.* potato (17)
papel *m.* paper (16)
   papel de avión *m.* air mail stationery (16)
   papel para escribir a máquina *m.* typing paper (16)
papelería *f.* stationery store (16)
paquete *m.* package (17)

para for, in order to (1)
   para que in order that
Paraguay Paraguay (3)
paraguayo(a) *m. (f.)* Paraguayan (3)
pariente *m.* relative (6)
parque *m.* park (7)
   parque zoológico *m.* zoo (13)
pasado past, last (13)
pasar to pass (2)
   pasar tiempo to spend time (13)
paseo *m.* walk (10)
   dar un paseo to take a walk (10)
pasta *f.* pasta (17)
pastel *m.* pastry, pie (1)
patata *f.* potato (2)
   patatas bravas *f.* cooked potatoes diced and served in spicy sauce (2)
patinar to skate (14)
   patinar sobre hielo to ice skate (14)
pedazo *m.* piece (17)
pedir to ask for (something), to request (8)
peine *m.* comb
película *f.* film, movie (5)
   película cómica *f.* comedy movie (5)
   película de aventura *f.* adventure movie (5)
   película de ciencia ficción *f.* science fiction movie (5)
   película de horror *f.* horror movie (5)
peligro *m.* danger
peligroso(a) dangerous
pelirrojo(a) redheaded (6)
pelota *f.* ball (16)
   pelota de tenis *f.* tennis ball (16)
pendiente *m.* earring
pensar to think (11)
peor worse, worst (18)
pequeño(a) small (6)
pera *f.* pear (17)
perder to lose (13)
perdón excuse me (1)
periodista *m. or f.* journalist (3)
pero but (2)
perro *m.* dog (5)
perseguir to persecute, to pursue
persona *f.* person (6)
Perú Peru (3)
peruano(a) *m. (f.)* Peruvian (3)
a pesar de in spite of
pescado *m.* fish (17)
picante spicy (3)
piedra *f.* stone
pimienta *f.* pepper (17)

pintura *f.* painting (5)
piscina *f.* swimming pool (7)
planear to plan (12)
plano del metro *m.* subway map (11)
planta *f.* plant; floor (4)
plata *f.* silver
plátano *m.* banana, plantain (17)
plato *m.* dish
playa *f.* beach (12)
plaza *f.* plaza, square (7)
pluma *f.* fountain pen, feather (4),
poco little (1)
poder to be able to (10)
policía *f.* police, *m.* or *f.* police officer (7)
   estación de policía *f.* police station (7)
política *f.* politics (5)
pollo *m.* chicken (3)
poner to put, place (16)
por for (11)
   por eso that is why (16)
   por favor please (1)
   por fin finally (14)
   por la mañana in the morning (11)
   por la noche at night (11)
   por la tarde in the afternoon (11)
   por supuesto of course (9)
¿por qué? why? (6)
porque because (6)
portafolio *m.* briefcase (4)
posesión *f.* possession (4)
póster *m.* poster (4)
practicar to practice (1)
   practicar el surfing to surf (14)
   practicar la vela to sail (14)
precio *m.* price (16)
preferencia *f.* preference (17)
preferir to prefer (7)
pregunta *f.* qustion (2)
preguntar to ask a question (9)
premio *m.* prize (9)
preocupar to preoccupy, to worry
preparar to prepare (9)
presentación *f.* presentation, introduction (2)
presentar to present, introduce (1)
primero first (7)
primo(a) *m. (f.)* cousin (6)
producto *m.* product (17)
profesión *f.* profession (3)
profesor(a) *m. (f.)* professor, teacher (3)
pronombre *m.* pronoun (1)
pronto soon
propina *f.* tip (12)

proteger to protect
próximo(a) next (10)
prueba *f.* test
público(a) public (7)
pueblo *m.* town, a people
Puerto Rico Puerto Rico (3)
puertorriqueño(a) *m. (f.)* Puerto Rican (3)
pues then (1)

Q

que that (1)
¿qué? what? (6)
    ¿Qué día es hoy? What day is today? (10)
    ¿Qué hay? What's new? (1)
    ¿Qué hora es? What time is it? (9)
    ¿Qué pasa? What's going on? (1)
    ¿Qué tal? How are you? (1)
¡Qué... ! How . . . ! (3)
    ¡Qué bueno(a)! Great! (3)
    ¡Qué comida más rica! What delicious food! (3)
    ¡Qué hambre! I'm starving! (2)
    ¡Qué horrible! How terrible! (3)
    ¡Qué pena! What a pity! (16)
quemado(a) burned
quemar to burn
quedar to stay (8)
querer to want (7)
    Yo quisiera... I would like . . . (1)
queso *m.* cheese (1)
¿quién? who? (3)
química *f.* chemistry (5)
quince fifteen (4)
quinientos(as) five hundred (12)
quiosco de periódicos *m.* newspaper kiosk (8)

R

radio despertador *m.* clock radio (4)
raqueta *f.* racket (16)
rara vez rarely (7)
razón *f.* reason
rebanada de pan *f.* slice of bread (1)
receta *f.* recipe
recibir to receive (5)
recordar to remember
recuerdo *m.* memory (3)
refresco *m.* soft drink (1)
regalo *m.* gift (18)
regatear to bargain (17)

regresar to return
regular regular; so-so (in response to greeting) (1)
reina *f.* queen
repaso *m.* review (3)
repetír to repeat (13)
República Dominicana Dominican Republic (3)
restaurante *m.* restaurant (1)
revista *f.* magazine
rey *m.* king
riquísimo(a) delicious (3)
rojo(a) red (17)
ropa *f.* clothes (18)
    ropa de marca *f.* designer clothes
rubio(a) blond(e) (6)
ruido *m.* noise
Rusia Russia (3)
ruso(a) *m. (f.)* Russian (3)

S

sábado *m.* Saturday (10)
sacapuntas *m.* pencil sharpener (4)
sacar to obtain, to get out (something) (14)
sal *f.* salt (17)
salir (de) to go out, leave (13)
salir con to go out with (13)
salsa *f.* sauce; type of music (3)
salud *f.* health
saludar to greet (1)
saludo *m.* greeting (2)
salvadoreño(a) *m. (f.)* Salvadoran (3)
sandalia *f.* sandal (18)
sándwich *m.* sandwich (1)
secretario(a) *m. (f.)* secretary (3)
seguir to follow, to continue
segundo(a) second
seguro(a) sure (18)
seis six (4)
seiscientos(as) six hundred (12)
semana *f.* week (11)
sentido *m.* sense
sentir to feel
    Lo siento. I'm sorry. (7)
señor Mr. (1)
señora Mrs. (1)
señorita Miss (1)
ser to be (3)
    Es de... Is from . . . , It belongs to . . . (3)
    Es la una y media. It is 1:30. (9)
    Son de... They are from . . . , They belong to . . . (3)

Son las tres. It is 3 o'clock. (9)
serie *f.* series, sequence (14)
serio(a) serious (6)
servir to serve (12)
sesenta sixty (7)
setecientos(as) seven hundred (12)
setenta seventy (7)
si if (12)
sí yes (1)
siempre always (1)
siete seven (4)
silla *f.* chair (4)
simpático(a) nice (6)
sin without
sin límite unlimited (11)
sino but
sobre *m.* envelope (16)
sobre *prep., adv.* above
soda *f.* soda water (1)
sol *m.* sun
sólo only (12)
sopa *f.* soup (17)
su(s) his, her, your, their (4)
subir to raise
Sudamerica *f.* South America (2)
suerte *f.* fortune, luck
suéter *m.* sweater (18)
suficiente enough (16)
¡Super! Super! (16)
sur *m.* south
suroeste *m.* southwest
sustantivo *m.* noun (1)

T

taco *m.* taco, corn tortilla filled with meat and other things (3)
talla *f.* (clothing) size (18)
también also (2)
tampoco neither (2)
tan so (8)
    tan / tanto... como as / as much . . . as (18)
tapa española *f.* Spanish snack (2)
taquilla *f.* booth (11)
tardar to take (an amount of time) (12)
tarde *f.* afternoon, late (7)
tarea *f.* task; homework (9)
tarjeta *f.* card (11)
    tarjeta de abono transportes *f.* commuter pass (11)
    tarjeta de cumpleaños *f.* birthday card (16)
    tarjeta del Día de la Madre *f.*

Mother's Day card (16)
taxi *m.* taxi (10)
té *m.* tea (1)
teatro *m.* theatre (7)
teléfono *m.* telephone (7)
telenovela *f.* soap opera (4)
televisor (a colores) *m.* (color) television set (4)
temer to fear
temporada *f.* (sports) season
tener to have (6)
   tener... años to be ... years old (7)
   tener ganas de... to feel like ... (10)
   tener hambre to be hungry (7)
   tener que to have to (6)
   tener sed to be thirsty (7)
tenis *m.* tennis (5)
tercero(a) third
terminar to end (13)
terremoto *m.* earthquake
tía *f.* aunt (6)
tiempo *m.* time (14)
   tiempo libre *m.* free time
tienda *f.* store (7)
   tienda de deportes *f.* sporting goods store (16)
   tienda de música *f.* music store (16)
   tienda de ropa *f.* clothing store (18)
tierra *f.* earth
tío *m.* uncle (6)
tocar to touch, to play an instrument (2)
   te toca a ti it's your turn
todavía still
todo(a) all (9)
   todos los días *m.* every day (1)
tomar to drink, to take (1)
   tomar el sol to sunbathe (14)
tomate *m.* tomato (17)
tonto(a) silly, stupid, foolish (6)
torre *f.* tower
tortilla *f.* omelette (Spain) or cornmeal pancake (Mexico) (2)
trabajador(a) *m. (f.)* worker
trabajar to work (1)
trabajo *m.* work
traer to bring
transporte *m.* transportation (4)
tratar de to try, to endeavor
trece thirteen (4)
treinta thirty (7)
tren *m.* train (7)
   estación de trenes train station (7)
tres three (4)
trescientos(as) three hundred (12)

triste sad (9)
tú you (familiar) (1)
tu(s) your (plural) (4)
turista *m.* or *f.* tourist (11)

U

un(a) a, an (1)
universidad *f.* university (7)
uno one (4)
uno(as) some (1)
Uruguay Uruguay (3)
uruguayo(a) *m. (f.)* Uruguayan (3)
usar to use (13)
usted (Ud.) you (formal) (1)
ustedes (Uds.) you (formal plural) (1)
usualmente usually (10)
útil useful
uva *f.* grape (17)

V

valiente brave
valor *m.* value
vaqueros *m.* jeans
varios(as) various (17)
vaso *m.* glass (17)
vegetal *m.* vegetable (17)
veinte twenty (4)
vendedor(a) *m. (f.)* salesman (woman) (17)
vender to sell (5)
venezolano(a) *m. (f.)* Venezuelan (3)
Venezuela Venezuela (3)
venir to come (9)
venta *f.* sale
ver to see (9)
   Nos vemos. See you. (farewell) (1)
verbo *m.* verb (1)
¿verdad? right? (2)
verdadero(a) true, real
verde green (17)
vestido *m.* dress (18)
vestir to dress
vez *f.* time, instance (9)
   una vez once (17)
   una vez al año once a year (9)
vía *f.* (railway) track
viajar to travel (1)
viaje *m.* trip (12)
   agencia de viajes *f.* travel agency (12)
vida *f.* life (13)
vídeo *m.* video (4)
videocasetera *f.* videocassette player (4)

viejo(a) old (6)
viernes *m.* Friday (10)
Vietnam Vietnam (3)
vietnamita *m.* or *f.* Vietnamese (3)
visitar to visit (7)
vista *f.* sight
vivienda *f.* housing (4)
vivir to live (5)
vólibol *m.* volleyball (5)
volver to go back (13)
vosotros(as) *m. (f.)* you (familiar plural) (1)
voz *f.* voice

W

waterpolo *m.* waterpolo (14)
windsurf *m.* windsurfing (14)

Y

y and (1)
yo I (1)
yogur *m.* yogurt (17)

Z

zanahoria *f.* carrot (17)
zapatería *f.* shoe store (18)
zapato *m.* shoe (18)
   zapato de tacón *m.* high-heeled shoe (18)
   zapato de tenis *m.* tennis shoe (16)

Glossary

English-Spanish

The numbers in parentheses refer to the chapters in which active words or phrases may be found.

A

ability **habilildad** *f.*
(to be) able to **poder** (10)
above **sobre**
accountant **contador(a)** *m. (f.)* (3)
across from **frente a** (8)
action **acción** *f.* (9)
address **dirección** *f.* (7)
adventure movie **película de aventura** *f.*
  (5)
adverb **adverbio** *m.* (1)
advertisement **anuncio** *m.*
after **después de** (1)
afternoon **tarde** *f.* (7)
afterwards **luego** (14)
against **contra**
age **edad** *f.* (7)
air mail stationery **papel de avión** *m.* (16)
airport **aeropuerto** *m.* (7)
all **todo(a)** (9)
almost **casi**
also **también** (2)
alteration **cambio** *m.* (12)
although **aunque**
always **siempre** (1)
ambassador **embajador** *m.*
American **americano(a)** *m. (f.)* (3), (from
  the United States) **estadounidense** *m.*
  or f. (3)
amusing **divertido(a)** (6)
and **y** (1)
angry **enojado(a)** (9)
animal **animal** *m.* (5)
(to) announce **anunciar** (9)
another **otro(a)** (11)
  another thing **otra cosa** *f.* (11)
(to) answer **contestar** (1)
any **cualquier** (13)
apartment **apartamento** *m.* (4)
(to) apologize **disculparse** (7)
apple **manzana** *f.* (17)
appointment **cita** *f.* (10)
architect **arquitecto(a)** *m. (f.)* (3)
Argentina **Argentina** (3)
Argentine **argentino(a)**
  m. (f.) (3)
(to) argue **discutir** (12)
around **alrededor**

(to) arrive **llegar** (8)
arrow **flecha** *f.*
art **arte** *m. or f.* (5)
as **como** (11)
  as / as much . . . as **tan / tanto. . .
    como** (18)
  as usual **como de costumbre** (11)
(to) ask a question **preguntar** (6)
(to) ask for (something) **pedir** (8)
at **a** (1)
  at night **por la noche** (11)
  at some other time **en otra oportu-
    nidad** (7)
  at the end of **al final de** (8)
at this moment **en este momento**
  (15)
  At what time? **¿A qué hora?** (9)
  at your service **a sus órdenes** (12)
(to) attend **asistir a** (13)
aunt **tía** *f.* (6)
avocado **aguacate** *m.* (17)

B

bad **malo(a)** (6)
bakery **panadería** *f.* (7)
ball **pelota** *f.* (16)
balloon **globo** *m.* (1)
banana **banana** *f.,* **plátano** *m.* (1)
bank **banco** *m.* (7)
(to) bargain **regatear** (17)
baseball **béisbol** *m.* (5)
basketball **básquetbol** *m.* (5); **baloncesto**
  m. (14)
battle **batalla** *f.*
(to) be **estar** (8), **ser** (3)
  to be in shape **estar en forma**
beach **playa** *f.* (12)
beans **frijoles** *m.* (3)
beautiful **hermoso(a)** (12)
beauty **belleza** *f.*
because **porque** (6)
bed **cama** *f.* (4)
before **antes** (12)
(to) begin **empezar**
behind **detrás de** (8)
belt **cinturón** *m.* (18)
beside **al lado de** (8)
besides **además** (17)

better **mejor** (9)
between **entre** (8)
big **grande** (6)
bicycle **bicicleta** *f.* (4)
biology **biología** *f.* (5)
bird **pájaro** *m.* (5), **ave** *f.*
birthday card **tarjeta de cumpleaños** *f.*
  (16)
biscuit **galleta** *f.* (17)
black **negro** (18)
blond(e) **rubio(a)** (6)
blouse **blusa** *f.* (18)
blue **azul** (18)
boat **barco** *m.*
body **cuerpo** *m.*
Bolivia **Bolivia** (3)
Bolivian **boliviano(a)** *m. (f.)* (3)
book **libro** *m.* (4)
bookshelf **estante** *m.* (4)
bookstore **librería** *f.* (7)
boot **bota** *f.* (18)
booth **taquilla** *f.* (11)
bored, boring **aburrido(a)** (6)
(to) be born **nacer**
bottle **botella** *f.* (17)
boutique **boutique** *f.* (18)
boy **chico** *m.,* **niño** *f.*
boyfriend **novio** *m.* (5)
brave **valiente**
bread **pan** *m.* (1)
  bread, slice of **rebanada de pan** *f.*
    (1)
breakfast **desayuno** *m.* (1)
briefcase **portafolio** *m.* (4)
(to) bring **traer**
brother **hermano** *m.* (6)
brunet(te) **moreno(a)** (6)
(to) build **construir**
building **edificio** *m.* (7)
bunch **atado** *m.* (17)
(to) burn **quemar**
burned **quemado(a)**
bus **autobús** *m.* (4)
  bus terminal **estación de autobuses** *m.*
    (7)
business **negocio** *m.* (3)
businessman(woman) **hombre (mujer) de
  negocios** (3)
but **pero** (2)
butcher shop **carnicería** *f.* (7)

butter **mantequilla** *f.* (1)
(to) buy **comprar** (13)

C

café **café** *m.* (1)
(to) call **llamar** (7)
calculator **calculadora** *f.* (4)
(to be) called **llamarse** (4)
camera **cámara** *f.* (4)
can **lata** *f.* (17)
Canada **Canadá** (3)
Canadian **canadiense** *m. or f.* (3)
canned goods **preservas** *f. pl.* (17)
car **coche** *m.* (4)
card **tarjeta** *f.* (11)
career **carrera** *f.*
carpet **alfombra** *f.* (4)
carrot **zanahoria** *f.* (17)
(to) carry **llevar** (4)
cat **gato** *m.* (5)
cathedral **catedral** *f.* (7)
(to) celebrate **celebrar** (9)
center **centro** *m.* (16)
chair **silla** *f.* (4)
change **cambio** *m.* (12)
(to) change **cambiar** (11)
chart **esquema** *m.*
(to) chat **charlar** (1)
cheap **barato(a)** (11)
cheese **queso** *m.* (2)
chemistry **química** *f.* (5)
chicken **pollo** *m.* (3)
Chile **Chile** (3)
Chilean **chileno(a)** *m. (f.)* (3)
China **China** (3)
Chinese **chino(a)** *m. (f.)* (3)
chocolate **chocolate** *m.* (1)
church **iglesia** *f.* (7)
city **ciudad** *f.* (6)
classical music **música clásica** *f.* (5)
clay **barro** *m.*
clock radio **radio despertador** *m.* (4)
close (to) **cerca (de)** (7)
(to) close **cerrar**
clothes **ropa** *f.* (18)
    designer clothes **ropa de marca**
clothing store **tienda de ropa** *f.* (18)
club **club** *m.* (7)
coat **abrigo** *m.* (18)
coffee **café** *m.* (1)
cold **frío(a)** (1)
Colombia **Colombia** (3)
Colombian **colombiano(a)**

m. (f.) (3)
comb **peine** *m.*
(to) come **venir** (9)
(to) comment **comentar** (3)
commentary **comentario** *m.*
commuter pass **tarjeta de abono transportes**
    f. (11)
compact disc **disco compacto** *m.* (4)
company **compañía** *f.* (3)
comparison **comparación** *f.* (18)
computer **computadora** *f.* (4)
concert **concierto** *m.* (13)
(to) cook **cocinar** (13)
(to) continue **continuar** (9), **seguir**
cookie **galleta** *f.* (17)
cool **fresco(a)** (17)
corn **maíz** *m.* (17)
corner **esquina** *f.* (8)
Costa Rica **Costa Rica** (3)
Costa Rican **costarricense** *m. or f.* (3)
country **país** *m.* (8), (vs. city) **campo**
    m.
cousin **primo(a)** *m. (f.)* (6)
cream **crema** *f.* (17)
croissant **croissant** *m.* (1)
(to) cross **cruzar** (8)
Cuba **Cuba** (3)
Cuban **cubano(a)** *m. (f.)* (3)
custard, caramel **flan** *m.* (3)
customer **cliente** (17)
custom **costumbre** *f.*
cycling **ciclismo** *m.* (14)

D

dairy **lácteo(a)** (17)
    dairy product **producto lácteo** *m.* (17)
dance **baile** *m.* (9)
(to) dance **bailar** (1)
dance club **discoteca** (7)
danger **peligro** *m.*
dangerous **peligroso(a)**
date **cita** *f.* (10)
daughter **hija** *f.* (6)
day **día** *m.* (10)
death **muerte** *f.*
delicious **delicioso(a), riquísimo** (3)
delighted **encantado(a)** (2)
dentist **dentista** *m. or f.* (3)
desert **desierto** *m.*
desk **escritorio** *m.* (4)
(to) die **morir**
dining room **comedor** *m.*
direction **dirección** *f.* (7)

disagreeable **antipático(a)** (6)
dish **plato** *m.*
divorced **divorciado(a)** (6)
(to) do **hacer** (10)
    (to) do an errand **hacer un mandado**
    (10)
doctor **médico** *m.,* **doctor(a)** *m. (f.)* (3)
dog **perro** *m.* (5)
Dominican **dominicano(a)**
    m. (f.) (3)
Dominican Republic **República Dominicana**
    (3)
downtown **centro** *m.* (4)
dozen **docena** *f.* (17)
drawing **dibujo** *m.*
dress **vestido** *m.* (18)
(to) dress **vestir**
dresser **cómoda** *f.* (4)
drink **bebida** *f.* (1)
(to) drink **tomar** (1), **beber** (5)
drugstore **farmacia** *f.* (7)
during **durante** (15)

E

each **cada** (6)
ear **oreja** *f.*
(to) earn **ganar** (2)
earring **pendiente** *m.*
earth **tierra** *f.*
earthquake **terremoto** *m.*
(to) ease pain **desahogar**
easy **fácil**
(to) eat **comer** (1)
    (to) eat breakfast **desayunar**
Ecuador **Ecuador** (3)
Ecuadoran **ecuatoriano(a)**
    m. (f.) (3)
eight **ocho** (4)
eight hundred **ochocientos(as)** (12)
eighteen **dieciocho** (4)
eighty **ochenta** (7)
El Salvador **El Salvador** (3)
eleven **once** (4)
(to) end **terminar** (13)
enemy **enemigo(a)** *m. (f.)*
engineer **ingeniero(a)** *m. (f.)* (3)
England **Inglaterra** (3)
English **inglés (inglesa)** (3)
Englishman **inglés** *m.* (3)
Englishwoman **inglesa** *f.* (3)
(to) enjoy **disfrutar**
enough **suficiente** (16), **bastante** (1)
entrance ticket **entrada** *f.* (11)

envelope **sobre** m. (16)
equal **igual**
equality **igualdad** f. (18)
eraser **borrador** m. (4)
(to) establish **establecer** (18)
event **acontecimiento** m.
every **cada** (6)
    every day **todos los días** m. (1)
example **ejemplo** m.
    for example **por ejemplo**
exchange **intercambio** m. (3)
excuse me **perdón** (1)
to exercise **hacer ejercicio** (13)
expensive **caro(a)** (16)
(to) express **expresar** (1)
expression **expresión** f. (1)
eye **ojo** m.
eyeglasses **gafas** f. pl.

F

facing **frente a** (8)
fair **feria** f. (9)
to fall **caer**
family **familia** f. (6)
famous **famoso(a)** (12)
fan (person) **aficionado(a)** m. (f.)
far (from) **lejos (de)** (8)
fat **gordo(a)** (6)
father **padre** m. (6)
favorite **favorito(a)** (16)
(to) fear **temer**
(to) feel **sentir**
    (to) feel like . . . **tener ganas de...** (10)
festival (religious) honoring a town's patron
    saint **Fiesta del pueblo** f. (9)
field hockey **hockey sobre hierba** m. (14)
fifteen **quince** (4)
fifty **cincuenta** (7)
(to) fight **luchar**
film **película** f. (5)
finally **finalmente, por fin** (14)
(to) find **encontrar** (9)
fine **bien** (1)
fireworks **fuegos artificiales** m. (9)
first **primero** (7)
fish **pescado** m. (17)
five **cinco** (4)
five hundred **quinientos(as)** (12)
flour **harina** f. (17)
flower shop **florería** f. (7)
folk dance **baile folklórico** m. (9)
food **alimento** m. (17), **comida** f. (3)
foolish **tonto(a)** (6)

football **fútbol americano** m. (5)
for **para** (1), **por** (11)
fortune **suerte** f.
fortune-teller **adivino(a)** m. (f.)
forty **cuarenta** (7)
four **cuatro** (4)
four hundred **cuatrocientos(as)** (12)
fourteen **catorce** (4)
France **Francia** (3)
free **gratis**
French **francés (francesa)** m. (f.)
    (3)
frequently **a menudo** (7),
    frecuentemente (10)
Friday **viernes** m. (10)
friend **amigo(a)** m. (f.) (1)
from **de, desde** (9)
    from time to time **de vez en cuando** (7)
frozen **congelado(a)** (17)
fruit **fruta** f. (17)
    fruit salad **ensalada de**
    frutas f. (17)
full **lleno(a)** (17)
fun **divertido(a)** (6)
future **futuro** m. (15)

G

garage **garaje** m. (3)
German **alemán (alemana)**
    m. (f.) (3)
Germany **Alemania** (3)
(to) get out (something) **sacar** (14)
gift **regalo** m. (3)
girl **chica** f., **niña** f.
girlfriend **novia** f. (5)
(to) give **dar** (8)
glass **vaso** m. (1)
globe **globo** m. (1)
(to) go **ir** (7)
    go ahead! **¡adelante!**
    (to) go along **andar** (13)
    (to) go back **volver** (13)
    (to) go camping **ir de camping** (14)
    (to) go down **bajar** (11)
    (to) go fishing **ir de pesca** (14)
    (to) go out **salir (de)** (13)
    (to) go shopping **ir de compras** (10)
    (to be) going to . . . **ir a...** (10)
gold **oro** m.
good **bueno(a)** (3)
    Good afternoon. **Buenas tardes.** (1)
    Good evening. **Buenas noches.** (1)
    Good morning. **Buenos días.** (1)

    Good night. **Buenas noches.** (1)
good-bye **adiós, chao** (1)
grace **gracia** f.
gram **gramo** m. (17)
grandfather **abuelo** m. (6)
grandmother **abuela** f. (6)
grape **uva** f. (17)
Great! **¡Qué bueno(a)!** (3)
green **verde** (17)
(to) greet **saludar** (1)
greeting **saludo** m. (2)
grenadine **granadina** f. (1)
group **grupo** m. (1)
Guatemala **Guatemala** (3)
Guatemalan **guatemalteco(a)** m. (f.) (3)
guitar **guitarra** f. (14)
gym **gimnasio** m. (13)

H

half **medio(a)** (17), **mitad** f.
    half kilo **medio kilo** (17)
ham **jamón** m. (1)
hamburger **hamburguesa** f. (3)
handsome **guapo(a)** (6)
happy **contento(a)** (9)
(to) have **tener** (6)
    (to) have just . . . **acabar de...** (2)
    (to) have lunch **almorzar** (12)
    (to) have supper **cenar** (13)
    (to) have to **tener que** (6)
he **él** (2)
health **salud** f.
heart **corazón** m.
Hello! **¡Hola!** (1)
    Hello? (answering the phone) **¡Bueno!,**
    ¡Diga! / ¡Dígame! (7)
help **ayuda** f. (8)
(to) help **ayudar**
her **su(s)** (4)
here **aquí** (4)
here is/are **aquí hay** (2)
high-heeled shoe **zapato de tacón** m. (18)
high school **escuela secundaria** f. (7)
his **su(s)** (4)
Hispanic **hispano(a)** m. (f.) (9)
homework **tarea** f. (9)
Honduran **hondureño(a)**
    m. (f.) (3)
Honduras **Honduras** (3)
(to) hope **esperar** (12)
horrible **horrible** (3)
horse **caballo** m.
hospital **hospital** m. (7)
hot **caliente** (1)

hot pepper **chile** *m.* (3)
hotel **hotel** *m.* (7)
hour **hora** *f.* (14)
house **casa** *f.* (4)
how **como** (11)
  how? **¿cómo?** (3)
  How are you? **¿Qué tal?** (1)
  How are you? (formal) **¿Cómo está Ud.?**
  (2), (informal) **¿Cómo estás?** (1)
  How can I help you (plural)? **¿En qué**
  puedo servirle(s)? (12)
  How is it / are they? **¿Cómo es / son?**
  (6)
  How is it going? **¿Cómo te va?** (1)
  how many? **¿cuántos(as)?** (6)
  How many are there? **¿Cuántos hay?**
  (4)
  How much is it (are they)? **¿Cuánto**
  cuesta(n)? (16)
  How old are you? **¿Cuántos años**
  tienes? (7)
  How . . . ! **¡Qué . . . !** (3)
  How terrible! **¡Qué horrible!** (3)
hug **abrazo** (1)
hundred **cien** (7), **ciento** (12)
(to be) hungry **tener hambre** (7)
(to) hunt **cazar**
husband **esposo** *m.* (6)

I

I **yo** (1)
ice cream **helado** *m.* (17)
(to) ice skate **patinar sobre hielo** (14)
idea **idea** *f.* (9)
if **si** (12)
impossible **imposible** (10)
in **en** (1)
  in front of **delante de** (8)
  in order to **para** (9)
  in order that **para que**
  in the afternoon **por la tarde** (11)
  in the meantime **mientras**
  in the morning **por la mañana** (11)
  In which direction? **¿En qué dirección?**
  (11)
Independence Day **Día de la Independencia**
  m. (9)
inside **dentro**
instance **vez** (7)
intelligent **inteligente** (6)
interesting **interesante** (6)
(to) introduce **presentar** (1)
introduction **presentación** *f.* (2)

(to) invite **invitar** (13)
It belongs to . . . **Es de. . .** (4)
It is 3 o'clock. **Son las tres.** (9)
It is 1:30. **Es la una y media.** (9)
It's at the end of . . . **Está a(l) final de. . .** (8)
It's not on sale? **¿No está(n) en oferta?** (16)
Italian **italiano(a)** *m. (f.)* (3)
Italy **Italia** (3)

J

jacket **chaqueta** *f.* (18)
Japan **Japón** (3)
Japanese **japonés (japonesa)** *m. (f.)* (3)
jazz **jazz** *m.* (5)
jeans **vaqueros** *m.*
jelly **mermelada** *f.* (1)
jewel **joya** *f.*
journalist **periodista** *m. or f.* (3)
juice **jugo** *m.* (1)

K

key **llave** *f.* (4)
kilogram **kilo** *m.* (17)
kilometer **kilómetro** *m.* (12)
king **rey** *m.*
kiss **beso** *m.* (5)
knapsack **mochila** *f.* (4)

L

landscape **paisaje** *m.*
language **lengua** *f.* (5)
large **grande** (6)
late **tarde** (9)
lawyer **abogado(a)** *m. (f.)* (3)
leaf **hoja** *f.* (16)
(to) learn **aprender** (5)
leather **cuero** *m.* (18)
(to) leave **salir (de)** (13)
leave (something) **dejar**
left **izquierda** (8)
legend **leyenda** *f.*
lemon **limón** *m.* (17)
lemonade **limonada** *f.* (1)
less . . . than **menos. . . que** (18)
Let's go . . . **Vamos . . .** (1)
Let's see. **A ver.** (16)
letter **carta** *f.*
lettuce **lechuga** *f.* (17)
level **nivel** *m.*
library **biblioteca** *f.* (7)

life **vida** *f.* (13)
(to) lift weights **levantar pesas** (14)
like **como** (11)
(to) like **gustar** (5)
Likewise. **Igualmente.** (2)
line **línea** *f.* (11)
(to) listen **escuchar** (1)
liter **litro** *m.* (17)
little, a **poco(a)** (1)
(to) live **vivir** (5)
location **lugar** *m.* (7)
long **largo**
Look! **¡Mira!** (3)
  (to) look at **mirar** (2)
  (to) look for **buscar** (8)
(to) lose **perder** (13)
lot, a **mucho(a)** (1)
(to) lower **bajar** (11)
luck **suerte)** *f.*

M

machine **máquina** *f.* (4)
mad **enojado(a)** (9)
magazine **revista** *f.*
(to) maintain **mantener**
majority **mayoría** *f.*
(to) make **hacer** (10)
  (to) make the bed **hacer la cama** (13)
man **hombre** *m.* (3)
market **mercado** *m.* (7)
married **casado(a)** (6)
mayonnaise **mayonesa** *f.* (17)
me **mí** (1)
meal **comida** *f.* (1)
means of transportation **medio de transporte**
  m. (4)
meat **carne** *f.* (3)
mechanic **mecánico(a)** *m. (f.)* (3)
(to) meet **encontrar, encontrarse (con)** (9)
memory **recuerdo** *m.*
Mexican **mexicano(a)** *m. (f.)* (3)
  Mexican food **comida mexicana** (3)
Mexico **México** (3)
midday **mediodía** *m.* (9)
middle **medio** *m.* (4)
midnight **medianoche** *f.* (9)
mile **milla** *f.* (12)
milk **leche** *f.* (1)
milkshake **licuado** *m.* (1)
million **millón** (12)
minus **menos** (4)
minute **minuto** *m.* (14)
Miss **señorita** *f.* (1)

modern **moderno(a)** (18)
Monday **lunes** *m.* (10)
money **dinero** *m.* (2)
month **mes** *m.* (11)
more **más** (2)
more . . . than **más . . . que** (18)
morning **mañana** *f.* (10)
mother **madre** *f.* (6)
    Mother's Day card **tarjeta del Día de la**
    Madre *f.* (16)
motorcycle **motocicleta** *f.* (4)
mountain **montaña** *f.*
    mountain climbing **alpinismo** *m. (14)*
movie **película** *f.* (5)
    movie, comedy **película**
    cómica *f.* (5)
    movie, horror **película de**
    horror *f.* (5)
    movie theater **cine** *m.* (7)
Mr. **señor** *m.* (1)
Mrs. **señora** *f.* (1)
much **mucho** (1)
    very much **muchísimo** (1)
museum **museo** *m.* (7)
music **música** *f.* (5)
music store **tienda de música** (16)
must **deber** (10)
my **mi(s)** (4)

N

name **nombre** *m.* (6)
    last name **apellido** *m.* (6)
(to be) named **llamarse** (4)
nationality **nacionalidad** *f.* (3)
native **indígena**
nature **naturaleza** *f.* (5)
near **cerca (de)** (7)
(to) need **necesitar** (2)
neighborhood **barrio** *m.* (7)
neither **tampoco** (2)
never **nunca** (7)
new **nuevo(a)** (12)
newspaper kiosk **quiosco de periódicos** *m.*
    (8)
next **próximo(a)** (10)
    next to **al lado de** (8)
Nicaragua **Nicaragua** (3)
Nicaraguan **nicaragüense** *m. or f.* (3)
nice **simpático(a)** (6)
    Nice to meet you. **Mucho gusto.** (1)
night **noche** *f.* (9)
    last night **anoche** (13)
nine hundred **novecientos(as)** (12)

nine **nueve** (4)
nineteen **diecinueve** (4)
ninety **noventa** (7)
no **no** (1)
nobody **nadie**
noise **ruido** *m.*
noon **mediodía** (9)
north **norte** *m.*
North American **norteamericano(a)** *m. (f.)*
    (3)
notebook **cuaderno** *m.* (4)
nothing **nada** (13)
noun **sustantivo** *m.* (1)
now **ahora** (9)
number **número** *m.* (7)
nurse **enfermero(a)** *m. (f.)* (3)

O

(to) obtain **sacar** (14)
of **de** (3)
    of course **por supuesto** (9)
    Of course! **¡Claro!** (5)
    Of course! (reaffirmed) **¡Claro que sí!**
    (10)
(to) offer **ofrecer** (17)
often **a menudo** (7)
oil **aceite** *m.* (17)
OK **de acuerdo** (9)
old **viejo(a)** (6)
older **mayor** (18)
olive **aceituna** *f.* (2)
    olive oil **aceite de oliva** *m.*
omelette (Spain) **tortilla** *f.* (2)
on **en** (1)
    on foot **a pie** (10)
    on the corner of **en la esquina de** (8)
once **una vez** (17)
    once a year **una vez al año** (9)
one **uno** (4)
one hundred **ciento** (12)
onion **cebolla** *f.* (17)
only **sólo, solamente** (12)
open-air market **mercado al aire libre** *m.*
    (17)
or **o** (12)
orange **naranja** *f.* (1)
order **orden** *m.* (12)
other **otro(a)** (11)
our **nuestro(a)** (4)
over there **allá** (17)
(to) owe **deber** (10)
owner **dueño(a)** *m. (f.)*

P

(to) pack **hacer las maletas** (13)
package **paquete** *m.* (17)
painting **pintura** *f.* (5)
Panama **Panamá** (3)
Panamanian **panameño(a)** *m. (f.)* (3)
pants **pantalones** *m.* (18)
paper **papel** *m.* (16)
    piece of paper **hoja** *f.* (16)
parade **desfile** *m.* (9)
Paraguay **Paraguay** (3)
Paraguayan **paraguayo(a)** *m. (f.)* (3)
(to) pardon **disculpar** (7)
parents **padres** *m.* (2)
park **parque** *m.* (7)
parking lot **estacionamiento** *m.* (8)
party **fiesta** *f.* (9)
(to) pass **pasar** (17)
    pasta **pasta** *f.* (2)
pastry **pastel** *m.* (1)
(to) pay **pagar** (12)
pea **guisante** *m.* (17)
peach **melocotón** *m.* (1)
peanut **cacahuete** *m.* (2)
pear **pera** *f.* (17)
pen, ball-point **bolígrafo** *m.* (4)
pen, fountain **pluma** *f.* (4)
pencil **lápiz** *m.* (4)
    pencil sharpener **sacapuntas** *m.* (4)
people **gente** *f.*
pepper **pimienta** *f.* (17)
to persecute **perseguir**
person **persona** *f.* (6)
Peru **Perú** (3)
Peruvian **peruano(a)** *m. (f.)* (3)
pharmacy **farmacia** *f.* (7)
pie **pastel** *m.* (1)
piece **pedazo** *m.* (17)
place **lugar** *m.* (7)
plain **feo(a)** (6)
(to) plan **planear** (12)
plane **avión** *m.* (12)
plant **planta** *f.* (4)
(to) play (a sport or game) **jugar** (11)
    (to) play basketball **jugar al baloncesto**
    (14)
    (to) play field hockey **jugar al hockey**
    sobre hierba (14)
    (to) play golf **jugar al golf** (14)
    (to) play hockey **jugar al hockey** (14)
(to) play (an instrument) **tocar** (2)
player **jugador(a)** *m. (f.)*
plaza **plaza** *f.* (7)

please **por favor** (1)
poetry contest **concurso de poesía** *m.* (9)
police **policía** *f.* (7)
   police officer **policía** *m.* or *f.* (7)
   police station **estación de policía** *f.* (7)
politics **política** *f.* (5)
pool **piscina** *f.* (7)
poorly **mal** (1)
popular dance **baile popular** *m.* (9)
possession **posesión** *f.* (4)
post office **oficina de correos** *f.* (7)
poster **póster** *m.* (4)
potato **papa** *f.* (17), **patata** *f.* (2)
   potatoes: cooked, diced, and served in spicy sauce **patatas bravas** *f.* (2)
pound **libra** *f.* (17)
(to) practice **practicar** (1)
(to) prefer **preferir** (7)
preference **preferencia** *f.* (17)
(to) prepare **preparar** (9)
(to) present **presentar** (1)
presentation **presentación** *f.* (2)
preserve **conserva** *f.* (17)
pretty **bonito(a)** (6)
Pretty good. **Bastante bien.** (1)
price **precio** *m.* (16)
prize **premio** *m.* (9)
product **producto** *m.* (17)
profession **profesión** *f.* (3)
professor **profesor(a)** *m. (f.)* (3)
(to) protect **proteger**
public **público** (7)
Puerto Rican **puertorriqueño(a)** *m. (f.)* (3)
Puerto Rico **Puerto Rico** (3)
purse **bolsa** *f.* (4)
(to) put **poner** (16)

Q

quality **calidad** *f.* (3)
quantity **cantidad** *f.* (17)
queen **reina** *f.*
question **pregunta** *f.* (2)

R

racket **raqueta** *f.* (16)
(to) rain **llover**
raincoat **impermeable** *m.* (18)
(to) raise **subir**
rarely **rara vez** (7)
(to) reach **alcanzar**
(to) read **leer** (5)

ready **listo(a)** (9)
reason **razón** *f.*
(to) receive **recibir** (5)
recipe **receta** *f.*
red **rojo(a)** (17)
redhead **pelirrojo(a)** (6)
relative **pariente** *m.* (6)
remember **recordar**
(to) rent a video **alquilar un vídeo** (13)
(to) repeat **repetir** (13)
(to) request **pedir** (8)
(to) rest **descansar** (9)
restaurant **restaurante** *m.* (1)
(to) return **regresar**
review **repaso** *m.*
rice **arroz** *m.* (3)
(to) ride a bicycle **montar en bicicleta** (13)
right **derecha** (8)
   right? **¿verdad?** (2)
   right now **ahora mismo** (15)
rock music **música rock** *f.* (5)
(to) roller-skate **patinar** (14)
room **cuarto** *m.* (4)
round-trip ticket **billete de ida y vuelta** *m.* (12)
rug **alfombra** *f.* (4)
(to) run **correr** (5)
Russia **Rusia** (3)
Russian **ruso(a)** *m. (f.)* (3)

S

sad **triste** (9)
(to) sail **practicar la vela** (14)
salad **ensalada** *f.* (17)
sale **oferta** *f.* (16), **venta** *f.*
salesman(woman) **vendedor(a)** *m. (f.)* (17)
salt **sal** *f.* (17)
Salvadoran **salvadoreño(a)** *m. (f.)* (3)
same **mismo(a)**
sandal **sandalia** *f.* (18)
sandwich **sándwich** *m.* (1), (French bread) **bocadillo** *m.* (1)
Saturday **sábado** *m.* (10)
sauce **salsa** *f.* (3)
sausage **chorizo** *m.* (2)
(to) say **decir** (10)
   (to) say good-bye **despedirse** (1)
schedule **horario** *m.* (11)
school **colegio** *m.* (7), **escuela** *f.* (4)
science **ciencia** *f.* (5)
science fiction movie **película de ciencia ficción** *f.* (5)
sculpture **escultura** *f.* (5)

season (sports) **temporada** *f.*
secretary **secretario(a)** *m. (f.)* (3)
(to) see **ver** (9)
   See you. **Nos vemos.** (1)
   See you later. **Hasta luego.** (1)
(to) sell **vender** (5)
sense **sentido** *m.*
sequence, series **serie** *f.* (14)
serious **serio(a)** (6)
seven **siete** (4)
seven hundred **setecientos(as)** (12)
seventeen **diecisiete** (4)
seventy **setenta** (7)
(to) share **compartir** (5)
she **ella** (2)
shirt **camisa** *f.* (18)
shoe **zapato** *m.* (18)
shoe store **zapatería** *f.* (18)
(to) shop **ir de compras** (10)
shopping cart **carrito** *m.* (17)
shopping center **centro comercial** (16)
short **bajo(a)**, (in length) **corto(a)** (6)
should **deber** (10)
sick **enfermo(a)** (9)
sight **vista** *f.*
(to) sign **firmar**
silly **tonto(a)** (6)
silver **plata** *f.*
(to) sing **cantar** (1)
singer **cantante** *m.* or *f.*
sister **hermana** *f.* (6)
six **seis** (4)
six hundred **seiscientos(as)** (12)
sixteen **dieciseis** (4)
sixty **sesenta** (7)
size (clothing) **talla** (18)
(to) skate **patinar** (14)
ski **esquí** *m.* (16)
skirt **falda** *f.* (18)
(to) sleep **dormir** (15)
slice of bread **rebanada de pan** *f.* (1)
slow **despacio** (8)
small **pequeño(a)** (6)
snack **merienda** *f.* (1)
   snack, Spanish **tapa española** *f.* (2)
(to) snorkel **bucear** (14)
snorkeling **buceo** *m.*
so **tan** (8)
   so-so **más o menos** (1)
soccer **fútbol** *m.* (5)
sock **calcetín** *m.* (18)
soda **soda** *f.* (1)
soft drink **refresco** *m.* (1)
some **alguno(a)**

someday **algún día** (12)
something **algo** (1)
sometimes **a veces** (1)
son **hijo** *m.* (6)
song **canción** *f.*
soon **pronto**
I'm sorry. **Lo siento.** (7)
soup **sopa** *f.* (17)
south **sur** *m.*
southwest **suroeste** *m.*
space **espacio** *m.*
Spain **España** (3)
Spaniard **español(a)** *m. (f.)* (3)
Spanish **español(a)** (1)
speaker **bocina** (4)
special **especial** (11)
species **especie** *f.*
(to) spend **gastar**
(to) spend time **pasar tiempo** (13)
sphere **globo** *m.* (1)
spice **especia** *f.*
spicy **picante** (3)
spirit **espíritu** *m.*
sport **deporte** *m.* (5)
sporting goods store **tienda de deportes** *f.*
(16)
sportsman (sportswoman) **deportista** *m.* or
f.
square **plaza** *f.* (7), (geometry) **cuadrado** *m.*
squid **calamares** *m.* (2)
stadium **estadio** *m.* (7)
stage (phase) **etapa**
star **estrella** *f.*
station **estación** *f.* (7)
stationery store **papelería** *f.* (16)
(to) stay **quedar** (8)
stereo **estéreo** *m.* (4)
still **todavía**
stocking **media** *f.* (18)
stone **piedra** *f.*
store **tienda** *f.* (7)
story **cuento** *m.*, **historia** *f.*
strawberry **fresa** *f.*
street **calle** *f.* (8)
strength **fuerza** *f.*
student **alumno(a)** *m. (f.)* (4), **estudiante**
m. or *f.* (3)
(to) study **estudiar** (1)
stupid **tonto(a)** (6)
style **moda** *f.* (18)
subway **metro** *m.* (11)
subway map **plano del metro** *m.*
(11)
subway station **estación de metro**

f. (11)
success **éxito** *m.*
sugar **azúcar** *m.* (17)
sun **sol** *m.*
(to) sunbathe **tomar el sol** (14)
Sunday **domingo** *m.* (10)
Super! **¡Super!** (16)
sure **seguro(a)** (18)
(to) surf **practicar el surfing** (14)
survey **encuesta** *f.* (12)
sweater **suéter** *m.* (18)
sweet roll, any kind **pan dulce** *m.* (1)
(to) swim **nadar** (13)
swimming **natación** *f.* (14)
swimming pool **piscina** *f.* (7)

T

T-shirt **camiseta** *f.* (18)
tail **cola** *f.*
(to) take **tomar** (1), **llevar** (4)
(to) take a trip **hacer un viaje** (13)
(to) take a walk **dar un paseo** (10)
(to) talk **hablar** (1)
tall **alto(a)** (6)
tape (cassette) **cinta** *f.* (4)
tape recorder **grabadora** *f.* (4)
taste **gusto** *m.* (5)
taxi **taxi** *m.* (11)
tea **té** *m.* (1)
teacher **profesor(a)** *m. (f.)* (3)
team **equipo** *m.* (13)
telephone **teléfono** *m.* (7)
telephone conversation **conversación
telefónica** *f.* (7)
television set, (color) **televisor (a colores)**
m. (4)
(to) tell (a story) **contar**
ten **diez** (4)
tennis **tenis** *m.* (5)
tennis ball **pelota de tenis** *f.* (16)
tennis shoe **zapato de tenis** *m.*
(16)
thank you **gracias** (1)
Thank you very much. **Muchas gracias.**
(1)
Thanksgiving Day mass **la misa de Acción
de Gracias** *f.* (9)
that **aquel(la), ese(a)** (17), **que** (1)
that is why **por eso** (16)
that one **ése(a)** *m. (f.)* (17)
that one over there **aquél(la)** *m. (f.)*
(17)
the **el** *m.*, **la** *f.*, (plural) **los** *m.*, **las**

f. (2)
theater **teatro** *m.* (7)
movie theater **cine** *m.* (7)
their **su(s)** (4)
then **entonces** (9), **luego** (14), **pues**
(1)
there **allí** (4)
there is / are **hay** (4)
they **ellos(as)** *m. (f.)* (2)
thin **delgado(a)** (6)
thing **cosa** *f.*
another thing **otra cosa** *f.* (11)
(to) think **pensar** (11)
(to be) thirsty **tener sed** (7)
thirteen **trece** (4)
thirty **treinta** (4)
this **este(a)** (17)
this one **éste(a)** *m. (f.)* (17)
thousand **mil** (12)
three **tres** (4)
three hundred **trescientos(as)** (12)
Thursday **jueves** *m.* (10)
ticket **billete** *m.* (11)
ticket, ten-trip **billete de diez viajes**
m. (11)
ticket, one-way **billete sencillo** *m.*
(11)
time **tiempo** *m.* (14), **vez** *f.* (9)
tin **lata** *f.* (17)
tip **propina** *f.* (12)
tired **cansado(a)** (9)
to **a** (1)
toast **pan tostado** *m.* (1)
today **hoy** (4)
together **junto(a)** (17)
tomato **tomate** *m.* (17)
tomorrow **mañana** (10)
tongue **lengua** *f.* (5)
tonight **esta noche** (7)
(to) touch **tocar** (2)
tourist **turista** *m.* or *f.* (11)
tower **torre** *f.*
town **pueblo** *m.*
toy **juguete** *m.*
track (railway.) **vía** *f.*
train **tren** *m.* (7)
train station **estación de trenes** (7)
transportation **transporte** *m.* (4)
(to) travel **viajar** (1)
travel agency **agencia de viajes** *f.* (12)
trip **viaje** *m.* (12)
trousers **pantalones** *m.* (18)
true **verdadero(a)**
(to) try (endeavor) **tratar de**
Tuesday **martes** *m.* (10)

tuna **atún** *m.* (17)
(to) turn **doblar** (8)
twelve **doce** (4)
twenty **veinte** (4)
two hundred **doscientos(as)** (12)
typewriter **máquina de escribir** *f.* (4)
typing paper **papel para escribir a máquina**
   m. (16)

U

ugly **feo(a)** (6)
uncle **tío** *m.* (6)
(to) understand **comprender** (5)
unemployment **desempleo** *m.*
United States **Estados Unidos** (3)
university **universidad** *f.* (7)
unknown **desconocido(a)**
unlimited **sin límite** (11)
until **hasta** (9)
Uruguay **Uruguay** (3)
Uruguayan **uruguayo(a)** *m. (f.)* (3)
(to) use **usar** (13)
useful **útil**
usually **usualmente** (10), **de costumbre**
   (15)

V

value **valor** *m.*
various **varios(as)** (17)
vegetable **vegetal** *m.* (17)
   vegetable salad **ensalada de vegetales**
   (verduras) *f.* (17)
Venezuela **Venezuela** (3)
Venezuelan **venezolano(a)** *m. (f.)* (3)
verb **verbo** (1)
very **muy, bien** (1)
   very much **muchísimo** (1)
   Very well, thank you. **Muy bien, gracias.**
   (1)
video **vídeo** *m.* (4)
videocassette player **videocasetera** *f.* (4)
Vietnam **Vietnam** (3)
Vietnamese **vietnamita** *m. or f.* (3)
(to) visit **visitar** (13)
voice **voz** *f.*
volleyball **vólibol** *m.* (5)

W

(to) wait **esperar** (12)
waiter (waitress) **camarero(a)** *m. (f.)* (1)

(to) walk **caminar, andar** (13)
   (to) walk on the beach **caminar en la**
   playa (14).
   a walk **paseo** *m.* (10)
walking **a pie** (10)
wallet **cartera** *f.* (4)
(to) want **desear** (1), **querer** (7)
   I would like . . . **Yo quisiera…** (1)
(to) watch **mirar** (2)
water **agua** *f.* (1)
water ski **esquí acuático** *m.* (14)
we **nosotros(as)** *m. (f.)* (1)
Wednesday **miércoles** *m.* (10)
week **semana** *f.* (11)
weekend **fin de semana** *m.* (13)
welcome **bienvenido(a)** (3)
well **bien** (1)
what? **¿qué?, ¿cómo?** (1)
   What a pity! **¡Qué pena!** (16)
   What day is today? **¿Qué día es hoy?**
   (10)
   What delicious food! **¡Qué comida**
   más rica! (3)
   What's going on? **¿Qué pasó?** (1)
   What's new? **¿Qué hay (de nuevo)?**
   (1)
   What time is it? **¿Qué hora es?** (9)
   What's your name? **¿Cómo te llamas?**
   (4)
when? **¿cuándo?** (9)
where? **¿adónde?** (7), **¿dónde?** (6)
   Where are you from? **¿De dónde es**
   (eres)? (3)
   Where is / are there . . . ? **¿Dónde**
   hay… ? (4)
   Where is . . . ? **¿Dónde está… ?** (8)
which? **¿cuál?** (17)
white **blanco** (18)
who? **¿quién?** (3)
whole **entero** (11)
Whose is it? **¿De quién es… ?** (4)
why? **¿por qué?** (6)
wife **esposa** *f.* (6)
store window **escaparate** *m.* (16)
winter **invierno** *m.*
(to) wish for **desear** (1)
with **con** (1)
   with me **conmigo** (10)
   with pleasure **con mucho gusto** (1)
without **sin** *m.* (11)
woman **mujer** *f.* (3)
word **palabra** *f.* (1)
(to) work **trabajar** (1)
work **trabajo** *m.*
worker **trabajador(a)** *m. (f.)*

world **mundo** *m.*
(to) worry **preocupar**
worse, worst **peor** (18)
(to) write **escribir** (5)
written **escrito**

Y

year **año** *m.* (11)
(to be) . . . years old **tener… años** (7)
yellow **amarillo(a)** (17)
yes **sí** (1)
yesterday **ayer** (13)
yogurt **yogur** *m.* (17)
you (familiar) **tú**, (familiar plural) **vosotros**
   (as) *m. (f.)*, (formal) **usted (Ud.)**, (formal plural) **ustedes (Uds.)** (1)
you're welcome **de nada** (1)
young **joven** (11)
younger **menor** (18)
your **su(s)** (18), **tu(s)** (4)
youth **juventud** *f.*

Z

zoo **parque zoológico** *m.* (13)

Index

de +, 189
él, ella, ellos(as), 31
embraces, 5
encantar, 380
entonces, 344
equality, 430
-er verbs
    imperatives, 196-198
    present tense, 116
    preterite tense, 314
ese, esa, esos(as), 403
ése, ésa, eso, ésos(as), 412-413
esperar + infinitive, 361
estar, 190
    + adjectives of condition, 214
    expressing present progressive, 353-354,
        361
    preterite tense, 322
este, esta, estos(as), 403
éste, ésta, esto, éstos(as), 412-413
evening, 207, 242, 261
extended family, 132, 134

familiar commands, 387, 392
family, 124, 132, 134
fewer, 424
finally, 344
finalmente, 344
first, 344
food, 9, 15, 47-48, 56
    beverages, 9-10
    expressing hunger or thirst, 178
    fruits and vegetables, 409
    meals, 20
    open-air markets for, 399-400
    ordering, 9-10, 47-48, 56
    snacks, 27
    supermarkets for, 408-409
for what reason?, 231-232
formal introductions, 36-37
frequency, 19, 162, 178
fruits, 409
furnishings, 84-85, 91
future tense, 361
    adverbs for, 261-262
    ir a + infinitive, 235, 361

-gar verbs
    negative **tú** imperatives, 392
    preterite tense, 335
gender
    demonstrative adjectives, 403
    indefinite articles, 12
    noun-adjective agreement, 57-58, 94, 138
    nouns and, 12
    possessive adjectives, 216
    profession nouns, 60

third person pronouns, 31
giving directions, 185, 193, 258
go (**ir**), 160
    imperatives, 198, 387, 392
    ir a + infinitive, 235, 361
    preterite tense, 310-312
going to do something, 235, 361
greetings and goodbyes, 3-5, 36-37
    on telephone, 165
gustar, 105, 380-381
    adverbs for, 7
    + infinitive, 6

hacer, 245
    expressing how long ago, 332
    imperative forms, 387, 392
    preterite tense, 306
    + **que**, 332
hambre, 178
have (**tener**)
    asking person's age, 178
    expressing hunger or thirst, 178
    preterite tense, 322
hay, 87
her, his, 216
holidays, 204-205, 212
home furnishings, 84-85, 91
hoping to do something, 285
hours, 207
how many?, 135
hoy, 241-242, 261
hunger, 178

imperatives, 196-198, 387, 392
indefinite articles, 12
informal introductions, 36-37
information questions, 135-136
interrogative words, 411
introducing people, 3, 36-37
ir, 160
    imperatives, 198, 387, 392
    ir a + infinitive, 235, 361
    preterite tense, 310-312
-ir verbs
    imperatives, 196-198
    present tense, 116
    preterite tense, 314
irregular second-person commands, 198
its, 216

job names, 60

la, las, 79-80
last names, 125
leavetaking. *See* greetings and goodbyes
less, 424
likes and dislikes, 103-104

encantar, 380
gustar, 6-7, 105, 380-381
    past, present, and future, 361
preferir, 169, 361
querer, 169, 361
sports, 331
wanting to do something, 237, 285, 301-302,
    361
location
    addresses, 176
    asking where something is, 135
    asking where something is from, 52
    directions to, 185, 193, 258
    time to travel to, 276-277, 279, 283
los, 79-80
love to do something, 169, 381

making plans. *See* planning
mañana, 207, 241-242, 261
markets, 399-400, 408-409
más, 424
meals, 20
meeting people, 3-5, 36-37
menos, 424
mercados, 399-400
metro, 258, 260
more, 424
morning, 207, 241-242, 261
movies, 112
music, 113

names
    countries, 52
    de in, 127
    last names, 125
nationality, 57-58
-ndo form of verbs, 353-354, 361
negative familiar commands, 392
neither, 39
night, 207, 242, 261
noche, 207, 242, 261
nosotros, nosotras, 17
nouns
    agreement with adjectives, 57-58, 94, 138-
        139
    collective, 80
    gender and, 12
    professions, 60
    specific, 80
numbers
    0 to 20, 86-87
    20 to 100, 176
    100 to 1,000,000, 279-280
    age, 178
    asking how many, 135
    expressing specific quantity, 404
    frequency, 19, 162, 178

Text Permissions

p. 195 Madrid city map and **p. 259** metro map reprinted from El Corte Inglés brochure with permission from El Corte Inglés; The following article adapted from the magazine El sol was reprinted with permission from Scholastic Inc., New York, NY: **p. 255-256** Estrellas musicales latinas

Photo Credits